CONTENTS

Continued in Volume Two

A white whale tangled in a net
Made murmur from the bloody sea,
To chide its trapper with regret:
'Why dost my brother thus by me?'

Anon a frolicsome sea-wave
Upset the wretch, and now did he
Make whisper, sinking to his grave:
'Why dost my sister thus by me?'

From **34. HUNTING THE BELUGA**
Volume Two

Volume One of

OLD HUNTING GROUNDS

AND OTHER STORIES

by

YURI KAZAKOV

Translated by Vladislav Zhukov

Published by the translator at
Mount Wilson, NSW

2019

Printed by Kindle Direct Publishing
an Amazon.com subsidiary

National Library of Australia Cataloguing-in-Publication entry:

Author:	Yuri P. Kazakov (1927-1982)
Title:	*Old Hunting Grounds and Other Stories by Yuri Kazakov*
ISBNs:	978-0-9874637-0-8 (Volume One)
	978-0-9874637-1-5 (Volume Two)
Contents:	Preface; Stories 1-22 (Volume One)
	Stories 23-38; Afterword (Volume Two)
Subject:	Short stories and travel sketches translated from Russian into English
Translator:	Vladislav V. Zhukov © 2013
Dewey Number:	891.7344

The first edition of the present compilation of stories by Yuri Kazakov was published sans place of publication by the translator in 2013; a second edition, revised and with the abridged title *Old Hunting Grounds and Other Stories*, was published by the translator at Mount Wilson in 2015.

Other translations by Vladislav Zhukov:

The Kim Vân Kieu of Nguyen Du (1765-1820), published in 2004 by Pandanus Books, the Australian National University. Second edition published in 2013 by Cornell University Southeast Asia Program Publications.
Javanese Gentry (from *Para Priyayi* by Umar Kayam), published in 2013 by The Lontar Foundation, Jakarta. Revised edition published by the translator at Mount Wilson in 2014 as *Gentry, Social Change in Java: The Tale of a Family*.
Pescara Tales (1902): Spirit and Flesh: Images of Abruzzo (from *Le Novelle della Pescara (1902)* by Gabriele D'Annunzio), published by the translator at Mount Wilson in 2017.

PREFACE

After six years of trying to interest publishers in producing a current issue of these stories by Yuri Kazakov—and sadly learning that the book trade these days is one that would hardly welcome or know what to do with a Nikolai Gogol or an Anton Chekhov, were the writings of such authors offered to it—I have finally taken the matter into my own hands and submit this compilation directly to the judgement of readers. I must acknowledge that in one or two editorial rejections, it was correctly pointed out to me that Kazakov had already been translated and, it was implied, to no long-lasting acclaim. Well, twenty-eight of the tales in these two volumes have indeed appeared in English, mainly between 1960 and 1970, a decade in which a number of striking literary releases from the Soviet Union—principally the works of Pasternak and Solzhenitsyn—appear to have excited hurried translations of whatever other Russian writers were then showing promise. Kazakov, I believe, suffered from the enthusiasm of amateur linguists, enterprising but too dependent on their dictionaries and unsure of nuance; and he, who himself had toiled as a translator, has left us some wry reflections on the quality of what passed as his work when converted into other languages. Kazakov and a new generation of readers deserve a more considered interpretation; and in fact I also present here ten of his short stories (or items of literary value by some allied definition) that have not, to my knowledge, been rendered before into English.

New information that could cast more light on this perturbing muzhik (thus apparent in his later photographs)—so obsessed with the minutiae, the delicate fading and renewing miracles of our sublunary existence—may have overtaken the comments I made in 2007 in the Afterword at the end of Volume Two; but that minor essay has been left unchanged for the sake of its main point dealing with a long invisible but highly generative element in Kazakov's personality. In any case, readers may safely ignore that Afterword, as indeed they probably wisely do anyway most such editorial accretions on original work, and instead concern themselves with the only text that matters. I invite them to do so forthwith, beginning as an introduction with a small tour de force that is surely some sort of record in being the product of a two-hour composition-exam sat in 1954 at the Gorki Institute in Moscow, and is a first sketch to have drawn discerning readers' attention to the then young writer.

V.V.Zh. 2013

[A background note may be excused on this one occasion. The reader should know that from the time of the 1952 Olympics (two years before this story was written) the U.S.S.R. began promoting sport as a serious arm of national policy, particularly stressing those divisions of athletics that could evince Russian 'might' and 'strength'. The policy presented opportunities to many an aspiring stalwart, who thereby hoped to free himself from the drudgery of the country's habitually grim factories and farms.]

1. AT THE WHISTLE-STOP

It was a cold, bleak autumn day and the rain had darkened the low structure of pine logs, the small station's only building. It was the second day of a mordant north wind that whistled past the dormer window of the station house, circled moaning inside the bell hanging on the platform, agitated the naked branches of the birch trees growing in a line beside the picket boundary. Beneath the trees a horse stood at a broken tethering-rail, head low, swollen legs braced apart. Gusts of wind whipped its tail horizontally, riffled its mane, lifted and dropped the matted hay in the cart behind it, jerked at the reins: the horse neither raised its head nor opened its eyes, seemed in the surrounding unrest to be fixed on some deep, sorrowful cogitation. But perhaps it was just dozing.

On the platform, a young man in a leather overcoat sat on a suitcase. A vigorous shock of hair done in the 'village cut' lifted untidily above his broad, pock-marked face, a face already set in an enduring expression of bad temper etched on it by life. He smoked a cheap cigarette with rapid inhalations, spitting often and rubbing his chin with red, stubby fingers, not lifting his eyes from a gloomy contemplation of the ground. Beside him stood a girl. Her eyes were swollen, and curved tendrils of displaced hair showed beneath the edge of her head-scarf. Her face was pale and tired, and she had the look of someone who had lost all hope and all interest in things around her and grown cold and indifferent, and it was only in her sad dark eyes that something continued to live, painful and unspoken. She was stepping patiently from foot to foot on slender legs booted in dirty galoshes, trying to keep her back to the changing wind while maintaining her gaze fixed on the male's sallow ear, pudgy and battered like a boxer's.

Leaves wheeled around the platform, banked up in mounds, fluttered away again with feeble rustlings, returned to whisper together, then, driven off by the wind once more, they scattered over the damp ground to fall into puddles, flatten on the water and lie still. Dankness and chill were everywhere.

'So, that's how it goes, then.' the young man said suddenly, 'How it turns out. Things, I mean,' and he smiled with his lips. 'Anyway, now it's me who calls the shots, who squares things. What's the kolkhoz to me, hey?... The house? Let my mother and sister have it, it's nothing to me. I'll show up at the Regional and they'll get me a trainer straight off; and somewhere to live. They call them weight-lifters, those characters over there—ha! I've been to the competitions, seen 'em: the best just barely make it to the higher leagues; and I've pressed to Master Standard—did it easy! Know what I'm saying?'

'And what about me?' the girl asked softly.

'About you?' The young man gave her an irritated glance and looked past her. He cleared some phlegm noisily from his throat and said: 'Now look, we've talked about all that already. Let me see how things go there first, and then I'll be back. I haven't got time now, I've got to lift for the records. I'll go to Moscow even, show 'em something. I'm only sorry I didn't get on to this caper sooner. If I had, I'd be long... How do they get on, over there? They train! Well, I've got it here, inside me. You wait a bit, I'll out-press the lot of them. I'll go international. Then just watch if I don't start to live. Yep, with a bit of luck... H'm. Yeah... And I'll come back, and... and then after that... Anyway, don't worry, I'll write.'

From the distance through a pause in the wind came the faint, indistinct sound of the train; and then the grey day's moment of uneasy silence was cut through by a thin, long whistle. And now the door of the station house banged open and the stationmaster came out on the platform. He wore a grease-stained red cap and his chin was hidden in the collar of a greatcoat, what was exposed of his face showing signs that he had been abruptly woken.

He gave the solitary pair a glance, took out a single cigarette from his pocket, turned it crackling between his fingers, sniffed it, looked up at the sky, and then put the cigarette away again. He yawned and called out in a gravelly voice: 'Which carriage?'

The young man swivelled his head slowly on his thick, short neck, and while searching for his ticket he stared with hostility at the stationmaster's figure, ending his examination at the latter's new galoshes.

'Nine,' he replied. 'Why, what's up?'

'No, no; fine... fine...' the stationmaster mumbled indifferently, 'nine, then? Right... nine. And the weather? A bitch. Oh-ho-ho...' and he yawned widely again; then he turned about and wandered off towards the storeroom at the end of the building, avoiding the puddles on the platform as he went.

The train appeared out of a line of forest beyond the fields, approached quickly, began to reduce speed, and shrilled out its call again, a tired, thin noise, and the young man got up and flicked away his cigarette. He looked at the girl. She was trying to smile but her lips would not obey her and they trembled.

'Now that's enough!' he growled, bending towards his suitcase. 'Enough, d'you hear?'

They moved slowly along the platform to meet the approaching train, the girl now looking up, suddenly smiling fervently, eagerly into his face, clutching at his sleeve and speaking rapidly in disordered phrases: 'You look after yourself, now... over there. Don't go lifting too much... or you'll tear a tendon, or something. Think about your health. Don't strain yourself. And I? I'll be waiting! I'll be looking at the papers... to read about you. Don't you even think about me. It's just that... I love you... that's only why I cry. I keep thinking...'

'Enough, now!' said the young man. 'We've talked about it all already. I'll be back soon enough.'

The locomotive passed them, shaking the ground, engulfing them for an instant in the damp warmth of its steam; then the carriages, worn old survivors of the war, passed too, more and more slowly: one, another, a third...

'There's nine!' said the girl excitedly, 'Let's just wait here... it's coming!'

Gently, the carriage stopped next to them. In the passageway stood unkempt, pale travellers, rocking lightly against each other with the train's last movements and peering out. At one of the windows a stout, unshaven man dressed in striped pyjamas was jerking at the frame, his low, puffy forehead wrinkled in concentration. The window would not lift, and the passenger frowned and wore an air of long-suffering. He managed to open the window at last, thrust his torso out and began peering in all directions, on his face the kind of concentrated smile that comes with short-sightedness. Seeing the girl, he smiled more broadly still and called out to her hoarsely: 'Say, missy, oy! What's this station?'

'Lundanka,' rasped the train-guard from below.

'They got a market here?' asked the figure in pyjamas, looking as before at the girl.

'No market,' said the guard. 'We're here for two minutes.'

'How come?' asked the passenger with consternation, still looking at the girl.

'Shut the window, please!' a fretful voice called from inside the carriage.

The man in pyjamas displayed his corpulent back to the platform, then he turned with a sad smile to the window, lowered it, and disappeared immediately as if he had fallen through a trap door.

The young man lifted his suitcase onto the first step of the carriage and turned towards the girl.

'Well... see you... you know...' he muttered glumly and thrust his hands into his pockets.

Tears trickled down the girl's cheeks and choking back a sob she pressed her face into the young man's shoulder.

'It's going to be lonely here,' she whispered. 'See if you can write... as often as you can. Do you hear? Write, and... and you *will* come back?'

The young man looked startled. 'We talked about it all already,' he forced out after a moment. 'Now, come on, wipe your face.'

'No, it's nothing,' whispered the girl. She sighed deeply, and with quick squirrel-movements of her fists rubbed her cheeks and looked up at him with total devotion. 'I'll be on my own. Remember what we said, now.'

'Sure, I remember, what's the big deal!' the young man mumbled sullenly, then he lifted up his eyes and looked about over the top of her head.

'And me, I'm yours for life. You know that, don't you?'

'We talked about it all before,' the young man muttered again, bending his head now to consider the ground between his feet.

The bell struck twice: a dull, muted sound.

'Citizens, on board please; you'll be left behind!' called the guard, and was himself the first to scramble up the steps.

The girl paled further and brought her hand up to her mouth. 'Vasya!' she cried, and looked around with unseeing eyes at the passengers, and they turned away quickly, 'Vasya! At least kiss me!...'

'Aw God...' grumbled the young man. Brought to bay, he bent over the girl; then, upright again, and with an expression of having just discharged a trying duty, he lifted himself lightly up on the step beside his suitcase. The girl made a quiet sound of pain, bit her trembling lip, closed her face with the palms of her hands, instantly brought them down again...

There was a hissing sound under the carriages. From far ahead, the locomotive gave a toot, and a distant weak echo repeated it. Barely perceptibly, the carriages began to move, the sleepers to creak. The young man stood on the step, looking loweringly down at the girl. Then he reddened and said quietly and distinctly: 'Listen... I won't be back!... Did you hear me?...' Through bared teeth he sucked in a long breath, said something else unclear and angry, and lifting his suitcase from the step he clambered sideways up into the passage.

The girl's body appeared to wilt, and she dropped her head.

The gaps between carriages flickered past beside her; beneath, sleepers wheezed hollowly; something went by creaking, noisily squealing. She stood unmoving, unblinking, gazing mutely down at a bright, iridescent slick of oil on one of the rails, a stain which she saw momentarily covered by the wheels, reappearing and being covered again. She looked at it in an absent muse, timidly, unaware herself that she was bending closer towards it, as if it beckoned, pulled at her. She tensed, pressed a hand to her unbearably painful heart, while her lips, still practically the lips of a shy young child, turned paler and paler.

'Hey—look out there!' a sudden angry shout sounded above her head.

The girl started, blinked, and the bright stain grew instantly lighter, the creaking of the sleepers and the knock of the wheels stopped; and lifting up her head she saw that the last carriage with its round, red guard-board on the buffer had passed, seemed now to be moving soundlessly as if floating on air, floating constantly further away.

And then, raising her eyes to the low, indifferent sky, she drew her scarf across her face, and in the immemorial manner of peasant women in grief she rocked, rocked as if drunk, rocked and wailed: 'He's go-o-ne!...'

The train passed through the clearing of fields and disappeared once more into the forest. Everything became quiet again. The stationmaster shuffled up, stopped near the girl, yawned. 'Gone, has he?' he asked. 'Ye-e-s, that's the way of it. They all go nowadays.' He fell silent and spat richly on the ground, grinding the spittle with his heel.

'And I'll be off too, soon,' he muttered. 'I'll apply to go south, that's what I'll do. Here, it's just boredom, rain. Down in the south it's warm, they've got those—what do they call 'em—cypresses...'

He looked at the girl, looked for a moment at her mud-caked galoshes, and then asked in an even, disinterested tone: 'You'd be from the Red Beacon, I suppose? H'm, yes... that's the trouble. And the weather? A bitch, and that's a fact too!'

He shuffled away, avoiding the puddles.

The girl stood a long time on the empty platform, looking straight ahead and seeing nothing: not the dark, sodden forest, nor the wan gleam of the rails, nor the brown, bending and lifting grass. She only saw the pitted, hard face of the young man.

Then she gave a final sigh, wiped her wet face and went out to the horse. She unhitched it, adjusted the girth, tidied the windblown hay in the cart, and then, her feet slithering slightly on the damp earth, she climbed up and took the reins. The horse backed, gave a feeble swing of its tail, turned the cart undirected, and with painful legs pulled out past the station's picket fence, past the bales of hay and the sleepers stacked in criss-cross piles, heading towards the start of the cart track.

The girl sat rigid, gazing over the fields and the hayricks. Then she looked back for a last time at the station, clambered into the rear of the moving cart, and lay face down on the straw.

2. A QUIET MORNING

The drowsy roosters had just crowed, it was still dark inside the izba, Yashka's mother had not milked the cow yet nor had the herder driven his flock to the meadow.

Yashka sat on the edge of his bed and peered sleepily at the window while its sweating glass turned vaguely blue with the beginning of day. Sweet are the slumbers before dawn, it is then especially that one's head lies heavy on the pillow and one's eyelids join tightly together; but the boy roused himself and stood up. Stumbling and clutching at a bench, then at a chair, he tottered about the izba, looking for the patched trousers and shirt he wore when he went fishing.

He dressed and had some bread and milk, collected two fishing rods from the inner porch and stood with them for a moment in the izba's doorway. The village lay softly swathed in a wide, downy quilt of mist, so dense that only the peasant cabins nearest to Yashka's were visible. Further away, other buildings could be just made out as dark discolorations; but even further, towards the river, nothing showed: as if no windmill had ever stood on its knoll there, and there had never been a fire-watch tower beside it or a school or, further yet on the horizon, the beginings of a great forest. All those had vanished, faded away, and only a small, secluded world remained, the centre of which was Yashka's home.

Someone had got up earlier than he, for hammer blows rang out from the direction of the smithy: clear, metallic notes that broke through the shroud of mist, flew as far as the big, unseen grain-barn, and then returned from it as dampened echoes. The echoing made it sound as if two persons were hammering: one loudly, one less so.

Yashka jumped down the steps, waved the rods threateningly at a rooster that hurriedly reversed under his feet, and feeling increasingly lively and awake he crossed the yard towards the threshing shed. There, he pulled a rusty chopper out from under a board and began to dig into the dirt floor. Almost at once he turned up worms: red ones, violet ones, cold to the touch, and whether fat or thin all equally determined to wriggle back into the loosened soil. But Yashka gathered them into a tin, and when it was almost full he covered the worms with a sprinkling of fresh soil. Then he went skipping down a path, scrambled over a wattle fence, cut through several back-yards, and so arrived at the barn in whose loft his new friend, Volodya, slept.

Yashka put two soiled fingers into his mouth, whistled, spat, and stood listening. No sound came from the barn.

'Hey, Volodka!' he called. 'C'mon, get up!'

From up in the loft came a stir and a rustling of hay, followed for a time by the sounds of indecisive movements and more rustling, then Volodya at last appeared. He felt his way down the ladder, reached the ground and stood uncertainly, treading on his untied laces. His sleepy face was creased on one side where he had lain, and his expression was vacant and set like a blind person's, there were shreds of hay in his hair, and some must have fallen inside the back of his shirt, because Yashka watched him stretch his neck, twitch his shoulders, and attempt to reach around himself to scratch his back.

'I say, isn't it rather early?' Volodya asked in a voice hoarse from his recent sleep. He yawned, supporting himself with one hand on the ladder.

Yashka bristled. He himself had woken a good hour earlier, had dug worms and brought the rods, and truth be known it was just to take this goose, this scrawny city-runt fishing, to show him a few of the good spots, that's all he'd got up for! And here, instead of thanks and getting on with it, he was hearing this 'early' palaver!

'For some it's early, it ain't for others!' he said, examining Volodya sourly from head to foot.

Volodya came to the doorway of the barn and put his head out, and as he looked at the misty village-scene his expression changed to one more animated, his eyes took on a shine, and he hurriedly bent down to tie his laces. But for Yashka, this morning which had started out so well was ruined.

'Going in your boots then?' he said with heavy sarcasm. He looked down at his own bare feet and considered for a moment one out-turned big toe. 'Will it be galoshes next?'

Volodya said nothing, but he crimsoned and went on tying the second shoe.

'Yeah, I guess...' said Yashka in a melancholy tone, leaning the rods against the barn wall, 'I guess they don't go bare-foot much in Moscow.'

'Well, what of it?' said Volodya, looking up from his crouch at the other. Yashka had one of those broad, country faces that can quickly take on a derisive and malicious look.

'No, nothing. Why don't you go and put on your overcoat as well?'

'Well then, I might!' muttered Volodya, and he reddened more.

Yashka's gloom grew deeper. It had been a total waste of time getting into this. Even Kolya and Zhenya Voronkov, real fishermen now, even they'd tell you there was no one in the whole kolkhoz smarter than he, Yashka, when it came to fishing. Take him to some spot and watch him pull them in: like shaking an apple tree. But this chump... He comes to see you last evening, all keen and bright and full of Moscow manners: 'Please this, thank you that...' Hell, I should wallop him one in the ear and that'd be the end of it. You're a dope, getting tangled with a townie who's never looked a fish in the eye, probably. He goes fishing in boots!

'You ain't got a tie now?' Yashka continued goading, and he gave a cracked-voice laugh. 'Our fish get sore when you call on 'em without a tie.'

Volodya had finally finished tying his laces. His nostrils worked with the offence of these insults, and he looked straight in front of him with unseeing eyes as the two of them left the barn. He too was ready to give up the thought of fishing, ready to burst into tears, in fact. But he had looked forward so much to this morning! The boys went down the lane, saying nothing and not looking at each other.

They went through the village, and as the mist gave way before them it revealed further houses and barns and the school and the long rows of milk-white structures in which the farming activities of the kolkhoz were carried out; and like a niggardly owner of all this, bestowing just a moment's display of his possessions, the mist then closed everything tightly again behind the pair.

Volodya was deeply miserable. He was unhappy at his own silly responses to Yashka's taunts, angry at Yashka, and he felt himself at this moment quite inept and pathetic. Embarrassed by his awkwardness, and to somehow mute those unpleasant sensations, he tried to harden himself with such mulling as: 'All right: let him go on, let him mock. They don't know me yet. I'll show them what I'm like soon enough, and after that they won't laugh so much! Big deal—going barefoot! Some imagination they've got here, to see that as a talent!' But at the same time he looked with frank envy and admiringly at Yashka, at his unshod feet, at the canvas shoulder-bag he carried strapped across his chest, and at the patched clothing he wore, the old trousers and grey shirt, kept long after their natural life just to go fishing in; he envied Yashka's tan, and even that gait of his: a certain curious, characteristic swing of the upper body and the shoulder-blades, a movement in walking that somehow seemed to involve even the ears and was considered rather smart among the village lads.

As they were passing a well with a wooden winder, its frame grown-over with green moss, Yashka muttered imperatively: 'Hold on a minute— we'll have a drink!'

The chain rattled, he brought up a bucket heavy with water, bent over the brim, and with a show of parched eagerness began drinking. He was not really thirsty, but he had some time ago decided that there was no water anywhere else better than this, and so each time he happened to go past the well he stopped and drank with an epicure's satisfaction. The water overflowed the bucket and splashed his feet, and feeling its coldness there he lapped one foot over the other, but he kept drinking and only paused to take breath.

'Here, have some!' he said to Volodya at last, wiping his mouth on his sleeve.

Volodya was not thirsty either, but he did not want to further provoke

Yashka, and so he too leant over the bucket and took a number of small sips from it, until he could feel the icy water beginning to give him an ache in the back of his head.

'How's that for real water now?' Yashka asked proprietorially when Volodya moved away from the bucket.

'First class!' Volodya acknowledged dutifully, shuddering.

'I'll bet you won't get anything like it in Moscow!' said Yashka with a sharp interrogative look at Volodya, who on his part could make no further response than to suck in his breath through his teeth and smile appeasingly.

'You ever catch much fish?' asked Yashka.

'I've only watched people catching them in the Moscow River,' Volodya confessed apologetically, and he looked at Yashka with timid expectation.

The admission softened Yashka somewhat. He gave the worms in the tin a stir with his finger and said matter-of-factly: 'Yesterday our club manager saw a catfish in the pool out Pleshansky way.'

Volodya's eyes lit up. 'Big?'

'You bet. A good two metres. Maybe all of three. He couldn't tell in the dark. Boy, did he have a fit, thought it was a crocodile. Say, you don't believe me?'

'Oh, you're kidding!' Volodya whispered excitedly, and it was evident in his eyes and by the way his shoulders twitched that he believed everything Yashka had said.

'No, but you think I'm lying?' Yashka said, looking puzzled at the notion. 'If you like, we'll go out there tonight. D'you want to?'

'Can we?' Volodya asked eagerly, and his ears reddened.

'Sure, why not?' Yashka spat and he wiped his nose on his arm. 'I've got all the gear. We'll go to a pond I know and pick up some loach. Get some dew-worms too. They've got chub as well at Pleshansky. Yep, we'll catch the evening bite, stay the night, and be ready for 'em at sunrise. We'll have a fire. What d'you think—coming?'

Volodya began to feel extraordinarily light and happy. For the first time in his life he felt how good it was to be outside in the early morning: one's breath came to one so pleasantly and easily, one wanted to break out into a run, dash down this lane which felt so soft underfoot after the pavements of the city, to run at full pelt and leap and squeal with delight! And what was that strange ringing he heard, somewhere behind him, like a repeated plucking on a tightly-drawn string, like a clear and melodic call, coming from yonder out in the meadows? Where had he heard it before? Or perhaps he had never heard it. But why then did this gaiety and this sense of being amazingly fortunate feel so well-known?

Something crackled noisily in the fields. A motorcycle? Volodya looked at Yashka.

'Tractor!' Yashka informed him confidently.

'Oh, a tractor. But why is it sputtering like that?'

'He's starting it. He'll have it going in a minute. Listen... there, there you are—did you hear that roar? Now he'll be on his way. That's Fedya Kostilev. He's been ploughing all night with the headlights on. He's had a nap and now he's starting again.'

Volodya looked in the direction of the sound and turned again to ask: 'Do you have this mist here all the time?'

'Nope. Sometimes it's clear and sometimes, like later on, closer to September, a frost'll fetch in and it's here before you know it. But that's all right, the fish bite even better when it's misty. Ha!—you can't pull them in fast enough.'

'What kind of fish do you have?'

'What kind, now? There's all kinds. There's carp on the reaches, pike; then there's perch, roach, bream. And then there's tench. You know them—tenches? Like little fat pigs. When I pulled one up the first time, my eyes bugged out.'

'Do you catch many here?'

'H'm. You can't tell. 'Nother time you pull up five kilo, 'nother time there's only enough for the cat.'

'What's that, that whistling up there?' Volodya stopped and looked up.

'That? That's ducks flying. Teal.'

'Oh, I know about those. And what's that?'

'Thrushes. They always jibber like that. They're doing a raid on Aunty Nastya's rowan tree in her garden. You ever caught thrushes?'

'No, never.'

'Mishka Kayunenok's got a net. Just wait a bit and we'll go catching 'em later. Thrushes, they're greedy birds. They come in in a horde to pick up the worms behind the tractor. You stretch out a net, throw some rowanberries under it, hide and wait. They fly in and straightaway maybe five'll get under the net. They're funny birds the way they carry on. Some are really smart. I had one all last winter and it could do all kinds of noises: a steamer, a crosscut saw...'

They left the village behind, and soon there were fields of young, unripe oats stretching before them, and a dark line of forest could just be made out now in the distance.

'Is it a long way yet?' Volodya asked.

'Nah, just over there. C'mon, let's move faster.' This particular exchange was repeated several times.

They came out onto a small hill, turned right, descended through a dip, followed a foot-track across a paddock of flax, and then, unexpectedly, the river stretched in front of them.

It was not a particularly big river. Thick growths of broom and white willow covered its banks, and where it coursed through shallow rapids the purling of the water made a very distinct sequence of sounds. Those shallow stretches emptied at intervals into deep, dark pools.

The sun had appeared, and from meadows on the other side of the river came the thin whinny of a horse. The morning brightened surprisingly quickly, everything around was acquiring a rosy tinge, the dew's hoar on fir trees and on exposed bushes had become more conspicuous, and the mist in reluctantly moving and attenuating at last left revealed hayricks dark against the smoky background of a now nearer forest.

From the pools came periodic and substantial splashes of fish jumping, and with each splash the sedge swayed in the disturbed water. Volodya was eager to start casting at once, but Yashka kept following the bank further along the river. They were soaked with dew almost to the waist before Yashka at last quietly announced: 'Here it is, this is the spot!' and turned down to the water's edge. As he did so he disturbed and sent rolling into the water a clod or two of the bank's damp, loose soil—and instantly some till-then unseen ducks flapped off with a great quacking! Their wing-tips left parallel rows of circles in the water, until, necks craned forward, they ascended and disappeared into the mist. Both boys were startled: Yashka jerked down into a crouch and hissed like a goose, Volodya licked his suddenly dry lips and moved closer to Yashka, for in addition to his alarm, now that Volodya was near the water he was also struck by the gloom reigning over the place. This was a wide pool smelling of dampness, of clay and ooze, and the water was impenetrably black. The sky above was almost hidden by tall, dense foliage, and although individual leaves in the highest branches were now rosy with sunlight, and patches of blue had become visible through the mist, yet beneath that canopy and all about the pool everything was humid, dark and cold.

'You know how deep this goes?' Yashka asked, and his eyes turned to Volodya were round with awe, 'There ain't no bottom!'

Volodya stepped a half pace back from the edge and shuddered. At that moment from near the other bank there was the sound of a fish jumping and thudding back into the water.

'There's no one goes swimming in this pool.'

'Oh? Why?' asked Volodya in a weak voice.

'It sucks you down. Put a foot in there—and that's the end! The water's like ice and it drags you down. Mishka Kayunenok says there's octopuses sitting down there on the bottom.'

'Octopuses are... only in the sea,' Volodya said uncertainly, and he retreated a little further from the water.

'Yeah, don't I know that? But Mishka saw one. He went fishing once, goes past here, looks—he sees a ten-taycle poke out of the water, and it starts feeling and groping along the bank. What d'you make of that, ha? Mishka didn't stop running till he got to the village! But it's all probably a lie, I know him.' With that somewhat unexpected conclusion, Yashka began to disentangle the rods and lines.

Volodya stared intently at the pool and tried to collect himself; but as for Yashka, he had already forgotten about any octopuses and now looked up with impatience, tensing his face with a pained expression, each time there was the loud splash of a fish.

Having separated the rods, he passed one to Volodya, doled him a few worms in a matchbox, and indicated with a jerk of his head the direction where Volodya was to cast.

Yashka cast, and then holding his rod in one hand and the loose end of the line with the other he stood on the bank with his eyes fixed on the float. A moment later Volodya cast as well, but the tip of his rod caught in a branch. Yashka turned a terrible glare on him and muttered something under his breath, before returning to his float. But where it had been— only some fine circles of water now spread from that spot! Yashka struck hard, whipping the rod smoothly back and to his right, feeling a satisfying elastic resistance from the struggling fish down below. But then the tension suddenly slackened, and the far end of the line broke surface with a whop! and a bare hook.

Yashka quivered with anguish. 'Got off then, did you? Got off...' By turns muttering and looking out on the water, he threaded with wet fingers another worm on the hook.

He threw out again, and again stood holding the rod, his eyes fastened unblinkingly on the float, ready for the next bite. But there were no bites, and even the splashes had stopped. Yashka's hands began to tire and he carefully rammed the butt of the rod into the soft earth of the bank. Volodya, watching him, did the same with his rod.

The sun rose gradually higher, and eventually it even peeped into the gloomy surroundings of the pool. When it did, the change down there was rapid: within moments the water glittered blindingly, and on each bank dew-drops caught fire on the surface of leaves and in the grass and on flowers. Volodya sat in his place, frowning with concentration. After staring at his float for some time he looked up and down the river and asked tentatively: 'What do you think, have they gone away? To another pool, maybe?'

'Course they have!' Yashka snapped back fiercely. 'It got off the hook and scared the others. And a good one it was too. I just had time to hit it and it pulled my hand right down! A good kilo it would have been.'

Yashka was embarrassed at having lost the fish, and in the usual way of these things was finding the cause of his misfortune in someone else: Volodya, of course. 'Some fisherman, gee!' he thought glumly to himself. 'Look at him sitting there... legs poking out everywhere. You go on your own or with someone that knows the game and then you can't pull 'em in fast enough!' He was trying to think of some cutting remark to make to Volodya—when he had to dart towards his rod: the float had bobbed lightly! Pulling the rod out of the ground, as slowly as if uprooting a sapling, he lifted it and stood poised, holding it balanced with its tip slightly raised above the horizontal. The float bobbed again, then lay on its side for a moment, then straightened once more. Yashka released his breath, flicked a glance around and caught a glimpse of Volodya, pale with apprehension, slowly rising to his feet. Yashka's body grew hot, specks of perspiration appeared along his nose and above his upper lip. The float trembled again, travelled sideways, dipped down halfway, and finally shot under completely, leaving just a thin spreading ring in the water. As before, Yashka struck lightly and firmly. He took a quick pace forward and attempted to straighten the rod, but now it and the line traced a curve on which a jerking float hung partway above the water. Standing half-crouched and feeling many quick, strong tugs, Yashka caught the rod with his other hand as well, the line gripped under that hand, and once again he swung smoothly to the right. Volodya sprang towards Yashka, with eyes desperate, wide and shining, and he squealed: 'Come on, come on, come o-on!...'

'Get away!' rasped Yashka. He was stepping back and being repeatedly pulled forward again.

The fish leapt out of the water, showed a broad, glinting flank for an instant, gave the surface a tight tail-slap that raised a small fountain of rosy spray into the air, and then shot down again into the cold depths. But Yashka was now holding the butt of the rod into his stomach and taking little backward steps, intoning: 'No wa-ay... not to-da-ay... you're a-comin', like it or not...'

He gradually brought the fish to the edge of the bank, with a little heave tossed it up on the grass and then leapt on it to cover it with his body.

Volodya's lips were dry and his heart was beating. 'What is it?' he kept asking, squatting beside Yashka, 'What have you got?'

'Bream!' Yashka uttered, panting. He carefully extracted it, large and cold, from under his stomach.

He had turned his broad-cheeked, triumphant face towards Volodya, when suddenly the smile on it, prelude to one of his rasping laughs, unexpectedly faded—his eyes widening and fixed on something beyond Volodya, he made a slithering lunge in that direction and gasped: 'Your rod! Look!'

Volodya whirled around and saw that the rod he had planted upright in the bank was now dislodging a lump of earth, was being slowly bent down, and was about to be pulled into the water by something powerfully jerking on the line. He bounded forward, stumbled, fell to his knees, and dragging himself further on them he just managed to stretch out his hand and grasp the rod at the last moment. The rod bent convulsively, Volodya in the act of standing up with it turned a round-eyed, bloodless face towards Yashka.

'Hold on to it!' Yashka bellowed.

But at that moment the bank under Volodya's feet moved, gave way, and losing his balance, dropping the rod, with his arms absurdly lifted and embracing the air as if to catch a ball, he uttered a ringing 'A-a-a-a!...'—

and fell into the water.

'You... you dope!' cried Yashka hoarsely, his face twisted with pain and fury, 'You bloody goof, you've scared the fish!...'

He picked up a grass-matted clod of earth to throw at Volodya's head the instant it surfaced.

But as he looked down on the water, and as he waited, his stance froze, and a queer feeling came over him, the kind a dreamer experiences when his whole body seems paralysed and unable to respond to some appalling *thing* his helpless mind has become aware of. For when Volodya finally emerged he was three metres from the bank and was floundering, thrashing the water with his arms, turning up his white face and bulging eyes to the sky, gulping water and spluttering, sinking again and rising, trying to shout something, but all that came from his throat was a gargled: 'Ya-kha!... Ya-a!...'

'He's drownin'!' Yashka understood with horror. 'It's got him!' He dropped the clod and wiped his hand on his trousers. Without taking his eyes from Volodya, and with a feeling of lassitude in his legs, he began retreating backwards up the bank, away from the awful sight; for into his memory rose Mishka's story of the giant octopus living on the bottom of the pool, and an icy feeling filled his chest and stomach. He knew now that an octopus had caught Volodya! Supporting himself on trembling arms, earth cascading from under his heels, trancelike, his eyes still turned down to the pool, he kept backing unsteadily up the bank.

He reached the edge of the flax, turned, and poised himself to take the first steps of flight towards the village, the hideous noises rising from Volodya below following him. But he had not taken three paces before he came to a stumbling halt. Running away was impossible!... Yet there was no one near, no one to cry to for help!... Yashka began a frantic rummaging in his pockets and in the shoulder-bag, to find something, a length of string perhaps, any conceivable means of responding to what was happening. He could find nothing. Ashen-faced, he stole back and looked over the edge of the bank, expecting to see some horror, while hoping at the same time that all had yet turned out well, had been somehow resolved down there. And he saw Volodya again. Volodya had stopped thrashing about and was now almost completely submerged, only the crown of his head with its spread mop of floating hair was visible, appearing and disappearing time and again. Not taking his eyes from the sight, Yashka let drop his trousers, and now only in his shirt, his bag still strapped across his chest, he shouted something unintelligible and almost rolled down the bank. He leapt into the water and in two strokes reached Volodya and grabbed him by the arm.

Volodya instantly clutched at him. His hands clawed Yashka's shirt and bag, his arms and body enveloped Yashka's, while, as before, he uttered those inhuman, terrible noises: 'Ya-a!... Ya-a-a!...' Yashka gulped water. Feeling Volodya's death-grip around his neck he tried to lift his own face out of the water, but Volodya, trembling weakly, clambered over him, weighed him down, attempted to climb on Yashka's shoulders. Yashka choked on more water and gurgled out a strangled cough. He needed air and was swallowing water instead! And then a wild, unprecedented terror gripped him, red and yellow circles flashed and expanded brilliantly before his eyes, and he understood that Volodya was drowning him, that his death had arrived. With all his strength he strove to wrench himself free, rolled, and with a shout as inhumanly frightful as any he had heard uttered a moment ago, he kicked Volodya in the stomach, surfaced, and saw through the screen of his own streaming hair the momentary sight of a bright, flattened-out roundness—the sun! Still entangled below with the weight of Volodya, he broke away and flung the other from him at last. With a panicked thrashing of arms and legs that raised a churn of brown foam, he took off for the bank.

He reached it and held himself beside it by some sedge. In a moment, recovered, he whirled around to look back. The turbulent water had stilled, nothing showed now on its surface; a few gay bubbles were trickling up from the depths, rising to the surface and popping there. Yashka's teeth chattered.

He looked about him. The sun shone brightly, leaves on the surrounding trees and bushes gleamed, webs that were strung between flowers shimmered with the colours of the rainbow, a wagtail perched on a twig was swaying its tail from side to side and with an eye like a shining bead peeped down at him. Everything was as it had always been, everything breathed calmness and quiet, a placid morning hung over the land. And yet, just now, a moment ago, something strange and beyond thought had happened: a boy drowned. And it was he, Yashka, who had struck the fatal blow, had drowned him.

Blinking water from his eyes, he let go the sedge, his shoulders moved spasmodically under his wet shirt while he breathed deeply, once, twice... and then dived. He opened his eyes under water and at first could not distinguish anything. He saw around him some unclear, wavering, yellowish and greenish patches of light, then an extent of what appeared to be grass illuminated by a ray of sunlight, but little of the light reached into the deeper levels of the pool. He swam lower into those depths, the grass brushing his arms and face; and it was there that he saw Volodya, lying on his side, a loose tangle of grass around one leg, his body slowly turning, rocking, presenting his pale, round face to the attenuated sunlight, one hand gently moving in a plucking motion as if feeling for something in the water. It seemed to Yashka that Volodya was feigning, that the faint gesture of that hand was a luring deception and that Volodya was watching him, ready to clutch at him the moment Yashka touched him.

Feeling that his lungs would burst, Yashka darted towards Volodya, seized the hand, grimacing with his need for air he wrenched Volodya upwards and was surprised to feel how effortlessly and obediently the body followed him. Surfacing, he gulped air greedily—the one and only thing he needed at that instant, the only important thing, was to breathe and find wondrously clean, sweet air filling his chest with every gasp!

By a series of lunges and gripping Volodya's shirt he towed him towards the bank. It was a difficult swim. When he felt the bottom under his feet he pushed Volodya chest-down over the edge of the bank with his face in the grass, then he dragged himself out of the water; finally, he pulled Volodya wholly up on the bank as well, flinching at the touch of the cold body, at the sight of the dead, motionless face; but he moved hurriedly, frantically, feeling himself devoid of strength and utterly wretched.

Turning Volodya on his back Yashka began pumping the boy's arms, pressing his stomach, blowing into his nostrils. He panted, grew more tired yet; and Volodya remained the same: pale and cold. 'Dead!' Yashka thought in panic, and horror grew in him. Could he run away somewhere, to hide? Anywhere, as long as he did not have before him that expressionless cold face.

With a snuffling sob of despair, he leapt up, gripped Volodya by the ankles, turned him about, and with his remaining strength dragged him a little higher on the incline of the bank; and there, crimsoning with the effort, he began shaking the body so that it quaked from end to end. Volodya's head bounced on the ground, the hair grew matted with loam... And at the moment when Yashka had used himself up, was about to drop everything and run hopelessly wherever his eyes led him—at that very moment a surge of water gushed out of Volodya's mouth, he groaned, a series of convulsions shook his whole body! Yashka dropped Volodya's ankles, he closed his eyes and sat down on the ground.

Volodya slowly lifted himself. He rose a little at a time, leaning on trembling arms, rose until he had attained a bent-over stance, and he remained thus for a long moment, like a runner ready to sprint forward in a race, and then he collapsed again. He was gripped by a frenzy of coughing, spattering water about him and writhing on the damp grass.

Yashka crept limply to one side a little, and from there he looked at Volodya. There was no one he felt kindlier towards at this moment, there was nothing on earth dearer to him than that pale, frightened and anguished face. A timid, loving light glowed in Yashka's eyes, and he gazed with tenderness at Volodya, while he kept asking him senselessly: 'You're all right now, ain't you?... How d'you feel now?...'

Volodya straightened a little and wiped his hand across his face. Looking at the pool and then at Yashka, he managed with an effort to stutter something in an unfamiliar, croaking voice: 'D-did you see... how I was d-drowning?...'

Then all at once Yashka's face twisted into a deep frown, then it crumpled; uncontrolled tears sprayed from his eyes and he cried, he howled, loudly and inconsolably, so that his whole body shook, so that he gasped for breath. Ashamed of his crying, he could not stop. He sobbed out of relief, out of joy at having survived a terrible thing, and because every-thing had come out all right, and Mishka Kayunenok had lied and there were no octopuses in that pool at all.

Volodya's eyes narrowed as he tried to concentrate, and his mouth opened slightly. He peered with alarm and bewilderment at Yashka and then managed to squeeze a question out of himself: 'Wha's matter?'

'Y-yes...' with difficulty Yashka blurted out in his turn, trying desper-ately not to cry any more, wiping his eyes with his trousers, 'you was d-drownin'... an' I had to g-go in for you...' and he bellowed even more help-lessly and loudly.

Volodya blinked again, a grimace now twisted his face too as he looked at the water, and his heart shuddered inside him while the whole event came back to him. 'I was d-drowning... d-did you see it?' he asked again, seemingly in astonishment; and then he burst into tears as well, his thin shoulders shuddering, feebly lowering his head and turning away from his rescuer.

The pool had been still for some time now. The fish had freed itself from Volodya's line, and his rod floated near the edge of the bank. The sun shone, the bushes continued to glisten with a sprinkling of dew, and only the water remained as dark as it had been at first.

The morning was advancing and the horizon shimmered and trembled in the currents of warming air. From fields far across the river, borne on gentle gusts of warm wind came the smell of hay and sweet clover, those balmy odours blending with even more distant but sharper forest-smells; and that gentle, genial wind seemed like the breathing of an awakening countryside, awakening to and rejoicing in a new, light-filled day.

3. THE HOUSE BELOW THE CLIFF

1

When Blokhin arrived in the rural town it was evening. He got out with his suitcase from the bus where it had stopped outside the District Committee building and he stood there for some moments considering his surroundings. A light snow was falling, the street lamps were dead, and the only illumination came from house windows throwing long yellow bands across the street.

After asking directions to the hotel from a passer-by, he went down a narrow lane, walked for some time past low, squat buildings that struck him somehow as reminiscent of barges, and finally came to the place. He knocked, and he heard someone coming down the internal stairs; but the door did not open. On Blokhin's request for a bed, a long moment of silent consideration followed on the other side of the door, until at last came the reply: 'There's nothing.'

'But where am I supposed to spend the night?' Blokhin asked, shocked, looking with irritation at the dully-glinting old-fashioned bronze knocker. 'Hey in there, open up!'

But there was no further answer. The person inside could be heard labouring back up the stairs, and Blokhin thought with resentment that the fellow must be some fair sort of a lump to make the stairs creak like that.

He left the hotel. Coming upon a roadside pedestal, vacant of whatever pre-revolutionary statuary it had once supported, he brushed the snow from it and sat down to think his situation over. He had arrived from Moscow, and since as a rule he travelled little he had hardly slept during the journey, tense and excited as he was and full of concern about how he was going to set himself up and how he was going to live in this distant place he was heading to. When he arrived by the Moscow train at the oblast's administrative centre, it was a further seventy versts by bus to this town. Blokhin had spent half a day looking for that connecting bus, had found it at last, and here he was. Now he was tired and despairing over what to do next or where to go. At the point when his feet were beginning to freeze, he saw a young woman approaching, and he decided to tell her his situation. She listened to him in thoughtful silence and then led him through more dark lanes and past snowed-over houses back up into the centre of the town.

They arrived at the regional Palace of Culture, a warm and well-lit building and at that moment alive with some sort of noisy activity. Little groups of what Blokhin took to be local youths wandered through the entry corridor and gaped into doorways, while from somewhere above came the sound of a loud and ill-tuned wind orchestra. The young woman vanished into a room, and a minute later the figure of what appeared to be a merchant from the previous era emerged. He wore a handsome goatee, and a heavy mayoral chain hung across his stomach. The young men fell silent and fixed their open-mouthed attention on him.

'I understand you are looking for a room?' that worthy asked politely in a surprisingly youthful voice, and then with a series of grimaces he began to tear off his beard. 'If you'd like to wait a minute, I can take you to one.'

He went away beardless, shaking his fist mock-menacingly at the lads as he passed them. Five minutes later he returned wearing an overcoat, to be revealed now as a rosy-faced and quite young man.

'Right then, we're away!' he said cheerfully, releasing a sigh of relief, evidently at leaving behind him the din and press in the building. And there and then Blokhin decided that this was a strange and gay little town and learning to live here ought not be an excessively difficult matter.

The young man took him past wooden fences and stone garden-walls, past a teahouse outside whose entrance rimed-over horses stood among the frozen heaps of their droppings, past white homes with black windows; and all the while his felt boots creaked on the snow and he talked to Blokhin about the place he was leading him to:

'The house is down the bottom, right close to the river, and the room is all right, it's liveable and all that. It's just that the woman's a bit of an odd 'un.'

'Oh?' said Blokhin.

'It's, well... But you'll not be staying long, will you? Things got a bit awkward when I was there once; but you shouldn't have any worries, just pay her, don't get involved, and that's it.'

'Is it a separate room?'

'It's separate. Are you here on an official trip?'

'I'm still studying. I've come for my practicum.'

'Oh, your practicum? Not with our Palace by any chance?'

'No, the library.'

'H'm, yes... a pity. Because we might have got some really interesting things going... Is that suitcase heavy? Let me take it.'

'No, it's all right, thanks. In this house, is there anyone else apart from the woman?'

'Her daughter.'

'Oh? Is she young?'

'The daughter?' There was a moment of silence before he replied: 'Yes, young. Quite young.'

And there the thought came to Blokhin: 'Ah, so that's what it's about, a girl. I'll bet he tried to get friendly and it didn't work out.' And he felt a growing curiosity, felt quite light in spirit, thinking that here he was going to a house where lived a young and no doubt pretty girl.

They descended into a wide natural cutting through the centre of which flowed the river, on the way down they passed some sparse, dark trees, turned left at the bottom and walked beneath the cliff-like wall of the cutting. On their right were bath-huts and houses, light showing occasionally through chinks in the closed shutters of the latter, and beyond the houses the river was not so much a presence to be seen as sensed: a broad, indistinct extent of snow-covered water.

'This is known as Embankment Lane,' Blokhin heard the other informing him. 'The land slipped from those cliffs a long time ago and people have built here. They go for locking themselves up in these parts. As soon as it starts to get dark, bang go the shutters. What a race! They've all got their own wells around here. They're Old Believers, you know, church dissenters and such, devil take the lot of 'em. And, you wouldn't credit it—the old ones keep a coffin and a cross in the back shed. Seems they worry about being polluted after they're buried. They're dead set on lying with their own kind, under their own crosses.'

'Why, how curious!' Blokhin said with genuine wonder.

'Curious to some,' the other muttered. He led Blokhin to a house with a tall covered entrance. Half the house was in darkness and the other half showed enough weak light to illuminate the snow-caps on each picket of a low wooden fence.

'There you are. Check it out. I'm off. If something doesn't suit, come to the Palace and we'll give you a hand. And for that matter pop in any time. Ask for Kolya Balaev, everyone knows me up there.'

He walked away whistling and disappeared into the gloom, and his whistling was audible for a little while. Blokhin found a besom leaning in the entrance of the house, brushed the snow from his boots and knocked on the door.

A young woman, barely more than a girl, opened to him. She wore a smock with the skirt gathered up for free movement and her sleeves were rolled up. She was breathing audibly, her hands were soiled, and a strand of hair adhered to one cheek. Seeing Blokhin she caught her breath, tugged the folds of her smock down, and pushed the strand away from her face with her shoulder. She led him into the kitchen and then left him to return to the front door. Locking it again seemed to take a long time.

'Talk to mother,' she said quickly to Blokhin when he began his explanations. Her voice was tremulous, and she blushed. She left the kitchen.

The mother came: a meagre woman with thin, tightly-pressed lips and a dismal expression, the perpetual look of one who seemingly had met some misfortune only minutes ago.

'A room? Yes, we rent rooms. Have a look if you like.' She led him to a glass-panelled door, opened it and turned on the light. 'A good room; an excellent room; clean. Are you on your own or with family?'

'On my own.'

'Well, we had a professor staying here last year. And two engineers. It's a good room, warm.'

The room was chilly, bare, and smelled very stale. Blokhin frowned.

'What would you be thinking? To stay long?' she asked, watching him carefully.

'A month,' Blokhin said shortly. Within a moment of meeting the woman he had begun to dislike her, while his mind kept returning to the girl who had opened the door to him.

'Well, it's an excellent room, quiet, you'll think you're living in the country.'

'And how much would it be?'

'Well, it's like this: when the professor lived here he paid two hundred roubles. Mind you, he was hardly ever at home.'

'Two hundred!' Blokhin repeated, frowning again. It was a lot.

'And then of course there's the firewood,' the woman added quickly. 'What, you don't think you'll need to heat the room?' Blokhin's expression had shown consternation. It changed to shock at the thought of freezing, and seeing his second reaction the woman went on, 'Ah, well, in that case I'll have to heat it; and wood, my dear man, comes to a pretty sum. We're living in evil times, you'll probably be aware.'

Blokhin felt the situation becoming more and more distasteful, but after the long trip he did so want to warm up, to find some haven, any place; and then, in fact, what choice did he have? He decided he must take the room. 'Why should I get bothered over some landlady?' he thought, 'She's got her life, I've got mine. And I'm not going to be here forever, am I?'

'Oh, very well. I suppose it's all right,' he said. At that moment he heard something fall in an adjoining room.

'Why don't you go out for a stroll and I'll get things ready in here,' the woman said to him, with her attention on whatever was happening on the other side of the wall.

Blokhin left the house with relief, and once out on the street quickly lit a cigarette. He did not really feel like going anywhere, and he went down to the edge of the river and stood there thinking.

He was twenty-six years old, just graduating from his institute, and lately he thought often about marriage but abhorred any notion of marriage without love. Somehow, though, love never seemed to come his way, and that was growing to be a concern with him, a failure which disturbed him and sometimes even oppressed him. As with so many young people, he for some reason had no confidence in anything remarkable ever happening to him in his own city or at the place where he studied: 'at home' in short. Whatever went on in his native surroundings was habitual and commonplace, the extraordinary lay somewhere far away; and for that reason, he loved the thought of travel, of voyaging, and each time he prepared for his infrequent trips he was almost certain that something very wonderful would occur on that particular occasion, someone would surely fall in love with him. Well, he went, and nothing happened; however, the hope lived on.

Now, looking across the snowy expanse of the wide river stretching away downstream, indistinguishable from the meadows on its banks, he thought about that girl who had shown such confusion when opening the door to him. And the more he thought about her the more animated those thoughts became: why, might not this be the long-awaited event, that astonishing turn of fortune envisaged in his reveries? Who was she? How had she lived until now, and what did she herself dream about and look forward to? He tried to recall her lips and the colour of her eyes, the form of her face; but he remembered nothing, felt only that she was attractive and that her discomfiture could mean much.

'Good!' he exclaimed audibly, and his voice startled him, and he looked around, and doing so he caught sight of the house, glowing with a light softened by distance. After Moscow everything seemed so silent and strange here. His mood suddenly lifted and he became quite excited. He finished his cigarette and flicked it into the air, it fell into the snow and he looked at it for some moments where it lay within the rosy stain of its own glow.

'Time to go back!' he thought, and he began walking towards the house, smiling in the darkness and listening happily to the crunch of his soles on the snow.

2

The floor of the room had been wiped over, and a narrow iron bed furnished with a grey, greasy pillow now stood by one wall. The woman followed him in. She kept glancing fretfully at Blokhin and then turning her wan face towards the wall, giving at those moments the distinct impression of seeing whatever was happening on the other side, in the kitchen.

'Will you be needing linen?' she asked.

'Well of course!' Blokhin replied with irritation, lifting his eyebrows and making no effort to conceal his surprise at such a question. His animosity towards this landlady was growing by the instant.

The bed was made up, a tablecloth appeared on the table, and the landlady departed. Blokhin calmed down, opened his suitcase, took his things out and arranged them; then he sat down with one of his books and began reading it. But soon he found it too dismal sitting there: reading did not suit him after all, what he wanted was a nice tall glass of tea and someone with whom to talk.

He put down the book. Leaning on his elbows, he looked out through the dark, sweating glass of the window, listened to the crackle of the wood in the stove; and then the thought came to him and held him that only yesterday he had been in Moscow, walking about the Arbat, and now here he found himself in someone's house, among strangers, people who after all were totally indifferent to him and to the things that had made him what he was, people who were unconcerned about what he did, who would probably never even remember him after he had gone away.

Blokhin's musing grew progressively more doleful; he thought that it was time he went to bed, although in fact he did not feel sleepy. He got up, paced around the room, felt the hot stove with the tips of his fingers, stood listening. Finally, he went out into the kitchen.

The girl, clad now in a dark dress, sat at the table, sewing. Seeing him appear, she flushed and made an initial movement as if she were about to stand up and leave the room; but she did not go, only lowered her head further over her work. Blokhin looked around the kitchen, sat down at the table and asked quietly: 'Where is your mother?'

'She's outside. Feeding the young pig.'

Her voice was gentle and low and she answered hesitatingly, as if not quite sure she had understood what had been asked. Her gold-blond hair was waved slightly at the temples and hung in curls over her forehead, and all the glossy mass of it, faintly suggestive of a source of luminosity within itself, was cleanly divided by a straight part.

'How old could she be?' Blokhin wondered, 'Eighteen? Nineteen?' He looked at those curls, the parting, at her slender neck, and he regretted not being twenty again, that he was not handsome, and he felt the inner impress of a wearying sadness. He wanted to sit there and just look at her. 'God, fancy now, you could really fall in love here!' he thought suddenly, unhappily.

'What do you do? Work? Study?' he began again.

The girl lifted her head. Blokhin saw that there were minute, pale freckles on her nose and brow, and that she had a very small mouth with red lips, and her eyes were innocent and limpid. And he also saw in those eyes that they had their own world, far from his, had their own life, foreign to him and at this moment out of reach to him.

'I work,' she said quietly in a tone devoid of any pretensions. 'As an accounts clerk, over on the other side of the river. I tried to go to an institute, but they wouldn't take me. I studied like mad, and it was all for nothing.'

'And life gets pretty dull, I suppose?'

'It's all right when I work, during the day. At night it's very dull. I'm always on my own, always. I don't go outside much, hardly ever to see a film or anything. My mother doesn't like to be left alone. I sew, like this... It's nice that you've taken a room with us, I don't like empty rooms. I was worried that you wouldn't like it here. It's out of the way. What's there to like here?' And she looked apathetically around the kitchen and her eyes seemed to darken.

It suddenly came into Blokhin's mind to say to her: 'You know something? I rather like you!' But he said nothing.

'Have you been to Moscow?' he asked after a pause.

The girl looked down and just shook her head. Blokhin began talking about Moscow: he spoke of the theatres, the institutes, the stadiums; and as he spoke his voice without his noticing it began to acquire a boastful edge; and the girl listened as children listen to a fairy-tale, and a weak glow came to her cheeks, her eyes glistened, she moved her sewing to one side, put her elbows on the table and looked without blinking at Blokhin as he continued his relation. Her unmoving eyes worried and unsettled him, but his recent despondency and boredom had left him and he was practically happy now.

The dark, snow-blanketed town, with its old, outdated, belly-alcoved merchant mansions; the teahouse, its yard odorous of hay, manure and snow, its patient, waiting sleigh-horses; the Palace of Culture and its out-of-tune orchestra and people in wigs; the things he had been recently told and the thoughts that had come to him on the way here; the empty wide river; finally, this house, the disagreeable landlady and her gentle, trusting daughter—all those struck him now as fascinating, unprecedented and somehow significant.

'How lucky you are!' said the girl with naive envy. 'Here am I, born in these backwoods, went to school: and now it seems to me I've never known anything or lived at all.' She smiled unexpectedly, wistfully and sadly. 'You wouldn't know how hard I worked all summer. It was hard even to write them something about myself, my autobiography. What could I say? Three lines: I was born, I've studied, I dig the kitchen-garden, do the wash, and in summer I go berry-picking. Whatever else has there been? There's nothing in my life. I go to see a film sometimes, or I listen to the radio: you hear that something is being done, someone or other has accomplished something, someone else has gone to the virgin lands, they play sport in the world out there, study wonderful things, places are all lit up at night, life is interesting. And I don't see any of that. Who told you about our house?'

'A young chap from the town, he brought me here. From the Palace of Culture.'

'Oh, I know. It was Kolya Balaev, wasn't it? Did he say anything to you?'

'No, nothing,' Blokhin replied, and he felt a sudden unidentifiable twinge. 'He didn't say anything. Why?'

'He lived here once. What a nice man. You know, I started to take part in the theatricals over there. We used to go walking together, talking, making plans... But my mother...' The girl suddenly reddened, 'my mother threw him out. She just literally threw him out. And as for me, she... But now we never meet.'

'You loved him, did you?' Blokhin forced himself to ask.

'No,' she answered after a moment's thought, 'No. I don't know how love feels yet, but what we had... it wasn't that.' A minute passed, and then she asked: 'Do you like our town?'

'It is rather a funny place. Those old houses that belonged to the merchants, the horses, snow, dark streets... we don't have that in Moscow.'

'Ah, Moscow,' the girl sighed, and a shadow passed across her eyes again. 'Our town is old, it's been here eight hundred years; and life here is somehow old too. Our big pride is that some Grand Duke died here. Isn't that something, now! There's a movie theatre and schools and a tech college, and in summer they all ride around on their bicycles; but life is just dull all the same. Around here, you go past houses, and it's all the world of those old merchants, how it was. They had their money taken away, but apart from that they haven't changed, all bearded. They sit in the teahouse in the evenings, drinking tea. On our road they are all Old Believers; and my mother is one too. She doesn't like people. There's a prayer-room not far from here where they meet and pray, mutter things together. I've been there too, but I don't believe in anything. Just out of spite. My mother didn't let me join the Youth League. So I sit here, sewing... and what the point of it all is, or whoever needs what I do, I don't know. Why do I live?'

Tears stood in her eyes and she quickly turned her face away to look at a wall. Suddenly from outside the window a sharply clear and regular beat came to Blokhin's ears, from its initial onset growing louder as it approached the house: it resembled a very loudly-ticking alarm clock.

'What on earth is that?' he asked.

'That?' the girl sighed, catching her breath, and she looked at the dark window. 'It's the night watch... it's his clapper.'

'His clapper?' Blokhin repeated, astounded. In his life he had never heard the thing before. 'Why is he doing it?'

'I don't know,' the girl replied with reluctance. 'He rattles it, rattles... and sometimes I think I hear that sound in my head.'

Tak-tok-tak-tok-tak-tok... the dreary noise was passing them now; and then it diminished and Blokhin looked with amazement and even with some apprehension at the girl sitting before him; and the thought of what a melancholy thing it really must be to live in this house possessed him for a moment.

'But how can all this go on?' he began aloud. 'It can't go on. What sort of a poor devil's fate is this? Why don't you... Yes, of course, I understand that your mother... But your mother is already old, her life is over; and then she had a different kind of life altogether, she would have been born before the revolution, she was used to living like this. But you! Go and talk to her, make her see. Look, if you want, I'll speak to her!'

'No, no, don't!' the girl said in a pleading voice. 'I beg you, don't! It won't do any good. Don't you think I've talked with her about it? Many times! But I'm alone here, there's no one to back me up. And I've got used to it, really. And I'm not the only one either; there are many others like me here, if only you knew! We get used to it. You see, we're brides, we need to be protected, to be married as well as possible when the time comes. But it's so hard sometimes, if only you knew! Mother's told you that we've had professors living here, I heard. She's lying. No one's lived with us. They stay for a week and then leave, stay and leave. While I've been here years. Sometimes I get angry, so that I would like to tear down this damned house with its ewes and its piglets!'

'Then get away from here—leave!' Blokhin said, now agitated.

'Leave? Don't you think I've wanted to? What's the point of thinking about that? Where would I go? Who would want me? I don't know anything, I have no skills, no relatives, no one in the whole world...'

Steps could be heard in the corridor, the girl instantly stopped talking and bit her lip. The landlady entered. She put down a bucket by the door, gave Blokhin and her daughter a cold look, hung up her overcoat and went to her room.

A minute later her voice addressed him from there: 'Will you be having tea?'

'No, thank you,' he said, and it was an effort to reply. He felt a strange constriction in his breast and some sort of bitter aftertaste there: the conversation had left him sickened and ashamed. The girl was no longer looking at him, she was pulling rapidly at a thread in her sewing, her small hands, coarsened with working outside in the cold, trembled. Blokhin could not bear to look at those trembling hands, he stood up and began to walk towards his room.

'Wait!' the girl exclaimed in a frightened voice.

He turned and saw her rising hastily and awkwardly from the table, holding her hands to her breast. She went to him, her temples and ears glowing red, and from her eyes it was evident that she too was ashamed of something.

'Why are you leaving?' she asked softly, looking at Blokhin in such a way that he began to be alarmed. 'I was telling you about me because...'

'Tanya!' the landlady snapped in a high-pitched voice from her room.

'Because I hadn't for a long time...'

'Tanya! Come here! What are you whispering about over there? Shameless girl!'

'I'm coming!' the girl shouted back in an angry and tormented tone, stamping her foot.

'What's that? Did you hear what I said?' Determined footsteps could be heard crossing the woman's room. The girl looked at Blokhin with eyes full of painful humiliation.

'We'll talk again, won't we?' she whispered quickly and went, leaving him with the sensation of her warm, childish breath.

He entered his own room, closed the door quietly and stood listening, not breathing. 'What a devil of a business!' he thought, releasing his breath finally. 'Here's a life for you! What on earth's going on? It's hardly credible, like a dream!' He tried to lie down: tomorrow he would need to take in hand the things he had come here to do, and he should think about his own affairs; but his mind was in a turmoil, and before him kept appearing the girl's face. 'So, she's called Tanya,' he thought despondently. 'And we never even got to exchange names.'

In a short while there came a careful knock on the door, and the landlady came in. She felt the stove, straightened the tablecloth, then sat down at the table and began a dreary complaint about life, her situation as a widow, the fact that nowadays the stores seldom had any sugar. It was small talk, annoying and tedious and the voice which conveyed it was unpleasant. Blokhin bore her observations with a frown and in silence. Then she went on to ask about his parents, his studies.

'So, you live in Moscow you say?'

'In Moscow.'

'Is it large, your place?'

'Very small. One room.'

'So. One room. Life's not so sweet for you either then. Married?'

'Not yet.'

'Do you expect to earn a lot?'

'I don't know.'

'You don't... you don't know? But how can that be?'

'Well... maybe eight hundred roubles, nine hundred.'

'Eight hundred. I see.' There was a rapid change in the woman's expression—repressed disdain? Something about her eyes—had she actually winked at him in some grim satisfaction at his answer?—said that the questioning was over; and in fact she got up and silently went out.

Blokhin lost no time in undressing, extinguishing the light and feeling his way to the bed. But he could not sleep. He tossed and turned on the hard, cold bed, rose more than once, sat beside the dark window, smoked.

From the other side of the wall came whispers, sobs. Floor boards creaked, something fell and rolled, someone went into the kitchen, clinked a mug, drank water probably. And outside, at even intervals, the dismal noise of the clapper neared and then grew weak again.

When he fell asleep at last, he dreamt that some horrible being walked around the house, tapping at the walls with a stick, trying to find a way in. But all the doors and windows were sealed with huge locks and there was no possibility of anything entering.

3

Next morning, Blokhin woke with a headache. The room had chilled during the night, the blanket was thin and retained no warmth and his feet were frozen; his back had become acquainted with every board beneath the skimpy mattress, and his sides pained. There was a crust of ice on the window. The house was quiet.

After dressing he went into the kitchen. A nauseating smell of stewed potato-peelings met him there. There was no water in the washstand and the samovar was cold. He went into the corridor and felt a door: it was locked. He went to another: it was locked as well. A third door did open, and Blokhin looked out at a shed and saw his landlady absorbed in some activity there. She was scratching a piglet behind one of its ears, and on her face could be detected the least play of a weak smile. The animal had its head and folded-down ear-tips inside a bucket and was pushing it along the ground, chomping audibly and twirling its tail.

The landlady saw Blokhin and her expression changed, she came towards the door and followed him into the kitchen. She was wearing heavy, dirt-caked jackboots, a padded coat, and the usual unlovely head-scarf possessed by every crone. Her hands and clothing smelt of dung.

'I've not been hired to bring you water,' she said. 'And I've given it some more thought, did some calculating. I've got to have two hundred and fifty from you for the room.'

'How come?' Blokhin asked, stunned.

'What d'you mean, how come? The bed linen's got to be washed, water brought for you, then there's the fire. How come, you say? You have the light on, and that's a strong globe in your room, a hundred candle-power. How much do you think that'll that cost me? I don't own a mint, you know, I don't print money. And another thing: I'll ask you to go outside to smoke, you smoke a lot, makes my head ache.'

'Will you make me some tea, please?' Blokhin asked, reddening.

'Am I supposed to start the samovar again? The charcoal, I'll tell you, costs something. You should get up earlier. You lie around asleep and then you'll be wanting the samovar heated ten times over. I'm a widow, you know. I've got nowhere to go, no one to help me. I'm beginning to regret that I ever let you have that room. You're a trouble of a lodger, you are, God be with you!...'

Blokhin turned around in silence and went back to his room. He began packing his things into his suitcase. The woman quietly entered and watched him. 'Well then, you're leaving the house, is that it?' she said finally.

Blokhin only gritted his teeth more tightly and did not reply.

'Well, I'm not keeping you, it's no worry to me, I can always find a tenant here, I don't have to wait for one to come from Moscow. Just pay me for the night and the fittings, the table runner and so on. I had a professor here; thankful he was, even went above the rent when he paid me. There were engineers here too, cultured people they were and all that...'

'It's like this...' Blokhin interrupted her, he had closed the suitcase and was putting on his overcoat, 'it's like this: I don't want to have any discussions with you. I was here one night. How much will that be? About seven roubles I should think? Eight?'

'What seven?' the landlady paled. 'What seven? You came yesterday?

Right, that means two days. And I've got to wash the sheets now because of you. Seven roubles? And the pillow case... I'll have twenty-five roubles from you!'

Blokhin took out ten roubles. 'Here, take this,' he said with a grim laugh.

'What's that?' the woman pressed her lips tightly together. 'I took you in out of my good nature and you hand me that? Well, choke on it! I don't want your money! Keep it, have yourself a good time on it, on my account, a widow!...'

'As you like,' Blokhin said, beginning to put the note back into his wallet and looking sideways at the woman.

Instantly, a fleshless, dark-hued hand with dirty fingernails snatched the money from him and made a fist around it.

'And you'd have been happy to do that? Ekh! And someone with an education at that! What were you saying to my daughter yesterday? Found yourself some little fool, did you? You want to drag her away from her mother?'

'Daughter?' Blokhin suddenly shouted at her, 'She's no daughter to you!'

'... thinks himself cultured, coming from an institute!' the woman un-heeding him was shouting back, her face becoming paler every moment. 'Where's your shame? Your eyes would pop if you ever opened them to look around you in God's light!... Coming to other people's homes to set up your own ways? Go get your own squat first, you vagabond, criminal! Spare me, Heavenly Mother! You've defiled my house, cursed antichrist! Get out of here, get out, get out!...'

Blokhin hurriedly left, passing through the corridor and out of the porch. In the quiet into which he emerged the creak of the snow under his feet was clean and crisp and he was struck by the smell of frost and by the unusual light of a sunny February morning. But what he felt in his breast was a foul and oppressive sensation, as if he had been caught in some sordid act.

The houses about him, the tiny bath-huts, those almost lost under a stilled torrent of snow, were all gay in the sun, sparkling with innumerable points of glass. The buildings nearest the street cast sharp, blue shadows across it, and the street, a shining band, was already streaked by the runners of sledges and spotted by the amber stains of horse dung, by the deep black of pacing ravens; and above, up on the steep wall of the cliff, growing by some amazing feat on small, snowy ledges, stood scattered firs with dove-grey boles. But Blokhin saw nothing of all that, all the beauty of a bright winter day was not for him. Breathing heavily, he was struggling up a steep, ice-encrusted path, stumbling and leaving behind him the imprints of his suitcase in the snow.

When he reached the top, he turned and looked down at the house in which he had spent the night, at the wide, blindingly-white river. 'Where to see Tanya again? How to meet her?' he wondered feverishly. 'I'll tell it all to Balaev,' he decided. 'He'll help. Something absolutely needs to be done!' His heart thudded with embarrassment, rage, with love for that gentle and timid girl. Suddenly he remembered the reason he had come to this town, his practicum, and ire and bitterness overwhelmed him. 'To hell with the practicum!' he thought with fury. 'I'll be sitting in the library, cataloguing, drawing up statistics on borrowing, advising readers—and here, nearby, a soul is perishing! There's a whole street of these damned Old Believers! And they too, probably, are readers! Some sort of damned practicum's needed around those houses, that's what! *There's* a subject needing examining, all right!'

Blokhin glanced down once more, his thoughts in turmoil, his eyes full of detestation, then he turned and began trudging in the direction of last night's hotel. He did not turn again, but if he had stopped to look back, he would have seen nothing: the house now lay hidden below the cliff.

4. "NIGHT"

I wanted to get to a lake where I knew there would be ducks, and so I had left home after dark to be there by dawn.

The country lane I walked on was soft with dust and repeatedly and gently descended and lifted again. Occasionally, I passed through some sparse little copse of pines, and there among the trees was an odour of resin and wild strawberries, a sultry odour that had been generated during the hot day but now had lost its pungency and was heavy and unmoving. Each copse yielded to a farmed field, then came another copse, and so it went on. No one overtook me and I met no one, I was alone in the night.

Sometimes a field had a crop of rye growing on it, and the plants were well-advanced, standing motionless and shining dimly in the darkness, and where the stalks grew close to the lane and the rye-ears bent to it I felt them brushing gently against my hands and my boots, and their touch was like a silent, shy caress. The air was warm and clean, stars shimmered vividly, there were smells of hay and dust, and from time to time a kind of acrid freshness drifted out of the meadows beside a river I was nearing. Beyond meadows, beyond the river, far behind the forested distance, summer lightning quivered faintly.

Then the soft and noiseless lane continued elsewhere on its own way, while I turned from it onto a narrower beaten path. The path was trodden in places to callus-like hard patches and followed closely and in fact rather fussily one bank of the river. Now came the damp river-smells, the smell of mud, and then a humid chill quickly permeated the air, and I began to hear the occasional muffled thud of colliding logs floating down from forestry camps far upstream. The noise when the logs met was like that someone makes quietly tapping a tree with the back of an axe to test the trunk for soundness. A long way ahead, in the direction I was going but on the other side of the river, I could see the bright spot of a campfire, the light sometimes disappearing behind trees and then appearing again, each time with the narrow, wavering streak of its reflection stretching across the water towards me.

Pleasant thoughts may come at unexpected moments in a night's journey. Things far away and fallen from memory return, faces of friends and kin gather around one, meditation enfolds and presses sweetly on the heart, and little by little everything in one's surrounds, influenced perhaps by those retrospections, begins to feel as if it had been met already some distant time in the past. There had been another occasion when one passed through gullies rendered cool by damp air, when one had walked through just such arid little copses, when the river had darkened thus, clods of earth had plopped into the undermining water, floating logs had met quietly together; another time when black hayricks appeared and disappeared in the distance, trees topped with crooked branches writhed in dumb battle with each other, and silt-banked pools had looked like still black windows. Some previous occasion? Yes, but try as one might, one finds it impossible to bring to mind where, when, in what happy period of one's earlier life that first experience of such things could have been.

I had been walking a good hour and a half, and it was still far to the lake. Walking at night makes for heavy going: you grow irritated with repeated stumbling over roots and mole-mounds, and the constant worry of straying from the path and getting lost in an unfamiliar stretch of woods wearies you. I was almost ruing that I had decided to make this night-trip, and had begun wondering if the sensible thing might be to find a suitable tree and sit under it to wait for dawn, when suddenly I heard a thin, trembling resonance, a sound like someone singing. Yes, it was singing. It was impossible to make out the words, only an extended 'O-o-o… A-a-a-o-o…' but I was cheered to hear that human voice and, mean what it might, I put on speed towards it. But for a while I seemed neither to get nearer the singer nor he to draw away, the song merely persisting in the same thread-thin and winding strain. 'Who could it be?' I thought. 'A rafter on the river? Someone fishing? A hunter?' Was this perhaps someone like myself, travelling at night, someone walking just ahead of me and singing to relieve his solitude?

I went on more quickly, pushed through a thicket of spruce, then through some aspen undergrowth, until at last below me, in a dip surrounded on all sides by densely-growing trees, I sighted a fire. Somebody was lying beside it, his head propped on his hand: he was looking into the fire and quietly singing.

I stumbled as I began to descend, and the breaking twigs made a crisp sound under my feet. The person at the fire abruptly fell silent, turned, rose quickly to his feet and stood peering in my direction, holding up one hand to shield his eyes from the firelight.

'Hullo, who's there?' he called. He was apprehensive, and his question was not much more than a whisper.

'That's all right, I'm just on my way to do some hunting,' I replied, approaching the fire, 'Nothing to worry about.'

'Oh, I wasn't worried,' he said, his tone changing rather too quickly to indifference. 'The place here's full of hunters, I see 'em all the time.'

The individual to whose singing I had been hurrying turned out to be a bow-legged stripling of some sixteen years, rather ugly, with a skinny neck, a prominent Adam's apple and large, jutting ears. He was dressed in a padded jacket, grease-stained cotton trousers, and on his feet were kersey boots. A small cloth cap with a narrow peak sat on top of his head as if glued there.

He looked me over for some moments with direct, country curiosity and asked: 'Have you come for the ducks?'

'Well, I was hoping to get to the lake,' I said, unslinging my shotgun.

'Oh, what one?'

I told him.

'Ah, now, it ain't far,' he told me, eager to be helpful. Then he turned his head towards the river and listened. 'Would that have been you was shouting a minute back?' he asked after a moment.

'No, why?'

'Oh, I dunno, someone was shouting. He shouted something, then stopped, then shouted again. I was gonna go an' look, but Lyoshka—that's my brother—got frightened, so I didn't'

He fell silent again and I heard the rapid steps of someone running towards us from the direction of the river.

A young boy's excited and worried piping came to us: 'Semyon! Semyon!...'

From the darkness and into the firelight burst the figure of the caller, a boy of about eight years, also dressed in a padded jacket, though one far too large for him. Seeing me, he halted on the spot and looked openmouthed from me to his brother.

'Well?' Semyon asked him in an uninterested, older-brother tone.

'Oh, Semyon, there's something on...' the boy looked at me again and drew breath, then turning to Semyon he continued in a rush: 'There ain't nothing on the outside ones, but the one in the middle's got something! I picked it up and it tugged!'

'Bull!'

'It's a big one. I saw its back go in and out of the water!' He made undulating motions with his hand.

Semyon hitched up his trousers, and with a gruff 'I'll just be a tick!' to me, he disappeared into the dark. The boy continued for a few more moments to stare at me without blinking, then he took one step backwards, then another, turned, and also disappeared, the tapping of his running feet audible in the darkness.

In a short time there came to me from the direction the two boys had gone mysterious sounds, stirrings, subdued voices, splashes; then there was silence, then steps, and the youngsters arrived back at the fire. Semyon carried at the end of an outstretched arm a not very large sterlet with a feebly flapping tail.

He stuffed the fish into a canvas sack and sat down near me. 'That's how we catch 'em here! Makes three now,' he said with satisfaction.

'I pulled one out,' said the younger boy. He dropped his eyes shyly and fiddled with a button on his coat.

'Did you, now?' said Semyon in a tone and look that suppressed further comment from the younger one.

The boy snuffled and bent further in confusion.

'My brother,' Semyon said by way of introduction, 'Lyoshka. You'd think he was a quiet 'un. Just pretends.'

Lyosha muttered something under his nose.

'What was that?' Semyon asked, opening wide his eyes, 'What d'you say?'

'Nothink,' said Lyosha, alarmed.

'Well, watch it!' the other said, and looking up at me from under his brows he suddenly smiled quite boyishly, mischievously, and his face was lighted by that change: his eyes shone, his teeth flashed, and even those ears of his seemed to move in the common enlivenment of his features.

And Lyosha laughed too, a tiny explosive sound; but he remembered himself quickly and bent his head again. Semyon put his hand in his pocket, hesitated a moment and then pulled out a crumpled packet of cigarettes, lit one and offered me the packet. I declined.

'Oh, you don't smoke then,' he said, disappointed, and turned away from me.

I took the opportunity to glance at him again. He was leaning back on his elbows and he suddenly gaped in a pleasurable yawn, drew his limbs in on himself and then sat immobile, looking dreamily into the fire, the cigarette forgotten. His face had taken on that kind of amiable, vague and entranced expression that people show when some dim, elusive thought drifts through the mind, indefinable yet accompanied by a warm and pleasurable feeling. The fire was diminishing, a film of reddish ash covered the dying coals, all around us stood the still presence of the night, except for an occasional sound that came down from some clearing above us where a horse trod on windfalls or sent out a muted rattle from the wooden bell on its neck.

Lyosha suddenly lifted his head. 'Someone's coming,' he said uneasily, and he moved closer to Semyon.

'Bull!' said Semyon, but he glanced quickly at my gun.

Some seconds passed in silence, and then we all heard a distinct snapping of trodden-on twigs. Semyon looked a question at me and smiled nervously.

'A bear probably,' Lyosha whispered, and he edged closer still to his brother; his eyes had widened and the pupils seemed huge.

'Burnin' the midnight oil are we, gentlemen-fishers?' said a suddenly loud, gravelly voice, and immediately we beheld the figure of an elderly muzhik with a shotgun, striding towards us and the fire.

Unconcerned by us he extended a leg to the dim firelight and proceeded to grunt and make unhappy throat-clearing noises while he considered the loose sole that hung from one of his boots. 'Devil drag thee

down!' he muttered, 'What a pest, what? You folks fishin' or something?'
Lifting his eyes to look at us his tone changed: 'Oh-ho, here's some pals
here,' he said, addressing the boys. 'Caught much?'

Semyon furtively dropped his cigarette into the fire and looked warn-
ingly at Lyosha, who let off another little explosion of laughter.

'Not many, Pyotr Andreich,' Semyon said politely, familiarly abbreviat-
ing the elder's patronymic. He smiled in embarrassment and added: 'Except maybe there'll be some more later towards morning.'

'C'mon, let's see, let's see.'

Semyon willingly tipped his sack bottom-up.

'Aha, sterlets,' said Pyotr Andreyevich merrily. 'Very good, very good;
bit small, but still...'

'Can't ever tell how it'll turn out, Pyotr Andreich.'

'Absolutely,' Pyotr Andreyevich freely agreed. And there the subject
appeared exhausted. He sat down, and with his eyes on the fire he too
seemed to wander away with his thoughts. With a series of mechanical
motions, he fished out a packet of cigarettes from a pocket, lit up, flicked
the match into the embers, and in the same abstraction watched it burn
with a bright little flame, go out, fall into fragments and join the rosy
ashes.

He was not really old, although his cheeks were deeply lined. He had
thin lips, a long, narrow nose, and there were some small nodules on his
low forehead. The immediate impression he gave was of severity and
tenseness. His gun was an old single-shot, the fore-stock being attached
to the barrel by windings of wire. From the top of the afflicted boot
showed an end of the foot-bindings he wore instead of socks.

'Are you making for Suglinka, that a-way?' Semyon asked him suddenly.

'Ay?' Pyotr Andreyevich came to himself after a moment. 'To Suglinka
you say? What would I go there for? Nope, I'm going further.'

'Because our mechanic just hauled back a bagful from there, a while
ago.'

'He caught two pike along the way,' Lyosha contributed. 'Bi-ig they
were!'

'That'll be Popov you mean?' Pyotr Andreyevich asked, and added: 'It's
all right for him, he's got a dog. No, I'll get me to Ovshanka, then you bear
a bit to the left, go careful for the river, and there's a little lake there I
happen to know, a wee little lake.'

'Near Ovshanka?' Semyon repeated thoughtfully. 'Never been that
way, no call. I mostly know this side of the river.'

Silence returned. Pyotr Andreyevich stood up now; shifting from one
foot to the other and coughing softly he considered something in the direction of the river. Lyosha lay near his brother, his arms and legs drawn
tight against his body, and it was very evident that he was enjoying himself
hugely in grownup company: it was visible in the way he curled himself

up, in his shining eyes, the repeated grin.

'D'you happen to know if the ferryman's there, at his place?' Pyotr Andreyevich asked Semyon.

'He is! He went upstream a bit back. They played the accordion. They're having fun. The son got married. With Motka Medunitzina. Her from the second workshop.'

'That little one with the pockmarks?'

'That's it. Dunno what he sees in her. Catch me marryin' one like that!'

'Some way yet before your turn comes to think about it,' Pyotr Andreyevich chuckled; and he turned his head towards where the ferryman lived, as if listening for the merriment. 'So he's having a party you say, that old ferryman now.' Then he became suddenly worried: 'Will he take me across? Nah, he won't, I don't think. Or will he? Probably drown us both if he does. They'll be that drunk, all of them most likely.'

Semyon turned to look in the same direction. 'Might,' he agreed uncertainly. 'But why don't you just undo the dinghy here and take it over yourself. He's got three, hasn't he—dinghies?'

'Ah, that's a fact!' Pyotr Andreyevich said, relieved. And then he looked down at his boot. 'And here's another curse as well! The sole's well and truly off. Is there a bit of string about? There I was going, it'd got dark you know, and crack! I trip over a root, Satan take it for kindling!'

Lyosha brought out a short length of string from inside his shirt, Pyotr Andreyevich tested it by a tug between his hands and then began winding it about the toe of his boot. 'What're you using for bait?' he asked.

'We're fishing the bottom,' Semyon replied readily, 'On lampreys.'

'Lampreys? Yep, that's the bait for 'em: they love it, sterlets. I was walking, back a bit, and I look, and there's some wolves howling across the river. Did you hear them? Their cubs are grown, likely.'

Lyosha became animated: 'A wolf took our neighbour's goat! In daylight! The goat was old, skinny. The wolf grabbed it, it let out a *me-e-e*, and that was it! Pulled it through the vegetable garden, through the paddock and into the woods. Uncle Fyodor jumped out with an axe, took one look, and you should have seen him wham it into the shed wall! It's still stuck there, no one can get it out.'

'It's true, that's what happened,' Semyon confirmed. 'But I'll tell you another thing: I was coming back from here, been fishing, and it's late, getting dark with just a bit of yellow left around the sunset, but you could see the track all right. Anyway, I went through that bit of timber growing just past the cemetery, you know it? I felt like someone had barged into me. I turned, and for a bit I couldn't work out what happened. Then I look—there's something near a bush that looks dark, eyes glowing out of it, a row of 'em, looking like bits of that mould that glows at night. There were three of them, sitting there and looking at me. My legs just sort of went like when you have a dream and you want to run but can't, you know? And I broke out in a sweat, it poured out of me! That's it!—I thought—the end. But nothing came of it. They just sat there.'

'It's because it's summer. They don't go for people then,' Pyotr Andreyevich said with total certitude.

'Uncle Pyo...' Lyosha began, then looked around at us and smiled hesitantly, 'Uncle Pyotr, you know, we heard you and thought it was a bear! There was all that crackling coming towards us...'

'Who thought that?' demanded Semyon, and he shrugged irritably. 'That's what you thought, so don't lay it on others.'

'No lads,' Pyotr Andreyevich said, smiling, 'A bear won't make for a fire. But then, you might wonder too who'd be beating around here at night. Bears and hunters, that's all. Are you hunting?' he asked me politely. 'Maybe if it's your first time round here you could come with me where I'm going? No? Well, that makes sense. I guess we're all keen to make just for our own little patch.'

He looked up at the stars and extended a broad, brown hand to Semyon: 'See you another time, I'm off or it'll be lighting soon. Oh, by the way, I heard you that last time at the club. Your dad must be proud of you, hey? It was grand!'

He slapped Semyon's shoulder, nodded to Lyosha and to me and went off into the dark, stepping carefully on his bound-up boot. Semyon sat with his face lowered, picking the calluses on his palms and snorting something to himself. His ears had turned red.

Lyosha stretched until his whole body arced. He yawned and rubbed his eyes and announced: 'I think I'm sleepy.'

'So sleep,' said his brother and he reached across and scratched Lyosha behind an ear. 'Sleep.'

'Yeah, I know you,' Lyosha said in an accusing tone and grinned at him. 'Tomorrow morning you'll go and see and you won't wake me.'

'I'll wake you. You're a kook.'

'Swear. On your Komsomol honour.'

Semyon looked down at his brother and smiled; then he too lay down on his back.

It was about two o'clock and the darkness had if possible become denser. One felt like lying and looking in turn at the fire, at the stars, at the just barely visible nearest trees, trying to divine what the infrequent, indistinct night-sounds might be: if that was a bird shaking itself and puffing out its feathers, or was that the sound of a cone falling; felt like lying and half-listening, while the passing moments conduced to reverie and to imagining many things.

'Lyoshka!' Semyon roused himself, 'Get some wood!'

Lyosha was alert and on his feet immediately and he disappeared into the darkness; a snapping of dry branches followed, and then he returned with a big armful. He drew out the lighter twigs and arranged them on the fire, squatted, and began to blow on the embers under them. His eyes bulged with the effort, sparks flew, and a cloud of ashes rose up.

'You'll strain your lungs,' Semyon said to him with a touch of real concern.

Lyosha lifted his head and gave us a quick vacant smile and then returned to blowing furiously again. The pile suddenly took, and there was instant light and a crackling that sent large sparks flying high into the air. It grew hot near the fire and everyone grumbled a little and moved further away from it.

I was interested to know what Pyotr Andreyevich had praised Semyon for, and so I asked him. Semyon mumbled something unclear: 'Oh, nothing much, just in general...' and he picked at his calluses again.

'He's writing music,' Lyosha came in quickly. 'He's even played twice at our school, and at the club too.'

'So?' Semyon turn on him. 'What's next out of you?'

'No, nothink.'

'Well don't go on.'

Semyon gave me a searching glance and then admitted grudgingly: 'I suppose in fact that I do like to muck around, play stuff.'

'Our pop bought him a *bayan*-accordion,' Lyosha burst in again. 'You should see him! He can play you anything on it!'

'Well, it's true,' Semyon acknowledged, 'I mean it's true that I play. But I've got this thought, like... It's a huge thought: how does a song get to be that way? You can do so many things with a song, turn it this way and that way, you know? Like no one's ever played it before? How do *I* do it, now? Well, I take a tune and add a new voice to it; and, see, now the song is altogether new, and that voice is all new too. And then you can sort of add another voice, gradually, and then that music is different again. But that's not the end, even then. All that's in the right hand; in the left, that's where the harmony is. The chords I mean. You play the chords and it sounds good, but if you listen with a bit of care you see that it's not really clean and clear there, you don't get the taste of what it's about, it's not really sharp and clean. And a song, and if it's a long one too, it's got to have its own taste and smell, like a river, or the forest has. I go and get those handbooks at the club, that have *bayan* numbers in them, and I play them, but... it's just not there, you see? They don't get hold of you inside; and then I can't go on, not their way, and I start to add things and make changes...'

He stopped suddenly and looked at me with suspicion, trying to see whether I was laughing at his words. Apparently reassured, he went on, frowning, twitching his brown fingers.

'I've got this plan: to make up a thing that's all about a night like this. Well, why not? I lie at night next to a fire and I hear it, the whole thing, playing in my ears, it all comes to me. I'd get it going like this: some violins would start out softly and very fine, very high, and that would be the silence. Then the violins are doing this long piece, and a horn, one of those

English horn things, comes in with that bit of a hoarse sound they have, comes in and plays such a melody that you close your eyes and fly over the earth, just wherever you want, and under you it's all lakes and rivers, cities... and everywhere it's quiet and dark. That little horn plays, and the cellos give it another voice: *they* sing it on the lower strings, talking like the way the pine trees hum. While the violins haven't stopped, they just keep drawing on, drawing on quite quietly. And this is where other instruments join in, and they begin playing louder, all together and louder: too-roo-room!... Toom-toom, ta-ta-ta-ta!... The whole orchestra plays, and it has never been heard before! And there's got to be instruments that sound like bells too, that's important. Then after that you've got to start clearing out instruments, a few at a time, and the music gets quieter all the time and finishes with the violins again. They'll draw on for a long time, till they die away altogether...'

Semyon was looking somewhere out into the darkness and licking his lips.

'And we've got to bring in that bell properly too, to ring in a way that's even, but very soft. That'll be the moon coming out of a cloud. We can see it and hear it that way, can't we?... I'd call the piece "Night." Or maybe it should be something more beautiful: "A Night's Tale," or "A Star in the Night". I couldn't try to tell you all about a night or about stars or mist on the river, but in music I feel I *can* do that! I feel those things like a pain in the chest, here. I lie down to sleep, and I don't sleep. Then I do, and I hear that music about those things playing in my mind. When I wake, I want to remember it all and just can't... I've got to study, that's clear! I work on a winch, pulling logs up on the bank. I sit there moving the levers; the winch makes noises, or a truck toots, or I hear the whistle to go to lunch, and I act like I'm in training, picking out the sounds: this one's a C, or that one's an F sharp...'

He stopped talking suddenly, smiled awkwardly to himself and set about tending the fire.

And then something strange and awesome grew in the air, came into being, broke the night's silence: a sound passed along the length of the river, agitating the brooding, starlit quiet, a bass-pitched, mighty and hollow 'E-he-e-e-y!...' travelled to our ears.

We three turned instantly towards the river and listened, uncomprehending. There was silence. And then once more the same potent bellow passed invisibly through the darkness: 'E-he-e-e-y!...'

'It's them bringing down the timber rafts,' Semyon said with relief. 'Just trying out their voices. They've got some really wonderful calls, don't they? You can hear noises a long way on the river at night. A dinghy might be a verst away and you'll hear the rowlocks squeaking. Or you hear things that you can't work out—like someone's cried out, or a sigh, or there's some wee tiny noise: 'Tee-ee-you, tee-ee-you, tee-ee-ee-you...'

It was a sound that I had heard myself during nights spent by

riverbanks and swamps. His mimicry was good, and I too had never discovered the source.

'Lyoshka's frightened, but I'm not,' he smiled. 'You get lonely being on
your own, but it's good too!'

'I'm not frightened at all of anything!' Lyosha said loudly, and he made
a fearsome face.

'So? Then go down to the Flagellants' Bog and get me some switches!...
Well, what're you waiting for? Go on, go on!'

Lyosha wrinkled his mouth, looked at the darkness over his shoulder
and giggled uneasily. Semyon let a pause pass.

'People here are pretty tough,' he began again, 'There's some that'll
fight anybody you like. But they're a funny lot too. You might think that
that feller on the raft was shouting a call to do with his job. Nah. He was
just sounding off. He'll jump ashore and yodel for a minute just to hear
how his voice spreads all over the forest.'

'Uncle, Uncle—have a shot at something!' Lyosha begged suddenly,
looking wistfully at my gun.

'Here. You have a shot yourself,' I said, handing him the gun.

'That's silly,' grumbled Semyon, 'He'll just waste a shell.' But the same
excitement was in his eyes as had come to Lyosha's. Lyosha looked
around, saw a tall aspen stump not far away and in a moment had planted
his old cap squarely on top of it.

As he was raising the gun, Semyon stopped him: 'Wait, wait, we'll get
the fire going, there'll be more light!' and he heaped dry twigs on the fire.
The glow dimmed for a moment and then thick, rosy smoke began to
creep out of the pile, slim blue tongues flickered through the gaps, and
then there was a sudden moment when the whole pile caught at once.

'Go for it now!' ordered Semyon, and with his hand shielding his face
from the fire he fixed his eyes on the stump and hat.

Lyosha aimed. He seemed to aim for a very long time: sniffing, drawing
in and releasing his breath, looking back down at the trigger, at his finger.
The anticipation of that shot grew into a painful weight, and I noticed one
of Semyon's hands had become a tense fist and his eyes had narrowed as
if he were looking into a bright light.

'You gonna shoot or...' he began impatiently.

At that moment the gun in Lyosha's hands kicked up, a long blue shaft
of flame flashed from one of the barrels, accompanied by the deafening
bakht! of the shot, and the cap leapt out of sight and an echo rolled over
the woods and the river. Up on the rise above us the horse snorted in
panic, its wooden bell rattled, and there was the noise of bushes being
forced. Lyosha put down my smoking shotgun and threw himself headlong
out of the circle of firelight

'That's some gun!' Semyon said with awe and delight as he took a step
to meet Lyosha returning with the cap. 'Some punch, that!'

The cap was solemnly examined in the firelight. Several pellets had gone through it, and cotton stuffing showed out of the holes.

Semyon paused in thought. 'You know what?' he said to me. 'If you want, I can take you to a place where there's never been any hunters, not since ever. I'll ask for a break from work and borrow our uncle's gun. We'll go there for a couple of days. It's a secret place. The birds haven't been frightened yet. You go through the scrub there, and on the right there's hazel grouse and heath cocks and wood grouse, and on the left there's a lake—and that's full of geese and mallard! They paddle out in the open and let you get close for a shot, and after that they don't fly off, just move away a bit. I went there with my uncle once and I know the way. There's no one there: no hunters, no berry-pickers, only bears that go there for the raspberries; but they're quiet bears, they look out at you through the bushes. There's cowberries growing there that if you stand in a clearing where the fires have gone through, stand on a hummock, then all the hummocks around look red. There's wild strawberries and no one comes for them, and the strawberries have gone black and over-ripe and they're so sweet—sweeter than sugar! When you're in the currant-bushes the smell of them is that strong it makes your head spin! And the heath cocks and the wood grouse there let you get real close, and then they fly off—tikh, tikh, tikh—one after another, and you can feel them on your face, how they fly past. And squirrels are another thing, jumping in the trees. Only now they're sort of gingery and the fur's not much good so we don't go after them. And another thing that's there, under the hillside—but you've got to go over a lot of fallen timber and across a gully—down there there's a spring—a "spout" we call 'em here—and all the different waters I've drunk, I've never drunk water like that, and that water, I reckon, must be really good for you.'

While Semyon was talking, Lyosha was restraining himself with greater and greater difficulty, until he finally gave up. Snuffling and with a pathetic frown on his face he let out a desperate wail: 'Semyo-on!...'

Semyon looked around with surprise at his brother. 'Well?'

'Semyon, ta-ake me too-oo...' Lyosha pleaded. His agony was clearly unbearable.

'What, take you?...' He looked at me. 'Do we take him?' he asked me, perplexed.

Lyosha's eyes, grown large and humid, fixed on me now. I considered the matter, considered it for a long time, and no doubt there was a severe expression on my face.

'Take him?...' Semyon asked again without enthusiasm, and he looked Lyosha up and down.

The boy's expression was on the point of disintegrating, his lips were pressed together.

'We'll take him!' I said finally.

Lyosha uttered the squeakiest of laughs, leapt up and wiped a sleeve across his eyes. 'Ha-ha!' he shouted exultantly. 'There you are, there you are!...' and with victorious glances at his brother he began skipping and dancing around the fire, repeating in various tones: 'Will he go? He will, he will!... Will he go? He will, he will!...'

I looked about me. To the east the sky had paled and there was the beginning of a greenish drift there. Dew had fallen and the air was crisp, individual trees had become distinguishable. No, there was still no light, but with every minute clumps of bushes grew visible, the branches of fir trees stood out, even the cones did. The night had ended and was being replaced by the earliest of half-light; it was the time of morning when village roosters sound their hoarse coo-ca-recoo!... and return to yet deeper sleep.

It was time for me to leave. I took my gun and said good-bye to the two boys.

No sooner had I left the campfire than damp and chilly air enveloped me from all sides, and my boots shone with dew. A magpie launched itself from the top of a whitening fir and noiselessly dipping and rising flew towards the east to meet the dawn.

I had managed to walk some way, had clambered up a tree-covered ridge and found on top the path to the lake, when once more the whisper of Semyon's song reached me. As before, I could neither make out the words nor catch the melody, but now I knew that it was a fine song, poetic and harmonious because it came from a pure, clean talent and from the beauty of the glittering stars, from a mighty silence and an odorous, fading summer. From another direction, 'Aaaa... o-aaaa!...' trembled a more distant rafter's call; and below me the river murmured sleepily, logs nudged lightly into each other; and it seemed to me for some reason that there on the river, hidden by eddies of mist, some wise old man sat in a boat and tapped those drifting logs with the back of an axe, testing by that sound their strength and freedom from taint.

5. THE HOMELY GIRL

The wedding reception was in full swing: it had been some time now since they had conducted the bride and groom to another cottage and the first roosters of the village had crowed; and still the accordion-player played, the log building where the party was being held trembled from the thunder of tramping feet, five lamps radiated heat and blinding light, and the heads of indefatigable children continued to pop up at the windows.

Much had been drunk and eaten, many tears shed, songs sung, dances danced; but after each more vodka and more zakuski were placed on the table, the accordion alternated with gramophone records of foxtrots and tangos, and stamping feet and prisyadka kicks with the more staid shuffling of shoe-soles; and still the gaiety ceased not, was heard yet more loudly in the road outside and further, in the fields and out as far as the river. The surrounding hamlets knew that at Podvorye they were having one hell of a good time.

All were happy, save only Sonya. She was miserable, her heart was heavy. Her pointed nose had reddened with the vodka she had drunk, her head was buzzing, and her heart beat with pain from the indignity of being ignored by everyone, from the awareness that all were happy, all were in love, one with another, and that she alone had no one who was in love with her, and of all the men who were there none had invited her to dance.

She knew that she was not pretty, was ashamed of her meagre frame—numberless times she had vowed that she would never again go to these evenings where they danced and drank and fell in love; but every time her resolve would break and she did go, hoping once more that her luck might turn.

In the past also, when she was younger and was studying at the institute, no one ever fell in love with her, not once was she escorted home, she was never kissed. She graduated and left home to work in the country, where she was given a room annexed to a school. At night she marked exercise books, read and memorised love poems, went to see films at the club, wrote long letters to friends... and was melancholy. In two years, practically all her friends married; whereas in the course of that time her face had grown wanner and her body more scrawny.

And now, almost as an unkind joke, she had been invited to this wedding, and once again had gone. She had examined with envy the fortunate bride, had shouted with everyone else, if in a less ringing voice, 'Gor'ko— it's bitter!', taunting and urging the couple to their ceremonial kiss; but in fact, any bitterness was hers, knowing that she would never play a bride's role at her own wedding.

They had paired her to a local veterinary aide called Nikolai, a sombre young man with chiselled, handsome features and dark eyes. They sat together, and at first he attended to her: Sonya drank and ate everything he brought her, conveying grateful looks to him with each offering, and it seemed to her that those looks must be full of subtle imports of secret tenderness. But for some reason Nikolai grew more gloomy, soon stopped concerning himself with her, and began talking with someone across the table. Finally, he left her altogether, danced with much shouting and swinging of his long arms, looked about him strangely, and came to the table only to drink vodka. Then after some time he went out to the porch and was not seen again.

Now Sonya sat alone in a corner, thinking about life and disdaining all these drunk, sweating, contented and happy people, disdaining them and feeling sorry for herself.

She had recently sewn a dress, a very good dark-blue dress. Everybody had admired it and said that it so suited her. And, see, the dress had not helped, and everything was just as before.

About three in the morning Sonya, forgotten by everybody, sorrowful and with mottled red blotches on her cheeks, went through the porch and out of the building. The nearby cottages stood black, the village slept, everything around was peaceful; except that from the open windows where they were having fun the sounds of the accordion, of shouts and stamping, resonated into the night.

Sonya's chin trembled; she bit her lip but that did not help. She jerked away from the doorway, staggered on beyond the space where the lamplight stained the grass grey, and barely made it to a birch tree that stood softly white in the darkness. She leaned her shoulder against it and sobbed like a child. She felt ashamed to cry like that, frightened that she would be heard, and so she jammed her scented handkerchief between her teeth. But no one heard her. 'That's enough now!' she told herself, tightly shutting her eyes. 'Stop it! No more! It's time to go.' And she wanted to go, and she rocked herself away from the tree, but her legs would not support her and she could not go.

'Wha's matter?' someone asked behind her.

Sonya held her breath. She snatched the handkerchief from her mouth, wiped her face on her shoulders without letting go of the tree, and looked about her in disorder. It was Nikolai, and he was unsteady. He lurched towards her, and on the point of falling grabbed her by the shoulder. His hand was grimy with soil.

'Ha!' he said drunkenly. 'You... is't? I... fell... on th' veg'table bed... there. Was...' he rocked and pressed himself on her, 'at wedding... Th' louse invited me!' he managed to blurt out. 'Ha!... I'll kill him! End... of... story! Thought he'd... buy me off... with a litre... Wrong, you skunk! You'll not buy me!'

Nikolai ground his teeth and uttered a string of oaths.

'Are you ill?' asked Sonya, frightened. 'Would you like some water?'

'Who? I feel bad...'

He broke free from Sonya and staggered around the corner of the building. Sonya began to pity him. She went back to the porch and brought out some water in a bucket, took it to him and began sprinkling it on his head. He bent submissively, made snorting noises, and continued muttering indistinct things.

After a while he returned to the porch in his shirtsleeves, sat down on the doorstep and lit a cigarette. Sonya followed him, cleaning his jacket.

'Are you better now?' she whispered, frightened that someone might come out and see her.

'A bit... Why haven't I seen you before? I know everyone here.'

'I don't go out much.'

'H'm. You live at the school?'

'I do.'

'Right, I'll walk you there, if you like.'

Nikolai stood up, put on his jacket, gave his head a shake and went into the porch to drink some water.

'What were you crying for?' he asked, returning, 'Somebody been bad to you?'

Sonya's heart beat with gratitude. She lowered her eyes.

'No, no one.'

'You just tell me. If someone touched you I'll break his ribs, the swine!' Nikolai took Sonya's arm, they crossed the dusty road, turned left and took a path that ran past wattle fences and kitchen gardens. There was dew out already and the grass was wet with it.

Sonya wanted to laugh. She seemed a changed person to herself. She wanted to rest Nikolai's head on her shoulder but was ashamed of such a thought, and when he staggered and pressed against her she hastily moved away.

'Listen—you are completely drunk!' she told him gently and reproachfully, as if talking to an old acquaintance.

'Rubbish!' Nikolai massaged his forehead and face with his hand, 'Who's drunk!'

They came to the school and entered the porch. Sonya fell into a state of confusion. She could not think what she should do now, go into her room immediately or remain there. At first she wanted to go in, but concerned that Nikolai might feel that he was being dismissed she stayed.

Nikolai for some reason grew drunk again, breathed hoarsely and held on to Sonya's arm.

'Well then, say something,' she said, lifting her face to him, pale in the darkness.

'Wha's to gab?...' he wheezed, and clutching her and squeezing her so that her ribs cracked he began kissing her with his wet lips.

'Let me go!' she whispered, breaking free, 'Let me go!'

'Shhh!' he hissed, pushing her into the dark porch, 'Quiet! Wha's matter? Well, wha's matter? Idiot!'

He pinned her to a wall of the porch.

'Kolya... calm down! Kolya dear! My God—what's happening?'

'You love me?...' she heard him mutter, and then: 'Stay still... bitch!'

'Don't, Kolya, don't!' she suddenly said in a voice of such sadness that Nikolai let go of her. He stopped and stood panting. He coughed a moment, took out his cigarettes and lit one, and by the light of the match looked at her face.

'All right now,' he said, taking care with his words. 'Don't go getting angry now. You... here's what you do. Come over to the threshing barn tomorrow. All right?'

'At what time?' asked Sonya in a whisper, trembling all over.

'Around seven. You'll be there?'

'I'll come.'

'All right then.' Nikolai inhaled deeply a few times, dropped the cigarette and ground it for a long moment with his heel. 'Well then... see you!' he said, and then kissed her again, but calmly now. He gave her face a rough stroke with his palm, and stepping out of the porch he disappeared into the darkness; a minute later she heard his singing, drunken and out of tune.

Inside, Sonya paced carefully about her room. She took off her clothes and drank some cold tea. She went in her nightdress to the mirror and looked for a long time at her face and at her pointed shoulders and jutting collar bones. 'My God, how horrid I am!' she thought, and flinched. 'I must really get some fish oil! Absolutely! Fish oil's the only thing!' She went to the table and began spooning butter into her mouth straight from the butter dish. It was nauseating, but she swallowed it and thought of Nikolai. Then she switched off the light and lay down. But sleep would not come. In Moscow there was a street-lamp across the road from her home, linden trees grew outside, and all night long their shadows fluttered on the window glass. Here there was nothing but dumb darkness.

'Is it love?' she asked herself aloud, and she turned to the wall.

The whole of the next day Sonya was in a turmoil. In the morning it rained, and while dictating pieces to the children she kept looking nervously through the window at the wet poultry and the pools of water; but the rain stopped, the sky cleared, and by evening the vehicles that passed outside the school were already raising tails of dust.

After work she sat down to write to one of her friends. She described to her how yesterday a young man had gone out with her and they had arranged a meeting for today. The letter developed into something quite long and cheerful. Having completed it, Sonya suddenly decided that she was in love with Nikolai. She took the letter to the post office, came back and lay down facing the wall.

She wondered whether Nikolai would come after all or not, and if he came how he would act and what he would say. And then she began to think in fright about what she should do if he started to kiss her again. Those thoughts so disturbed her that her hands shook when she began to dress. She put on yesterday's dark-blue dress, arranged her hair a little, and dabbed on some scent. The palms of her hands were damp with perspiration.

Walking through the village, it seemed to her that she was being observed from every window and that everybody knew where she was going and why. She was flustered and wanted to increase her pace but restrained herself. It was only when she was out at last among the fields that she began to breath freely. It was warm there, a slight haze of dust above the lane made the sun seem as if it was setting behind purple vapour. But on a boundary path that adjoined the lane an oil-besmirched tractor-driver was tinkering with the motor of his machine, and catching sight of Sonya he straightened up, wiped his hands on his trousers, lit a cigarette and seemed to follow her passage with thoughtful interest.

Entering a damp gully where the lane had been fouled by the traffic of cows, Sonya had to slow her pace to pick her way through the mire, and she suddenly grew frightened that Nikolai might arrive before her and leave without waiting. She began to hurry, and then to run. She stopped when the barn appeared in the distance and was relieved to see that there was no one near it. She paused to catch her breath and took off her shoes, wiping them with some grass.

She decided that she would not sit at the front of the barn, facing the lane, and went instead around to the back, which looked out on the distant river. It was pleasant there, the sun had been on that side during the day, and now the wall radiated warmth. But soon a boy carrying two fishing rods arrived nearby and started to dig for worms. Sonya, blushing, returned to the front. People passed in carts, coming from town, and they looked towards her, while the boy, as if bent on annoying her, hung about for a long time. She became quite flushed. Finally, apparently having dug up all the worms he needed, the boy left, turning a number of times to look back at her with what seemed to her an amused expression. 'Yes, he's guessed!' Sonya thought in panic. 'It's a good thing he's not from my school!'

Once again she stole around to the rear of the barn. She picked a wilted daisy, its petals drooping down like the fins of a little rocket, and she began to pluck them in turn and recite: 'He'll come. He won't come...' The conclusion was that he wouldn't come. But the worst of it was that Sonya did not know which way Nikolai might approach from, and so more than once she stood up, walked to the front of the barn, looked in all directions, only to return to her hide again. By the time Nikolai did appear she was completely exhausted. He came up from the river, his hands in his pockets and a jacket draped casually over his shoulders. As he neared her and saw her his face took on the concentrated expression of someone trying to remember something, then it spread over with an increasingly evident pain. He extended a limp hand to her, not looking at her: 'Why, hello there...' he said.

'I'm very happy to see you,' replied Sonya, not daring to lift her eyes.

'Been here long?'

'No.'

'H'm... Well, let's go where it's cool.'

They went around to the front of the barn and sat on some hay piled by the wall. The sun was disappearing, objects were fading, and the shadow of the barn now stretched a long way over the fields.

'Did you get home all right—yesterday?' asked Sonya, attempting an understanding but sympathetic smile at Nikolai.

'O-ow,' yawned Nikolai, taking off his jacket, 'Yeah, as usual. Didn't get enough sleep, that's all.'

'You were bad last night,' said Sonya, gently.

'What do you expect?' said Nikolai, and without any great warmth embraced her and drew her to him. Then, about to kiss her, he changed his mind at the last moment.

'It will be dark soon,' Sonya said, submitting to his hold. She could feel the hollow beat of his heart.

'We'll go to the pea field a bit later, ha?' Nikolai jerked his head vaguely to the right. 'There's a hut there. Want to come?'

'There is no need for that, Kolya,' Sonya said quietly, and she sighed.

'Hoo,' Nikolai suddenly exhaled, 'I'm dead tired. Here, let me lie down.'

He stretched himself out, booted feet thrown apart, and propped his head on Sonya's knees. After lying like that for a moment he reached around and clasped her side with his hand.

'How come you're so skinny?'

Sonya stopped breathing for a moment.

'It's my constitution,' she said, desperately trying to smile.

'Constitution my foot! You've probably got something. It's like with the animals: once they get sick, you can feed them all you want and they still finish up skeletons.'

Suddenly it all seemed pointless to Sonya. She swallowed several times to rid herself of a bitter, nauseating sensation.

'Why are you so coarse?' she asked abruptly in a low voice. 'Or do you think that you can do what you like with me?' She turned sharply away and began to redden. 'Don't you dare talk to me like that! Do you hear?' She bit her lower lip and wiped her eyes vigorously with a sleeve. Then, looking back tensely across the fields she made a fretful movement with her knees and said: 'And go away! I'm not an animal! Take your head away! Do you hear? Leave me!'

Nikolai sat up, bewildered. 'Now then...' he mumbled, 'I apologise. There you are. If I'd known... I didn't want... all right, I am a louse. It's my work, that's what it is. You get into habits.'

'No, it's not the work,' said Sonya, now calmly and sadly, 'It's because...' she pulled at her handkerchief, her fingers trembling, and she turned away, 'It's because you decided that once I had come, well, what's the point of any politeness.'

Nikolai rubbed the back of his head and said nothing.

'What were you angry about, last night?' Sonya asked, after a silence.

'Yes, well...' Nikolai grew sullen, 'I've got some things to sort out with him, that swine. Grabbed Zoyka from me and married her. Did you see the bride yesterday? I used to take her out!'

'But you must have many girls who love you, probably,' said Sonya.

'Ha!' Nikolai made a bitter face and leant his head back against her knees. 'I know all about that love of theirs!'

'Why be like that, Kolya?' Sonya said quickly, 'You've got to believe in people! Look around you, we have so many fine ones here!'

Nikolai lifted his head and spat.

'Don't you believe that?' asked Sonya in a disappointed tone.

'Believe what?'

'In the goodness of people.'

Nikolai laughed: 'Don't women just love to muddy the waters though! The goodness of people!' He turned away, yawned and closed his eyes.

In that big, slothfully-spread, strong-necked figure and in that handsome face, immobile and craggy in the growing darkness, she seemed to see something lasting and indomitable, a cast-iron strength gathered into it from numberless generations. With a trembling hand Sonya passed her fingers through Nikolai's hair and looked down yearningly at him, even as she felt shame and blushed.

'Kolya, you're a good person, I know you have a good heart...' she began to say, barely audibly.

'Quiet! Wait!...' he cut her off and lifted his head to listen to something; then he sat up, leaning his arm heavily on Sonya's knees.

Two people were coming along the lane, talking together in murmurs.

'Hallo there!' Nikolai shouted to them.

'What on earth... Kolya!' Sonya whispered, hiding her face in her hands.

The pair stopped.

'Where are you fellers off to?' Nikolai shouted once more.

'Going to a party. Who's that? That you, Nikolai?'

'Yeah, in person. Where's it at?'

'At Sosnovka.'

The two on the lane lit cigarettes, then the movement of the points of light told that they had recommenced walking. Nikolai looked on after them for a moment.

'Hey, wait!' he suddenly shouted again. 'I'm coming too!'

He stood up hurriedly, dusted his jacket and draped it on his shoulders, cleared his throat and extended his hand to Sonya.

'Well... good-bye! Bound to meet again,' he said, and turning, keeping his jacket in place with one hand, he trotted off after the others.

Night had fallen. To one side just above the horizon an eggshell new-moon was rising; pale tendrils of mist from the river had started to creep up on the flats and to broaden there; all sounds had died, except that once near the back of the barn some small running creature made a pattering noise: top-top-top-top...

Sonya sat slumped against the wall, looking up at the sky. She was shaking. She unbuttoned her collar, but that did not ease her. She tried to cry, but the sound torn out of her breast seemed such a frightful growl that it shocked and stilled her to rigidity. Finally, she rose with one hand on the wall and stood for a moment, then began to walk home.

No sooner had she left the vicinity of the river than the ground became drier and the air warmed again. She was on the lane to the village once more, but now the stars were providing what light there was. There was a faint odour of hay and road dust; by the glow of the Milky Way haystacks and the smaller ricks of flax could be made out in the fields on each side; a rye-field shone palely, newly harvested and still in disorder.

'Oo-oo!...' Sonya moaned to herself, in that same low and frightening tone, 'Oo-oo!...'

She could utter nothing else nor think of anything else. She passed through another low, damp area and then up out of it. The tractor that she had seen being repaired earlier was now ploughing a field some distance from the lane: the cast of its lights and faint murmur of the motor could just be made out.

Then she started to feel better.

She suddenly saw the piercing beauty of the world and how so slowly the stars pour across the sky; she felt enveloped by the splendour of the night, in which the glimmers of distant bonfires joined by their vacillating lights in an equable great unity with those stars; bonfires which, she marvelled now, might at this moment have good people sitting and standing sociably around them; and thinking like that, she felt the tired, quiet fortitude of the earth. She thought about herself, that she was after all a woman, and, whatever else, she had a heart and a soul, and someone would be lucky to discover those in her one day, possibly.

Oh, that ignorant, ignorant fool! What strength and delight she suddenly felt within herself, how light, how filled with energy she seemed, how determined grew her steps! In the darkness perhaps she was beautiful, alone under the blaze of the star-canopy and the streaks of falling stars.

The darkened village appeared ahead. Most people were now asleep, only an occasional cottage showing a light. From a gate a large white dog came trotting out. Seeing Sonya, it approached her, curved silently behind her to sniff her legs. 'Ha! Just try biting me!' she thought, and breathless with intended vengefulness and new bravery, she turned to face it. But the dog did not bite her, it merely panted for a moment near her heels, and then ran off into the night. Sonya continued on her way, feeling even more pleased with herself.

6. THE PILGRIM

1

He was walking by the side of the highway, gazing into the distance where long woolly summer clouds lay banked above gently sloping hills. A persistent head wind puffed out his short, soft, sun-bleached beard and made his eyes water, so that he often wiped away the tears from his cheeks with a coarse, dirt-ingrained finger, after which, never blinking, he resumed peering ahead through the dazzling heat haze. Cars overtook him, their tyres on the asphalt strident as fiends, but he showed no signs of wanting a lift and trudged on, his figure obstinately distinct against the grey road shining sleekly from the passage of countless vehicles.

He was young and tall, somewhat stooped, and he walked with a long-legged and determined gait. His rubber boots, his fur hat, frayed in places and more appropriate for winter, his knapsack, his heavy, worn-to-a-sheen overcoat, were all carried lightly and did not irk him or hinder him.

What did he think about—or did he think anything—as he paced on past villages and copses, as he went by streams and green fields and brown fields in fallow? His blue eyes rimmed by red eyelids did not look at anything with particular interest or for very long, their glance skimming over distances and pausing only among white clouds, eyes that might be dimmed by wind-tears momentarily, and then, expressing nothing, peered on ahead again. His stick was a piece of nutwood, the end streaked grass-green, and he walked tapping it on the asphalt, past shrubbery that looked as if intent on reclaiming the road, past old birches that might have wandered in a fit of abstraction to the road's edge or be retreating thence silently, never long impressing their presence on the expanses of roadside clearings.

The sun showed the time to be past midday. It was now hotter and drier than it had been that morning, the wind was laden with the smell of warm hay and of the asphalt, and the traveller still maintained his stride, his stick tapping and tapping, and it was impossible to say where he was heading or how much longer he would walk.

Then at last he glimpsed some way off to one side a white outline: the bell-tower of a church. Once it was seen, he was soon able to turn into a dusty lane, and down that lane he now walked more attentively. Coming to a clear, deep stream he sat down in the shade of a bush, slid off his knapsack and brought out of it some boiled eggs and bread and began eating. He chewed slowly, looking each morsel over with care before putting it in his mouth. When he had finished eating, he crossed himself, waved his hand across his beard and moustache to shake off any crumbs, lifted himself up heavily on his feet and went to the stream to drink. After he had drunk and rinsed his face he returned and moved deeper into the shrubbery. He lay down with the knapsack under his head, turned up his collar, slid his hat over his face, and instantly fell into a sleep of great tiredness.

2

He slept long, waking when the sun was already settled on the hills. He rubbed his rheumy eyes and yawned for some time, scratching himself and looking around, unable to comprehend at once where he was or why he should find himself there. His face, distended with sleep, was empty of any expression save stupor and listlessness.

A vehicle loaded with milk cans passed along the lane, going towards the highway. The traveller followed it with his eyes until it disappeared, and as he did so his face grew livelier. He quickly shouldered his knapsack, walked back to the lane and began following it in the direction of the village he had noticed earlier.

He crossed the stream by a bridge, and on his right now appeared a green spread of oats, lush and just beginning to darken in the late day; past the oat-field a line of firs stretched ahead on each side of the lane, and the sun in going down was leaving behind a thin, blood-red band that glowed through the dark crowns of the firs. To look at those two together, that band and that darkness, was troubling, and the traveller hurried on, raising dust with his boots, for he had a fear of darkness and did not like the night.

Now the smells were different: of grass cooling and lane dust, there was the languid scent of sweet clover, the honeyed one of thousandfoil yarrows, and from the fir trees the heavy odour of resin. The sky above was clear, profound, and the descent into twilight was like the evening falling into reverie; on one side, a milky new-risen moon had appeared and it stood out distinctly.

The lane now crossed a tongue of forest and wound in and out of dark gullies. The traveller walked more quickly, nostrils working, his panting like that of an animal, and he looked about himself continually. Twice he gave voice to the beginning of some ditty but soon fell silent again, overborne by the sombre quiet.

At last he came to the smells of habitation and passed pasture land and slowed to a calmer pace, looking alertly towards what might lie ahead. The brush and the trees grew more scattered, were left behind, and he arrived at a substantial village: the same stream ran below it and a church stood on a hill. The slopes above the stream were taken up with animal enclosures, and from those despite the advancing darkness still came noises of settling life, a murmur of activity like that around a hive at late evening.

He was approaching a barn, when he saw a woman leave the enclosures and begin walking up to the village. He stopped to wait for her, and when she neared him he wrenched off his hat, bent in a deep bow, and in the act of lowering his head looked quickly and searchingly into her face. His speech was strangely declamatory: 'Greetings, mother! The Lord protect thee!'

'And to you, greetings,' the woman replied, slowing down. She straightened her scarf and licked her lips uneasily.

'You'd be local?'

'Eh, I? Yes, local... And yourself, which village might you be from?'

'I come from far. I go to holy places, a pilgrim.'

The woman looked closely at him, was on the point of saying something, but began moving off in silence. The man walked in step beside her, his face as he talked acquiring an ascetic severity: 'And would the chapel be open?' he asked, glancing up at the rose-gold cross on the bell tower.

'The church, you ask? Closed. How else could it be. No one goes. It's the MTS now, they've turned it into the motor tractor station. We did have a priest, but he was an old thing. Died going on twenty years now.'

'And so ye live in unbelief?'

The woman showed more signs of discomfort, adjusted her scarf again, sighed helplessly and lowered her eyes. The pilgrim quickly made a second examination of her. She was not altogether old but her face and hands were swarthy and weather-coarsened, the angles of her thin shoulders could be detected through her worn and faded cardigan, and her breasts had lost any prominence.

'How else could it be?' she repeated morosely after a moment. 'The young ones... well, you know how it is with them in these times, they don't believe. And then there's also that we have to work day in day out the whole year and there's no strength left for our own affairs. There's a priest that does the rounds. We pray at the burials, and that's about as far as belief goes around here.'

'Aye, indeed, that is the way of it,' said the pilgrim; then, dwelling on the words, he pronounced: 'Oh, ye people, ye people—my heart grieves to see it! Would that I kenned not what ye do with your lives. Your own graves ye ready thus!...'

The woman stopped, and they stood together in gloomy silence. The path had grown dark and only the water in a nearby pond still showed dull glints where two tardy ducks floating beside a bank snatched greedily a last cropful from the hanging sedge.

'Would there be a Christian here at all then, to give a God-fearing man shelter?' asked the pilgrim mournfully.

'To stay the night, you mean? Well... I suppose you could even stay at my place. It wouldn't wear out the bed, I expect.'

Neither of them said anything more until they came to the woman's cottage. But at the moment when she was about to open the door she paused and asked: 'How are you called, then?'

'Yohan!' he said, reverting to a stern rhetorical tone.

The woman sighed again, and they entered the dark, rank porch and passed into the cottage.

'Take off your coat, rest,' she said to him, and she went out again.

He dropped his knapsack, took off his overcoat and sat down to remove his boots. He sat there for a time, smelled with a pained face the bindings he unwound from his feet, scratched each wide, venous instep, looked around the room.

When the woman returned, he was sitting in his shirt-sleeves and reaching inside his knapsack. He brought out of it a copy of the New Testament and a thick exercise book inscribed with the title 'The Memorial of Blessed Yohan' above a large cross hand-drawn on its cover. Having felt again inside the knapsack and produced a stump of pencil, he opened the exercise book, thought for a moment, and asked in an interrogatory tone: 'Has there been a death in this house?'

The woman started. She stared rigidly at the strange, bearded figure before her. 'There has been,' she said hardly audibly. 'In spring... my boy died. He was a driver for the kolkhoz. He was trying to drive over the stream...'

'Name?'

'What?' asked the woman, uncomprehending.

'The name, the name! Thy son's name!' he said loudly, irritated.

'Ah, the boy... Fedya, he was called. They told him: "Wait, don't go, the load won't rot!"—he was carrying parts for the MTS—"Go round by the bridge, the ice is ready to give!" He wouldn't listen. Hot-headed he was. Drowned... my little boy... drowned...'

'I will pray for him!' Yohan interrupted her, and he wrote in large letters 'Fyodor'. 'Thy name? How do folk call thee?'

'Nastasya.'

'So... Nas-ta-sya. Do you live alone?'

'There are two of us; there's my daughter—although, she's no daughter, she's Fedya's wife, and I can tell you that she and I...'

'You had a husband?'

'I had, of course I had. Killed at the front, in '42.'

'Name?'

'Mikhael he was called.'

'So.' Yohan paused. 'And how do we call thy daughter-in-law?'

'Lyuba. It means "love", you know.'

'I know,' said the man, writing. 'Is she a good one?'

'Eh? What's that?...' asked Nastasya, not understanding again.

'Does she behave? Believes in God?'

'No, she doesn't believe in God, she's in the Komsomol. But I have to give it to her that she's proper enough. She did a course to do with animals, at an institute, so she works over at the farm. And then they've got her involved in the club. We've got a social club, so she has to look after that in the evening. She gets tired—away all day, then off again at night. Of course, you can't deny that it's a hard thing for a young person alone. They were only together a year. The boy, my Fedenka... he comes back from the army... says, "Mummy... Mum, dear", he says...'

Nastasya's face puckered, her dry lips trembled, and tears trickled down her dark, bony cheeks. The man remained coldly silent.

'But do sit down, please. We'll have tea...' said Nastasya through her tears. 'I'll give the samovar a blow.'

'Are there any icons here?'

'Yes indeed—the Blessed Women Anointers of Christ's Body, and the Three-Handed Madonna.'

'Where? Take me to them!'

'They're in the other room. This way.'

She opened the door into a clean chamber. Yohan followed her with a joyless expression, treading heavy-footed on the floor mats. He picked up the 'Memorial' on the way.

'Go!' he said, catching sight of the icons. 'I must pray.'

He dropped on his knees with a thud and threw back his head so that the tuft of hair on his chin pointed up. Nastasya left, very quietly.

'Ah, Lord!' intoned Yohan in a deep voice. 'Ah, Lord!'

And he fell silent. He remained kneeling there, looking through the window at the still apple trees, listening to the sounds of Nastasya rattling plates in the other room and getting the table ready; and that stillness, those small noises, this long, summer descent into dusk, were strangely pleasing to him, swayed his heart into a placid contentment. O how many villages he had seen, where had he not found lodgings at night! Everything was different wherever one went: people, manners, speech. And only the dusk, the smell of habitation, of bread, the village-sounds, were the same everywhere.

Yohan looked through the window, craning his neck to better see through the dimness. Below, beyond the kitchen gardens, flowed the stream, past the stream there were fields, the forest. A mist was already flowing down from the tree line, milky strands were unrolling towards the stream and spreading sideways over the water-meadows.

'Ah, Lord!' he sighed, still listening to the subdued kitchen-noises and looking out of the window into the distance.

Nastasya peeked carefully into the back room and saw the tousled, long-unbarbered head of the pilgrim, the sunburnt neck, the broad, hard-angled shoulder blades and the bare soles of his wide feet. But he stayed motionless, silent in some world of thought, his body propped up on his long arms, knuckles on the floor. She withdrew again, leaving the samovar by the door, and went out to do her milking.

Now he heard at the porch the sound of lighter steps, and he instantly thought: 'The girl!' and carefully turned his head. There was the noise of the door being thrown open, and then the footsteps died at the door of his room. Yohan lowered his bearded chin, crossed himself with wide sweeps of his arm, looking towards the dark imagery of the icons, feeling that the new arrival was observing him, surely with wonder.

Silence. Then the steps retreated quickly back to the porch. He sprang up and glided close to the inner door of the porch, one brown ear poised forward.

'Mama!'

'What's the matter?' The steady buzz of the milk against the side of the bucket stopped.

'Mama, who's that in there?'

'Oh... somebody just passing through. A pilgrim. Looking for the Lord. He asked to spend the night.'

'A pilgrim? Old?'

'He's got a beard. Doesn't look all that strong. His eyes are young.'

'Could be a tramp do you think?'

'What a thing to say, Christ be with you! He's a godly man. He prays.'

Silence. Except for the faint grunt of a piglet somewhere. The quick, even, metallic buzz of milking resumed.

'Has the pig been fed?'

'No, I haven't had time with this milking. I've made up his mix, it's there behind the stove.'

'I'll give it to him.'

In the dimness Yohan hurried away from the door and into the back room, fell again on his knees and lifted up his bearded chin as before. 'A harlot!' he said to himself furiously. 'She'll throw me out, won't have me here for the night!'

But around the cottage the quiet sounds of domestic life continued. Inside, darkness accumulated in the corners, things became indistinct, the figures in the icons, those in photographs, the printing on a framed diploma, everything was being lost to the gloom, was taking on a vaguely troubling mysteriousness as the forest-dark entered the little building. When it was night, and the moon had grown white above the trees and begun cautiously to peer into the windows, a brightly burning lamp was brought in, the samovar sang again on the table, Yohan came out of the back room, crammed the New Testament and the 'Memorial' into his knapsack, sat down on a bench and began studying Lyuba.

3

They sat down to table. Yohan ate greedily and much, with noisy swallows and movements of his beard and ears.

'Eat, eat...' Nastasya kept saying, moving food towards him.

And each time he lifted his bloodshot blue eyes from the plate, they settled on Lyuba; and she was aware of his glances, her cheeks flushed, and she grew restless and frowned.

She was pretty, with a soft, sun-tanned freshness. Remnants of girl-hood were still visible in her person: an awkwardness of movement, a difficult to define fleeting look in her eyes, breasts that were yet girlish. He glanced often at her, there was something in her that he liked; and he began to think that it might be a good thing to shave his beard, marry such a wench and take up domestic life, sleep with her in the hayloft, kiss her till the roosters crowed; and his heart thumped and he felt a ringing in his head from the thinking of such things.

'Eat, don't be frightened,' Nastasya urged him, 'Try the little mush-rooms, they've come early this year.'

At last satisfied, Yohan crossed himself, bobbed his head to the woman and the girl in a gesture of thanks, pushed back his chair, almost belched but controlled himself, saving it for later, and he proceeded to roll a ciga-rette, dropping strands of tobacco on his knees and collecting them again with care.

'I smoke, you see,' he said sadly. 'I smoke. The devil will devour me. How many times now I've sworn to stop, laid penances on myself—I can't.'

Lyuba burst into laughter, then quickly turned away from the table and went to the stove. Nastasya, squirming with annoyance, half-raised her-self from the chair, lifted appealing eyes to the man, and rounded on her: 'What's got into you? Well? Have you gone mad?'

Lyuba kept silent, her eyes invisible behind her lowered eyelashes: she was trying not to laugh.

'Yes,' Yohan came in with passion, 'Many have become wise today. They don't believe, and yet the devil is by their side. They diminish every-thing. Life is just fuss and vanity. No one thinks any more. It's all machin-ery. The machines have eaten the humans! It's all written there, in the Apocalypse.'

Lyuba, openly amused now, was looking directly at him.

'You look at me?' said Yohan, harshly now, feeling in his breast a gay anger towards her, 'You don't like me? Never seen anyone like me before? Displeased I ate with you?...'

'God be with you, what things you say!' said Nastasya in a shocked tone.

'I don't care about the food, nor about you staying,' said Lyuba in a resonant, confident voice. 'That's mother's affair. But to be honest, all this is ridiculous, of course. What are you walking around for? Aren't you ashamed? Grown yourself a beard! How does a beard add to holiness? My word, but it's like one of our amateur plays at the club, right here in this house!'

'And you, you wouldn't like to be free, to just go?'

'I? No, I like to work.'

'Work...' The man drew his breath in sharply, turning his eyes towards a corner of the room, 'You're a silly girl! What's the benefit of your work, the work of people like you? You don't believe in God, and yet he is and always will be, forever and ever! Work... Oh, ye people, ye people! I travel around, I see...'

'Yes, that's easy enough to do,' Lyuba interjected calmly.

'I travel around and see things,' continued the man more loudly, 'What do you do? How do you live? Has life become better on earth? No, worse! I tell you sincerely—worse! More thieves, more debauchery. I read the Holy Text—here it is. That would be a book for you!' and he thumped the knapsack. 'But you don't get that in your technical colleges and institutes—you do not!'

'And we don't need it,' said Lyuba, and she yawned. 'We'll get along without it. I'm tired, I'll go to bed. Good-night, Mama.'

She left the stove, took something out of a chest of drawers and went past the man, leaving with him the faint odour of her healthy, clean, woman's body. She went into the porch, banging the door shut behind her.

'There's a lass who knows her mind,' said the man, with a voice of someone holding himself in check. 'Spirited.'

'What can you do with them? They're young,' Nastasya sighed, and she began clearing the table. 'They think differently, nothing worries them. But don't be offended. It's not an easy life they have. Young, pretty, a widow.'

'Ye-es...' Yohan conceded, 'It seems that the Good Lord has decided it should be so. I too had no thought of becoming a pilgrim. Of course, my view on life was different from the start. I come from Pskov, from the village of Podsosonye—never heard of it? Parents killed in the war, may theirs be the heavenly kingdom! I was left alone. What can you expect? I wandered around miserably, worked, got a job clearing mines. One blew up and got me in the stomach, right here under the lung. Just got out of that alive, an invalid. And what's an invalid's lot? He gets a little light work occasionally if he's lucky. No education: you've got to study a long time to become an engineer or agronomist or that kind of thing. Things went bad with me at the kolkhoz, I got fed up. I've got a soul that can't be satisfied. It's pulled me to far places. And to prostrate myself before God. Yes, I too did not believe once. There was an old fellow at the kolkhoz who used to take the milk around, a true believer he was. He made me see. I began to read books. You read this, you read that, it all becomes clearer. "Go, my son"—that's how he talked to me—"Go," he says, "to the holy places; pray, save us all from perdition; and save yourself!" And I went, and it's the fifth year now and I'm still on that road. Many indeed are the people on that road, clean and holy folk. I've become lighter in spirit, I walk near God, and I won't deviate from that road now. No, I won't deviate!'

'And will you go a long way, next?' asked Nastasya in a sleepy voice.

'Well, tomorrow I want to get to Borisovo, to kiss the Miraculous Cross there. Much have I heard of it. And where have I not been! I lived among the monasteries in Kiev, getting my bread from the charitable people there. I was at the Great Monastery of the Caves, a place of marvels, and many prayed there. And the Trinity Monastery of Saint Sergius, I was there, too. And I even went as far as Estonia, and I've been on the Vetluga. But there the people are a sullen lot, priestless, heretical—I dislike them, uncharitable heathens...'

And suddenly he thought of Lyuba: 'Why, she's gone to bed out there, inside the porch!...' and his heart pained sweetly.

'Yes, mother!' and his voice grew happy and animated, amazed that everything was falling into place so well—he had chanced on a hostess who was a believer; and there, sleeping in the porch alone, was a young widow—'Yes, mother! I have gone much around the world; but if I were to speak truly, before the God of heaven, there's no place like our Russia. You go about her, the skylark sounds, he flutters there, then over there... The clover is flowering; here a daisy is looking up at you... You chance on good people, they ask about you, call you to spend the night with them, invite you to eat... Or you go through the forest—and our forests are so full of scents! The bumble bees drone, wasps buzz around on their affairs—that's what's good, that's sweet! There's no boss above you, no regulations. You get up—and then you just go! What are people to me? Who are they? Yes, and my memory is bad, I forget everybody, I don't remember them. No, I don't remember them at all. See: I spend the night somewhere, I get up, pray to God, bow my thanks to those who had me, and—onwards! But, then, there are those who don't let you inside, who call you a tramp. It pains me, that, God be with them, but it pains! But there are still many good people, believers who give you their address, welcome you—"Come, live with us, be merry!" But I don't want to live in any one place, everything pulls at me, something draws me on. Especially in spring. No, I just can't.'

He fell to musing, was silent and sat leaning on his arms propped each side of him on the bench. The woman began to doze, her head nodded, she started, blinked. The clock ticked in the back room, each tick distinct in the quiet.

'I'm falling asleep,' said Nastasya apologetically, and yawned, 'Like it or not, I have to get up at first light.'

She stood up creakily and began arranging a wide wooden bed, explaining with sad irony: 'Imagine, at my age I've got to be the first one at the pens, I'm on the roster to do the milking. God knows why I've taken it on. But anyway, lie down here, heaven be with you, you'll be tired yourself as much as anyone.'

'No but don't worry, just something on the floor's all I need,' he muttered the protest without conviction. 'Just make up something and that's all.' And he looked longingly at the bed, now being covered with a feather quilt.

'Lie down, lie down and don't give it a thought! I don't sleep on it, I don't like it, it's too wide. Lyuba sleeps on it sometimes, I'm always over there by the stove, so do take it.'

'Well then all right, Christ save thee,' Yohan said, his reluctant tone barely hiding his satisfaction, and he began to undress.

Nastasya moved about a little longer, shifted things, tidied up, her huge shadow looming and receding on the wall like an apparition in a dream. Up in the ceiling a fly or two buzzed, disturbed. Then she went to the table, screwed up her eyes, blew out the lamp, and the cottage fell into darkness.

4

'Is she asleep now, in the porch?' the pilgrim kept thinking, and he was unsettled by an intense desire, could not lie still, kept turning, looking at the bright splashes of moonlight on the walls. At last he got up, a pale figure in the dark, draped in his long smock-shirt which served him also as nightwear.

'Should've gone out before bed...' he mumbled back into the room, feeling for the door handle. He entered the blackness of the porch, stood a moment to get used to the dark, and listened until he heard the sound of Lyuba's breathing where she slept. 'There!' he thought happily, and crossing the porch he slid back the bolt on the outside door and stood on the step.

The village was mostly dark and quiet. There were a few cottages where people had not yet gone to bed and where a light still burned, and from some distance away came the sound of talking and laughter. The moon glowed with all its strength but was still low, casting the sharp shadow of the cottage a long way beyond the path that led to the door. In the moonlight the stars shimmered hazily. It was beginning to grow cooler. A tractor working late somewhere in the fields made a chirring noise and it was difficult to tell the direction of the sound. The voices and laughter were coming nearer, and soon tiny points of light that were cigarettes appeared in the darkness. The pilgrim turned quickly, passed through the porch again, entered the living area but did not close its door, thinking: 'I'll wait and let the old woman sleep deeper a bit, and then...' He lay down and closed his eyes.

Outside, there was the sound of hushed voices and an accordion droned for a moment, not very loudly. Then came a timid tap on the window glass. Craning his neck, Yohan looked up and saw through the window the figures of two girls. There was more tapping on the glass, soft and apologetic. In the cottage the others slept on, no one stirred.

'Well, what's happening?' a male now spoke. 'Is she asleep or what? Come on, do it louder!'

The fellow himself knocked with his knuckles more forcefully on the window frame, and then leapt back, laughing.

'Devil take them! Who brought them here?' Yohan thought with chagrin.

There was a patter of bare feet in the porch, and Lyuba entered unsteadily in her chemise. She went to the window and opened it.

'What do you want?' she called out sharply.

'Lyubushka dear,' said a girl in a cajoling voice, 'we thought you wouldn't be asleep...'

There was a gust of cynical laughter from around the corner of the cottage.

'Truly, we thought... Give us the key, please. We want to go to the club to dance.'

'Do let us have it, Lyubushka...' joined in the other girl, laughingly and pathetically, 'or we'll all just shrivel up. It's summer and we've got no films; we never get to see anything.'

'No, I won't!' said Lyuba with finality. 'Go to bed!'

Yohan did not move. Hardly breathing, he looked at her figure outlined in the moonlight, saw her firm arms and shoulders, her breasts.

'We don't see any films or get to do any concerts...' continued the second voice unhappily.

'Lyubushka, just for an hour,' begged the first. 'Look at the time: it's early!'

'What early—it'll be dawn soon!'

'What dawn!... What dawn!...' cried out a chorus of excited voices outside. 'Kolya, Kolya, tell us what the time is.'

'Twenty to eleven,' someone around the corner said hoarsely, and guffawed.

'I won't give you the key!' said Lyuba, firmly. 'The chairman has forbidden it: they had it on the agenda today. You'll be dancing till morning and then they won't wake you up to go to work. You should be sleeping!'

Lyuba closed the window with finality; as she left on the way to the porch, her white calves flashed past Yohan's bed. The girls outside stood murmuring among themselves for a little longer and then moved away.

'Didn't let you have it, mm?' drawled someone around the corner, and added in a sing-song:

Thereupon she told him sweetly:
Laddie, leave your wooing me...'

The accordion droned in full volume this time, and someone in a cracked falsetto full of weariness and theatrical pain gave vent to the cruder remnant of that verse. Then the voices separated, grew fainter in the distance, and everything became very quiet.

In the yard a rooster called three times. The pilgrim sat up, rolled a cigarette, smoked it carefully enclosed in his curved palm, dropping the ash on the floor. At last he put the stub out in a flower pot, waited a little longer, got up and went noiselessly to the stove. He poked Nastasya with his finger and listened. Nastasya slept on, whistling gently through her nose.

Then he made up his mind. He went to the porch, entered, closed the door carefully behind him, and with a cold and unsettled sensation in his stomach began moving slowly towards the place where Lyuba slept. Having felt her bed with his hands, he stretched himself out on its edge, turned to pull away the thin blanket, slipped an arm under Lyuba's chemise, and planted his lips firmly on hers.

She woke into life with a jerk. Twisting her face away from under his beard she hit him in the chest and cried out. He fell upon her with his whole body, closing her mouth with his hand, hissing: 'What's the matter, what's the matter with you, it's me!... don't be frightened, it's me!...'

'Let me go, you tramp, you holy devil—let me go!' Lyuba uttered in a jumble of words, and tearing herself away she sat on the edge of the bed with the skirt of her chemise between her legs.

'Wait... I'll marry you, don't make a noise, listen to me...' he hissed again. 'I'll marry you, tomorrow even. I'll shave my beard, I'll work in the kolkhoz... I'll go to the baths,' he added, as it flashed through his mind that it had been a long time since he had gone to a public bath to wash. 'Come to me, I'll be good to you...'

'Mama!' shouted Lyuba, jumping up from the bed and pressing herself against a wall, 'Will you get away from me, you filthy devil?' She was trying by abuse to hide her terror from him.

'I will love you!' Yohan whispered, now sadly, for he was realising that nothing was going to come of this. 'I'm healthy, young, there's a man's strength that boils inside me. I'll cut off my beard, I'll do it right now! Just think, there aren't any young men left nowadays in a kolkhoz. You'll rot. Or you'll have to settle for an old widower, or some boy. Come here, come! I'll kneel down on the ground before you if you want!'

'Mama!' Lyuba cried again. 'God, what madness is this?'

There was a rustle inside.

'Be quiet!' Yohan made hushing gestures in the dark, 'I'm going, I'm going. Be damned to you, witch, evil one!'

He rose, groped for the door, and staggering entered the moonlit living area.

'Who's that?' the woman's sleepy voice called out from the stove. 'A? Who's that?'

The pilgrim did not answer and lay down, trembling all over, grinding his teeth, tears rising to his eyes from the pain of his disappointment.

The woman settled down again and grew quiet, was soon snoring softly.

'Bitch!' hissed the pilgrim. 'Bitch! Jezebel! Got me all excited, hey?'

Out in the porch something rattled, rolled, thudded; footsteps could be heard up in the ceiling; there was the grating noise of something being dragged, and then silence fell again.

'She's gone up into the ceiling, the trollop!' he hissed to himself. 'And she's pulled the ladder up, too. Well, devil take thee! Be damned, accursed one!'

He smoked again, not attempting to hide the cigarette now, mouthing imprecations in a whisper. Time passed: there was a period of transition when the light of the moon was overtaken by that of the dawn and in that pallor things grew more visible. For long after lying down he could not sleep, turning over many times on the soft bedclothes.

5

A rooster woke him at full morning, pouring out a cataract of crowing just under the window. He did not give any thought to washing but just sat yawning and scratching his head; then he remained there immobile for a time, trying to remember what he had dreamt. But he could not. The sun was warming the room and it had become stuffy, smelled sourly, and flies flew about in it. In the daylight, things had returned to their common and monotonous selves again, yesterday's mysteries had disappeared. He dressed, sat at the window, smoking and musing dully.

Nastasya entered, opening the door noisily, looking grimly and strangely at him. She went to the stove, picked up the fire tongs and rattled the damper, bending down and pumping her sharp elbows rapidly and irefully. 'The girl told her about me,' he thought to himself. 'Ah, well, what can you do? I'll get no breakfast now. Time to go, I suppose.'

He got up slowly. An expression of sadness and penitence came easily to his face. He put on his overcoat and took up the knapsack. Leaning on the tongs, Nastasya looked on, her lips pressed together in a thin thread. At the doorsill the pilgrim at once grew happier. Restraining a smile of sudden joy, he turned and bowed low as he had done to her the first time. 'Christ be with thee,' he said in full seriousness, 'God save thee and be merciful to thee. And I shall pray for you all.'

'You red-eyed hound!' Nastasya spat out, her face flushing crimson in variegated blotches, and she turned away.

The pilgrim put on his hat and went out.

As with other times when he was going away from some place, he grew gayer with every step. The road called to him, and what had occurred the day before soon faded and was forgotten. 'Night and day, time floats away!' he intoned to himself happily as he went through the gardens and down to the stream. At the bank he soon found a ford and on the other side walked up the broad, gentle slope to the edge of the forest from which milky strands of mist had unwound on their way to the flats the previous evening. For a little while he meandered vaguely among the trees, following first one route then another, until he finally emerged at the highway and began striding beside it in an easterly direction.

He did not know where the road might take him, but he felt once again light and happy in his soul, moving with the insensibly rapid pace of a person used to much walking, swishing his stick through the roadside grass and bushes, tapping it against the trunks of trees, softly singing something merry to himself. And the memory of his night-time misfortune, and the restive, fleeting sense of melancholy which he had felt yesterday as he knelt in the darkened cottage, pricked his heart, but soon only occasionally and almost imperceptibly.

And so, he walked the whole day; and when evening came he begged again a place to sleep in, in a distant village.

BLUE AND GREEN

1

'Lilya,' she says, and her voice is pitched low, a contralto voice; and then she offers me her small, warm hand.

I press it carefully and let it go, then mutter my own name. At least I think I do, tell her my name: it may have slipped my mind to say it in that first moment. Her hand leaving mine is pale in the evening light. 'What an amazing, what a delicate hand!' I think to myself with wonder.

We are standing at the entrance to a deep courtyard. I'm struck by the number of windows that face out into this square, dim courtyard. Some have got blue frames and some have green ones; and then there are pink ones and some are just white. There's music coming from one blue window on the first floor, they've got their radio on up there. Jazz, I think... I really like jazz. No, not to dance to, I can't dance, but I do like listening to it, to good jazz. Yeah, fine, and is that a big deal? I don't know... Anyway, there I am, standing there like a post, listening to the music coming from that blue window on the first floor.

After we exchanged our names, or whatever did happen, there's this long silence. Maybe she's thinking that I'll say something very intelligent, or something or other amusing, like people do in these situations; or maybe she's waiting for me to ask her a question so that she can start a conversation. But I stay silent. I'm taken up by that strange rhythm, by the sound of that trumpet. A kind of silvery sound. And while it's playing, I can tell myself I don't need to interrupt it with small talk.

But we move off at last, the four of us, out to the lighted street: my friend and his girl, and Lilya and me. We are off to a movie, the first time I've been to one with a girl. They introduced me to her, she gave me her hand and told me her name, and now we are walking together, two total strangers who have become very aware of each other.

The music is gone and there's no excuse left. My friend is dropping back with his girl and I panic and try to walk more slowly—but those two walk even slower! I know he's doing it on purpose—it's mean, leaving the two of us alone like this, I never thought he'd play that kind of trick!

What can I say to her? What sort of interests could she have? I look at her quickly, sideways, and see her eyes reflecting the night-lights, and her dark hair—probably rather coarse, I wouldn't be surprised. They say strong hair goes with self-assurance. I noticed a moment ago that her thick brows were drawn together a bit. Yes, she has certainly a determined look. But her cheeks were kind of rounded and tense, like those of someone trying not to laugh. So—what *am* I going to say to her?

'Do you like Moscow?' she suddenly asks, giving me a sort of severe look.

I start. Surely, I've never heard anyone with such a voice before! I pause, gather myself, reply. Naturally I like Moscow! And especially the side streets and the boulevards around the Arbat. Although I like the other streets as well.

After that I say nothing again for a long time. We come into Arbat Square and I begin whistling, walking with my hands rammed into my pockets. Let her think what she likes. Going out with her is no big deal. I mean, it's a hundred times more interesting with the other fellows. And if it comes to that, I live nearby and I can go home any time. I'm not forced to go to the cinema and put up with watching her trying not to laugh at me!

But anyway, we arrive at the theatre. It's still fifteen minutes to the start and we stand inside the foyer and listen to some singer performing her act. Around us is a big crowd and they are all talking quietly and not taking notice. I noticed quite some time ago that people don't listen very carefully to foyer entertainments, they seem to have some sort of superior attitude to them. It's only those at the front who listen and clap, while those at the back eat ice-cream or sweets or just talk together. Since I won't be able to hear the singer properly anyway, I look at the illustrations on the wall. I've never paid them any attention before, but now they interest me terribly. I think about the artists who drew them. Yes, it's a fine thing that they've been hung there, those illustrations, in this foyer. A fine thing.

Lilya looks at me with bright, grey eyes. It's strange: I try to make a point of not looking at her and yet I can't stop coming back to her face. How beautiful she is! But no, actually she is not beautiful, it's just that she has those bright eyes and those rosy cheeks: when she smiles, they come out in dimples. And when her eyebrows relax and part, then she stops seeming so stern. Her forehead is high and smooth, although when I see that she's thinking about something it has little lines too.

But I just can't stand dumbly beside her any longer! And why is she looking at me like that?

'I'm off for a cigarette,' I say, casually, and depart for the smoking-room. There, I sit down and let out a long sigh of relief. Strange, but when the air is so full of smoke, is grey with it, then for some reason one after all stops wanting to smoke. I look around and see there are a lot of people in the room: some are talking quietly together, others smoke in silence with concentration; they take quick, deep pulls, stub out their half-smoked cigarettes and hurry out again. What could they be hurrying to?...

Now, I've discovered an interesting thing: if you smoke too quickly, the cigarette will taste sour and bitter. The best thing is to smoke slowly and with moderate draws, letting the smoke float up into the air. I look at the clock—another five minutes to the start.

No, I'm just a dope. Others get acquainted easily, talk and crack jokes. I know they talk about football and God knows what—argue over cybernetics. Yeah, I'd like to see me talk with a girl about cybernetics!

But Lilya is a hard person. You can tell: I saw it in that hair of hers. Now me, I've got soft hair. Yes, and it must be from my weakness of character that I sit here and smoke when I don't want at all to smoke. But I'll just go on sitting here quietly. What's there for me to do in the foyer—look at the pictures on the wall all over again? Senseless pictures, I don't know what they want to go on hanging them up there for; I'm glad that I never took any notice of them before!

Oh God, there's the bell. I emerge slowly from the smoking-room and search out Lilya among the crowd. Without looking at each other we go into the hall and sit down. The lights go out and the movie begins.

When we leave the theatre my friend and his girl disappear completely. That has the effect of taking away from me any last ability to think. I simply walk and keep silent. There aren't many people on the streets now. The traffic is faster. The sound of our footsteps comes back from the walls and carries a long way.

And that is how we get back to her place and stop at the entry to the courtyard. It's late and not many of the windows show a light, the yard is darker now than it was two hours ago. Many of the white windows are dark and the pink ones as well, but the green ones are still lit, and that blue one on the first floor is lit, although there is no music coming from it now. We both stand for some time without saying a word. Lilya is acting strangely: she lifts her face, looks up at the windows as if counting them, almost turns her back to me, starts to do something with her hair. Then I say, very nonchalantly, carelessly, that it might not be such a bad idea if we met again next day. I'm glad that in the darkness of the courtyard she can't see how red my face must be.

She agrees. I can come to her: her window looks out on the street. She has holidays now; her parents are away in the country and things are pretty dull. So, yes, she'd be happy to go out.

I ponder whether it would be the correct thing to press her hand in parting. She puts out her slim hand herself, a pale movement in the dark, and again I touch it and feel how warm it is and quite trusting.

2

Next day I go to Lilya, just on dusk. This time the courtyard is full of kids: two of them are on bikes, about to ride off somewhere or else just arrived, while others are standing around. It seems to me that they know very well why I've come. I find that it's hopeless: I can't pass through that yard, and so I go to her window by way of the street. I look into the window and cough.

'Lilya, are you there?' I say loudly. I notice that my voice is indeed loud, and steady as well. It's quite remarkable that my voice is so firm.

Yes, she's at home. She's there with a girlfriend. They are arguing about something interesting and I must come in to decide the question.

'Come in, quickly,' Lilya calls to me.

But I can't bear to go around through the yard.

'I'll come through the window,' I say with decision, and with a little spring I'm up on the sill. It's a light and graceful movement, that little spring, and it's only when I'm throwing my leg over the sill and into her room that I notice the astonishment and amusement on the face of the girlfriend and Lilya's bewilderment. I gather instantly that I'm involved in some kind of blunder and I freeze, there on the sill, one leg out in the street, the other in the room. I sit like that, staring at Lilya.

'Well then, get in!' says Lilya impatiently. Her brows have come to-gether and her cheeks are flaming.

'Actually, I never like being indoors in summer,' I mutter with dignity, 'I'll wait for you outside.' I jump down and retreat to the footpath across the street, opposite the entry to her courtyard.

How they are laughing at me! Why did I come? Why set yourself up to be laughed at? Best clear out—run to the end of the street and around the corner before she comes out. To run or not? I look each way along the street: should I take to my heels? Then I see Lilya. She is coming out of the courtyard with her friend and looking towards me, the laughter in her eyes not yet quite gone out and the dimples trembling on her cheeks.

I don't look at the friend. What's she coming with us for? What am I going to do with two of them? I don't say anything and Lilya begins a con-versation with her friend. They talk and I stay silent. When we go past hoardings, I read them carefully. Hoardings can be read from right to left and also starting from the bottom, and then you can get some very queer and sometimes even really barbaric combinations. We arrive at the corner of the street and Lilya's friend starts saying her good-byes. I look at her gratefully: how kind she is, how wise!

She leaves, and we two go to Tverskoy Boulevard. How many lovers have walked on it over the ages! Yes, and now we are here. But of course we're not in love, that's silly. Or not yet. Or on the other hand for all I know maybe we are, I really don't know that much about it. We walk a metre apart and I notice that the limes have finished blossoming. Still, there are lots of flowers growing in the street-beds. Those don't smell at all. I wonder if anybody knows their name. But I really must find some-thing to say to her.

We begin to talk about things, and actually I'm soon surprised by what a great deal we have to say to each other. It's incredible how one thing leads to another or how our thoughts run on. We talk of ourselves, of people we know, jumping from one subject to another, forgetting what we just said a minute ago. But that doesn't matter, we are suddenly aware that we've got lots of time, there's a long evening ahead of us, and if anything's forgotten we can come back to it. And, maybe best of all, it can all be remembered again later, when alone.

Suddenly I notice that Lilya's dress has come undone. She has a really wonderful dress, I've never seen anyone wear one like it, fastened from collar to belt by tiny studs. And now a few of them have come undone and she hasn't noticed. Now, she can't possibly go around the streets with her clothes undone! But how should I go about telling her? Perhaps I should simply do it myself? Say something light-hearted and do it, like the most ordinary thing? O how nice it would be to be able to do that! But no, it's impossible, it's just not possible. I turn away and tell her that she should button herself up. She instantly falls silent.

I light a cigarette. I smoke for some time. Generally, at difficult moments the best thing to do is to smoke a cigarette, it helps a lot. I venture a glance at her. The studs are now done up, her cheeks are burning, while her eyes have grown dark and severe. She is looking at me, too, as though she is seeing some great change in me or as if I had just discovered something important about her. But the crisis subsides and we go on walking, and now we walk closer together.

One hour follows another and still we walk, we talk and we walk. You can walk endlessly around Moscow. We come to Pushkin Square, and from there go down to Trubnaya Square, then follow the Neglinka to the Bolshoi Theatre and go on to the Great Stone Bridge. I could walk forever, but I ask her if she isn't tired. No, she isn't, this is all interesting for her. Now the street-lamps start to go out, only those on one side still glow, and the sky in the pre-dawn seems to grow lower and more starry. And then, quietly, it begins to lighten. On the boulevards couples sit close to each other, on each bench one couple. They sit silently, and I don't know why they are so silent but I look at them with envy and I wonder: could Lilya and I possibly ever sit like that?

There are no pedestrians on the streets, only the militia. Now and then one of them clears his throat with disapproval as we walk past. They seem on the point of saying something to us but hold back. Lilya at those moments lowers her head and increases her pace, and for some reason I find that amusing. We walk almost touching now, and when she lowers her head like that, I see little puffs of curly hair on her delicate neck. Her arm sometimes touches mine: insignificant touches, but I feel them.

At last we say good-bye in her quiet, echoing courtyard. Everyone is asleep, there's not a light in any window. We lower our voices until we are practically whispering, yet our words sound loud to me and I'm afraid that someone may hear.

I arrive home at three on that summer morning. It's only now that I start to feel the stiffness in my legs. What must she feel like, in that case! I switch on the table-lamp and begin reading *Hatter's Castle*, which Lilya has lent me. It's an excellent book. I read and for some reason her face keeps coming back to me from the pages. At times I shut my eyes and hear her gentle, deep voice.

It's now completely light and I can't read any more. I lie down and look out through the window. We live on a high floor, the sixth floor: you can look down on the roofs of other buildings, and in the distance, from the point where the sun rises in summer, the star on the tower of the Kremlin is visible. Just the star. I often look at it for a long time. At night when all Moscow is quiet I hear the Kremlin chimes. At night you can hear everything quite clearly.

I lie there looking at the star and thinking of Lilya.

3

A week later I leave with my mother for the North. I had been looking forward to the trip for a long time, since spring; but now life in the woods is full of new meaning for me, full of particular significance.

The first time I went into a forest, into a real, uninhabited forest, I was filled with the joy of a pioneer, an explorer. I have a gun: they bought it for me when I passed ninth grade. I wander completely alone and never feel lonely. I like people well enough, I enjoy being with them, enjoy laughter; but there in the woods, I don't know why, I'm content to be by myself. Sometimes I get tired, and then I just sit and maybe look at a wide river or look up at the pale sky of early autumn.

It's August already and there's often bad weather now here in the North. But even in bad weather I leave our lodgings as soon as the sun rises, and I go into the forest. There I'll hunt, or I might get an urge to gather mushrooms, or I'll simply pass from one clearing to another, looking at the field daisies, of which there are so many in these parts. Why, there's really no end of things to do in the forest! Like, you can pick a comfortable spot on the bank of a lake and just sit there, motionless. The ducks fly in and land on the water with a hiss, quite close. At first, they'll float upright with their necks stretched forward, then they'll begin to dive and splash, sometimes clustering together and at other times swimming about on their own; and I follow their movements with my eyes only, not moving my head. Then, sunlight might suddenly break through the clouds and through the leaves above me and stretch quivering gold fingers deep into the water; and then you can see the long, rust-coloured stems of the water-lilies, and near those are quite large fish, caught motionless in the sun's light, not moving a fin. You'd think they were daydreaming, maybe remembering the wonderful days of summer, days of thunderstorms and May beetles. Or maybe they're just sleeping like that. I feel strange when I look at them, as if I were myself unable to move, the way it happens sometimes in dreams.

Yes, there's so much to do in the forest. Like simply lying there listening to the hum of the pines, lying and thinking of Lilya, or even talking to her. I tell her about hunting, about the lakes and the woods, I tell her how marvellous is the smell of the smoke after I've fired my gun, and she understands me, although in general girls don't like and don't understand hunting.

Sometimes, returning at night and crossing the fields can be quite scary: I carry the gun loaded, but I still look about me often. I'm troubled then and all kinds of things enter my mind. It might be very dark, although if you look for quite a while up in the sky you will finally see a weak, silvery light, but on the ground it's very dark. Above, owls circle and don't make a sound. I can just see their velvet-black silhouettes but try as I might I can't hear the sound of their wings. I once shot one. It hit the boundary-path hard and made snapping sounds with its beak for a long time in the darkness.

After a month I return to Moscow. From the station I stop home only long enough to drop off the suitcases and then I go to Lilya. It's evening and a light shows in her window, so I know she's at home. I get to the window by going past some scaffolding: it looks as though they are doing work on her building. I peer through a gap in the curtain.

Lilya is sitting alone at her desk, reading a book by the light of a table-lamp. Her face is thoughtful and sad. Leaning on her elbows, she turns a page and looks up at the lamp while she winds a strand of hair around her finger. How dark her eyes are! Why did I once think that they were grey? They are dark, almost black. I stand under the scaffolding and all around me is the smell of plaster and varnish, and that resinous smell comes to me like a distant call from my hunting times, like a recollection of all that I had left in the North. Behind me I hear the steps of passers-by. People go past on their way to some place or other, hurrying, their steps clicking on the asphalt. They all have their thoughts and their loves, and they all live, every one of them, individual lives. Moscow deafens me: I've grown unused over this last month to its noise and lights, its smells and crowds. And with a timid happiness I think: how good it is that in this huge city I too have someone I love!

'Lilya!' I call out, but not too loudly.

She starts, her brows lift. Then she rises, comes to the window, moves the curtain aside, bends to me—and, near, I see her dark, happy eyes.

'Alyosha!' she says slowly, and just-visible dimples appear on her cheeks, 'Alyosha! Are you there? Are you really there? I'll come out. Do you want to go for a walk? I would dearly like to go for a walk with you! I'll come out right now!'

I find my way out through the scaffolding, cross back to the other side of the street and watch her window. Now the light goes out; there's a short interval, and then in the black opening of the passageway Lilya's figure comes into view. She sees me straight away and runs across the street. She takes my hands quickly and holds them for a long moment in her hands. She seems to have tanned and to have lost some weight. Her eyes have grown larger. I listen to her breathing after her run.

'Let's go walking!' she says. I suddenly realise that the last reserve, the last hesitations in our speaking to each other, are past and gone, we have become close; and as I realise it, I desperately want to sit down or lean against something, so suddenly have my legs grown weak. Even after the most tiring days of hunting they never trembled like this.

But I feel awkward about going with her. I've just dropped in for a moment to see her. I'm badly dressed. I've come here straight from the trip. My shoes are battered and my suit is scorched in places. When you sleep by a campfire you very often singe your jacket or trousers. No, I can't possibly go out with her now.

'What nonsense!' says Lilya, totally unconcerned, and she pulls me along by the hand. She needs to talk with me. She is completely by herself, her friends are still away, her parents have gone to the country, and she is terribly bored and has been waiting all this time for me. What's a suit got to do with it? And, by the way, why didn't I write? Does it please me when others are distressed because of me? No, she doesn't mean that, she meant simply: when others are concerned for me.

And so we are off, walking around Moscow again. It's some strange, mad evening; it begins to rain, and we hurry to take shelter in a passageway echoing with the traffic and we stand inside it, looking out on the street, panting after our run. The downpipes are noisy with rainwater, the footpaths gleam, drenched cars drive by, and each time small red and white snakes of reflected light slither from them towards us across the wet asphalt. The rain soon stops and we come out, laugh, jump puddles; but the rain starts again, and again we take shelter. Drops of rain glisten on Lilya's hair; but even more brightly glisten her eyes when she looks at me.

'Did you think about me?' she asks me, and says immediately: 'I thought about you almost all the time even though I tried not to. I don't know why but I couldn't stop. There I was, simply thinking and thinking. You see, we haven't known each other very long, have we? I was reading a book, and suddenly I thought: would you like a book like this? Oh, I'm a real idiot! Did your ears turn red? They say that if you think long enough about someone the person's ears will turn red. I didn't even go to the Bolshoi. My mother got me a ticket and I didn't go. How could I sit there, enjoying the music, and you were somewhere up there in your North by yourself. You'll tell me all about the North, won't you? I'd like to go there too, where you've been. Do you like opera?'

'And how! I might become a singer soon. People say that I've got a good bass voice.'

'Alyosha! You, a bass? Sing something—please! Sing softly, so no one will hear, just I will.'

At first I refuse, then finally I give in. My voice isn't firm to start with, then it settles down. I sing romances, and then a Northern *barabushka*; I sing and don't notice that the rain has stopped and that pedestrians go by now and look at us. Lilya too notices nothing. She looks on and on into my face, and her eyes shine unbearably brightly.

4

Being young isn't good, it's not good at all. Life goes by quickly, you're seventeen or eighteen and you've still done nothing, you are still only getting around to doing something. It's not even clear if you have any sort of talent to do that something with. And, there you are, you want to lead a huge, intense kind of life! You want to write poetry, such poems as the whole country will want to know by heart. Or you want to carry out who knows what kinds of exploits: fly in a rocket out into space or whatever. What can I do? What can I accomplish, so that my life should not pass and be wasted, so that every day should be one of battles and triumphs? I live a life of constant melancholy, agonised by the thought that I'm not a hero, not a discoverer of anything, not a great thinker. Am I capable of real feats? Have I got willpower?... On one occasion I hold my hand over a candle, to the point where I hear a spitting sound and smell the singed flesh, while Lilya clutches her cheeks and looks speechlessly at me.

Or, am I capable of enduring hard, mundane, daily work; do I have the strength to put up with, to withstand, long, laborious years? The worst is that no one understands my trouble. They all look at me as at a boy, tousle my hair even, as if I were a ten-year-old. And only Lilya, just Lilya, understands; with her alone I can be totally frank.

We've been back at school for a long time now, she in the ninth and I in the tenth grade. I've decided to take up swimming and become the champion of the USSR, and after that of the world. I've been going to the pool three months now. The crawl is the best of all the styles, the most dashing, I like it very much. And in the evenings I like to just think about all kinds of things.

In winter there's a short moment when the colour of the sky and of the snow on the roofs becomes dark-blue, even violet. I stand at the window and look out through the open casement at the violet snow, breathing the frosty air, and I don't know why but at such times I begin to imagine voyaging a long way to unknown lands, scaling mountains. I see myself hungry and grown whiskery with a red beard. I'm baked by the sun, or the cold invades me to the very marrow, I even come to the point of dying; but at that final moment, yes, I succeed in bringing to light some new secret of nature! There's life for you! Oh, if only I could be accepted as a member of some expedition!

I start to do the rounds of Moscow bureaux and government offices. There are many, and all have striking and mysterious names. Yes, they send out expeditions: to Central Asia and the Urals and to the North. Yes, they do need workers. What are my qualifications? Oh dear, I don't have any qualifications. Very sad, but they can't help me at all: I must study, there's nothing else for it. Labourers? Labour is hired at the particular location. Good-day sir, and best wishes to you!

And so, I return to school and do my lessons. Fine, I'll finish tenth grade and go on to some institute, it's all the same to me now. I'll go to an institute and become an engineer or a teacher; but in my person the world will have lost a mighty explorer!

It's December: I spend all my free time with Lilya. I love her even more. I had no idea that love could be endless, but it's true. With every month she becomes dearer to me, and I would make any sacrifice for her now. She rings me up often. We talk long on the telephone, and as we talk I imagine her face; and after talking I just can't get interested in textbooks, I can't calm my heart, and I'm liable at those times to fall into God knows what fantastic, sweet reveries.

The hard frosts and snowstorms have started. My mother is preparing to go to the country. My aunt who lives just outside the city has an ancient and very warm shawl and I'm to go to her and get it.

Sunday morning, I leave home, but instead of going straight to the station I drop in to see Lilya. We go to the skating rink and after that we warm up at the Tretyakov Gallery. The Tretyakov in winter is very warm and cosy and they have benches where you can sit and talk quietly. We wander about the halls, looking at the paintings. Serov's 'Girl with Peaches' is my favourite. The girl looks very much like Lilya. Lilya blushes and laughs when I tell her that. Sometimes we completely forget the paintings, talking in whispers and looking at each other or down at our hands. In one of those intervals it starts to get dark: the gallery is closing. We go out into the frost, and then I remember that I was supposed to have gone for the shawl! Stunned, I tell Lilya about it. Well, fine, no problem: we decide we'll go together on the *elektrichka* out past the city limits and get it.

And we go, happy in the thought that we don't have to part yet. We get out at a snow-covered platform and follow a lane through fields. Ahead and behind us are the forms of people who got off the train with us. We can hear their voices and laughter, see the flair of their cigarettes. From time to time someone in front throws down a cigarette-end. When we come to it its speck of light is still visible, and around it is a small rosy stain on the snow. We don't tread on it—let it light the dark a little longer. Then we cross a frozen stream, and the wooden bridge groans under us with a hollow, echoing sound: there's a very hard frost about.

The lane passes through growths of timber, and the night gets darker. On each side the spruces and pines are totally black. It's considerably darker here than in the fields, with only an occasional light from a cottage throwing down a yellow streak across the snow. There are other cottages which are silent and unlit: probably no one lives in them in winter. The smell of winter-hardened birch buds and clean snow is strong: you never get that in Moscow.

At last we come to my aunt's house. And now for some reason it strikes me that I can't possibly go in to her with Lilya.

'Lilya, can you wait for me a moment?' I ask her uncertainly. 'I'll be very quick.'

'All right...' she agrees, 'But don't be long, I'm totally frozen. My legs are frozen, and my face. No, don't worry; I'm glad I've come with you. But you won't be long, will you?'

I go, leaving her on the dark lane by herself. I don't feel very good about that.

My aunt and cousin are astonished and happy. Why am I so late? How tall I've grown! A man, for sure. I'll stay the night, of course?

'How's mother's health?'

'Very well, thank you.'

'Papa works?'

'Yes, papa works.'

'Still in the same place? And how's uncle?'

Lord, a thousand questions! My cousin looks at the train-timetable. The next train back leaves at twelve o'clock. I must take off those things and have a good cup of tea. And then I must let them look me over and I must tell them all about everything. What is it—a year since I was with them last? A year—a long time!

They force me to take off my outer things. The stove heats up, the lamp glows brightly under its rosy shade, the hoary old pendulum-clock ticks away. It's warm, and I would dearly like some tea ... but out on the lane Lilya is waiting for me!

At last I speak. 'I'm in a terrible hurry... yes, I'm in a dreadful hurry; and I'm not alone. There's someone waiting for me outside... a friend.'

How they scold me—I am without manners! How can you leave someone outside on such a night? My cousin runs out into the yard: through the window I hear her steps crunching on the snow. A moment later there is more crunching, and she brings in Lilya. Lilya is totally white. She is so pale that I can't bear to look at her! They take off her things and sit her by the stove. They put warmed felt boots on her feet.

Little by little we thaw out completely and then we sit down to the tea. Lilya grows crimsons with the warmth and with embarrassment. She hardly lifts her eyes from her cup; only, sometimes, she looks at me with a look of terrible seriousness. But her cheeks are trembling, and the dimples come and go—I know already what that means, and I feel very happy!

Full of tea, we rise from the table. It's time to go for the train. We put on our outer clothes and I'm given the shawl. Then suddenly a new thought occurs to them: they make Lilya take off her overcoat again and they wind her up in the shawl and force the overcoat back on. She looks very round now, like a wooden doll, with most of her face covered and only her sparkling eyes visible.

We go outside and at first we can't see anything. Lilya holds on to me tightly. Away from the house we begin to make out the path. Lilya suddenly bursts out laughing, laughs uproariously. She even falls, twice, and I have to help her up and dust off the snow from her sleeves.

'What an expression you had!' she hardly manages to say, 'The look on your face—like an ostrich or something—when they brought me in!'

I too roar with laughter.

'Alyosha!' Her tone is suddenly alarmed, 'Do you think—somebody might hold us up?'

'Who?'

'Who knows who, there are all kinds of people about. Bandits... They could murder us!'

'Rubbish!' I say loudly. Actually, I think I say it rather too loudly. And I don't know why but suddenly I feel that it's freezing now. The cold seems to have grown even sharper while we were drinking tea and talking. 'Rubbish!' I repeat. 'There's no one here!'

'But what if there is someone?' Lilya replies quickly and looks around us.

I look around too.

'Are you scared?' she asks, and her voice seems to ring in the night.

'No. Are you scared?'

'Oh, I'm terrified! What an idiot I was to come. They'll strip us of our clothes, I feel it, I have a presentiment.'

'Oh, you believe in presentiments?'

'I do. Oh, why did I come? But no, just the same I'm happy to have come.'

'Are you?'

'Yes. Even if they strip us and kill us, I won't mind. What about you?'

I say nothing and only squeeze her hand more tightly. O, if only something were to really happen so that I could show her how much I would do for her!

'Alyosha...'

'Yes?'

'I want to ask you... only, you mustn't look at me—don't look at me! Now, what was I going to say? Turn away!'

'Well, all right, I've turned. But you better keep an eye in front for the two of us or we'll trip over.'

'That's all right, in this shawl if I fell I couldn't get hurt anyway.'

'Well?'

'Alyosha... have you ever kissed anyone before?'

'No. I've never kissed anyone. Why?'

'Absolutely never?'

'I kissed someone once, but that was in the first grade. I kissed some girl. I don't even remember her name.'

'Really? You don't remember her name?'

'No, I don't remember.'

'Then it doesn't count. You were just a boy.'

'Yes, I was a boy.'

'Alyosha… do you want to kiss me?'

Despite everything, I trip over. I face forward to walk and look for the way ahead with great care.

'When? Now?' I ask.

'No, no! If we get to the station and nothing happens to us, then I'll kiss you. At the station.'

I say nothing. The cold, I think, has eased. I hardly feel it. My cheeks are burning. It's actually quite hot. Or is it that we've been walking so quickly?

'Alyosha…'

'Yes?'

'I've never kissed anyone.'

I look at the stars in silence. Then I look ahead towards the yellowish glow from the lights of Moscow. It's thirty kilometres to Moscow but you can see the glow.

'It's a shameful thing, probably… kissing? Did you feel ashamed that time?'

'I don't remember, it was long ago… but in my opinion it's not as shameful as all that.'

'Yes, it was a long time ago. But nevertheless, it is probably a shameful thing.'

We come out into the fields. This time we are alone and they are completely empty. There is not a soul to be seen in front or behind us, no one is on the lane to drop a burning cigarette-end, the only sound is that of the packed snow crunching loudly under our feet. Then, suddenly, a point of light flickers ahead, glows faintly like a distant candle. It glows, swings for a moment from side to side and goes out. Then it appears again, nearer now. We look at the light and realise what it means: it's a hand-torch. We make out a number of small, dark figures. They are heading towards us from the station. Maybe they've arrived on the train? No, no train passed, we didn't hear the sound of any train.

'There you are…' says Lilya, and presses against me. 'I knew it. They're bandits.'

What can I say to her? I say nothing. We go forward towards the dark shapes, we slow our steps. I observe them, count them. Six. I rummage in my pocket and make a fist around the shank of my door-key. And suddenly a sense of rapture and valour floods hotly over me, I am choking with worry, my heart beats like thunder. They are talking loudly about something, then at some twenty paces from us they fall silent.

'I should have kissed you. It would have been the best thing,' Lilya murmurs sadly. 'I'm very sorry…'

And then we come to them, on that path between the empty fields. They stop, their torch glows again, weakly, and then its reddish beam slides along the snow towards us and up to our faces. We squint while they look us over, silently. In the dim starlight I can make out that two of them have their overcoats open. One smokes with quick draws on the last of a cigarette and then spits the stub from his lips. I wait for a cry, a blow. But there is no cry. We pass each other.

'The chick ain't half bad, hey?' one remarks in a tone of regret. 'Don't hold back, man! Or we'll snaffle her offa you!'

Lilya looks down and I can see that she's grinning.

'You were scared, weren't you?' she asks a little later.

'No, I wasn't. I was only scared for you.'

'For me?' She gives an odd, sideways glance at me and slows her steps, 'Well, I wasn't a bit scared, I was only sorry for the shawl.'

And then we say nothing more, right up to the station.

At the station Lilya stands on tiptoe and brings down snow on herself in breaking off a pine-twig to take home. She crams it into her pocket and then we go up the steps to the platform. There's no one around. At the untended ticket-office one bulb is still switched on and by its light the snow on the platform glistens like salt. We stamp our feet: it's very cold. Something snaps with a loud report and a fragment goes skittering along the frozen wood of the platform. Lilya suddenly moves away from me and goes to lean on a railing. I stand at the edge of the platform, right by the rails, and crane my neck to look for the lights of the train.

'Alyosha…' Lilya calls to me. Her voice sounds strange.

I come over. My legs are trembling; suddenly I'm terribly afraid.

'Cuddle up to me, Alyosha.' she asks. 'I'm completely frozen.'

I embrace her and hold her tight and my face almost touches her face. I see her eyes very near. This is the first time I have seen them so near. Hoarfrost is on her lashes. Some strands of hair have escaped from under the shawl and there is frost on those too. How big her eyes are, and what a startled look they have! The snow creaks under out feet. We stand immobile, but it creaks. Why are we silent? But, actually, why say anything?

Lilya moves her lips. Her eyes darken to blackness.

'Why aren't you kissing me?' she whispers weakly. The vapour of our breathing merges.

I look at her lips. Again, there is that vulnerable movement, and they part slightly. I bend my head down and kiss her, kiss her for a long time while I feel how the whole world silently turns. Her lips are warm and soft and yet rough too. During the kiss Lilya looks at me beneath her long, lowered eyelashes. She kisses and looks at me, and now I see how she loves me.

That is how we kiss that first time. Then she leans her cold cheek against mine and we stand like that without moving. I look over her shoulder at the dark, wintry trees beyond the platform. I feel her warm, girl's breath on my face and feel the rapid beat of her heart, as she probably feels the beat of my heart.

In the distance there is a quiet hoot and the flash of a small, dazzling star. The train approaches, carriages pass near, raising a cloud of snow-dust. We enter a warm, lighted carriage, close the doors with a thud behind us, and sit down on a warm seat. There are not many people in the carriage. Some are reading, rustling their newspapers, others snooze and rock with the movement of the carriage. Lilya is silent, and during the whole trip she stubbornly looks out of the window, although the glass is frosted-over, it's night outside, and there is certainly nothing to see there.

5

You can probably never tell exactly to the minute when love came to you, and I can't decide when I fell in love with Lilya. Was it when I wandered alone up there in the North, perhaps? Or was it that night when I looked at her through her window and saw that sad expression on her face? Or did it happen during that kiss on the platform? Or was it when she first held out her hand and said her name, Lilya, so gently? I don't know, I only know one thing: that I can't be without her now. All my life is now divided into two parts: up to her time, and then after that. How would I live and what would I be without her? I don't even want to think about that possibility, as I don't want to think about death taking away any of those who are close and dear to me.

Winter passed beautifully. Everything was ours, everything was in common: the past and the future, happiness and the whole of life to the last breath. What a wonderful time, what days, what dizziness!

But comes spring and I start to notice things. No, I don't notice anything, I only feel, painfully, that something new is happening. It's even hard to describe. Simply, there is this discovery that we have different personalities. It has grown now to this: she doesn't like my views, she laughs at my daydreams, laughs cruelly; and we quarrel on several occasions. Then... then everything goes downhill, more quickly, more terribly. More and more often Lilya is not at home, more and more often our conversations are unnaturally gay, are empty. Each time I feel her going further from me... further.

How many young girls there are in the world! But you know one, only one whose eyes you look into to see those glints, that depth—liquid eyes. Only one whose voice touches you, moves you to tears; only her hands are such hands as you feel even frightened to kiss. She speaks to you, listens to you, laughs, is silent—and you see that she needs you alone, that she lives only with you and for you, that she loves only you, as you love her.

And then, with dismay, you notice that her eyes—which once gave up to you all their warmth, their sparkle, their life—those eyes are now indifferent, inward, and she herself has gone away from you to some far place out of your reach, a place from which she will not return. It's like death. Your holiest ambitions, your glorious, secret imaginings are not for her, and you yourself, with whatever complexities and beauties of soul you may have, are not for her. You pursue her, you strain every nerve, but she eludes you, for some indefinable reason you miss the target each time. She has slipped away, gone somewhere far into herself, into her own enchanting, unique world, and you have no access to it—you have erred and Eden is denied you. What despair, what a sense of grievance, of self-pity, of sorrow grips you! You feel let down, cheated, luckless, destroyed! It's all gone and you are left empty-handed, fit only to fall down and howl with pain and helplessness. And if you fall down, and if you howl, she'll look at you with frightened eyes, marvelling, pitying eyes—anything may appear in those eyes now but the one look which you need and that you'll not get. Her love, her life are not for you. You might become a hero, a genius, a person of whom the whole nation is proud, but that one look she'll never give you.

And so, it's spring already. Lots of sun and light, blue skies, on the boulevards the limes are beginning to send out their aroma. Everyone is lively, everyone is preparing for the First of May. And I, like everyone else, am also preparing. I have a hundred roubles that I hoarded up—I'm rich! And before me are three free days. Three days which I will pass with Lilya—surely at such a time as this she'll not still be going to the library to study for her exams? No, I won't go anywhere, I don't need any other company, I'll spend those days with her. It's such a long time since we were together. I still believe, believe and place my hope in a turn of luck.

But no, she can't go with me. She has to go to the country to visit a sick uncle. Her uncle is sick and he's alone: he'd like to have his relatives around him for May Day: and so they are all going, her parents and herself. Excellent! To go to the country for the holiday is just marvellous. But I had so much wanted to be with her. Perhaps the second of May? The second? She considers it, frowning, and reddens a little. Well, yes, perhaps she might get away. Of course—she would like to, very much! Especially since we haven't seen each other for so long. So, let's make it the evening of the second, outside the Telegraph Office on Gorky Street.

At the designated time I stand outside the Office. What a crowd there is around here! Above my head is the globe of the world, turning quietly. It's barely twilight but its lights are already on: blue, with the continents in yellow. Other lights illuminate the display of ears of corn: a golden glow with shimmers of blue and green. Under those changing lights people's faces are quite beautiful. In my pocket I still have those hundred roubles: I had not spent anything yesterday; who knows to what places we might not go to tonight, Lilya and I, to a park or to see a film? I wait patiently.

New fellows keep arriving, new girls. Some meet immediately and leave, hand in hand. Others look around, chew their lips, adopt an expression of indifference. But they are nervous. I know. I alone am calm. I, of course, am calm.

On the street, right in the middle, there is a great movement of people. How many girls and fellows are there: all singing, shouting things, playing accordions. There are flags on all the buildings, slogans, lights. They sing songs, those ones out there. And I could sing with them too: you see, I have a good voice, a bass voice. Once I thought I might become a singer.

Suddenly I see Lilya. She is threading her way towards me, is coming up the steps, and all are looking at her, she is so lovely: I've never seen her more lovely. My heart begins to pound. She looks quickly at people, her glances fly from face to face, looking for somebody. She is looking for me.

I take one step towards her, just one step, and then a sharp pain strikes me in the heart and my mouth goes dry. She is not alone. Beside her is a young fellow in a proletarian beret and he comes up now and stands looking at me. He's a handsome one, this chap, and he holds her arm. Yes, he holds her arm, when I only dared to take her arm in the second month.

'Hello, Alyosha!' says Lilya. Her voice trembles a little and there is embarrassment in her eyes. But it's not a great embarrassment, quite small. 'Have you been waiting long? We're a little late, are we?' She glances at the great clock under the globe and frowns slightly. Then she turns her head and looks at the fellow. She has a very tender expression on her face when she looks at him. Did she once look at me like that?

'Now you two, get acquainted, please!'

We say hello to each other. His handshake is strong and there's self-assurance in it, dominance.

'You know, Alyosha, there's no hope for us tonight. We two are going to the Bolshoi now. You're not offended, are you?'

'No, I'm not offended.'

'Will you come with us a bit? You won't have anything to do now anyway, will you?'

'I'll come. It's true, I won't have anything to do.'

We merge into the flow of people and go with it to Okhotny Row. Why am I going? What's happening to me? Where am I going? They are singing all around, accordions are playing, loudspeakers are booming from the rooftops. But why am I here, where am I going?

'Well, and how is your uncle?' I ask.

'Uncle? What uncle?... Ah, you're talking about yesterday?' She bites her lip and looks quickly up at the fellow. 'He's getting better. We had a good First, we had such fun! We danced. And you? Did you have a good First?'

'I? Yes, very good.'

'Well then, I'm glad!'

We turn towards the Bolshoi Theatre. I don't give her my arm now. It's this handsome one who gives her his arm. And she is no longer with me, she's with him. She's gone away a thousand miles from me now. Why do I need to clear my throat all the time, why are my eyes smarting? I must be going down with something.

We come to the theatre, stop, are silent. There's absolutely nothing to say. I notice that he has pressed her elbow lightly.

'Well, we're off. Good-bye!' says Lilya, and she smiles at me. What a vacant, meaningless smile it is.

I shake her hand. Whatever else, it's such a beautiful hand. They turn and go unhurriedly into the colonnade. He bends close to her to tell her something, smiling. And I stand there and look at her going. She has grown quite a lot during this last year. She's already seventeen. She has a graceful figure. When did I first notice her figure? Ah yes, in the dark entryway, that time when I had returned from the North. Her figure had surprised me then. And then I delighted in it at the Hall of Columns, and at the Conservatorium. And at the school ball when I at last began to learn to dance. That wonderful winter ball! And now she's walking away and she doesn't look back. She always used to look back when she was leaving. Sometimes she would even turn back, would look at me questioningly and ask, 'Did you want to say something else to me?'

'No, nothing.' I would reply, laughing, happy that she was there again.

She would look around quickly and say, 'Kiss me!'

And I would kiss her, she with the odour of frost on her, and we would then be in some square or at the corner of a street. She liked those madcap kisses in the street. 'What would they know?' she would say of the people who might see us kissing. 'We could just be some brother and sister for all they know.'

Now she doesn't turn to look back. I stand there, and people pass close to me, they go around me, like around a post, a thing. Now and then there's laughter. They go past in pairs and threes and in whole groups, not one is alone. It's unbearable to be on the street alone in the middle of celebrating crowds. Those who are alone most probably stay at home. I stand and look on after her. Now they've disappeared into the lighted portico. They'll be listening to the opera this evening, enjoying their nearness. Above me, in the violet sky, the Bolshoi's foursome of winged horses are flying, are flying and unable to fly away. And in my pocket I have a hundred roubles.

6

A year has passed. And I've almost forgotten about Lilya. Or more precisely, I have tried not to think about her. What's the use of thinking?

I met her once in the street. I felt myself turning pale and a chill ran down my spine, but I held myself erect all right. I tried not to look at her too much, I clenched my teeth. You see, I've lost interest completely in her life. I didn't ask her how she was getting on, and she didn't ask me. Even though a lot, a great deal, had happened to me over that time. A year—that, after all, is a long time!

I study at the institute. I study with great care, no one distracts me from my studies, no one calls on me to go out. I do a lot of community work. I train at the baths and have qualified for the first grade now. I've mastered the crawl during this time. The crawl—the most impetuous of the styles. Actually, who cares? What's the crawl got to do with it?

One day I get a letter from Lilya. It's spring again and I am light of heart. I love spring. I've done my exams and am now in the second year. And here I get a letter from Lilya. She writes that she has got married. And suddenly I remember the time when I was drowning. It was in childhood: some witch-like, weird and evil force swooped on me and with loud gurgles of maniacal laughter began to hold me under the water. I tried to bite, to snatch breaths, to twist and writhe, and all the time there was something green everywhere around me, I was choking, swallowing water, I couldn't cry out...

What was I just saying? Ah yes, she has married. She also writes that she's going to the North with her husband and would very much like me to see her off. She calls me 'my dear' and signs herself 'Your old, old friend, Lilka.' Lilka.

I sit for a long time looking at the wallpaper. We have nice wallpaper with intricate little designs. I like to look at them. Of course I'll come to see her off, seeing that she wants it. Why on earth not? She's no enemy of mine, she's done me no harm. I'll see her off—especially since everything has long been forgotten. How many things go on in life: are you expected to remember everything that happened to you a year ago?

And so, I'm heading for the station, on that day and that hour as specified in her letter. It's the same station from which I too had once left for the North, with all the same smells, the same atmosphere of uneasiness and vague premonitions that hang over those departures for far places.

I catch sight of her unexpectedly and start. Strange, that I should start like that, seeing that it's finished, that it's all finished. She is standing there in a light-coloured dress with short sleeves, and a first tan has already touched her arms and face. Her arms are still as soft and supple as they ever were. But her face has changed: it's become the face of a woman. She's not a girl anymore; no, not a girl. With her are her people and the husband—the same chap. They are all talking loudly and quickly and with lots of laughter, but I notice that Lilya is glancing fretfully about her: she is waiting for me to arrive.

I approach. She immediately takes me by the arm.

'I'll just be a moment,' she tells the husband, and smiles sweetly at him.

He nods and looks at me in a friendly manner. Yes, he remembers me and extends his hand amiably to me. Then Lilya leads me aside.

'Well, Alyosha, you see how it goes?' she says gaily, 'I'm a grown lady and I'm off and good-bye to Moscow!' and she looks dolefully at the station tower. 'I'm glad you came. I just suddenly wanted to see you. Strange how somehow everything... You've grown a lot. How have you been living?'

'Fine,' I say, and try to smile. But the smile can't seem to form, my face feels wooden.

Lilya looks attentively at me, light creases form across her forehead. That's how she is when she's considering something.

'What's the matter?' she asks.

'Nothing. I'm simply very glad for you. Have you been married long?'

'Just a week. It's such joy!'

'Yes, of course.'

Lilya laughs. 'Now, how would you know?... But wait a moment—you do have such a strange look!'

'O, it might seem that way. It's the sun. And, then, I'm a little tired: the exams, you know. German...'

'Oh, that damned German.' She laughs. 'Do you remember how I used to help you?'

'Yes, I remember.' I move my lips to shape a smile.

'Listen, Alyosha, what's the matter?' Lilya asks anxiously, bending nearer.

And once again I see close-up her marvellous face. From which something has gone. It has changed, it's now almost strange to me. Has it grown better? I can't decide.

'You're hiding something,' she rebukes me. 'You weren't like that in the past!'

'No, no, you're mistaken,' I urge, 'It's just that I didn't sleep much last night.'

Lilya looks at her watch. Then she looks around. The husband is nodding to her.

'A moment!' she shouts to him, and again takes my arm. 'You know, I'm so happy! Be glad for me. We're going to the North, to work there. Do you remember how you used to tell me about the North? Well, there you are... Are you glad for me?'

Why, why is she asking me about that? Suddenly, she starts to laugh.

'You know, I've just remembered. Do you remember that winter, on the platform? We were kissing? I was kissing you and you were shaking so much that the platform creaked? Ha-ha-ha. You looked so silly.'

Lilya is laughing and looking at me with gay, grey eyes. In daylight her eyes are grey. It's only at night that they seem dark. I watch the dimples that are trembling on her cheeks now.

'What idiots we were,' she says without much emphasis, and she looks towards her husband. There is tenderness in her glance, and when she turns to me there is still a remnant of that tender look, but unrelated to me, and with some secret added element in it now which is unfathomable to me.

'Yes, we were idiots,' I agree.

'No, not idiots, that's not the word. We were simply silly children. Isn't that so?'

'Yes, we were silly children.'

At the front of the train a signal-light glows green. We walk towards a carriage.

'Well, good-bye!' she says. 'I mean till we meet again, of course. I'll write to you, definitely!'

'Good.'

I know that she won't write. What for? And she knows that too. Her eyes slide away for a moment and she reddens a little.

'Well, I'm still happy that you came to see me off. And of course without any flowers! You never did bring me a single flower!'

She lets go my arm, takes her husband's, and they step up into the doorway of the carriage. I remain with her kin on the platform. The parents are asking me something, but I can't understand them. Up front, the electric locomotive gives a long, low hoot. The carriages start to move. A line from a pop song about being left a train-ticket as a souvenir passes through my mind... It's incredible how gently an electric locomotive can move carriages! Everyone is smiling, waving handkerchiefs, caps; they shout, walk beside the carriages. Two or three accordions are being played simultaneously in various parts of the train; in one wagon there is singing, loud and uncoordinated. Probably students. Lilya is already far away. She is holding on to her husband's shoulder with one hand and waving to us with the other. Even from that distance you can see how graceful her hands are, still see her sad-happy smile.

The train goes. I light a cigarette, cram my hands into my pockets, and move with the stream of returning well-wishers towards the passage that leads to the square. Outside, with the cigarette clamped between my teeth I stand looking at the metal lamp-posts. They shine like silver in the sunlight: it's positively painful to the eyes how they shine, and I lower my eyes. It might as well be faced now: all that year there had still been some residue of hope in me, and now it's all finished. Well, I'm happy for Lilya, truly, I'm happy! It's only that for some reason my heart aches.

Nothing unusual—a girl gets married. You see it happening all the time, girls getting married. An excellent thing. The only thing wrong is that I can't cry. Last time I cried was when I was fifteen. Now I'm twenty, and my heart is in my throat and keeps rising and I can't cry.

I step out into the square and what arrests my eyes is the face of the Kazan Station clock. Instead of numbers it has those strange symbols which I have never been able to work out. I need to drink something and

I go to the kiosk. I almost order a sweet drink but change my mind and ask for plain water. Awkward business drinking pop when your heart is in your throat. I lift the frosty glass and take a mouthful of water, but I can't swallow it. Then I manage to swallow it finally, one mouthful. I think I feel better. Then I go down to the Metro. Something has happened to my face: I notice that people are staring at me.

At home I think of Lilya for a time. Then once again I begin looking at the pattern on the wallpaper. If you look closely at it and your mind wanders for a moment, as when you think about something, the pattern returns to you with many curious figures. You might see jungles, and elephants with uplifted trunks, or the outline of strangers wearing berets and raincoats, or the faces of people you know. Only Lilya's face alone is not on the wallpaper.

About now, she's probably passing the platform on which we kissed that first time. Only, in this season the station is surrounded by greenery and its boards are dry and warm in the sun. Will she glance at it? But why would she want to? She's looking at her husband now. She loves him. He's very handsome, her husband.

7

Nothing lasts forever in this world, even grief. And life doesn't stop. No, life never stops, it occupies your soul and disperses your sorrows like vapour, your little, human sorrows. Very little compared to all of life: the world is admirably constructed that way.

I'm graduating now. My youth has ended and gone a long, long way away forever. And that's fine, too. I'm an adult and capable of anything, and no one tousles my hair now. I'll soon be going up there to the North myself. I don't know why, but the North is always calling to me. Probably because I hunted and was happy there once.

Lilya I've forgotten completely, as you would expect, considering how much time has passed. It would be very difficult to go on living if things were never forgotten. But luckily many things are forgotten. Of course she never did write to me from the North. Where she is exactly, I don't know, and I don't want to know. I never think of her. I have a good life. Admittedly I never became a poet, or a singer—but we can't all be poets, can we? Sporting competitions, conferences, field work, exams—they take up all my time, I don't have a moment to spare. And in addition I've mastered dancing now and have come to know many good-looking and intelligent girls. I go out with them, have fallen in love with some of them and they have fallen in love with me.

Yet, I sometimes dream of Lilya. She comes to me in my dreams and once again I hear her voice, her soft laugh, and I touch her hands, speak to her: of what, I don't remember. Sometimes she is sad and in a sombre mood, sometimes happy, the dimples then trembling on her cheeks—

very small dimples, hardly to be detected by a stranger—and at those times her dark eyes are liquid, lambent. And then I come to life again and laugh with her and feel young and awkward, feel as if I've become seventeen once more, become happy again and in love for the first time in my life.

I wake up, those mornings, and remain lying there for a long time with my eyes shut and I don't do my morning exercises then. I go to the institute, attend lectures, take my turn at the Student Committee Office or I might present something at a Komsomol meeting. But for some reason those are tedious days and I want to be alone.

But that doesn't happen often. And then—those are just dreams after all. Dreams, dreams... those unbidden dreams that keep coming... They say that sleeping on your right side stops dreaming. I'll try sleeping on my right side.

Dreams... a curse on them!

8. TEDDY, THE STORY OF A BEAR

1

The big brown bear was called Teddy, that was the name they had given him. The other animals had names too, but Teddy could not remember those; try as he might he always mixed them up and recognised with certainty only the sound of his own name: always responding and approaching when he was called to do whatever they told him to do.

His life was unvarying. He worked in a circus, had indeed been working there so long that he had lost sight of when he first began to do that. He was kept in a cage, but more or less out of habit, for it was long since he had become quite tame, and so securing him was really not necessary, he having grown indifferent and incurious towards things around him and only wanting to be left alone and in peace. But since he was an old, experienced artist he was not often left alone.

In the evenings he was let out into a brightly-lit arena in the centre of which a tall man with a powdered face paced up and down with a mannered, leisurely stride. The man wore white breeches, soft black knee-boots, and a lilac coat with gold embroidery on the front. All those—the breeches, the coat, the white face, and the man's imperturbable expression—always had a deep effect on Teddy. But most of all, the bear feared the man's eyes.

Once, long ago, in those days when he was still very young, Teddy was apt to break out in most awful bear-rebellions, howling sorrowfully, tearing at the bars of his cage, and then the severest measures could not quieten him. But the man with the white face would come, stand at the cage and look at Teddy, and each time the bear would soon grow subdued beneath that look, and within an hour he could be led out to his rehearsals.

Now, Teddy did not rebel any longer and he performed obediently all kinds of awkward and pointless and often rather unpleasant tricks. And the man in the breeches no longer threatened him with his look, and when he talked about the bear he would never call him anything but 'good old Teddy' and his voice then was very gentle.

Teddy would come out into the arena wearing a leather muzzle and he would bow to the spectators and they would greet him with a delighted buzz. A bicycle would be wheeled up to him and he would mount it, throwing a hind paw over the saddle. Then he would push off, pressing heavily on the pedals and gripping the handlebars tightly and would thus go around and around the arena. The music played loudly and the audience laughed and clapped.

He could do a few other amusing tricks. He could squat on a large ball and tread with his paws in a rapid shuffle that rolled the ball with him on top of it about the arena. He could climb up to and then balance on a thin strip of metal. He boxed with other bears, each animal wearing gloves that had been bound to its front paws. Teddy was devoid of any sense of humour—or at least his humour was of another, un-human, kind—and he could not understand why all those people demonstrated such delight when he himself only performed with aversion those uncomfortable and distasteful acts.

He often had trouble sleeping at night. A weak light-bulb burned wanly out in the passage of the animal annexe, where an old caretaker, who always smelt deliciously to Teddy, snored loudly. The animals snarled and whistled in their sleep, a strong wild smell came from the cages, and out of the dark corners of the annexe large impudent rats would emerge into the open areas, stop and sit back on their hind legs, and then their shadows extended a long way across the floor.

Awake, Teddy would remain thoughtful, growling to himself occasionally, and after a while he would begin his toilet. He would lick his paws and his stomach evenly and over a long time, and when those had become completely wet and sticky he would start on his sides and back. But it was hard to do his back, and then he soon tired and gave himself up to sad meditations.

He remembered when he was small, recalling his mother, a handsome she-bear with soft paws and a long, warm tongue. But the period of his youth came back only vaguely to him now; he only remembered a smallish stream with yellow, sandy banks where the sand was fine-grained and warm. He also still recalled the sweet-and-sour taste of ants, which it had never been his fortune to savour again since those days.

As well, the tasty dinners which he sometimes got in the circus stayed long in his memory. Once it happened that a small donkey became ill; all night it wheezed and choked in its stall, until when morning came it had fallen silent. Some men with sullen faces arrived to take the dead donkey away. Then, that evening, Teddy got not his usual oatmeal gruel but a bowl of some strongly-smelling boiled meat, and that event passed into his recollection as a holiday.

And he thought of many other things as well, and vague images visited him, anger and great bitterness sometimes filled his breast, and then he wanted to howl, to go somewhere to do things that animals do; and on those nights he sighed sonorously the whole night through, and the next day he would be especially listless and ill-humoured and would came out of his cage unwillingly to carry out his rehearsals.

2

Then one day the circus left to go somewhere distant by train, and Teddy went with it. He had travelled around so often already that nothing astonished him any longer, and the only thing that still bothered him was the smell of petrol that the circus lorries emitted.

Everything proceeded in the normal way. At the station the cages with their animals sealed inside were rolled into goods wagons; there was shouting, arguments, the sound of things being nailed down—altogether, the usual lot of noise. At last the wagon doors were slammed shut, and soon everything began to shudder and sway in a rhythmic manner and the desire to sleep became overpowering. The shuddering and swaying continued for two days and then ceased. When the doors were opened and the cages began to be unloaded onto lorries everything now was different, smelled different, and that did not surprise Teddy either.

It was decided to feed the animals before taking them further. An attendant came, cleaned out the cages and then brought food. Having pushed into Teddy's cage some boiled potatoes, bread, and a small basin of oatmeal gruel, the attendant was distracted by something and went away, forgetting to fasten the cage.

Paying no attention to the open door, the bear ate greedily, grunting quietly with pleasure, for he had become very hungry. Having eaten and licked his chops he began according to his habit to nudge the dishes towards the door, and only then did he notice that it was open. He was very surprised. He poked his head outside the cage, looked to the left and to the right, yawned, and then returned inside and closed his eyes. But a moment later he got up and once again stretched his head out of the cage. He sniffed the air and looked around, seemed to vaguely recollect something, thought a bit, then left the cage and jumped from the lorry to the ground. There, having first agreeably stretched himself, he began to circle the vehicle inquisitively. By that time, the driver was approaching. He had his cap under his arm and was chewing something. The breeze blew from his direction, and Teddy, scenting the smell of sausage, trotted forward to meet him. Seeing the bear, the driver stopped chewing and froze. Teddy rose on his hind legs and growled gently. At that, the driver turned, dropped his cap and took to his heels towards a long, low building with a sign over the door, bellowing in terror as he ran: 'Help! Help! I'm done for!'

Teddy lowered himself again, and being uncertain of the situation he thought that the prudent thing might be to turn about and go back, intending to climb up into his familiar cage; but now people poured out of the building and began shouting wildly at him. Teddy faced them in bewilderment, searching among all that crowd for a known face, but saw none.

He became very frightened and began running. He loped past the horse-floats, and the horses saw him and shied and whinnied, and Teddy now also sent forth a roar of his own and increased his pace.

He ran through someone's kitchen garden, leapt over a wattle fence and tore across fields towards the distant forest. He ran quickly, ears flat against his head, snorting, feeling a sharp, unfamiliar pleasure in this movement. Arriving at the first stand of trees he stopped, panting, and looked back in fright: the station was now out of sight, there were no people, no vehicles, just the empty fields and in the distance a dark line of roofs.

The bear felt a yearning for the known; he wanted to re-join the circus, to live in that dark passage and listen at night to the snoring of the tasty-smelling caretaker; but he was frightened to go back, and so he stood there, growling softly, poised on his hind legs and swaying from side to side.

Then he turned around, looked towards the forest, snorted a few times to clear his nose, and sniffed the air. From all around him came a sweet, resinous odour and there was a smell of mushrooms and there were many other unsettling and exciting smells. He went into the thickening trees, went slowly through the underbrush, looking about him each time he came to a clearing in the hope of seeing an attendant, or the man in the white breeches who would speak gently to him and say: 'Tedd-ee!...' But no one appeared, no one called to him, everything was silent. And from the green depths ahead, from within that silence, came another, increasingly distinct and powerful call. Perplexed by the two opposed feelings of fright and awakened curiosity, Teddy entered the forest.

3

Fortune did not favour Teddy: he had chanced on a populated stretch of harvestable timber. Here, the State Forestry Commission was very active, there were large swathes cleared of trees, and things repugnant to the nature of a forest offended the eye everywhere: a narrow-gauge railway, discarded lengths of cable, oily rags, rutted trails, echoing corduroy walks. Here were practically no birds or wild animals, and at night there were many sounds hostile to the forest and its silence: the noise of motors, metal striking on metal, high-pitched locomotive tooting.

To Teddy the forest felt savage and foreign, and at first he only wanted to meet with people again. Yet, at the same time, something opposed his going towards the sound of machinery. Everything unsettled him, he did not eat, hardly slept, and he became very thin. A number of times he tried performing those acts which had become ingrained in him, in the hope that someone would appear from the treed surrounds and feed him. He stood on his front paws, rotating the back ones in the air as though rolling a ball, and he did circuits of a clearing thus. Then he turned somersaults, danced, 'died', and on returning to life he looked around, highly pleased with himself and waiting for titbits. But no one was delighted with him or praised him, no one appeared with the magical oatmeal, and so his little bear-eyes filled with sad wonder. Ultimately, driven to despair by his ignorance of the forest, he would have gone to find people; but now occurred an event which only increased his feeling of apprehension towards them.

One morning, Teddy wet with dew and out of humour was delving about in the bottom of a gully, scratching up some scraps of grass and eating them, when lifting his head he suddenly found himself eye to eye with a man standing just above him. Teddy, surprised, rose on his hind legs. He even gave a grunt of pleasure. But the man did not show any signs of friendliness, nor did he say anything resembling 'Tedd-ee!...' as the bear expected. He paled, tore from his shoulder the shotgun he was carrying, lifted it, and there was an issue of fire, a crash of thunder, and something painful whipped about Teddy's ears. He roared and fell on his back, beating at the air with his paws. While the bear howled with pain, indignation, and astonishment the man, having done his brutal deed, took to his heels; and even through the sound of his own bellowing Teddy could hear the rapidly diminishing thud of the other's feet and the crackling of the undergrowth as he fled. A moment later Teddy was seized by a wild rage and he lunged after him, but his enemy had managed to hide somewhere or had cleared out, and so Teddy did not find him. From that moment the bear began to fear people and to seek out even more unfrequented places.

But to find such greater isolation, in an untouched forest, Teddy needed to swim across a river, a thing still strange to him, while in the meantime his situation was growing continually more desperate. Several times he left the trees and approached the bank of that river. On each occasion he stayed a while to look unhappily at the logs floating downstream, then turned and went back into the trees on his side.

4

And in that way, two days passed and two nights. On the third night Teddy, coming out to the river again but at another spot, stopped in surprise: he saw a raft with a cabin on it moored by the bank. The moon was bright and by its light he saw an encampment of white huts with dark windows. No one was about, and the only sound to be heard was the lulling gurgle of water passing between the logs of the raft. Teddy raised himself on his back paws and levelled his nose at the camp. An irresistibly delicious odour of rye bread and potatoes wafted from the cabin on the raft. Teddy licked his lips and rocked on his hind paws, rocked some more and thought hard.

He was afraid to go there, where the smell originated, because he knew there were people about, people who hated him and were in turn abhorrent to him: his painful ears did not allow him to forget that. But the temptation was powerful. The bear passed up and down along the bank, testing the water several times with his paws, and eventually he found himself right opposite the cabin. Oh, what a most wonderful odour was this!

The raft did not quite float against the bank, and for boarding there was a gangplank at one end, but in his impatience Teddy paid no attention to it. He entered the watery gap and in a moment had clambered up onto the logs. Stepping gingerly on each one, the bear arrived at the cabin and did a circuit of it. From inside, a loud snore came to his ears. Teddy remembered the watchman at the circus and took courage. He looked into a window but could see nothing. Then, resolved, he pushed open the door, squeezed inside—and immediately had to swallow, his mouth watered so from the delicious smells of all kinds of things: old foot-bindings, bread, potatoes!... The food was on a table. Teddy approached the table, knocked from the top of a cast-iron pot the warm, condensation-beaded plate which covered it, upset the pot itself, growled softly, and then without a further moment's loss began swallowing mouthfuls of bread, almost choking in his haste.

'Hey!' exclaimed the man from a bunk, his snoring suddenly cut off, 'Who's there? That you, Fedya?'

The bear, surprised, fell backwards on his rump; then converting fright to fury he growled in earnest and slammed his paw down on the table. Both pot and plate fell on the floor. Something just recognisable as a person rolled out of the bunk, scuttled on hands and knees through the door, then darted across the raft to the shore.

Teddy understood that there was going to be trouble, but he continued eating hurriedly, champing his jowls noisily, snarling, dribbling saliva on the floor, aware all the time that he was committing a crime against men.

After a minute, as the bear was finishing the last of the bread, a great uproar erupted on the shore: it was time to leave!... But he still had not eaten enough—he must pick up a few more potatoes from the floor! And after that he could not find the way out immediately! When he finally squeezed through the door, there was a large group of men confronting him on the bank. When they saw the bear they all shouted together, as they had done that time at the station, and Teddy stopped, confused. The way to the bank was cut off.

He tried to slip around the side of the cabin, hoping to jump to the bank from the other end of the raft, but he was met by a long, bright tongue of fire and the boom of a shot. He panicked and ran around the back of the cabin. Men ran after him, half encircling him, forcing him towards the edge of the raft. Another shot thundered behind him, and a piece of bark chipped off a log hit him sharply in the stomach. He roared, leapt in the only direction left, and with a mighty splash that raised a column of silver spray in the moonlight he went into the water. He had never swum in his life: his head went under, and when he came back to the surface he did not know what to do at first. But his paws moved of themselves, he paddled with all his might and kept his nose out of the water, pointed at the stars. The current carried him gently downstream, while the men remained on the raft and could be heard shouting for a long time. The bear worked his paws more and more strongly, he sneezed and puffed and kept his nose up.

When he had been about a half-hour in the warm, glinting water he saw that he had come to a stretch of forest which was dense and dark. This was no longer like the one the bear had recently left. This was a forest without large cleared areas and cut timber and had only the rarest human habitations. Feeling the bottom under him, Teddy clambered heavily up onto the bank and stopped. The water poured in streams from his coat. Looking about him he saw, far upstream, faint lights and something that stood out pale in the darkness, and he understood that that was where there were people and their camp and the raft; and he understood, too, that on that side of the river it was dangerous and noisy, while this side was quiet and good. Remembering the gunfire and the potatoes which had been left on the floor of the cabin, he growled a little; then, after shaking himself a few times, he climbed up a steep slope towards the big, motionless pines and firs.

5

This was a colossal forest, extending dozens of versts up and down the river and eastwards to the spine of the Urals and north to the very tundra. It climbed up and down ranges of hills, only parting sometimes around lakes or infrequent clearings where small villages of two-story log houses might be found. It was an empty region, not much visited by people, one in which all kinds of animals and birds freely ranged.

Here there were many wolves and foxes, squirrels and hares, and here elk and lynx—creatures of the yellow enigmatic eyes—were to be found. The region contained expanses which were untrodden and indeed could not be traversed, where fallen trees lay on the ground for years, rotting and sinking gradually into the soil.

Fires sometimes occurred, flaring up for no known reason, spontaneously at appointed periods as it were. They stormed over huge areas, devouring trees and grass, and then animals perished by the thousands; and after their passage of destruction the fires, also seemingly by their own volition, gradually died down, leaving black cinders and ash and the occasional charred trunk of a tree. Then, following on that very soon, a tough, red grass would begin to appear, and then to luxuriate in the burnt areas, and soon after this there would be bilberries and red whortleberries on the hummocks, and then birch and pine seedlings, dog-roses and raspberries overgrew the burnt surroundings; and now where the fire had been no longer seemed so terrible to the native animals, such growths returning to become an inexhaustible larder, feeding the dusky wood-grouse, the shy hazel-grouse, heath-cocks and hares. Elks would come here too, leaving their deep little hoof-prints in the pallid moss.

There was a ferment of life in such a forest, a wilderness that had not yet been darkened by the advent of men. Yet, of course, there was an unending war here too, where the law of fang and claw reigned, and oh how many bones and feathers rotted in secluded nooks and corners of this lovely domain! But the struggle within the animal kingdom, though hazardous enough, was not as hopeless as that with man.

Once in a while, infrequently, shots would crash out, and at such times the sound would roll long and ringing around the hills and over the river, returning from the other side, weaker and attenuating. Then the squirrels dropped their cones to fly up to the topmost branches of trees, where from that vantage they might be able to look around them with their eternal inquisitiveness; hares, lying in their harbours, stood up like little posts; elks pricked their ears and stopped grazing for a moment, listening, and then moved away silently to another place; lynxes, dreaming in the depth of thickets, opened sleepy yellow eyes and twitched nervously the tufts on the tips of their ears; and only the wolves, most knowledgeable about humans, dropped everything and ran like grey shadows to nearby knolls, and long sniffed, trying to catch and fearing to catch on some faint breeze man's abhorrent scent.

6

That whole night Teddy headed north, following the bank of the river and relating to it like a sailor to his compass. He was frightened to go deeper into the forest, for it contained many uncertainties, while the river was something known: it had saved him once and was a thing to feel trustful towards. Sounds and smells came to him from all sides, and those were impressions which he needed to understand. Some were well-known to him. Twice he crossed the track of lynxes, and he immediately remembered the lynx at the circus, although her smell, then, was more acrid: animals in captivity always have a stronger smell. Then he flushed some hazel-grouse from their nocturnal perch on one of the lower boughs of a large fir, and although he was startled he quickly settled down when he saw that they were nothing other than birds. The tracks of foxes he also immediately identified. But, finally, the many novelties which kept him constantly on his guard so tired the bear that he found himself a dry spot in a small clearing surrounded by young firs, lay down, and slept there till morning.

Strange as it may seem, such a large animal was, at this stage and in his situation, totally helpless in the forest. After many years the forest had become foreign to Teddy and he had forgotten everything of that little he had managed to learn about it as a cub. All nature's allotment of instincts was dormant in him, and the most insignificant event requiring an immediate response from him confounded him now. He was always hungry, his stomach, used to a plentiful, filling diet, was empty and distressed. But the attendant who had fed him in the circus was no longer here, he had to find his own food, and he did not know how to do that or what could be eaten.

Probably no one feels or understands the way a wild animal does the full import of having a mother. A mother teaches her young how to hide, how to fight, when to run away; she makes known to them their enemies and their allies; she knows where the bilberries and ants are, where wild strawberries grow, the precise location of the tastiest, juiciest roots, where to look for mouse holes, where to go to find fish and frogs. She knows where the clean water is, she knows the isolated places and the sunny clearings with the soft, tall grasses. Mysterious scents are clear to her, the enigma of migrations known. And she knows something else— that not one forest-animal ever lives to an advanced age: all eventually are overtaken by a terrible doom, and it is necessary to be deft, daring and cautious to preserve oneself as long as possible and leave after one one's progeny.

If Teddy had not grown up among humans, firstly in a zoo and then a circus, if he had been taught about life by a fierce she-bear—fierce towards everything around her but tireless in her kindness to him, a small bear-cub—he would by now have become a mighty animal, knowing all that a wild animal needed to know and could know. But Teddy had learned life from a man who wore white breeches, and his ultimately untameable, savage spirit had been suppressed from the time of his youth. He had managed to learn many things that were inaccessible and frightening to the natural denizens of a forest—in a town he was undoubtedly more experienced and knowledgeable than any of his forest-fellows—but what use was all that to him in the world he had come to now? Now, here, he had returned to the state of a small, helpless and pitiful infant-bear, knowing nothing and fearful of everything around him. The only difference lay in that he was no longer a tiny cub but a stoutly built adult-bear, with yellow fangs and a rump rendered shiny from long living in a cage—and in the lack now of a kind, wise mother to defend him and to instruct him.

7

He was woken by birds. They were small and their fluttering was barely audible, coming from above in the dew-wet branches. A long way to the east and over the hills the sun was rising. A transparent veil of mist hung about the pines, dew drops glinted, the air was fresh and clean when

Teddy emerged from his night's refuge and hobbled onwards in a northerly direction. Unused to forest wanderings, his paws on this second day ached, but he went on stubbornly because there was still something in the area where he was that did not satisfy him. He did not think, but moved northwards, without any more sense of purpose than birds have when they flock preparatory to their migrations. A rooted instinct urged him towards a land where he had never been, where there would be ample sunlight and food, clean water and silence.

In the middle of the day, as the bear was crossing a sunny clearing, his nostrils were struck by an unusual odour which woke a swirl of dim memories. But what was the source of that delightfully sweet scent? Teddy turned eastwards and went that way some distance—the smell disappeared. He returned, puzzled and worried, to the same place. Again, that seductive smell! Then Teddy began circling, and after some considerable time he realised that the odour came from an ant-hill. The smell which his nostrils had caught was the smell of ants and he had recognised it although he had not experienced it for so long.

What a delight, ants! Is there anything in the world tastier? Fat and tart, delicately pungent, tempting the appetite and arousing thirst, and satisfying both in turn... one might go on eating them forever!

Teddy thrust his nose into the nest, snorting with happiness, so powerful and near was that wonderful smell. He dug in deeper with his nose, noisily champing, eyes reduced to slits, wet tongue toiling in and out. In a moment large, ginger-hued ants had enveloped his muzzle with their furious numbers, had crawled inside his ears... but Teddy merely shook his head, lowered his tail tightly as a precaution and went on munching even more vigorously and steadily. At length he had to stop, if only to draw breath, and he sat back on his hind paws. Right then it occurred to him to do something that had long gone from his memory: he began to tear up the ant-heap. Now the ants deluged his paws—and it only remained for him to lick them off! That was incomparably more convenient—the ants no longer got into his nose and ears, nor earth and pine needles into his mouth. Teddy only halted when there was nothing left of the nest.

Having done with that, he continued on his way, over a hill mysteriously covered in dead firs, a whole forest of naked branches, and then down into a ravine, in the bottom of which he stumbled on a raspberry patch and there he remained until nightfall.

At first, Teddy was alarmed by the winging past of hazel-grouse and woodcocks, the sound of fish splashing in the small lakes, the noises that trees make, and the crackle of elk passing over forest litter. He was worried by unknown and peculiar odours, sharp and yet almost imperceptible. But overcoming his fear he invariably proceeded to investigate each sound and smell, so that if he should meet it again he might safely approach it or avoid it or simply pay it no further heed.

In this present life of his there was one happy circumstance which went unrecognised by him at first: he need fear no one but man, he need fear no wolf or lynx or the diminutive marten, all those terrible creatures that carry evil to smaller animals and to birds. No one dared touch him, and he had no need to hide or to run away, to run and feel behind him the light and terrible sound of pursuit. On the contrary, all feared him, since here in the forest he, himself unaware of it, was the largest and most dangerous beast.

That fact he understood considerably later, when he came one day upon the carcass of a young elk being torn at by two large wolves. Seeing the wolves, the bear stopped, undecided about what he should do. The wolves growled angrily and impotently and immediately moved away, giving place to the bear. And all during the time Teddy enjoyed his meal of elk, the wolves circled near but did not dare approach. Then a joyous awareness of his might awoke in him, and even after he had fed to satiety he returned more than once to the carcass, noting with satisfaction how the wolves leapt away from it.

8

Stopping in one place a day, in another, two, Teddy travelled further and further north. The pine trees began to grow taller and more wide-trunked; raspberries, field strawberries and whortleberries increased; villages were even scarcer. A limitless wild beauty, an untouched depth of wilderness and undisturbed silence spread all around and seemed almost to pose the question: What more than this could you want? But from Teddy's almost forgotten cub-hood there remained memories, tantalising and vague, which still whispered that even here some element was missing; and so he continued to long for that imponderable goal, some home-region of his own, his bear-Eden.

When he found from his point of view a particularly nice spot, Teddy made his rounds. He uprooted old, mouldering stumps, pulled the nests of mice and squirrels to bits, turned over stones covered in dry, white moss to reveal the slugs and worms underneath. In two weeks Teddy learned a lot. He began to sleep lying with his head towards the direction he had come from; he learned that besides berries and roots mushrooms were very good to eat also; he no longer chewed everything that he came across indiscriminately as he had done in the first days; he now knew that the juiciest roots grew in damp places; he began drinking only clear, running water; he learned how to use the wind, his sense of smell becoming so keen that he could now identify very subtle or old odours; and he also learned by bitter experience that not everything in the forest is edible, that there are berries and mushrooms which it is better to leave alone. He became stronger, wearied less quickly, and the soles of his paws, so painful in those first days, were now calloused, and his claws, which had been kept short in the circus, had grown out. He moved about quietly, almost noiselessly—except that on the odd occasion he was carried away by some fancy and would begin to break everything around him, whatever chanced in his way—and then the uproar filled the whole forest!

At the start, Teddy slept more at night, as he had been used to doing in the circus, but later he noticed that life in the forest was much more interesting at night than in the day. The tracks of martens, of hares, and foxes were fresher, things rustled in the grass, made busy noises in the bushes, there were pattering sounds through the ravines and clearings, the darkness gave birth to strange cries. In addition to that, at night the flies and midges which so vexed him in the daytime disappeared. And so he began to wander about at night, and in the day he slept in secluded places.

9

One night, Teddy happened on a small field sown with oats beside an old, abandoned road some distance from a settlement. He immediately understood that this was no vegetation which just happened to grow there, that it was in some way connected to men.

He skirted around the field. The oaten ears faintly piqued him in a pleasant way. Having gone around the field and found nothing that interested him, he left; but in a short time he returned, entered right inside among the oats, lay down in that soft and moonlit little island and began snatching at the oats with his maw. Thus, he discovered the taste of growing oats, which somehow put him in mind of the now almost forgotten oat-gruel of the past. At first, he ate greedily the whole of the plants, both the grain and the stems; then he began to suck at and chew the ears alone. He left at first light after having trampled a large bald patch into the oat-field.

He liked the oats very much, and the next night he returned and feasted on them until dawn. He would have come the following night again, but was distracted when as he was passing through a small swamp he happened to frighten a couple of dozen frogs. The pursuit in the dark was long and messy, resulting in his becoming so muddied that he had to spend the time up to that morning cleaning himself.

Teddy did not know that on that same morning men drove up the old road in a cart, looked long at the field, cursed and left; and that in the evening those same men returned with axes and boards, and while trying not to be too noisy they set up some contraption on an old pine tree conveniently branched for their purpose.

'Perfect, that tree! Made to order!' someone among them kept repeating, and grim, cruel smiles passed across their faces.

Then they moved away a little, smoked, dropped their cigarette-ends that were like small coals into the humid grass, got rifles out of the cart, and while two of them climbed into the pine the third drove off. A pail hanging under the cart jingled, the one driving away lifted his voice in a song, and the singing and jingling returned for some time to the ears of those who remained.

The moon had risen above the forest when Teddy woke. He continued lying for some time, quiet in the absolute silence, only turning his head and nosing the air. Then he rose, yawned, stretched himself, and remembering the oats he headed towards the field with his unhurried, swaying gait. He stopped occasionally, attracted by some smell, poked his nose into grass, tore out a sweet snack of root, champed on it: he had not learned to eat quietly.

He had almost arrived at the place and could already glimpse through a thick stand of aspen the whitening band of the field with its dark smudge in the middle, the spot where he had been revelling during the last two nights; he had only to continue another ten or fifteen steps more. Then, he suddenly stopped.

No, he had not seen nor had he smelt anything, but it was exactly as if a faint shadow had flickered and caught his attention, conveying some signal to him. His instinct warned him—a change had occurred here while he had been away!

Teddy turned right and circled the field from just inside the trees, never losing sight of the dimly gleaming ranks of oats. The fur up and down his spine stood on end, but he did not give vent to a deep roar as might have been expected: something told him it was best not to roar. The field was empty and everything around remained still. An almost imperceptible breeze come from somewhere scarcely bent the grass; it was faint, but the odour of the oats grew stronger by it and Teddy's nose in turn more humid and colder.

But he did not lick his chops, did not open his maw, although it watered he swallowed silently. And now he came out onto the moonlit road cut across by dark shadows of trees. The fur on the nape of his neck had settled, but now it rose again: his nostrils were struck by the odour of tar, horse, tobacco, and men. He stopped and sniffed for a long moment. He knew at last that there had been people at that place, with a horse; they had stood here, smoked and gone. A little bolder now, he went further down the road, crossed it again and came upon the field from the other side.

He was certain that the people who had been here the previous evening had gone; but, strangely, the feeling of danger did not leave him nor did the fur on his nape lie down. He wanted to go away from this place which filled him with such unease, and he actually turned; but instead of going into the forest he turned back again, uttering a quiet grunt.

Teddy had no mother, and no one else could have taught him that one must leave without delay things that cannot be understood. And the lack of that elemental education explains why he had returned and now stood in the shadow of the fir trees; and the smell—the delicious, delicate call of oats—deadened his fear and drew him to itself, lullingly, prevailing over caution.

The bear slowly and hesitantly emerged completely from the shadows and approached the grain; but at that moment there was an audible click and then a rustle above him and to one side. Teddy had no time to leap back where he had come from or even to lift his head, there was a mighty flash and the echoing thunder of a shot—terrible to hear in the silence of the night—and something burning struck his left front paw, knocking it from under him, and he fell.

There was another clattering noise and Teddy understood at last that he was in for it, that this was his most dangerous enemy, man—that he had to escape! As infuriated as he was at that moment, he leapt up and threw himself towards the safety of the dim forest. He lunged forward, intending to run as quickly as he could; but, to his surprise, at the second hop he fell over again, while two more shots from the crooked pine thundered after him and things flew humming piercingly, thudding very near him and a little to his front.

But now neither the shots nor the sound of their impact frightened him but only the fact that he could not run and had fallen. He leapt up again meaning to race clear of the oat field, and again something incomprehensible and terrible happened to him and he landed with his snout in the earth. Only now did Teddy understand that his front paw was as if it did not exist, had gone numb, did not move and could not be leant on. He then shifted the weight of his body on the other front paw and so he began to run more quickly, and then more quickly still, with a terrible noise of breaking undergrowth, not choosing his path, snorting with terror, swaying on his way, stumbling, falling forward on his chest—away from there!

He ran for a long time, imagining all the while that he heard the crackling noises of gaining pursuit, and he added to his speed, wearing out his strength; and when he had finally become incapable of running further he stopped and turned about, roaring, to meet his enemy. He growled and crouched down, his ears flat on his head, his now unbearably painful paw pressed under him. His eyes burned, his sides heaved, all the fur on his spine and flanks stood on end from terror and fury. Because of the noise of his own panting he could not hear well, and he stopped breathing so that he might listen. Not hearing anything but distrusting the silence, thinking that the enemy was in concealment, Teddy roared again, turned and went on, looking back often.

But no one pursued him, the forest had grown unnaturally quiet, frightened by his roars, and there was not a whisper of sound anywhere now. As he went, Teddy licked his paw. The warm blood aroused him, the pain decreased a little and he licked more assiduously, finding in the taste some strange pleasure.

And that saved him. After waiting for day to dawn, the hunters, rifles at the ready, followed the bloody track and guessed exactly what had happened: here he had hurried on, broken the underbrush; there he had torn up the earth with his claws and left blood sprinkled on the grass. They saw where he had crouched, facing them—and at that place there was an especially large pool of blood, the grass was bent and sticky with it. But then the signs grew fainter, the blood-drips were less frequent and soon disappeared, and the hunters, having lost the trail and after beating through all the nearby ravines, returned to their village empty-handed.

10

By then Teddy was lying in a little dry island in the dark of the forest, a long way away, suffering. His paw swelled and hurt, and all that day he could not move from that place.

Night came, but the pain in his paw would not allow him to sleep. In addition to the torments of his situation, he was possessed by another, new apprehension, but could do nothing, only sniff the air to seek for the cause of his worry. The forest had grown strangely quiet again, had withdrawn into itself, not the slightest sound could be heard, and that dead silence increasingly oppressed the bear and kept him constantly on his guard.

Some indefinable disturbance passed through the forest, and the air grew close. At first infrequently and then more and more often there were flashes of summer lightning whose brilliance soon encompassed half the horizon. They were soundless and mysterious apparitions and were unseen in the thick woods, except where the highest tips of the pines responded to them by glowing momentarily with a pale and transparent light. Then, quietly in the distance, thunder began to growl. Teddy answered with his own sullen growl and turned restlessly under a fir tree. Finding himself surrounded by an ill-boding silence, while from afar the rolling thunder was becoming more marked and now almost continuous, Teddy's yearning to hide himself in some secret concealment grew. But there was nowhere to hide, and he could only press himself closer against his tree.

The storm arrived incredibly quickly: a blackness drew like a curtain across the stars and extinguished their glimmer, visible until that moment through the branches of the trees; the dark was cut through by white flashes of lightning, striking somewhere in the nearby hills; something kept exploding and crashing, harshly and terribly—Takh! Agrrrrr-bakh!—as though the heavens coughed.

A wind from the upper sky poured down through the clouds, the tops of the pines and firs answered with a hiss, even as below them there was yet silence and nothing moved. The wind passed on and almost immediately following it came rain. This was no ordinary rain of a temperate rustling in the leaves, as had been known to Teddy previously, this rain poured down all in one instant, filling the forest with the roar of cascading water, a roar above which nothing else could be heard except the thunder, thunder which overwhelmed every other sound with its triumphant bellow.

Towards dawn the storm passed, and soon the forest, penetrated by the sun of a new clear day, blazed with light. Glittering drops fell from high branches down onto lower ones, from there to the grass, and from the grass finally to the ground, which drank every drop. All morning the forest was alive with that patter and rustling.

Poor Teddy! Tormented by pain, by the terrors of the storm and the dread of humans, sleepless, wet and wretched, he sat under the old fir and could not find enjoyment in the arrival of the sun; he could not, from the pain, even think of going somewhere to seek some food for himself. And he lay like that, helpless and alone, a day and another night and a day again, until his wound started to heal a little and raging hunger drove him out of his covert.

Somehow hobbling on three paws, dismal and fearful, he wandered about the hills; and each bush, dry branch, root, and even the high, coarse grass, as it caught at his wounded paw ignited his rage. But after the passage of a few more days the bear began cautiously to use that paw to move upon, and gradually his gloom left him and he began to be more buoyant and to find his courage again.

There was one more occasion for him to meet with people. He was moving along a river bank with his unhurried amble, it was a warm night and he was coming across a particularly large quantity of raspberries; but Teddy was grumpy. Before this, he had chased a groggy heath-cock, the bird dulled by sleep. It had flapped about, unable to take off, had thrust itself into the undergrowth, collided with trees, fallen, and Teddy had almost got him; but the cock still managed to fly up into a birch tree, and Teddy had been unable to reach him there. Now he was ireful.

He went down into a gully, drank from a stream, went up the other side—and suddenly he smelled smoke and heard human voices. He continued quietly towards the smoke, soon coming to a clearing where a large fire burned brightly; and there he saw two tents, and some hobbled horses grazing. This was a party on a scientific expedition, but Teddy could not know that of course. In high amazement he sat down on his rump to better observe everything. There were people sitting and moving about near the fire, talking loudly and laughing, casting large, constantly shifting shadows on the trees.

He loped around the clearing and came closer to the tents; and then, unexpected to himself, he suddenly growled, loud and angrily. Instantly, the horses snorted and sidled together from all directions to form a tight group, while from one of the tents out leapt a dog and bounded towards Teddy. But after closing to within ten metres of the bear the dog suddenly halted and set up a wild and fearful barking.

Teddy retreated a little and attempted to approach the tents from another side, but the dog ran at him again. The people by the fire jumped up, and two of them who had darted into a tent ran out with rifles. As soon as Teddy saw the red glint of firelight on the barrels, he turned and took to his heels. The dog ran after him persistently, ecstatic with triumph and the excitement of pursuit. Teddy left the clearing behind and turned into a patch of swamp and there rounded with outrage to face the dog. The dog instantly fell silent, wheeled about, and went for its life back towards the tents. Teddy wanted to return to the camp and tear it to pieces, but remembering the rifles he went down to the river and there soon became engrossed in the search for something to eat.

By this, the bear had travelled some two hundred kilometres in a northerly direction, not stopping long at any one place. He was now no longer helpless as in the first days. The smells were known to him now, things puzzled him less frequently and he coped increasingly well with the quandaries and discoveries he met in daily life. Thus he had come to know that one could invariably rely on jays and magpies, although they are generally judged to be the silliest of birds; he had learned to plumb the meaning of this or that kind of cry uttered by a woodpecker; and if he noted from a distance a crow perched on a tree, cleaning its beak, and slightly beneath the crow magpies sitting motionless with their tails hung downwards, looking attentively at something below themselves, he lost no time heading for the spot, not even preceding his move in that direction by a sniff of the air, for he knew now that wherever satiated crows rested, there was bound to be something nearby of profit to a bear as well. Also, although he was no great tree-climber, when he found a pine with a convenient spread of branches, he never lost the opportunity to grapple up it to take a look at the neighbourhood from a high perch.

Having mastered in a short period of time many things that he would never have encountered in the city, and now grown fit and prudent, he had become, it would seem, a genuine wild animal, complete in his capabilities and experience. But that was not quite the case, not yet.

One morning, having come to a brook to drink, Teddy halted as if thunderstruck—in the vicinity of the brook he sniffed the scent of another bear! It was an old smell, probably two days had passed since that other one had been there. But the weak odour carried such menace that Teddy forgot his thirst and stood peering around for a long time, while the fur along his spine would not settle. It appeared, then, that he was not the sole ruler of the forest, that there was another, and this other, it was wise to assume, constituted a menace. From that day there was no peace for Teddy.

More and more often he came upon rent anthills, chewed and trampled leftovers of raspberry and whortleberry brakes. When he scented from a distance the smell of carrion and then approached it, Teddy would find that the other one had been there first and all that in fact remained of the carrion was its smell. Now, everything in the forest had the odour of the foreign bear, and that odour infuriated Teddy to madness. His anger, growing by gradations, became so acute and so permanent that a reality was increasingly obvious to him: the area could not contain the two of them, one of them had to go! But this was such a fine place, had so much food!... And so, Teddy decided he must expel his enemy and he sought everywhere to encounter him. He found much fresh sign and even more that was old, but he was unsuccessful in coming upon the other in the flesh.

Their confrontation occurred unexpectedly. One morning, Teddy was looking for a spot where he might lie up for the day, and he was then about to cross a tiny clearing among the pines, its floor all overgrown with white, dry moss—when his nostrils were suddenly struck by a hateful and powerful smell of bear! Lifting his head, Teddy looked in the direction the smell was coming from, and he finally saw his enemy. Oh, how he was going to teach this insolent fellow—he would soon sort him out! The other—in that initial moment obscured by some trees—entered the clearing.

He was a colossus of a bear, so massive that Teddy at the sight of him froze like a stunned rabbit! Just a moment earlier, fierce, thirsting to come to grips, Teddy had been a murderous animal. But what counted his ferocity in comparison with the appearance of his rival? This was a real wild beast: shaggy, bearded, iron-clawed, a mountain of muscle, and with such a savage gaze that Teddy, who was himself hardly puny, grew rigid with fear.

The bear stood with his head hung low, seeming hunchbacked in that attitude. He stood silent, looking steadily at Teddy. No sound was uttered, there had been no further movement, but Teddy understood already that it was himself who must leave forever this marvellous region. Could there ever be any dream of competing with such a monster?

And that which Teddy understood, in the same second understood also the other bear. And not that alone: he understood that Teddy understood. No, he did not fall upon Teddy to slaughter him, but simply growled quietly. And that growl was a whole octave lower than Teddy's lowest growl. To a man, the growls of bears sound much the same, man's ear is incapable of distinguishing the fine nuances in growling. Teddy immediately knew what the other wanted. The noise the bear made—not loud, even a somewhat disdainful sound—stood for a curt 'Beat it!' Disobeying meant that Teddy would within the space of a minute fall on the white, dry moss with a broken neck and his breast ripped open.

And Teddy made no sound in reply. He turned around and beat it. When he was about to disappear among the trees he looked back for the last time. The bear still stood as before, unmoving and looking in his hunchback pose like a hayrick against the compact rank of pine trunks behind him.

Teddy left forever that region of abundant ginger-coloured ants and red whortleberries, left it in order not to bump into its bearded emperor. He had been proved the weaker: had there been a fight to the death he would have lost, and on that basis he could in fact consider himself lucky to have got off as he did.

11

The leaves had almost all blown down from the birches and aspens and covered the ground in a thick rustling carpet, birds were gathering in flocks, the raspberries had gone, mushrooms grew plentifully, and now began the time of morning frosts, when Teddy, lumbering over innumerable hills and having turned rightwards to follow a tributary of the big river, came out one morning onto a vast natural clearing.

A stream ran through its lower areas, there were stands of huge pines that hummed quietly, the last of the daisies bloomed and turned hopefully towards a weak sun. The shores of this new stream had many stretches of fine golden sand, showing the tracks of grouse and the places where they took their dust-baths. The water tinkled melodiously and continuously, and Teddy, pausing to listen to it, understood suddenly that he had found the Promised Land, had finally come to the region of his cubhood. Nothing more beckoned him, he did not want to go further, his trek had ended.

No, it was not in fact the land of his birth. But everything was precisely as it had been long ago when Teddy, who then had no name and was simply a silly little cub-bear, used to overeat on ants and strawberries, and his mother rinsed him in a stream, holding him in her teeth by the scruff of the neck, and afterwards with her long, rosy tongue rubbed his swollen stomach. Those were wonderful, inexpressibly happy days, and Teddy, as if anew, had returned to them. But, of course, it was not the same. That cub-hood had been lost somewhere in the dim past, it could not return, could not be revived by any glinting of sunlight or green lustre of grass. Ah, if he could but have become that small being again, rediscovered his mother, cried perhaps by her soft, warm side!... Sad, but no; such things are impossible.

Wandering over it by day and by night, Teddy gradually covered the whole of that region, marking for his own purposes the boundaries of his kingdom. He explored creeks, marshes, gullies, low meadows, wooded edges and secure, hidden places. He met plentiful signs of wolves, elk, squirrels, otters, hares. Towards some of those he showed no concern, others annoyed him, and then he dug up the ground and threw it about, or tore at the bark of trees, all to announce his right to the land, the forest and even the air.

The wood-grouse and heath-cocks flew off from under his very nose with much fuss and scatter of dead leaves, but now nothing astonished

him and he accepted it all as something necessary and become long familiar. He no longer smelled animal tracks with unease and curiosity, but
simply noted them in passing: 'H'm, elk went by here. There were three.'
Or: 'A vixen ran through here... in a hurry, and carrying a partridge between her teeth.'

His coat took on a nut-brown tinge, the fur grew longer, becoming
woolly and shiny as it did so. His paw no longer hurt and he could depend
on it equally with the other when he needed to push over a rotten stump
or turn some heavy fallen log. He travelled around much, driven by a terrible hunger. But here everything was in abundance, and he often had periods when he felt a sensation of great satisfaction, knowing himself as
never before free and powerful.

A noble thing is freedom, a thing like the sun and the huge starry heavens. Freedom is like the warm, even-blowing wind, or like water in a
stream, flowing fast, full of its own voices. There is no need to fear anybody or do anything that one does not want to do. One can get up when
one wants, go wherever a prospect opens. One can stop and follow for a
long time with one's eyes a caravan of geese flying over a river. Or one
can climb on a hill, open to all the winds, where all the scents converge,
choose a particular scent from among the others and follow its call wherever it leads. One can amble into a ravine where so many trees stand hollow, their heart-wood eaten out by worms, and, rejoicing in one's mighty
strength, push those trees over, dry and lifeless, and listen to how they
fall with such a sad, tearing rush.

12

November came, the month of hard frosts and the beginning of the au-
tumn-mating of the elks. Circling about the hills, Teddy listened with
great irritation to the roaring of the males. On a number of occasions he
saw one in the distance, an aristocrat among elks, a beast with giant
antlers, moving without fear among the underbrush and up on bare
ridges, snorting and trumpeting almost ceaselessly. The bear grew to like
the noisy neighbour less and less. Teddy was a cautious animal and infrequently forgot himself, becoming rowdy only on some particularly ex-
igent occasion; but as for others, strangers, making an uproar—that, he
could not abide, and he soon grew to hate that elk as he once had hated
the other bear.

One day, he came across elk-sign and immediately guessed that the
giant elk had recently passed this way with his does. He happened to be
in a particularly irritated mood as it was, and a great desire to expel the
upstart overwhelmed him now. After angrily scattering the droppings left
by the little band, he set off on their trail. Cresting a ridge, he lost them,
but he returned to the bottom again and after completing a long semicir-
cle he came across their scent once more. Soon he saw them. They were

browsing in a thicket of thin aspens, reaching with their velvet lips towards the most tender of the upper foliage.

Teddy growled and threw himself at them. The does leapt sideways away from him and headed down the slope with long delicate bounds, while the buck-elk did an unexpected thing: he grunted and turned around to meet the bear. At other times he would of course without a second thought have followed the does. But now, after many victories over rivals, and ruled in this season by the fever of elk-love, he went boldly to meet his enemy; and thus they came together in the clearing. Teddy roared angrily. The elk answered with a snort and hissing aspirations. All his coat trembled with his keenness for the fight, his eyes filled with blood, his nostrils quivered, and the light vapour of his exhalations rose and was carried away by the breeze. He was at the peak of his strength, his huge antlers branching out with projecting vanes, while behind them poised a powerful neck and a slim, sloping rump.

Teddy, who had not expected such an encounter, was taken aback. He was not frightened, he only checked his advance momentarily to consider how he was to fall upon the other. But the elk, understanding that pause in his own way as irresolution, suddenly lowered his head, gave a snort and charged. Teddy had no time to jump clear, and the blow knocked him off his feet. The elk then instantly reared up high—and here Teddy's life might have ended if he had been struck in the head by the hooves darting down on him. But the elk missed his mark and only hit a shoulder. The hard bear-bone sustained the blow without breaking—but who could entertain any further notion of fighting? The point now was just to get out of this alive!

Realising he had misplaced his blow, the elk tried again, but Teddy rolled away, and the hooves missed him this time altogether. Then the elk bent his head and charged as he had done the first time. Teddy evaded, jumping behind a bush. The elk could not stop immediately and by the time he had turned again the bear, impaired somewhat by a limp, was bolting down the slope.

The victory—an unimagined victory—had gone to the glamorous elk! But now this was not enough for him, he wanted to destroy his attacker or drive him far away, so he followed Teddy, caught up with him easily and managed to butt him a few more times as he fled. Then, as if he had suddenly remembered something, the elk halted, snorted and returned to his does, while the unfortunate Teddy, bruised all over, took himself off to a place in the forest where the fallen trees were piled thickest, and there long he groaned and wheezed and suffered over again the shame of his impressions. He had not long ago been driven away by that other bear, today he had barely survived an elk!... The worst of it was that now he had to be careful of all elks in general, because seeing that one had defeated him it meant that the same must occur should he meet another. His life after this became insupportable. As if deliberately to plague him, the tracks of elk appeared before him everywhere. Wherever he went, to find whortleberries or an ants nest, or to a brook to drink, on meeting one of their tracks he immediately turned about and departed.

But that impossible situation could not continue very long. Suddenly, all his savage progenitors awoke in him, fiercely demanding that he should find and slaughter his enemy. He began to prowl around the forest, seeking the tracks of the elk, angrily tearing at the earth and at trees with his claws as a declaration of his rule. For long hours he lay stock still in ambuscades. On one occasion having found much new elk-sign at a creek he lay down in the middle of a patch of bushes which grew nearby and proceeded to wait. Body pressed low, he eyed the trail through the twiggy growth. A thick layer of damp yellow leaves matted the ground, for the trees were now completely bare, except for the dark, dense firs standing out especially distinctly now against the rest of the depleted and almost transparent forest. The morning had been frosty, but by this hour the rime had melted. The day was lowering and cold.

In the second half of the day, from up above, light crunching noises and a snort or two came down to Teddy's hide. He lifted his head, inhaled, and smelled elk. His ears flattened back, the fur along his spine lifted. He pressed himself closer to the ground and gathered his hind paws under his belly. The elks paused: once, twice. What they were up to—listening or pulling down twigs to eat—Teddy did not know; he continued lying there patiently. At last, antlers rose above the bushes, and then the buck himself appeared. Behind him came three does. They stopped, looked down the slope attentively, swivelling their ears, and then descended to the watering-place, the buck in front, does following.

But it did not all go Teddy's way, the buck scented the bear and immediately halted rigid. Teddy leapt from his ambush with a muffled growl. The elk grunted and threw himself at the bear, who managed to jump aside and hook the elk's flank. The blow from the bear's paw seemed light, glancing even, but the claws tore the skin, and a line of blood instantly appeared on that side. Scenting the blood, Teddy grew frenzied. For the first time in his life he wanted to tear living flesh, to hear the choking death-gasps of his prey. The elk meanwhile had turned and now threw himself at Teddy. The bear was heavy, but the impact of the mighty antlers hurled him through the air like a kitten. He was sent rolling over, much as had happened in the previous combat; but the elk had not completely escaped, and now a new wound bled on his neck. Teddy leapt, delivering such a mighty roar as made his whole body vibrate, aiming himself at the side of the elk, since by now he had understood that the antlers were a weapon against which he was powerless.

They continued the struggle, tearing up the damp desiccated grass, the earth, trampling down everything around them. But the elk clearly was weakening, blood spurted from several wounds, smoking in the cold air. At last Teddy succeeded in taking him from the side. He fastened on the powerful lower nape while at the same time his hind paws clawed into the elk's flanks. Then, clinging with left front paw and his teeth to the nape and growling through clenched jaws, Teddy levelled a great thrusting blow down on the upper neck with his right paw. The vertebrae tore apart and the elk crashed to the ground. The bear ripped the elk's chest—but even with his chest torn and a broken neck the elk still tried to rise and throw off the bear, such was his strength!

Rumbling in his throat and coughing from the swallowed blood of the now dead elk, it was a long time before Teddy could come to himself again. Then the bear, still growling continuously, went into the forest; but he soon returned and attempted to drag the elk away. The body was heavy and awkward to drag, so he began to throw branches and other dead windfall over it where it lay. Having thus in some fashion over-strewn his dead enemy, and in addition grubbed up the soil all around the heap, Teddy left the spot, departing with an attitude of finality. No one had taught him to do what he had just done and he had never done it before, but now he knew that that was what one did.

Two days later, having forgotten all about the elk, he happened to pass not very far from the spot, when suddenly the wind carried to him an agreeable odour. Then he immediately remembered everything, turned that way and ate his fill from the cache. There had been wolves there before him, as Teddy could see from the tracks left by them, and so he went no further but slept nearby. For a whole week he kept returning to the elk and he slept there, feeling now he was the true lord of all that surrounded him and certain his territory was as sacrosanct as that of the bearded bear.

13

But after a long interval, and for the last time, nostalgia for the world of men came back to trouble him like the ache of an old wound. A force even mightier than instinct drove him suddenly out of the forest, and exactly as he had recently sought to be alone and free he now began to seek a meeting with humans.

For four days he loped with astonishing swiftness south-eastwards until he finally came out at an open place. Before him rose a large, gently-sloping hill covered in some bright-green winter crop, and along the border of the clearing, not far from where Teddy stopped, ran a highway on which automobiles sped frequently and horse-carts passed in slower progress.

Teddy stood there on his hind paws and rocked with the sad need for men. But it was not just men but that man of strength who wore white breeches whom he pined for. He wanted that man to come to him and scratch him behind the ears and say to him caressingly: 'Tedd-ee!...' and then with that dominating hand put a lump of sugar into his maw.

And so the bear stood there a long time, nothing like the former Teddy;

he stood as if apprehending anew the great and mysterious meaning of life and, with that, taking leave of his past in it. He did not go out to the road, to people, nor did he do any of those hilarious tricks that he had learned in the circus. He grieved mutely. Then, it was as if something had turned inside him, a last burden had dropped, a last thread binding him to humans had parted, and he went back into the forest. Four days later he had returned to his domain.

It became colder with each passing day. Teddy now slept much and went about less frequently. Each morning the smaller lakes and the back-waters of the streams were enclosed further in a border of crisp and ring-ing ice. Hunger, the everlasting director of his movements, now suddenly took on a lesser importance, something else bothered him increasingly. In the circus they had not allowed Teddy to sleep through winter, for he had to perform. But here he came under the laws of the forest, nature's laws: he needed to sleep. He kept moving around, sampling, seeking the right setting; but wherever he looked he found invariably that something did not quite suit: here, not comfortable enough; there, too open...

One night, snow fell, and in the morning all was white, the far hills shone as if through a mist, and Teddy's desire to sleep grew even stronger. Even his own tracks in the snow failed to amaze him.

Once, he settled down on some dry leaves under a fir tree and slept for three days; but he woke and began wandering again, pausing to look sadly at the lively black crows in the white landscape.

Finally, he found what he needed. It was a commodious pit strewn with fallen leaves and conifer needles. Its mouth was overgrown with bushes and in addition the soft finial of a fir tree had snapped off and fallen right over the pit, as accurately as if some wandering lumberjack had travelled to this wilderness to lay it so. The lower arms of the segment were so dense that when Teddy got under them he could hardly see the sky. But this was not enough. He emerged again and dragged up all manner of windfall and piled it on top. He worked long and it was evening by the time he descended inside. There, he turned this way and that way and could not seem to find how he might lie most comfortably; but he lay down at last and it seemed good and he began to lick himself all over.

Darkness arrived slowly, the snow fell silently, and when it became completely dark and the snow on the tips of the surrounding pines had lost the last of its sunset colours, Teddy finally slept.

And what did he dream? Did he dream of the circus and his long artist's life, divided, it could be said, into two: by the darkness of the passage in the animal annexe, and the blinding lights of the ring? Or were his dreams those of journeys and railway wagons, the knock of the wheels, the smell of coal and petrol; or of the people laughing and shouting excitedly, and the man in the white breeches? Or were they about his new, free life, sweet ants, tinkling cold brooks, terrible storms, shots, the bear that had driven him away, the battle with the elk? Did he dream of his youth? Did the mild and summoning scents of the forest, their subtle meanings, waft down into his den? Who knows.

He did not wake the next day, nor the day after that. The snow kept falling and each day the bushes became downier, the tracks more difficult to detect, the pines and firs whiter, and only the branches of the birch trees remained bare where the heath-cocks long gathered in the evenings. The hard frosts arrived, and winter—the real winter of the North—was at play in the forest.

But Teddy's sleep grew deeper, his breathing slower, the vapour of his breath now no longer rose above his den; which soon, under its covering of snow, might only be stumbled upon, its location indicated by just an air-vent and the yellowish rime on the twigs around that small orifice.

9. OLD HUNTING GROUNDS

1

They had spent the night in the upper sleeping-platform of an empty, abandoned foresters' hut, making their bed on a mat of compacted leaves so old that they had lost their odour. Pyotr Nikolaevich woke when a weak light began to filter down through the gaps in the roof timbers. His son Alexei lay soughing gently, arms twisted awkwardly, a padded jacket over his face, his long, thin legs and big feet thrown apart. By his side the butt of a shotgun jutted out from under his blanket.

Pyotr Nikolaevich put on his boots, then carefully and with some hesitation felt his way down from the platform: there were rungs missing from the attached ladder and he was aware that he could take a fall. Having made it to the floor he went to the open doorway of the hut and stood there looking at the paling east, at the motionless trees and the shrubs heavy with dew. Then he went out and walked slowly around the hut.

There had been an enclosure for cattle here, he thought to himself, when drovers used the hut. There had been a smell of wood-smoke then, of milk and dung; there were hoof-marks everywhere and you had to watch out for the cow pats.

But five years ago it had all been abandoned, and now the fenced yards were collapsing in places, a kind of wide-leaved pale-green nettle grew profusely around the hut, and everything told of departure, neglect and of a place of human habitation reverting to wilderness.

Pyotr Nikolaevich returned to the front of the hut. The door had been torn from its hinges, and he passed freely through the doorway and went inside. There was no glass left in the windows except for one remnant sweaty fragment turned smoky-blue by the sun and the rain; leaves had heaped up in the corners; the door of the stove had gone, together with the cast-iron inner plates, and the firebox gaped with a cold, black starkness. Why had the people left? Where did they pasture their animals now?

Pyotr Nikolaevich went to one of the corners, sat down on its leaves and lit a cigarette. He smoked slowly, gazing moodily and unhappily at the threads of smoke drifting up through a thick, dusty cobweb stretched across the empty window-frame above him. The hut smelled of the stove's dried-out clay and of old timbers, while from outside came the smell of grass; and that at least was a clean odour, although somehow also saddening in its way. His cigarette went out unnoticed as he fell into thinking about the time when he, then young, had first hunted in these parts.

He was twenty then, as irrepressibly excited as a colt, almost ill with happiness. For a whole month, alone or with his father, he had wandered about these singing regions, sleeping at night in bush lean-tos or in hayricks the unbroken deep sleep of youth, to wake at first light and find all of life before him: life vernal-fresh, endless and joyous. He had wandered beside lakes and over meadows and through dim pine-forests, feeling an unspeakable blessedness in his own youth and strength, ready to dive into icy water after a wounded teal, to walk a dozen kilometres in the hope of bringing down some nimble snipe. And then, on top of that, probably the most important thing, he had been in love at the time, had thought of the girl ceaselessly and with a sweet anguish. And it seemed to him, in the nature of those who are young, that all this happiness was not the genuine thing yet, not quite real happiness yet, that a far greater happiness, happiness beyond words, was still ahead of him in life.

So much had passed and disappeared since then, so much had been lived through and even gone totally from his memory; yet this quiet, clear corner of country and that time when he had roamed over it remained with him as the best he had known of life, the cleanest; and he remembered each of those days and each spot where he had met success in hunting, still recalled prominent trees, secluded springs, even remembered what he had thought then.

Now he had returned, not alone but with his son, and all the time they journeyed here he was agonizingly happy that he was going to see it all again. And it had all gone sour: he could hardly recognise anything, things had aged, faded. Look where he would, there was something not right, not right. Only the dawn and the dew on the grass, the smells, those were still the same, those remained always the same. Yes, and it was strange, strangely wonderful, he thought, that thousands of people, many perhaps not even born yet, would one day after him wake and look, as he had just done, at the day beginning like this, at the mist on the meadows, and they in their turn would breathe too these same strong, rueful odours of the earth.

2

His son woke and began moving about on the platform, then the ladder creaked and there was the sound of light feet meeting the floor.

'Father! Come over here!' Alexei called to him softly.

Pyotr Nikolaevich, breathed a sigh, rubbed his face with his hand, got up and went across the hut to his son. Alexei, in skiing trousers, his long legs braced, was looking up with an apprehensive and excited expression. 'Shh!' he cautioned his father, at the same time gripping him by the arm.

'Can you hear them?'

'No-o... What it is it?' Pyotr Nikolaevich asked, straining his ears.

'But—can't you hear them?' Alexei asked incredulously, his voice breaking out of what had started as a whisper, and he looked at his father in round-eyed disbelief, 'Wasps! They've got three nests up there. We missed them last night in the dark, but I grazed one just now, and what a buzz went up! Can you hear that?' Once again Alexei looked up animatedly.

'Ah, yes, mm, they're buzzing all right!' Pyotr Nikolaevich confirmed and smiled. But he still heard nothing and only felt now a slightly bitter edge to his melancholy. 'There you are—now your hearing's going as well!' he thought. Then, to put an end to this morning mood of his, he said briskly: 'All right now, that's all very well but we've got to get moving. It's late. The packs, the guns—let's have them.'

'Coming!' said his son and mounted effortlessly up the ladder. From above, with equally fluent movements and with an expression of adult seriousness, he handed down first one pack, then the other, the two guns and the heavy cartridge-belts, pulled on his new boots, and seemed to have hardly drawn a second breath by the time he dropped back on the floor.

'Off we go!' Pyotr Nikolaevich said with decision, and himself led the way towards the limits of the old pasture, past which he remembered there ought to be the start of a trail.

But they spent some time in an unsuccessful search for it, and the dew had penetrated their boots by the time they struck out more in hope than certainty towards a dark line of tall pine trees. The native fields beyond the pasture were white with daisies, and the grass there was thick and caught at the feet. 'What a good lot of fodder's going to waste here. All this, and no one to mow it,' thought Pyotr Nikolaevich, still dispirited. 'Everything's reverting.' Behind him Alexei stumbled over tussocks, yawning audibly from time to time. Something in the boy's pack kept clinking, and the faint, recurring sound touched a vague chord in his father's mind, stirred something there that he could not pin down.

The moment they entered the pines the old trail became visible at once. Under the canopy hung a sombre darkness, except for an uncertain bluish light faintly discernible at the distant limits of the wood. There, Pyotr Nikolaevich now remembered, the pines grew thickly on the bank of an old dried-up riverbed. In a little while they heard from the meadowsweet in that direction the simple, two-tone call of a bird: 'pee-pee, pee-pee...'

Alexei, yawning, stumbled again. 'Is it still far?' he asked dully.

As if waiting for that precise question, a wood-grouse burst out explosively from a thicket right beside them! Its flight traced a curve like a series of short unconnected strokes as it passed behind tree trunks, the bird's clear, strident cackle diminishing along that trajectory. The two hunters stopped, transfixed for an instant, and Pyotr Nikolaevich felt his heart leap—so, there were still some wood-grouse left here, after all!

'Phew, that gave me a shock!' he laughed, 'Never mind, come on, we'll go after them later, there'll be plenty of time.'

But Alexei was not listening: he had turned from the trail and was moving stealthily over the soft moss, feeling his way through the whortleberries and holding his gun raised. Then Pyotr Nikolaevich paused to watch his son. He followed his movements with a tense interest, prepared at any instant to hear a shot; but after some moments he shouldered his own gun again and continued alone, walking quietly along the path.

He emerged from the pines, found a fallen log and sat down on it to have a cigarette. Before him lay a small misty field, beyond it was more forest, then there should be another field with a little island of fir trees, after that a tussocky damp meadow with coarse sedge at the far end, and then, finally, the lake. There he had hunted long ago.

Soon Alexei appeared, slinging his gun and brushing something from his face.

'Well? Nothing?' asked Pyotr Nikolaevich, smiling.

'Not a thing!' Alexei answered, grinning delightedly as if reporting the contrary. 'But it's so wild here! Mushrooms everywhere, berries—what a place! Are we really going to stay here a whole month? Boy!'

Pyotr Nikolaevich looked at his son, and the expression on his face softened. 'We'll live here a month and it'll be just fine,' he told him. 'You like it? I was worried you mightn't. But no, you'll be all right.'

The overgrown trail crossed the field and they followed it to the next patch of forest; but now Alexei went in front and Pyotr Nikolaevich walked behind him; and looking at the boy he thought how much he had grown lately and what a fine idea it had been to bring him here.

3

The sun had risen high, what dew remained lay in the shadows under bushes, and now the hunters approached the lake. They had not hurried particularly, enjoying instead the silent seclusion of the places they passed, savouring each in his own way a sense of the unknown lying ahead and around them. They had lingered more than once where stretches of wood opened into the perspectives of clearings, had sat on logs, conscious of the quiet ascent of the sun, noting in that tranquillity the creaking, glassy call of cranes, the tapping of woodpeckers, sometimes the shriek of a falcon. Finally, pausing in the clearing by the lake, Pyotr Nikolaevich took off his cap, smoothed down his thinning hair and stood absorbing the scene around him. How things had changed!

The lake had diminished and seemed to have aged somehow, one shallow and pinched end was altogether choked with sedge and rushes, the trees on the bank appeared to have grown more dense and taller now, their crowns bending well over the water, and there were more pond lilies than he remembered.

'Well, then—greetings to you all!' he addressed the scene ruefully in his mind. 'Hello to you, shrubs and trees and water! Hello, flowers and sedge! Here am I, come back among you. You waited so long, I dreamt of you so often, and now I've returned!'

Uncertain and with some difficulty, he found the clearing's edge where within the band of trees bordering the lake he and his father had had their campfire years ago—a fire which they kept almost continually burning, where they used to dry themselves after bad weather, where they had cooked their soupy stews and brewed tea. Beside that fire they had re-loaded cartridges, had quietly sung songs, harmonising their two voices. Turning to look back at the clearing, he saw that it too had grown smaller and strange to his recollection; and it was impossible to say whether the growth surrounding it had actually encroached so much, or just that, as with practically everything that had long receded into the distant past, memory had made that space seem more noteworthy than it ever was in reality. Frowning back the tears which he felt about to well from his eyes Pyotr Nikolaevich waved his son away. 'Go around the lake... go look... go, go!'

Alexei gave his father a startled glance, reddened, and walked away quickly, his boots swishing through the grass, his thin back hunched. Pyotr Nikolaevich dropped his pack, sank down on his knees and began feeling with his hands among the grass. 'There must be something left—surely!' he thought, determined to believe that. 'There was such an amount of ashes here, coals and charred bits and pieces... the fire even scorched one of the low branches of the tree we had our shelter under!' He glanced up: in the sunlight above him conifer needles glinted like silver, fine iridescent spider-webs stretching tautly among them; hard russet-green cones slept bedded in the branches; gnats jostled in the air. He bent to rake the grass apart with his fingers, pushed the long, tough stems of daisies away; but he could find nothing, only the damp earth, old, musty leaves, tiny, oily-yellow mushrooms; ants ran about and wild strawberries trembled like drops of blood on their short stalks. 'Yes, it's natural, I suppose,' a bewildered and unhappy Pyotr Nikolaevich, reasoned with himself. 'The cycle of life. What did you expect? Everything passes, changes. But was it actually just here, where we were that time?' He rose and looked around. Their lean-to had been set up a little apart under a fir tree: where to look? It had been such a fine structure, cool in the daytime and warm at night. He and his father had done such a good job of making it. Which fir was it now? Had he really just dreamt everything?

There was an occasional murmur in the tops of trees that stood beside the lake shore, and patches of pale-blue sky showed and disappeared among their moving branches; the paler underside of aspen leaves flick-ered with each draught; a warm, sunny light trembled intermittently on shadow-lapped trunks. At the base of those trunks spread the domain of windfalls, of fallen but still fresh-looking birch detritus, dead ferns. Pyotr Nikolaevich forced his way under one fir after another, scratching his face and his hands, looking back repeatedly at the clearing, taking care to orient himself to the spot he had first recognised. His gun got in the way and he unslung it and leant it against a tree. He came across many mushrooms and trailing brambles of stone-berry, and a moist mushroom-odour and spicy smell of needles rose to his face. Without thinking, he tore up strands of stone-berries and sucked them, feeling their cool, citric taste in his mouth, the tang of them in his nose. At last he returned to an old, thick fir, from which he looked back at the clearing, and it seemed to him that this after all was the one. Somewhere up the trunk there should still be the notch that had held one end of their shelter's roof-ridge, he remembered that mark well. But now among the vigorous swellings of sappy burls he could make out nothing. Then Pyotr Nikolaevich knelt again and began broodingly sifting through the litter of years that had piled up beneath the tree; and he found what he was looking for. One after another, rotting, dark-hued poles, the ends still showing where they had been hacked with a hatchet.

So, there it was, all that was left of a fine, well-built shelter, just some rotting poles.

Pyotr Nikolaevich got up, brushed his knees, pushed through some underbrush to the clearing again, and stood there a moment examining the fir from bottom to top, peering at it through its lower branches up to the crown. How ancient it was, what a great deal of lichen grew on it, and much of the top had lost its colour too; pretty soon what had once been a green, downy young tree would wither all over and die. Yep, and thus life passes on, he thought.

He found where he had left his gun, got it and returned to the clearing and stopped, not thinking, looking down at the daisies. Then it came back to him how he and his father used to signal to each other. He broke open the gun, extracted the two shells, brought the gun's chambers close to his lips—and in a moment over the forest flew a summoning, poignant, song-like sound, flew and died away somewhere far over the lake.

'Oho-ho-o-o!...' a boyish bass responded from quite near.

There was a rustle, and Alexei came into sight. He had an apologetic look, and Pyotr Nikolaevich understood that he had not gone away anywhere, that he had sat nearby, waiting until his father found what it was he had been looking for.

'How did you do that?' the boy asked with wonder.

Pyotr Nikolaevich showed him, and Alexei with alacrity and joyously opened his own gun, hooted into it with all the force of his young lungs—and again that perturbing sound rang, rang as it seemed from a distance of thirty years, over woodland and lake.

'Well now. This is where we'll live,' Pyotr Nikolayevich said quietly.

'Is this where you lived with grandfather... that time?' Alexei asked, reddening.

'Get the hatchet, we've got to make a start on our shelter,' said the father evenly, and without looking at his son he began rummaging in his own pack.

4

They spent a long time cutting poles, setting them in place, repositioning them more than once, fastening them together; and then they covered the resulting frame with a double layer of fir boughs. And from the start they took care that the shelter should stand under the fir tree just as the earlier one had stood. Pyotr Nikolaevich kept remembering more things that his father had done, and he did those things precisely in the same way. And just as he had once done and learned, so he noted that his own son was attentively and with an expression of awe assisting and committing to his own memory all that they were doing.

Towards mid-afternoon—after the shelter was quite finished and the ground inside had been covered with fir branches, their raincoats and padded jackets been laid over those, everything in the packs been taken out and arranged, and they had pulled off their boots to rest in comfort— the weather began to threaten rain. Dark clouds gathered quickly above them, closing off one by one each patch of blue sky. The forest across the clearing grew silent and darkened, and that made being inside their refuge even nicer. They expected the rain to be heavy, but it began as a gauzy mist of fine drops which hardly did more than touch the flowers and leaves, then it strengthened to a steady, warm drizzle.

The two hunters sat content in their shelter, happy and tired, happy to know that they had set themselves up and could outwait any bad weather; they sat feeling the quiet around them and listening to the whisper of the rain on the leaves. Everything outside grew quickly damp, but now not with the clean, saddening dew-smell of the morning: now the humid air was heavy with the odour of mushrooms, of wet soil, of birch leaves and the bitter smell of aspen bark.

Alexei soon curled up to sleep close to the thick fir trunk, his face turned to a corner of the shelter. Pyotr Nikolaevich shifted nearer to the low entry and looked out at the leaves hanging in wet strands from the closest birches and at the bent-over daisies in the clearing. He sat as he used to in that past, his arms around his knees, softly crooning to himself. He sang quietly the old, poignant Russian songs that told of separations, of death, of unlucky love, of the wide, free steppes, of homesickness and lonely nights. He sang and remembered many things in his life, dwelling at times on some thought and touched by a mood that was sweet and hidden in origin; he sang looking up at the sombre heavens and ahead towards the wood, now subsided into stillness. Then he stopped singing and began thinking of his son. He did that for a long time, and he could not be certain whether tenderness or something like envy predominated in those thoughts.

He started to nod, and then overcome by tiredness he lowered his head on his knees. But even in sleep a sense of sadness would not leave him, a regret for the irrevocable passing of things. One of his arms hung down from his body, and the hand had numbed and swelled and now looked lifeless. The rain dripped on, kept pattering on the aspen leaves and on the grass, everything grew more suffused with moisture, and the only place where it was still dry was under the big fir where their shelter stood.

5

They both woke when evening was approaching. The rain had stopped and they took their guns and went into the wet forest. The branches dripped with heavy drops and their patter could be heard from a distance. It was coming to sundown and a weak yellow light passed between the trees, a golden transparent vapour rose from the ground, and birds were taking a last opportunity to see off the day with their calls. More vapour hung over the lake when they returned to it, the sedge and bushy growths bordering the shore winked with pearly glimmers, and the water just stirred with barely detectable ripples—for there were ducks paddling somewhere!

They spent some time carefully moving along the shore until they saw the ducks, floating near the edge of the lake some distance away. Keeping well hidden, they observed them through a pair of binoculars, then they backed out, quickly and silently followed the lake around to a spot above the flock and began to descend. Dark water grew visible through gaps in branches—and on the surface of the water, illuminated by the yellow light of the low sun, floated the ducks!

'Wait, wait—let me!...' came Alexei's pleading whisper, 'Let me!...'

Pyotr Nikolaevich moved aside, and as he did so he remembered that he too had implored his father in the same tone, and his father had often made way for him. Alexei laid the barrels of his gun across a branch, aimed, then his shoulders jerked with the shot—a thunderous explosion followed by scattering echoes, while a small cloud of smoke rolled forward over the water.

The two, father and son, now no longer cautious, tore their way down through the bank-growths and over crackling sticks, and when they broke out on the shore they were just in time to see three ducks in rapid flight diminishing across the lake. Two ducks remained floating on the water: one was motionless, rolled over on its back, its white breast-feathers yellowed by the light; the second, turned on its side, was attempting to dive but could only manage to dip its head into the water and flap its wings feebly. The smoke of the shot blended with the lake-vapour in a drifting shroud over the water.

'Wait a minute, we'll cut a branch and scoop 'em in!' Pyotr Nikolaevich said excitedly; and he laid down his gun to take hold of the hatchet.

But Alexei was not listening. Frowning with concentration, not taking his eyes for a moment from the flapping duck, in the grip of the thrill and worry of his first kill, he was pulling off his boots, shaking the foot-wraps from his feet, and undressing. And then Pyotr Nikolaevich understood, and he put down the hatchet, found a rotten log to sit on, and lit a cigarette.

The boy dropped the last of his clothing, his thin, shivering body quickly overspreading with gooseflesh. He entered the water, carefully feeling the bottom and moving the stems of pond lilies aside with his hands; then, hissing, unable to tolerate the cold any longer, he flung himself forward and began swimming. When he came to the ducks, he turned his face—and it was radiant—towards the shore.

'Father!...' he shouted, breathless with the cold of the water, 'Come in for a swim!... You know what?... That smoke... from the shot... smells wonderful! Like hydrogen sulphide... and mixed... with your tobacco!... Oho-ho!...' Ecstatically he dived under, his feet flaying momentarily above the surface, then he rose, spluttering and snorting, and swam back, flinging the ducks one after the other onto the bank.

And Pyotr Nikolaevich suddenly remembered, and could not help feeling a chill as it came back to him, that on just such an evening as this he had shot a duck on another lake some two kilometres from this one, and he too had swum out to the duck, and his father had sat on the bank, resting and smoking, and the smoke from the gun had merged over the water with the tobacco-smoke, and it had all smelled so wonderful and so strange that he had shouted back about it to his father. He too had threshed in the water out of acute delight and had made just such a commotion.

Yes, it was all the same. And life was good as in the past, and it would go on and be good: dawns would still flame and turn crimson-purple and then greenish, sunsets would burn with a quiet light, the flowers would bloom and the grass grow and new people would come to the old hunting grounds.

Such a mingled sense of joy and sadness overwhelmed him at that moment, that he could feel his heart beating. He could not sit there smoking any longer, and he dropped his cigarette and strode away over the wet grass, blindly into the depth of the darkening, silent forest.

And long his son remained in the lake, smacking his cupped hand down on the water, splashing, shouting things in various voices, his noise evoking echoes. And the boy looked across the lake, to the opposite shore, grown mysterious and clad gradually in the blue haze of a departing day. Finally, he came out of the water, shivering and livid with cold, and he dressed quickly, hopping first on one leg and then the other. He stroked the warm ducks, turned them and looked them over, examined their wet, webbed feet, their half-closed, turquoise eyes, the drops of blood on their beaks. Then, spotting the still-burning cigarette, he glanced furtively around and put it to his lips; and while he inexpertly puffed on it, squinting his eyes and coughing, he was smiling at this day of complete, unclouded happiness.

10. NIKISHKA'S MYSTERIES

1

The peasant cabins were fleeing from the forest. They had come to the seashore, and where they could go no further they stopped, frightened and huddled close together, looking with wonder at the sea...

The cabins, the izbas of the northern villages, are often indeed thus: overlooking the sea, set near one another, storybook-affective. Footsteps echo on the corduroy walkways of their narrow lanes—the sound carries, and the old women come to their windows to look out and listen... Is he bringing back a salmon? Is he going to the woods with a basket? Perhaps he's just passing by... In the season of the strange white nights it might be a young man shouting with laughter and pursuing a girl; and again everything is heard, is known, who is pursued and by whom. Those well-crafted log structures, strong and old and flanked by tall outbuildings, remember everything, know everything. A White Sea dweller, a *Pomor*, goes coasting aboard his shallop, which on these shores is known by the Karelian term *karbas*: the village sees his wide, dark sail returning and knows he went to look at his salmon trap. Other fishermen arrive in a motorboat with their harvest from the deeper waters, and the village is aware of them too, what they are bringing and the manner it was caught. An ancient of these backwoods dies: he is seen off with remnants of curious ritual read out of a hoary volume, is dropped into a sandy, sombre grave; and again the village observes it all, takes in the sobbing of the wife with appropriate discretion.

They all love Nikishka in the village. He is somehow different from everybody else: quiet, gentle; and he retains those qualities despite the fact that village-children are often such snipes, such persistent mockers. He is eight, mop-headed with light blond hair, has a pale, freckled face, large, translucent, limp ears, and his eyes are of two colours: the left is yellowish, while the right could be called turquoise. He might be looking at something, and you could take him to be a rather slow-witted little chap; then he changes his posture, and now the impression is that of a wise old-timer. Quiet, thoughtful Nikishka. He stands apart from the other children, does not play, likes to listen to adult discussions, he himself rarely joining in and then only with questions: 'And what's that? And what's that for?' He only ever becomes talkative with his father and mother. He has a fluting voice, pleasant as a reed pipe, but his laughter is in a bass register and sounds half-witted: 'Hee-hee-hee-ee!...' The children mock him, whenever something or other happens they run around him and shout: 'Nikishka-the-Silent, silent Nikishka, laugh for us, do!' Then he becomes quite annoyed and offended and goes and hides in one of the outbuildings and sits there alone, rocking and whispering something to himself. Well, sitting there is pleasant after all: in the dark, with no one coming in, one can think about all kinds of things, while all around one are keen smells of hay and wood-tar and dry seaweed...

A horse stands saddled outside Nikishka's porch. It has been chewing at some green shoots in the wicker-fence, plucking at them with its large, yellow teeth. Now, bored, it is still, with its eyes closed and its head hung low, back slumped and one hind leg bent, an occasional deep sigh flaring its nostrils. The horse stands, dozes; and the village knows already: Nikishka is ready to ride to his father out on the grounds, twenty versts along the beach; he is going at dry water, past cliffs and forest stretches.

Nikishka comes out on the porch with his mother. He has a small kitbag on his back, the cord drawn over one shoulder, across his chest and diagonally down one side, and he wears knee-boots, has a hat on his head and his mother has wound a scarf around his thin neck. The weather is cold already: October weather, perceptible when you are outside.

'Now keep to the shore, just keep close to the shore...' says the mother, 'Don't turn anywhere. Along the way you'll see the cliffs. You go past the cliffs and the path jumps out at you, and then you're nearly there. Don't miss it now; look carefully, all right? Only twenty versts. Not far.'

Nikishka says nothing, clears his nose with a loud, wet sniff, listens distractedly to his mother, clambers up on the horse. He is in the saddle, he has his feet in the stirrups, he twitches his eyebrows,

'No-o!' he utters on a rising tone.

And the horse moves off, waking up as it goes, ears swivelled back, wanting to know what this small burden is that sat on it a moment ago. They rock along past neighbouring izbas, the shod hooves clattering over the little bridges along the lane: clip-clop. The izbas end and a sprinkling of bath-huts appear. There are many of these, each with its own yard and all are different. You can see if the owner is a careful person, then the hut is a good one; if not, then the hut is not so good. And now the bath-huts have finished and the paddocks of oats are past and there comes the glint of the sea on the right. The horse steps with crunching paces on the sand and the damp seaweed. It sidles away from the sea, rolling its eyes: it does not like the sea, keeps wanting to go further to the left, away from the water. But Nikishka asserts himself, pulls on the right rein, bangs his heels against the horse's sides. The horse submits, trots onward at the very edge of the water, neck low, snorting through its nostrils.

There are ridges of stone not far offshore, and now that the tide has gone out many of them are bare and black and wet. Around them the waves break into foam, boiling and becoming white combers that roll landward and diminish at the tideline with a feeble murmur. But inshore the water is quiet, the bottom clear, fragments of mother-of-pearl flicker and disappear, transparent little waves lick gently at the sand. Sea-gulls roost on the nearer rocks, looking sleepily at the sea: they rise on their legs to take off unhurriedly when Nikishka approaches, skim smoothly just above the water, then with wings up and tail fanned they quickly drop down to settle on the water. The low sun of autumn shines with a dazzling light, and the sea shimmers beneath it and seems to belly towards its glow. Ahead, long points of land stretch far out, float on blue vapour, seem suspended above the sea.

Nikishka looks about him, his two different eyes sparkling and his lips forming a smile; he looks at the sun, at the curved, fiery sea and laughs: 'I see you there, sun. Hee-hee-hee-ee!...'

Sandpipers fly along the shore, uttering their plaintive, shrill cry. They land on swaying long legs, right at the water's edge. A wave retreats, they follow it down the wet sand; it returns, and they turn back too.

'Coolee-coolee...' Nikishka twitters, in imitation of their name, and he stops the horse to gaze at the birds, noting how trim and well-groomed they are, how their beaks look like awls.

And what may not be found on the seashore! There are red jellyfish, still wet, left by the outgoing tide, looking like bloody pastry, and there are others with four violet prickles in the centre; there are sea-stars, too, with crooked, pimply arms; and there are droppings of seagulls: long or convoluted, white and tinged with lilac. Seaweed lies in heaps at the high-water mark and is already beginning to decay with a humid, heavy odour. And then suddenly one comes across the track of bare feet! Here, the feet dragged themselves down through the sand to the edge of the water; there, they turned back towards the forest, and on the way changed course for a moment to trample around a strangely formed dark growth of driftwood that protrudes from the sand... Now, who could have been here? To what purpose?

On the left, above the beach, stretches an endless ribbon of washed-up logs, white and rinsed by the rain and by the waves, bleached by the sun, iced-over in winter and then warmed and dried again by the summer sun. Nikishka remembers hearing that many years ago on the lower Dvina a logging boom burst and all the logs that the men had collected ran down the river and they could not catch them, and afterwards the sea threw them up on the shore everywhere. There they lie to this day: no one comes to get them and they are no good to anyone, except maybe some fisherman or the odd hunter who sometimes will use bits to make a fire.

Nikishka is happy and the horse just keeps crunching along and snorting occasionally. Sometimes, without being aware of it, it stands on a jellyfish, and then driblets squirt out from under that hoof and rest unabsorbed and rounded on top of the sand, looking like fragments of some precious stone. The beach ahead is empty, it is empty behind, empty on the left and on the right. On the right is the sea, on the left the forest.

And what is there not, in the forest! In the forest there is heather, and there are many crooked pine trees, small and mean-growing trees. And there are birches too that are worryingly misshapen in that way as well. There are sweet berries: whortleberries, bilberries. And mushrooms: the butter-mushrooms are sticky, the saffron milk-caps are firm, and there are eat-'em-raw russulas with a shock of pine needles usually perched on their brittle tops. And bears go about in the forest, and other animals too. But there are no birds, only those little hazel-grouse that call to each other all the time. Old Father Sozon says: 'They've flown away, the birds, God knows why. There was a time you could just wander into the forest with a basket and come back with it full of them. But lately the birds have flown away, who knows where. Yes, God be with them, they've all gone.'

Streams run out of the forest, big ones and little ones. The big ones have bridges over them. The wood in them is rotten now and the horse sniffs at the beams, listens to the noise of the water below, takes a step, stretches its neck forward, looks back...

'No-o!' says Nikishka softly.

The horse takes another step. The sound of its passage over such bridges is dull, dead, like walking on a tomb. And the water down there is dark, the colour of strong tea. All the streams run out of marshland, there is no clear water here, they are all like that, and the sea where they come out throws a yellow scum back on the sand.

And now there is something dark up ahead, Nikishka rides nearer and a schooner grows out of the sand. The masts have gone and the keel is out of sight, sucked right down. The schooner lies on one side, deck rotted away, and sunlight plays through the gaps in her hull, so that the seaweed and sand inside are visible. There is nothing else in her. A wave approaches, covers that cargo, swirls and splashes, gurgles, bubbles, and then flows out again, the smaller streams making thin, rushing sounds as the water recedes towards the rocks.

Freedom and space are everywhere, the atmosphere is blue and tangy with sea odours, and there is no one for many versts. Sometimes the remnants of a fishing hut, old, empty and abandoned come into sight. Moss covers the walls, the windows are tiny, just big enough to poke a head through, the decrepit roof has settled and the hut itself sags on one side, while the opposite side has lifted and its windows look up at the empty sky; the racks for drying the nets have collapsed and everything is disintegrating. Only the cross, the old, traditional cross of the White Sea coast, black, eight-angled, protrudes awesomely: a guard put there for eternity, never to be relieved, a frightening thing—don't look, don't look, and pass on quickly!

But Nikishka is not really frightened. He knows wood-elves live in those old shelters, and they are a peaceful, melancholy race. They get dismal, having to sleep the way they do during the day. Now as they sleep they hear Nikishka riding past and they wake and they yawn and come to peer cautiously out of the little windows. One has a black beard, another a grey beard, a third—well, you can't tell what sort it is. They will be muttering in their own way among themselves, wondering: 'Now, where's that Nikishka riding to today?'

Over yonder, there is something black in the sand, a piece of driftwood, or maybe a dark, protruding boulder. The horse has seen it already from a distance and has pricked up its ears, pulls its head sideways and tries to deviate, frightened.

'You better not pull to that side,' says Nikishka to the horse. 'It's nothing. It's only some tree that grew and now it's gone rotten and finished up in the sand. See, it's just driftwood. See, it's nothing to worry you.'

The horse listens attentively, twitches its hide, snorts—and carries Nikishka onwards; and so they continue, further and further. The horse has heeded Nikishka: all the animals listen to him.

Now the cliffs appear. Steep, black, their walls constantly breaking off into the sea; where there has been a slip and a ledge has formed, little pines and birches stick glued there by their roots, looking down at the sea, awaiting woe. And under the cliffs there is a rocky layer and the lines of rocks creep down to drink at the sea, and rocks are piled on top of other rocks in surprising ways. The horse goes forward increasingly carefully, sniffs, selects where to place its hooves.

It had been going and going—and suddenly it baulks, will not go forward or back or to the side, won't go anywhere! Nikishka gets down, takes the reins in his hand, walks among the wet boulders. The horse stretches its neck forward, flattens down its ears, skips after Nikishka—then suddenly quails, its shoes clattering on the stone, legs trembling! And the waves roll noisily under it: shoo-ooo!... they roll in; sssssssss!... they retreat; then, shoo-ooo!... they roll in again.

No, the horse can't possibly go on! It is in the grip of its imagination: to the right yawns bottomless water whence the waves rush and thunder, and underfoot there is this submerged stone—there is no way to retreat, no escape! It stops in horror, makes snorting noises, bares its yellow teeth. Nikishka is displeased, tugs at the reins, pulls with all his strength, 'No-o!' he cries. The horse does not move, looks at Nikishka with smoky-violet, rolling eyes.

Nikishka feels ashamed. He goes up to the horse and strokes its neck and whispers something soothing and quiet to it. The horse listens to Nikishka's whispers, it listens to the sound of the sea, pants so that its flanks heave. Where to go? To the right: the sea. To the left: the cliffs. Behind: the stone. In front: the stone... It braces itself and prances forward... and the regular clatter of its shoes begins again.

At last they are out of the agglomeration of stones, Nikishka leads the horse to a boulder, he clambers up into the saddle, and the hoofs crunch again on the sand and the seaweed. The land ahead sends out repeated promontories like long, grasping fingers. Nikishka rides towards one—a distant blue point—comes to it, curious to know what is behind it—and behind it is another point further ahead again, protruding out into sea, and behind that, another and another, and so on without end.

Now they have come to the beginning of a path: undetected by Nikishka the horse turned onto it by itself. And that leads Nikishka into thought, and he begins pondering while he looks about him: he wants to learn the mystery that will make known and explain to him at one instant the meaning of all that he sees. Yes, if you don't know that mystery, that secret, then well may you look, but you will look sadly; you may look with your eyes, listen with your ears, smell even, but... And as he gazes around, mesmerised, Nikishka falls deeper into dreamy musing, while the path goes further and further into the forest, and after the sea everything becomes silent and the light grows golden. Under the horse's feet the tongues of light are yellow, red, orange, and there is a smell of moss all around and of mushrooms. The milk-caps are amber here and they are everywhere, and there are coral milk-caps too. The whole forest glows, only the fir trees are green. And look how the heather spreads in flat little islands!—everything is spellbinding. And on the ground, boulders poke up dark-brown through their overgrowth of moss, and deformed firs and birches stand apart among them, all grey and twisted into unnatural contortions, strangely like the writhing arms of bare apple trees.

Oh, if only someone would come to meet him! But no one comes, Nikishka passes alone through an inert forest. Will he come to some habitation soon? There is no one to ask, the pines and firs are silent, the stones look at him enigmatically from out of the ground, all now is stones and dampness, there is nothing but the path, trodden deep, an old and solitary route. And Nikishka remembers the old woman in the village telling how a long time ago strange people were going through a dead forest; among them were fugitives and sick people and people who had met misfortunes and known mortifications, all kinds of people they were, and they were all going to one place by many remote paths, they were making for one shining abode, the Solovetsky Monastery. But where that monastery was, Nikishka never heard: somewhere over where the sun sets, but who knows where.

And suddenly, in the midst of this hush, this dead silence, this conversation of the lifeless, a song sounds. There is the tapping of an axe, and a faint, irregularly-borne smell of smoke. The horse, ears pricked up, gives a ringing neigh and trot-trot-trots forward—it has sniffed a place where there are people! Nikishka rides out of the forest, and there ahead is a little log hut, his father's fishing cabin. Everything about it is new, everything is strong and well put together, and from the flue rises a thread of smoke. Nets dry on racks, there is a smell of fish, a karbas is on rollers, its black sides gleaming with the gloss of oil.

There on the path sits his father. He is putting the finishing touches to a stern-oar, whittling the last shavings from it with an axe, and he is singing.

2

He sees Nikishka and gets up: a giant in high boots, dressed in oiled-canvas overalls, a knife at his belt. His hands are red, his face is brown and bearded and the beard is bleached quite fair. Under his bushy brows his eyes are sharp and attentive.

'Well here's my wee son who's arrived!' he says gaily. 'Just so, I had a dream. Well, how are they going over there, back home? All alive?'

'All alive!' says Nikishka, and he gets down from the horse, rocks, stamps his feet. 'The chairman let Uncle Ivan have the horse, mama sent me, I went, I rode and rode, I'm ridden to bits, my back hurts.'

'Ah, you're our mighty one!' says the father, and his huge hand strokes Nikishka's shock of flaxen hair, 'I heard a noise of someone coming, but who it was I couldn't mind—and it turns out it's our Nikishka! And you weren't frightened to come?'

'No, it wasn't anything! I saw birds, I saw mushrooms, I talked with the horse. He's a wise horse. Here, here's this, mamma packed it.' Nikishka disburdens himself of the kitbag. 'What were the stones looking at me for? Do they think too? I bet they turn over at night when they're not sleeping comfortably; just look how you get sore after lying on one side for a while!'

'Stones, eh?...' the father pauses to think, 'Stones, I would guess, are alive too. Everything's alive!'

'And do you know what the birches are saying?'

'Well, they talk in their own way, in birch-fashion, you bet. You've got to know their language or else how are you going to know?'

'Where's Uncle Ivan?'

'Uncle Ivan's gone to the next fishing ground, out Kerzhenka way. Some of the fishermen went past in a dory a while back and they took him with them. They've got a bath there and we don't have one, so uncle Ivan went there.'

'When is he going back to the village?'

'He's going back to the village tomorrow, to get treatment. His foot, see, got all battered. He'll go back on the horse next dry water.'

'And what about me?'

'You'll stay with me. Do you want to? We'll catch salmon.'

'I'll stay!'

'There you are. I'll go and unsaddle the horse.'

The father goes, catches the horse, unsaddles it, and with a length of rope brought out from the hut he tethers it to a birch tree so that the horse cannot wander away into the forest.

Nikishka goes into the hut. There is a strong smell of fish there. In the stove the coals are smouldering, almost out, and on the table there is bread and there are bowls and spoons. The walls are covered in posters, there is a pile of newspapers on a shelf, the hut is clean and swept, and mittens and foot-bindings and a pair of trousers hang on a drying-line. Nikishka goes out, goes all around the hut, looks into a shed. The shed is open, it does not get closed, there is no one to close it against.

Nikishka just wants to go into the shed to sit there and think everything over, all that happened today—when, lo, he sees that there is something alive in the shed, something glimpsed ginger-red, like a dim flame! A pair of eyes glint out like the flush of that corner of the sky where the sun is setting. A dog! Big, shaggy.

Nikishka squats on his heels, peering all-eyed at the dog. He looks around quickly—the father is out of sight. He talks to it.

'Adyaaa!... Oorrrr... goo-goorrrr... gam!'

The dog remains silent, sniffs, cocks its head sideways, one ear up, the other hanging down, tail thumping—it likes Nikishka. Having talked enough, Nikishka comes out of the shed, the dog trotting after him as if it had known him for ever. He looks up at his father: how tall he is, how sunburnt, the light playing around his massive figure is like forest vapour irradiated by the sun.

'Well then, me lad!' says the father merrily, 'We'll go after the salmon shortly! Just wait till I finish the oar.'

Nikishka goes away a little, lies down on the warm sand, and the dog comes and lies next to him, panting rapidly. He closes his eyes, and everything seems to rock. He seems to be still on the horse, the seagulls are taking wing above the sea, the cliffs are beside him, he is in the forest, here are the black crosses, the elves peering out of the fishing hut mutter: 'Look at that! It's Nikishka going to his father to catch salmon. He's carrying tea and sugar!' And someone is quietly singing, the voice sometimes carrying louder, then soft again, like a lullaby; and the sun shines and the waves keep saying shoo-ooo!... coming in, and sssssss!... going out; there is a strong, heady smell of rotting seaweed, and the sandpipers cry: 'Pee-peeee!... Pee-peeee!...'

Nikishka lies there, not quite asleep, not quite dozing. The sand is warm, the dog is warm, it looks at him with its fiery eyes and says to him: 'Nikishka, let's go into the forest!'

'I'm going out to watch for salmon!' Nikishka replies.

And the dog keeps urging, 'Let's go into the forest, I'll tell you secrets: what the birches whisper about. We'll listen to what the stones think, we'll know.' Nikishka is drawn and yet in doubt, whether to go to the sea or the forest; but now his father comes up to him with the new oar in his hand.

'Get up, lad—we're ready.'

Nikishka stands and goes with his father towards the water. And the sea is happy and glints and flashes, plays, grows bluer; now it rises, beck-oning, now it spreads itself flat again. His father presses his chest against the karbas and pushes it into the water: he has put Nikishka in the stern and he himself is pounding through the water in his boots. Now he is in the boat too and has taken the side oars, giving Nikishka the stern oar to dabble over the back, to scull with as best he can. They have heaved off the beach, turned, and are away, rocking up-down, up-down. The shore sways, the dog left on the shore runs along it then back, and the father rows powerfully and the water splashes past the cheeks of the boat, burst-ing sideways in sprays.

They coast carefully up to the trap and tie to a pole. The father stands up and looks with a keen eye over the side, down at the secret place, the trap. Nothing there.

'Empty,' he whispers, unperturbed.

Nikishka looks around: it is quiet here, a faint breeze blows evenly, the sun glows, the sea is blinding, the shore is very far away and dark, petering out at its extremities. It seems to Nikishka that he has been here before, has sat here long ago, for years, waiting for the salmon, thinking of some-thing... Or did he dream it all, once?

'Tide's starting to come in,' says the father; then in a singsong to him-self: 'Rising-in-its-own-good-time.'

'Blue skies sheer...' Nikishka murmurs the adult lore quietly, 'sea-bot-tom clear.'

'Aye, how else! She likes a clear bottom, that one. Doesn't want rocks or weed down there. She likes to go along the bottom at half tide. High tide or dry water don't suit, doesn't like them, and so she comes at half tide.'

'And is that—there—a mallet?'

'That? It's a mallet, sure. To hit her with. She's a powerful one, strong, you'll never get her up otherwise, you'd get into a stew, and so we hit her with the mallet.'

'And what if she jumps away?'

'Oh, how? You see, we've got the trap for that. You see that strip down there? That's the net. Those are the walls, all staked down and with draw-cords. And below again... look, down there, look!'

Nikishka hangs over the side, screens his two-coloured eyes with his hands, looks into the water, into its depths, sees greenish specks of light on the bottom, sees the thin mesh of the net.

'See? Underneath, that's also the net, see—that's the bottom of the trap. The walls and the net at the bottom are the trap, and over there is the gate—yonder where them two poles stick up, that's the gate. She comes, goes inside the gate and into the trap, and that's where we hit her, in the trap. We row to the gate, block the way out, lift up the net and hit her.

'I know,' says Nikishka, remembering something.

'I tell you this and I tell you that, and you know,' says the father nodding. 'You're the boy that knew everything.'

'Why do the other kids tease me?'

'They're just little dopes, don't listen to them. They like mischief, silly tricks, while you're good and quiet and clever, and so they tease you. Don't listen to them, you're smarter than any of them.'

'That's because I think a lot.'

'Well now, don't you think too much; and on the other hand don't think too little; when you want to think, think, and when you don't want to, don't think, that's all.'

'Well, I'm thinking now: where does all the water in the sea go when it's ebb tide, before it comes back at high tide? Rivers flow into the sea, but the sea—where does it flow to?'

'The sea? H'm...' The father rubs his beard, looks towards the horizon, considers. 'The water, see, goes out at the mouth of the White Sea, then into the Arctic Ocean. And from that ocean it spills into the other oceans.'

'Are there many other oceans?'

'Many, lad; and all kinds of countries, too, on the land.'

'And have you been to them?'

'I have! To Italy and to France, and I've been to Norway, when I was a sailor.'

'What's Italy like?'

'Italy now? Italy, lad, is nice. It's hot there, lots of sun, all kinds of fruit grow there, sweet and nice to eat. Everybody's dark from the sun there, they walk around without many clothes, and there's no winter at all.'

'None at all?'

'It's as I say: there's no snow, no frosts, nothing. Sun the whole year long.'

'That's really nice,' Nikishka says, and sighs: 'Oh, I'd like to go and live there.'

'And you will,' says the father. 'When you grow up you can go and study to become a captain, then they'll give you a big ship at Archangel and you can shoot down by Norway, go around the land and straight into the Mediterranean Sea.'

'Were you a captain?'

'No, I was a sailor. I've been everything: a lumberjack, a hunter, a fisherman, a fur trapper...'

'Oh, look over there! What's that?'

'Where?'

'There, it looks like...'

'Oh! That's a seal. A seal, lad, who's come to take a look at us.'

'I know. And where does he live?'

'He lives in the sea. In the daytime he's busy with the fish, and at night he swims ashore and sleeps on the rocks in hidden places and on shifting sandbanks.'

'How come they club them? They don't eat them.'

'His skin is good, and he's got a lot of fat. It's easy to club him, he's silly: people can creep up to him and pick him off with a rifle. There's all kinds who go after him: another time they'll go after him in a karbas, another time on an ice-breaker. Nowadays, mainly on an ice-breaker.'

'And in the dark weather, is it frightening on a karbas?'

'Oy, it's frightful. When you grow up I'll take you trapping, then you'll get to know our wee northern sea. Yonder, there where you see those glints...' the father extends his hand, 'where the sun stands, there's a tiny island, Zhizhgin it's called: the seals gather there. The fishermen on this coast always make a bit of their living out of Zhizhgin. There's a trappers' cabin there on a sandbank; the fishermen come in on their karbases, they stay there, live on bread, waiting for the change in the weather. In good weather they run into the sea, shoot the young seals, sleep at night on the ice. If it happens that the dark weather arrives—why, then it takes you off! It takes you away, it does. You shout yourself hoarse, say goodbye to it all. The lucky ones escape if the wind turns round or drops; others are driven out of the straits—past the Kanin Nose it takes them, yes, out into the ocean. And out there a plane might spot them, otherwise...'

'Salmon!' whispers suddenly Nikishka.

'Hah!' The father gets up and kneels over the bow, looks down at the trap. 'And you're right! Well God be with us—I'll be lifting the net, you keep the karbas steady there, don't let it move!'

He quickly unfastens the boat and rows it around the trap, alongside the gate. There, he bends and reaches down, his arms deep in the water, while Nikishka holds tightly to a pole. Down in the depths, something is dashing about silently, something huge, powerfully alive. The poles shake and the net-lines stretched between them hum. The nylon net rustles as Nikishka's father begins pulling it in. Nikishka, neck craned, looks down. The space left to the salmon diminishes. Now it has leapt twice out of the water! The father holds a length of gathered net in one hand and gropes behind him with the other for the mallet. Finding it, he raises it, waiting for the moment to strike. But the salmon thrashes about in an even greater frenzy, more powerfully, rams with great thuds against the side of the karbas, will not yield and drenches the two in the boat. Now the whole length of the salmon is visible as in a bowl of suds—if the fish were able to cry out it would shriek in terror! With a wide swing the father strikes down on its head and instantly it all ends, the salmon goes passive and turns on its side. The father hooks his fingers in its gills and with some effort pulls it into the karbas and flops it with a heavy slap down between Nikishka's feet. Nikishka looks at its grown-still eyes. It is still alive, its gills still quiver, its scales contract: a big, silver creature with a dark back, up-turned lower mandible and large, black eyes.

The father lets drop the net back into the water, pushes the karbas away from the trap, wipes his face on his sleeve and his fish-smelling hands on his trousers. He looks happily at the salmon and at Nikishka.

'That's the way we deal with her!'

Nikishka sits above the fish, pale and bewildered. The karbas is tied again to a pole and resumes its rocking: up-down. The father is silent and with his strong red hands laid on his knees rests.

Nikishka becomes a little used to the dead salmon, and then remembering his father's remarks about the seals he says: 'No, I guess I'll be a captain... I don't want to club the seals; they are gentle...'

'Yep, a captain would be the shot,' agrees the father, and peers up at the sky. 'Look at those clouds coming in now, the sun's getting covered. We'll go back soon. Captain's all right. Or engineer: that's good too.'

'What does an engineer do?'

'How, what's he do? He builds things. Now that would be a fine thing, yes, if you were to come back here an engineer. Then we would build an asphalt road along this coast together, and you'd make moorings, there'd be lights burning, cars whizzing about...'

Nikishka falls into thought and gazes at the distant shore: how dark it is, how empty of people! 'All right,' he decides, 'I'll be an engineer.'

'There you are! Now, we'll just sit for a while and then—home. I've got a bit of fish back there; just this morning at dry water there was some fry in the trammel. We'll cook up a fish soup and we'll drink tea and then we'll have a good sleep. But now let's not talk any more, we'll just look out for the salmon.'

Everything is silent: the sea is silent, the karbas rocks noiselessly, the shore is silent, not a sound comes to them from there. The low sun has gone behind clouds, everything has gone darker, mournful. And no one is to be seen anywhere: all is emptiness and undwelled. The seagulls fly about; back on the shore, in the forest, the hazel-grouse are quiet in their concealed places. In the karbas rock two fishermen and a salmon asleep.

3

The stove hums and crackles, the hut is warm, while on the other side of the windows dusk is falling. The father has lit the lamp and with a bucket of water between his legs sits gutting and scaling fish for the soup: spotted cod; dark, hunchbacked spiny sculpin; long-bodied navaga. And Nikishka dozes: he has talked himself out, has listened and rocked himself to tiredness and is now drowsy and his thoughts float God only knows where.

The weather is changing rapidly. A high south-easterly is blowing, the sea is noisy, everything is growing greenish out to the west, the sky above takes on an azure tone, the air is like glass; and now arrives an incredibly clear evening of stars studded among the inconstant lights of heaven.

The ginger dog sleeps near the stove, occasionally jerking in its sleep. Nikishka rouses himself to listen with half an ear to his father, who is talking about something, talking in a soft voice, a voice long known to Nikishka and familial. He talks of fish and the sea, of boats, the village; he talks about winds: the north-easterly that rises at midnight, the littoral north-westerly, the prankster south-westerly, the scant and impoverishing south-easterly... Big father, bent low over the bucket; his hair, which is the same fair colour as Nikishka's, hangs over his eyes, and his beard has flared out. He sits motionless, only his hands move, the knife glints, the fish fall glinting into the bucket, his shadow quivers on the wall. He talks on in a low voice, while Nikishka closes his eyes and sees the land he has grown up in: the sea, the forest, lakes; he sees the sun, the silent birds, the variety of strange animals; and it seems to him that he is just on the point of learning some secret, something known to no one else, that a whispered word will quietly sound and the silence will break and every-thing about him will speak to him, everything will instantly become under-standable to him. But no word comes, the mystery is not revealed, and Nikishka hears his father's even tone and sees and hears many other things in his abstraction.

He sees what the ginger dog is dreaming: it is dreaming of the forest, and of terrible beasts, unknown, monstrous, that fall upon it from all sides. It runs, barks, horrified; only one thing can save it—Nikishka! Ni-kishka hears the stones beginning to murmur among themselves, hears the sea-noise grow. The trees in the forest are shaking, someone is shout-ing—he sees in a storm his father rocking on an ice-floe, calling dismally! A gigantic, fierce salmon appears, swimming shoreward along the bottom, and on that clear bottom come behind it from deeper waters other salmon: they are all seeking, pulled by a strange attraction, the secret place of his father's trap...

The logs in the stove hum and crackle. His father goes outside to tip the water out of the bucket and is audible on the other side of the wall as he gathers an armful of firewood. He comes back into the cabin, the wood rattles down by the stove, the ginger dog jumps up, Nikishka shudders and opens his eyes.

'Asleep, lad?' the father bends over him. 'Then you haven't seen what's happening outside—the lights are here! Some show! Go look!'

Nikishka goes out. It is dark and cold now, a damp wind blows. The sun has gone down long ago, the forest is invisible, but overhead a gemlike stain extends far across among the stars. It looks as if a band of the west-ern cloud that had earlier been illuminated by the setting sun drifted loose and floated by some breath-taking process directly above the earth. And as Nikishka gazes at it with his head tilted back the cloud slowly and irreg-ularly extends, swells in the middle and bends like an opalescent rainbow spanning the sky from east to west. The door of the hut bangs open and the dog runs out to Nikishka and behind it comes his father, and he too lifts up his face.

Vague milky shadows begin to pass across the cloud of colours and, where overlaid, it alters and acquires an increasingly denser and denser blue. It seems then to Nikishka as if the cloud strains, tries to gather to its centre remnant flame-like ruby tints in semblance of the departed sun. The colours shimmer more and more strongly, radiance pours down from a narrowing arc... but the effort is unavailing, it is all going out, and large, blue-dim and dismal shadows wholly overflow the bridge of light.

Nikishka looks on, the father looks and is silent, the dog looks and is silent too. The horse is silent, standing asleep by the birch tree, everything is still; only the sea, a moment ago bright with the heavenly fire, murmurs and murmurs.

Now the lights have gone out and Nikishka returns into the warm cabin, gets up on the bed and draws his feet under him; the dog lies down by the stove; the father puts a kettle of fish and the teapot on the stove.

Nikishka will soon be sleeping and he will dream wondrous dreams. The village will surround him with its cabins whose windows are eyes; the forest will come to him, and the stones and the cliffs; the horse will appear, the ginger dog, seagulls will glide, sandpipers will run on their rapid, twig-like legs, and the salmon will emerge from the sea. All things will come to him and will stand waiting and gaze at him, waiting in silence for his assenting sign, to reveal to him wordlessly together the secrets of their unitary mute soul.

11. ARCTURUS THE HUNTER
In memory of M. M. Prishvin

1

How he arrived is still unclear: he just appeared that spring and began to be noticed about the town. He was not a nuisance, nor did he show any desire to attach himself to anyone or to fawn on anyone, he appeared to be, as one might say, a free agent.

Some said that the gypsies who had passed through at that time had abandoned him. Strange people, gypsies: come early spring, off they go on those treks of theirs. Some nowadays go by train, others on boats or rafts, a third kind still plod along the roads in horse-drawn wagons, levelling unfriendly looks at the cars that shoot past next to them. People with southern blood they are, yet they seem to be found in the most desolate northern corners. They suddenly set up camp outside a town, are seen about the markets for a few days, fingering the local merchandise, haggling. They go from house to house, tell fortunes, quarrel, laugh. Swarthy folk, handsome, with rings in their ears and bright clothing. And then they disappear as unexpectedly as they came, and the town sees them no more. Others will come, but these first ones will not be seen there again. The world is wide and gypsies dislike returning to a place they have been to once.

And so, many in the town were persuaded that the gypsies had left him behind in spring. But there were those who thought that he had floated in on the ice during the spring thaw. He had stood there, black among the blue-white medley of broken ice, motionless in the middle of all that general progress, while above him flew the migrating swans, calling, as they passed, that metallic cry of theirs: 'Clink-clank!'

Everyone waits for the swans with some anxiety, and when they fly over at dawn, when they rise on the horizon and pass over, at one with the force which moves the waters in the spring floods, and, passing, issue that great cheery call, 'Clink-clank!', people follow them with their eyes, and then the blood begins to course faster in the hearts of the watchers, who know now that spring has come at last.

The ice came down the river, soughing and crackling, the swans cried, and there he stood on a floe, with his tail between his legs: intent, unsure, nosing the air and listening to what was happening around him. When his floe neared the bank, he grew fretful, then leapt, clumsily pitching into the water. But he clambered quickly up the bank, shook himself, and was soon lost behind the piles of lumber stacked all about that area.

Well, one way or another he arrived that spring, when the days were filled with the sparkle of sunshine, the tinkling of the thaw's many rivulets, the smell of bark; and he stayed on in the town.

One can only conjecture about his past. He would probably have been born on a bit of straw under someone's porch. Evidently his mother was a pure-bred bitch in the line of those hunting hounds they have in Kostroma: that is to say, dogs relatively low in stature and long-bodied. With distended belly and her time come, she would have crept under that porch to fulfil in concealment her great maternal role. Those above would have called to her, but she would not have responded, would not have come out to eat, remaining completely self-involved, sensing that at any moment would occur something which was the most important thing in the world for her, more important even than hunting and than people— and people, mind you, to such a breed of dog are sovereigns and gods, to be promptly, with alacrity obeyed!

He was born blind, as all pups are, and immediately his mother licked him all over and put him close to her warm belly, while that belly still strained with birth-spasms; and while he lay there, becoming accustomed to breathing, a row of brothers and sisters kept being added to beside him. They wriggled weakly, mewled, tried to dog-whine, and they were all like him: smoky in colour, bare-bellied, with short, trembling tails. Soon it was all over, each pup had found a teat and grown quiet, and there would have been nothing more to hear beyond the gentle sounds of snuffling and sucking and the panting of the mother. Such was the beginning of their lives.

In due course, their eyelids parted and they learnt with huge excitement that a greater world lay out there than the one they had been aware of up to that moment. His eyes opened too, but he was never allowed to see that world. He was blind, wall-eyed, a thick grey film covered his pupils. A hard and bitter life lay ahead of him, and indeed it would have been a terrifying life if he had known that he was blind; but he did not know that, it was not given him to understand his state, and he accepted his life the way he had received it.

For some reason it happened that he was not drowned. Killing a helpless pup, useless to anyone, would have been of course the kindest way to deal with it; instead he was left to live and to suffer such ordeals as prematurely hardened and inured to pain both his body and his spirit.

He had no owner to give him a home and feed him and show concern towards him as one does with a friend. He became a rootless dog-vagrant, morose, clumsy, distrustful—his mother, once she had weaned him, lost all interest in him, as she did also in his siblings. He learned to howl like a wolf, with that long-drawn, dismal, melancholy sound they make; he was dirty, often afflicted with some ailment or other; he scratched about among the rubbish behind eating-places, receiving kicks and tubs of dirty water flung over him, as did other such homeless and hungry dogs. At those times he could not escape with any speed, for his legs, strong as they were, were essentially useless to him. It seemed to him as if he was always running into things that were sharp or cruelly hard. When he fought with other dogs, and that happened very often indeed in the course of his life, he never saw his enemies and could only throw himself and snap at the sound of their breathing, their snarling or squealing, or at the soft thudding of the other dog's trampling pads; and then, often enough, he lunged and bit at thin air.

We cannot known by what manner of name his mother distinguished him—for surely every mother, even among dogs, knows her offspring by some natal name of her own idiom? But be that as it may, as far as people were concerned he had no name and seemed a totally ephemeral thing. It is uncertain whether he would have remained to live very long in the town or gone away or simply died in some gully—perhaps, if one can imagine it, reproaching in his last moments of misery some canine seat of providence?—but a man became involved in his fate, and that changed everything.

2

That summer I was living there, in that same small northern town set on the bank of a river. White steamers passed along the river, and dirty brown barges, there were long log-rafts and broad-beamed karbases with tar-stained sides. There was a jetty that smelled of sacking and rope, damp-rot and fish: roaches were prevalent in the local waters. Rarely was it that anyone moored at that jetty except occasionally workers from the collective farms outside the town, coming in on market days, or cheerless officials dressed in grey raincoats, arriving from the regional capital on some business with the sawmill.

Surrounding the town were low hills, gently sloping and covered with the trees of a forest whose huge, pristine expanse was being logged in the upper reaches of the river, whence timber floated downstream. There were stretches of meadow-land in that forest, and solitary lakes with great ancient pines growing on their shores, pines whose branches never ceased whispering quietly, unless a cold humid wind from the Arctic Ocean happened to be blowing, harrying clouds over the land, and then the pines buzzed threateningly and their cones volleyed down on the ground.

I rented an upper room in an old house in the outskirts of the town. The owner was a doctor, a taciturn sort of chap, perennially busy. He had originally lived there with a large family, but his two sons had been killed at the front, his wife had died, and the last child, a daughter, remained now permanently in Moscow. So the doctor lived alone and spent his time treating children, his main patients. He had one oddity: he loved to sing and would with the thinnest of falsettos draw out and lose himself in the sweet, high notes of all sorts of arias. There were three rooms below, but he seldom entered them, preferring to have his meals on the veranda and to sleep there as well, and so those rooms remained gloomy and smelled of dust and pharmaceuticals and old wallpaper.

The window of my room opened on a wilderness of a garden, over-grown with currant bushes, raspberries and burdock, and nettles grew against the fences. In the morning the sparrows were lively outside my window, and clouds of thrushes swooped down on the currants; but the doctor was not concerned, and he never picked the berries. Sometimes a neighbour's fowls flew up on the fence and with them the flock's rooster, whose crowing was like a general proclamation to the neighbourhood; neck stretched, tail quivering, he would perch there, peering intently about the yard, until finally unable to restrain himself longer he glided down, followed closely one after another by his hens; and they would all set to, scratching the soil under the neglected bushes. There were cats there too, prowling in the burdocks or settling themselves in ambush with an eye on the sparrows.

After I had lived in the town some two weeks I had still not got used to those quiet streets, with their boardwalk footpaths and grass growing be-tween the planks, nor to the creak of wooden stairs, nor, at night, to the occasional hoot of a passing steamer.

It was an unusual town. The white nights lasted there almost the whole summer. Its river-front and streets were peaceful, contemplative, so that you could hear the clear, staccato tapping of feet when the odd night-shift worker passed by, and sleepers might be woken at any time by the foot-steps and laughter of couples. It felt as if the walls of the houses were sensible of, and the town itself attentive to, the life of each inhabitant. At night our yard smelled of the currants and of dew, while from the veranda came the gentle snoring of the doctor, and out on the river the engine of a launch muttered, and the nasal call of its hooter would cross to me, re-cumbent and listening: 'Doo-doooo!...'

About that time, a newcomer joined the company at our house. It hap-pened this way.

Returning one day from his round, the doctor saw the blind dog sitting trembling among some lumber, a rope-end hanging from his neck. The doctor had seen him before, but now he stopped and looked him over musingly, made smacking, dog-calling noises with his lips, whistled. Failing all, he took hold of the rope and pulled the dog home. There, he washed him with soap and warm water and fed him. As was the dog's wont, he flinched and quivered as he ate, his tail down. He ate greedily, choking in his hurry. His head and ears were covered in pale scars.

'Well, off you go now!' said the doctor once the dog had had his fill, and he nudged him towards the edge of the veranda. But he would not go: he just stood there, shivering.

'H'm...' muttered the doctor, and he sat down in his rocking chair.

Evening arrived, the sky dimmed but did not darken completely and the major stars came out. The hound lay on the veranda floor, dozing. He was very thin, his ribs were visible under the hide, as was his spine, and the shoulder blades protruded sharply. From time to time he opened those lifeless eyes, pricked up his ears and swivelled his head about, sniffing at odours; then he dropped his head on his paws and those eyes closed again. The doctor, at a loss, sat looking at him and rocked on in his chair, considering what he might call the dog. What to call it?—why, was it not better to get rid of it immediately, before it was too late? What use was a dog to him? In this reflective mood he happened to look up, and there low on the horizon he saw the blue glimmer of a large star.

'Arcturus...' he murmured to himself, and the dog twitched his ears and opened his eyes.

'Arcturus!' said the doctor again, and his heart began to beat faster. The dog lifted his head and made an uncertain movement with his tail.

'Arctur! Arctur! Here boy!' the doctor called happily, immediately employing a confident and masterly tone. The dog got up, approached, and carefully nudged his nose into the doctor's knee. The doctor laughed and put his hand on the dog's head... and so, that unspoken name once known to his mother vanished and the dog received a new one given him by a man.

Now, dogs are all different, like people. There are beggarly dogs, living on what scraps they can pick up, there are free-spirited dour tramps, there are silly hysterics, forever yapping. Some dogs are self-abasing pleaders for any mite of attention, ready to wriggle up to anybody who whistles. Such slavish fawners will writhe up to you, tail fanning, only to tear off with a panicky squeal if hit or simply waved at. I have seen staunchly devoted dogs, meek ones, capricious ones, swanks, stoics, sycophants, distant dogs, crafty dogs, and dogs empty of any trait. Arcturus was unlike any of them. The feeling which that dog had towards his master was unusual, it was lofty—why, it was downright poetic! It was a feeling of love possibly exceeding love of life: pure and only seldom revealed in its perfection.

There were moments when the doctor was in a bad humour or indifferent, and often enough he smelled disagreeably of eau-de-Cologne; but in general he was kind to Arcturus, and then the dog glowed with affection for him: his fur seemed at those times to turn to fine wool, his body would tingle with pleasure, and on such occasions, had he been another dog, he might have leapt in the air and run barking around and around, half-choking with happiness. But no, Arcturus remained composed, ears limp, tail still, placid body at peace, while his heart beat quickly and hard. When his master began belabouring him with hearty thumps, began to tickle and stroke him, laughing all the while his broken-winded chuckle—that was very heaven! His master's voice on those occasions—drawn out or sharp, bubbling or a whisper—was like the sound of water and the rustle of trees.

Or else perhaps it was like no other sound; and yet that voice seemed to set off glimmers, vague odours, as a falling raindrop sets quivering the water in a pool, inciting something which Arcturus felt had always been there, had been there so long that it was impossible to know when or where it had originated. Probably, this happy sensation came closest to that he had known when as a blind puppy he suckled at his mother.

3

I soon had occasion to be well acquainted with the life of Arcturus, and then I discovered much that was curious. I think now that the hound had somehow become aware that there was something incomplete in his being. On appearance, he was a fully-grown animal with powerful legs, a dark back and gingerish shadings on his stomach and muzzle. Big and strong for his age, nevertheless all his movements bore signs of hesitancy and strain, and his nose, his whole body, expressed a confused interrogation. He knew very well that all other creatures around him were freer and swifter than he was. They ran quickly and confidently, walked smoothly and firmly, never crashed to the ground or knocked into things. Just by their sound, the steps of those others were different from his own: he himself always moved carefully, slowly and in a somewhat twisted attitude, so that he might lead as much as possible with one or the other of his shoulders. Innumerable objects became obstacles to his passage, whereas hens, pigeons, other dogs, sparrows, cats and people and many other creatures went up steps smoothly, jumped ditches, turned into alleys, flew away and disappeared into regions he could have no inkling of. An unending state of uncertainty and caution were his lot: I never saw him walk or run freely, without concern and quickly, unless it was perhaps on a wide road or a meadow or on the familiar veranda of our house. And if he had acquired understanding of animals and people, and could relate to them to some extent, then cars, tractors, motorcycles and bicycles were totally incomprehensible and terrifying. Steamers and launches excited curiosity at first, but once he had accepted that they would always remain an unsolved mystery, he took no further notice of them. And of course he could have no interest in aeroplanes.

But if he had no sight, then as far as the sense of smell went no other dog could approach Arcturus. The hound gradually learned all the odours of the town and would orient himself unfailingly by them, and there was never an instance of his becoming lost and not finding his way home. Yes, every single thing had a smell: there were innumerable smells, each one declaring itself to the dog almost as a reverberation, a sound. Every object had its unique aroma: some unpleasant, others bland, a third, delightful. Arcturus need only raise his muzzle and sniff in the direction from which the wind came, to immediately identify rubbish heaps, slop pails, wooden houses, stone houses, fences and sheds, people, horses, birds—all as precisely as if they were seen.

By the river, behind the depot, there was a reef of grey stone seeming to grow out of the ground, and that was a thing Arcturus particularly liked to sniff all over. The stone itself was not especially interesting, but its cracks and pores long held the most amazing and unexpected odours, odours that appeared and remained for weeks sometimes, when only a strong wind might blow them away eventually. Trotting by it, Arcturus would inevitably turn sharply towards it and begin a long investigation, snuffling and growing excited, leaving and returning again to add in his mind some new detail of knowledge about that stone.

And another thing: he could hear the minutest of sounds, such as would pass any of us unnoticed. He would wake up at night, raise his eyelids, prick up his ears and listen; and he would hear every rustle for kilometres around: the zing of mosquitoes, the buzz from a wasp's nest in the attic, a mouse scratching in the yard, a cat treading softly on the roof of a shed. And the house was not soundless either, or lifeless, as it was for us; for it lived, it creaked, hummed and cracked, it trembled imperceptibly during cold nights, the dew-run from its roof trickling into a down-pipe fell with infrequent but sensible drops onto a flat stone on the ground beneath it. Then, from below us and far away, came to him the faint lap of the river, and from the boom by the sawmill the sound that densely-crowded floating logs made when they rubbed together. There was the thin squeak of rowlocks—someone was crossing the river in a dingy!—and then, really distantly, from the surrounding villages, roosters crowed weakly in invisible farmyards. Yes, this was a level of life unseen and unheard by people, but familiar and comprehendible to him.

And he had another quality: he never whined or came whimpering to you to beg for your pity, however cruel life had been to him. I was walking just out of town one evening: it was warm and calm, as occurs at that time of day during our peaceful summers. There was a cloud of dust some distance away, the sound of mooing, faint, drawn-out yells and the crack of whips: cattle were being driven back from the meadows. Suddenly I saw a dog running directly up the road towards the herd, and I immediately recognised Arcturus by his usual tense and uncertain gait. He had never gone beyond the town limits till now, and I thought: 'Where's he off to?' Then as the cattle neared I noticed signs of disquiet growing among them. Now, cows do not like dogs—fear and loathing of dog-wolves are inborn in them—and here, seeing the dark figure of the dog running towards them, those at the front stopped on the spot. Immediately, a bull pushed forward: thickset, pale yellow, with a ring through his nose. Legs straddled, he lowered his horns and gave a hiccupping bellow, as he did so twitching his hide and rolling the bloodshot whites of his eyes.

'Grishka!' someone shouted from the rear of the herd. 'Run up the front, quick, the cows have sto-oped!'

Arcturus was trotting up the road in his ungainly way, suspecting nothing, and he had come now quite close to the cattle. Worried for him, I called him back. His momentum carried him a few steps further, and then he stopped and sat on his haunches, his body turned towards me. At that moment the bull gave a snort and with unexpected acceleration charged at Arcturus and hooked his horns under him. I glimpsed a black silhouette flying across the background of the sunset, and then the dog flopped down right among the cows! It was like a bomb going off!—cows flinging themselves in all directions, snorting, the horns of one rattling against those of another, individuals at the rear still pressing forward, the whole thing a melee, with dust rising up in columns. I waited tensely and painfully to hear a last death-yelp... but I heard nothing.

By now those herding the cattle had run forward, and cracking their whips and shouting in various pitches and tones they soon had the road cleared, and I saw Arcturus. He was lying in the dust, himself looking like a heap of dust or of old rags left there on the road. Then he moved, he rose and staggered over to the side of the road. There the old head-herdsman spotted him.

'Aha!... you devil!' he cried with malicious glee. He uttered an oath and simultaneously with long-refined expertise landed on Arcturus a most mighty blow of his whip. Arcturus did not yelp, he only shuddered. He turned for a moment his blind eyes towards the herdsman, then he found the strength to drag himself to the ditch, and into that he collapsed.

The bull was still straddling the road, pawing the ground and roaring, and the herdsman gave him just as expert and stinging a cut—as a result of which the beast instantly calmed down. The cows too quietened, and the herd moved on unhurriedly, a fragrant dust redolent of milk rising about them. Pats of dung remained behind on the road.

I went up to Arcturus: he was filthy and breathed heavily, his tongue lolling out and his ribs moving beneath the skin. There appeared to be some damp weals along his sides, one back-paw had been crushed and now trembled. I put my hand on his head and talked to him, but he did not respond. His whole being expressed pain, bewilderment and grief. He could not understand why he had been trampled on or why he had been whipped. Now, most dogs would whimper in such a circumstance; Arcturus did not whimper.

4

With the passing of time he might well have become a house-dog and turned fat and lazy; but an event took place, a fortuitous happening which was to give the rest of his life something of a heroic bent. It occurred as follows.

I went one morning out to the forest to look at the last departing flushes of summer, following which I knew would soon come the forest's fading. Arcturus tagged along persistently despite some attempts of mine to shoo him back. Each time, he sat and waited while a gap grew between us, and then he caught up with me again. I soon became tired of his incomprehensible stubbornness and decided to take no more notice of him.

Yet the forest, I saw, amazed him. In town, everything was now familiar to him: the boardwalks, the wide roadways, planks laid along the riverside, smooth trails. Here, all kinds of unknown things met him: there was tall grass, already beginning to coarsen, there were prickly bushes, rotten stumps, fallen trees, resilient young firs, there were rustling leaves scattering over the ground. Things reached out to him, pricked him, caught at him from all sides as if they had all agreed beforehand to drive him away from there. And then there were the smells—ah, the smells! How many those were: new, frightening, faint ones, strong ones, smells whose meaning he did not understand. Stumbling upon all these odorous, rustling, crackling, spiky things, Arcturus quivered, snuffled through his nose, pressed against my legs. He was at a loss, frightened by all this.

'Poor Arctur...' I said to him quietly, 'poor dog. You don't know that we have a bright sun, or how green the trees and the shrubbery are in the morning, or how the dew can glisten on the grass. You don't know that even now we're surrounded by flowers—white, yellow, blue, russet—and that among the grey firs and yellowing leaves there are rowanberries and clusters of dog-roses whose hips are beginning to redden. If you could see the moon and the stars at night, well, maybe it would please you to bay at them. How could you know that horses and dogs and cats can be of so many colours, that fences are brown or green or simply grey, and that windows at the time of sunset can glisten as they do, or what a sea of fire the river becomes at that time. If you had been a normal, healthy dog your master would have been a hunter and in the morning you would have listened for the grand song of the hunter's bugle, and you would have witnessed such passionate shouting coming from men as they never produce outside the chase. You would have pursued wild beasts, barking almost to choking in your frenzy, and in that furious trailing of a hot scent you would have served your lord the hunter, and no higher purpose would you have wanted in life. Poor Arctur, poor dog...'

I spoke softly in that vein to him, so that he would be less frightened as we went deeper into the forest. He gradually calmed and began to investigate the bushes and stumps with more confidence. And how much there was to find that was new and extraordinary, what excitement now seized him! Soon, animated by his important discoveries, he no longer kept tightly beside me, and only occasionally turned his dead white eyes towards me and listened to ascertain that he was going in the right direction and that I was still following him, and then each time he recommenced circling on his investigations.

We came to a meadow and continued our ramble there; and here a tremendous animation took hold of Arcturus. Snapping at the grass, stumbling over tussocks, he flashed from bush to bush, panting noisily, barging through obstacles and paying no further attention now either to me or to the sharp twigs. Finally, losing any last restraint and closing his eyelids tightly, he thrust himself with a great noise of crackling into a thicket and disappeared inside it, where I could hear him thrashing about and snorting. 'He's onto some scent!' I thought to myself and stopped.

A first loud but rather uncertain bark came from the thicket, followed by others. 'Arctur!' I called out to him, worried. At that moment something happened: he yelped, gave a long howl and charged on into the furthest depth of the thicket. His howl changed to an excited barking, and from the agitation at the top of the mass of bushes I could see that he was forcing his way through to the other side. I was concerned for him and tried to head him off, calling loudly to him—but my cries seemed only to add to his excitement! Stumbling, my feet catching in growths, I ran after him, across one clearing and then another, until as I came out into an open hollow I saw him bounding out of some low bushes and charging back towards me. He was unrecognisable, running in a comic manner with high leaps in the air, with nothing in his gait that resembled that of any other dog. But, say what you will, he was pursuing—confidently, barking, choking in his excitement, breaking out into high-pitched young-dog whines!

'Arctur!' I called to him. He paused, and in that instant I collared him. He tried to break free, snarling, and he almost bit me; his eyes were bloodshot, and it was all I could do to calm him and distract him from his passion. He was messy and scratched and his left ear drooped—evidently he had collided with things—but his frenzy was such, he was so aroused, that he seemed not to feel any hurt.

5

From that day, his life took a different turn. Each morning he disappeared into the woods, alone, sometimes returning at nightfall, sometimes the next day, and always worn out, battered and with bloodshot eyes. He grew bigger during this period, his chest broadened, his voice turned resonant, the pads on his feet hardened and his legs became as strong as steel springs. How he hunted there, on his own, how he managed to avoid serious injury to himself, I never understood. And did he feel that in those lone excursions of his there was something missing? Did he yearn for some expression of approval and support from a master, for those effusions whose necessity is bred into the life of a normal hunting hound?

Never once did I see him return satisfied. His pursuit, that of a blind and handicapped dog, was of course restricted and uncertain. The forest was his silent enemy: it struck at him, whipped at his head, at his eyes, it threw itself at his feet to trip him up, it brought him to a standstill. No, he never caught up with his quarry, sank his teeth into the neck of his foe, only the foe's scent was left him: wild, worrying, enticing, at once unbearably attractive and hateful, one scent among a thousand others, leading him always onward and onward.

How on earth did he find his way home each time, after he regained his senses at the end of those mad chases in that great envisioned hunting realm of his? What feeling for space and topography, what potent instinct was necessary to allow him, having grown calm again, to return to us— completely worn out, battered, gasping broken-voiced—from some place many kilometres away in the depths of the forest, where there was only the whisper of grass beneath the pines and the smell of dampness in the ravines?

Yet, as I have said, every such hound is bred to need a man's approval. Such a hunting dog pursues an animal and in doing that forgets everything else. Nevertheless, even at the moment of its greatest rapture, it knows that somewhere nearby, gripped by the same passion, following the same spoor, runs a human hunter, its master, whose shot will finally conclude everything. At such moments, the voice of that hunter goads and maddens the dog even more; the hunter too drags himself through the growths; as he runs, his hoarse voice is sooling-on the dog, encouraging it to keep engaged with the scent; and when all is over, he will throw the dog a shin-bone, will look at the dog with wild and intoxicated happy eyes, and will shout with delight: 'What-a-dog-we-have-here! Hey?' and pull its ears.

Well, Arcturus was on his own in that sense, and he suffered because of it. Love for the doctor, his owner, never grew integrated with his own hunter's passion. A number of times I saw him emerging in the early morning from where he slept beneath the veranda and begin circling the yard, then sit under the doctor's window, waiting for him to wake. That was his habit at first; and if the doctor got up in good humour and saw the hound outside and called: 'Arctur!'—what a routine that would animate! Arcturus would come to the very glass, craning his neck and presenting his muzzle up to it, swaying from paw to paw. Then he would dart into the house, from which soon all kinds of bustling noises would issue: happy sounds, the doctor's arias, the tramping of their feet from room to room, and so on.

Even later, for some time after our visit to the forest, he still waited for the doctor to rise. But now something new disturbed him insistently: he twitched nervously, shook himself, scratched, looked up, stood, sat again, whined softly. Then he would begin to run about in front of the veranda, turning ever wider circles, sit once more under the window, even give a couple of sharp barks of impatience, prick his ears, and with his head tilted to one side and then the other, listen. Finally getting up, he would stretch irritably, yawn, and then make for the fence, pressing with a determined wriggle through a hole in it. A little later I would see him a long way away out in the fields, trotting as usual with his even yet tense and uncertain manner. He was off to the forest.

6

I happened once to be passing with my gun along the high bank of a narrow lake. The ducks that year were more than usually fat and numerous, and snipe could be found in the lows, so the hunting was easy and satisfying. I found a convenient stump and sat on it to rest; and when a steady breeze which had been blowing until then died, and there endured for a moment the purest dreamlike silence, I suddenly heard a strange sound coming from a long way away. It came to me as evenly as the toll of a bell, as clear as the sound of a silver bell whose warm and mellow tones, winding around the groves of fir trees, growing louder through the pines, carrying to all parts of the forest, imparted a harmonious solemnity to everything about me. The sound became gradually more distinct, and as I considered it I realised that it was a dog baying from somewhere deep within the tract of firs across the lake. The baying was quite clear but weak and distant, sometimes dying altogether, then stubbornly returning, nearer and louder.

I sat on, turning my head, looking around me at the yellow and already sparsely-leaved birches, at the grey moss on the forest floor, admiring on the background of that moss the eye-catching crimson of fallen aspen leaves; and as I surveyed my surroundings I listened to that silver tolling; and it seemed to me that the squirrels in their harbours, the woodcocks on the sandbank, the birches and the dense stands of green firs, and below me the lake as well, all listened with me, that even the woven spider-webs quivered to that sound. And in that extraordinary music I recognised something familiar: and then I knew that it was Arcturus, hunting.

So that is how I heard him. That weak, silvery, reiterated echo, often scattered by the intervening trees, could make one believe that there were a number of dogs giving forth. At one point it seemed he must have lost the scent and the baying ceased. The silence continued for long minutes and the forest became empty and dead. I could almost see the dog circling, his eyelids blinking over those white eyeballs, he trusting to his sense of smell alone... Or had he spiked himself, run into a tree perhaps, was he now lying somewhere out there with his chest stove in, without the strength to rise, all bloody and miserable?... But then the chase commenced again with new strength, now unmistakably nearer the lake.

The situation of the lake was such that all local paths and spoors passed near it, none could avoid it. I had seen many interesting things close to that lake, and now I prepared myself for the unfolding of some event, and I waited. And soon on the other side, in a small clearing darkened by reddish-brown sorrel, out jumped a vixen. She was a dirty-grey colour, with a threadbare brush, and she paused there for a moment, one front paw raised, while she listened prick-eared to the approaching pursuer. Then, unhurriedly, she ran across the clearing, down into a dip at the edge of the forest and disappeared into the undergrowth. Now Arcturus bounded into the clearing, a little to one side of the trail, his angry bark ceaseless. As usual his gait was characterised by those high, ungainly leaps. On the scent of the vixen, he drove down into the dip and its undergrowth, whining and yelping, then he fell silent while it seemed he must be extricating himself from some difficulty in the bushes. But soon that low and measured sound, that toll of the silver bell, began again. As in some strange theatre, hound and fox in a representation of immemorial enmity had flashed across a stage and disappeared, and I was left once more surrounded by silence, broken only by the dying echoes of distant barking.

7

Word of this strange dog soon spread through the town and its surroundings. He was seen as far away as the banks of the Losva, he was seen in clearings beyond the wooded hills, on remotest forest-paths. They talked about him in the villages, on landings and ferries, and the ferrymen and sawmill workers argued about him over their beer.

Now a series of hunters began to visit us, folk who as a rule approach rumours with scepticism, knowing themselves the credibility of their own tales. They looked Arcturus over, discussed his ears and paws, talked about endurance and speed and other matters of relevance to their interest, sought out imperfections in the dog, and then tried to buy him from the doctor. They would have liked to probe and pull at Arcturus, to feel his muscles, to inspect more closely his pads and his chest; but he sat at the doctor's feet, looking grim and on guard, and none dared stretch a hand towards him. And the doctor grew red in the face when he told them with undisguised irritation for the tenth time that the dog was not for sale and it was about time everybody knew it. The hunters left in a pique and others arrived in their place.

One day, when Arcturus was lying under the veranda, having just injured himself particularly painfully, a real old mossback of a hunter appeared down in the garden. He was minus an eye, the left—the lid on that side had been sewn surgically to close the socket—there was a bare hint of a tartar's beard on his chin, he had on his head a crumpled fur hat of the kind called 'three-ears' because of its two side-flaps and one at the back, and he wore the usual battered boots of his fraternity. Spotting me, the old one blinked and dragged down his hat from his head, scratched the latter and looked up at the sky.

'The weather nowadays...' he muttered vaguely, 'h'm, the weather... yes.' He cleared his throat with a rasping noise and paused at that point.

I guessed what was up and asked: 'Would it be the pup that you've come about?'

'Yes indeed, my word!' he said, growing lively and covering his head again. 'Now you look at it this way—what's the doctor want with the dog? It's nothing to him... Whereas me, well, I'll tell you—I need a dog! Badly! The hunting's starting soon, and so on... I've got one already, see, a hound, but he's no good, a dope, can't keep on a scent and no voice to speak of... Whereas this one... Blind? Why, he's got a talent like witchcraft, the way he follows 'em! The Tsar would have such a dog, by the holy cross!'

He was panting with excitement by this. He blew his nose through his fingers and went into the house. Five minutes late he emerged again, red-faced and baffled. He stopped near me, uttered a grunt or two, lit up and smoked for a moment, looking indignant.

'So, he refused, mm?' I asked, knowing the answer.

'And how!' he said, hurt. 'Where's the sense of it? I've been hunting since I was a boy—there, see: lost that eye... and I've got sons that hunt, and so on and so forth. We need—I tell you—a dog! For the season! But no—he won't hand it over!... Fifty roubles I offered—how's that for a trade! But it don't suit him, he won't let me have it! Nearly howled at me, did you hear him? I should be the one to howl! The hunting's just about started and no dog!'

He looked unhappily around the yard, at the fence; and suddenly something flashed across his face, a cunning and calculating expression, and he immediately became calmer. 'Where do you keep him, anyway?' he asked with casual interest, and his eye twinkled.

'Now, you wouldn't be thinking of stealing the dog, would you?' I asked.

The old one grew flustered, took off his hat, wiped his face with the lining and looked at me searchingly, then his face creased in an artless smile.

'God spare us!' he said and gave a cackle. 'It's easy to be taken wrong here, to get into trouble with people. So that's what you thought! Well, what good's a dog to him anyway, hey? Tell me that!' He began to move towards the gate and then stopped, and there was a sudden expression of joy as he looked back at me. 'And what a voice! What a voice—d'you follow me? Clear as a bell, I tell you!'

Then he came back, moved close to me, and while he winked at me with that eye and then squinted towards the windows of the house, he hissed to me: 'Just you wait—that dog'll be mine yet! What's a dog to him? He's a bright chap, he's no hunter. He'll sell it to me, by the cross, he'll sell it! Lady Day's a bit ahead yet, in October. We'll come up with something. And you thought... What an idea!'

No sooner had he left than the doctor came out. 'What was he saying to you?' he asked in a worried tone. 'What an unpleasant old man! Did you see that eye of his? A real bandit! I wonder where he heard about the dog.' He was rubbing his hands together nervously, his neck had grown flushed and a strand of grey hair had fallen across his forehead. Arcturus, hearing the doctor's voice, emerged stiffly from under the veranda and came limping to us.

'Arctur,' said the doctor, 'you'll not want to leave me for someone else, will you?' The dog closed his eyes and poked his muzzle into the doctor's knee. He could hardly stand. He sat down, lowered his head and almost fell asleep right there. The doctor looked at me happily, laughed, and tweaked the dog's ears. But he did not know that the hound had already left him, left him not for someone but for something else, left him from that moment he had first gone into the forest with me.

8

How nice it would be if all wonderful stories had happy endings. And does not the hero, even a dog, deserve a long and happy life? No one is born on this earth without a purpose, and such a dog, a hunting hound, is born to pursue wild animals and be their enemy, to seek them out for the reason that they never came to man and never became man's friends, as dogs once did, but remained untamed instead. Now, a blind dog is not to be compared with a blind person: no one helps it, it is alone in that darkness, powerless, doomed by nature itself, which is always cruel to flawed things; and if such a dog still manages to serve, and serve passionately, its destined role—and that is merely the same as saying, if it continues to exist—what can be better and more noble than that? But, alas, Arcturus was not meant to continue that existence for long. At the end of August the weather turned bad, I began making my preparations to leave, and it was then that he disappeared. One morning he left for the forest, and that night he did not return, nor the next day or the day after that.

When a friend who has lived with you, whom you saw daily, and perhaps indeed to whom you often paid scarce attention, goes away and never returns, all that is left to you are memories, however little they avail the sudden void. And I began to remember those many days spent together with Arcturus: his constant uncertainty and bafflement, his awkward, side-on gait, his bark, his habits—silly and harmless—his love for the doctor. I even remembered his odour, which was the smell of a clean and healthy dog. I remembered those things and was sorry that he had not been my dog and I had not been the one to name him, that it was not me he had loved or my house he returned to at night after recovering from the fervour of the chase.

The doctor grew quite worn in those days after the dog did not return. He immediately suspected the old man, and we spent a long time searching him out until we found him at last. But he swore oaths on all that was sacred that he had not set eyes on Arcturus, and he volunteered to come looking for him with us. The news of the dog's disappearance flew around the town, and it turned out that he had been known to many, and many had been fond of him and were prepared to help the doctor find him. People followed up all sorts of contradictory rumours: that someone had seen a dog resembling Arcturus, someone else had heard his baying in the forest; the children the doctor had treated, and many unknown to him, searched the countryside, shouted, checked inside forestry huts, guns were fired. A dozen times a day visitors came to ask the doctor if the dog had returned yet, whether that extraordinary hunter had made it home.

I did not join in the search. Somehow, I could not believe that Arcturus could lose his way, he had too good a nose for that, and he was too fond of his master to just attach himself to some backwoodsman or other. He had certainly perished. But how? Where? That I did not know. There is no end to the places where one can meet one's death.

And after a number of days had passed, the doctor understood as well. He fell into melancholy, in an instant as it were, and at night he stayed up long, unable to sleep. The house without Arcturus became empty and silent. The cats had no one to startle them now, and they promenaded freely around the yard. No one came any longer to sniff at the reef of stone by the river: it jutted out of the ground uselessly and somehow dolefully, darkened by the rains, its secret odours of no interest to anybody.

12. A WOMAN OF THE COAST

1

September days by the White Sea grow dark early, the twilight is short and nights are cold and as black as slate. Occasionally the sun just before it sets breaks through the clouds, slants a last dying brightness across the sea and over the hilly coast, and for a moment or two the windows of the high-walled peasant izbas throw back a yellow reflection of that flush. The sunlight spreads and thins to a veil that then seems to sink into the water, leaving in the west the remnants of the sunset, a wan band darkening into purple. A high, cold sky glimmers weakly and unsteadily, while the land, the wooden village, the hill-slopes and stockyards—their squares bordered on the inland side by a bristling low forest of little saplings thick as a hairbrush—all shade into darkness, and only the freshly-barked logs by the administration building continue a little longer to answer that iridescence, and the wood-chips, crunching underfoot on the paths, to keep their curiously oily gleam.

Down on the shore, a couple of diminutive glows grow visible: wood fires where squatting boys are baking themselves a treat of potatoes. Windows brighten with lamp-light. But soon everything goes out again, the fires, the lights in the windows, and the village slips again into another long night of autumn sleep.

But at midnight it suddenly becomes lighter again: long luminous clouds launch out trembling fingers across the sky's zenith, move silently and alarmingly, changing from one pale colour to another, casting reflections on the sea. Then they disappear just as quickly as they came, and again the darkness closes in on everything, to endure stubbornly until the reluctant dawning of the following day.

The villages are empty in the daytime: the children are at school and there are no men. Some of the latter are at the coastal fishing-grounds, others have gone far out to sea after cod, some are in the fields. A village only becomes lively at holiday times, or when a crew arrives with a large catch of herring or salmon: then that first night the radio-loudspeaker crackles and wheezes on its post beside the club, the sparse streetlights are turned on, an accordion, usually in the hands of someone with a heavy touch, will send out a monotonous drone, there is laughter of girls, someone starts a song... But after a day or two the village empties again; and that is the way things will be until the end of autumn, when the fishermen begin to return from the grounds, the motorised vessels from the deeper waters, and all the fieldwork has ended at last.

Then the izbas fill again with the smell of salted cod and haddock, and on feast days there is vodka and home-brewed beer and the smoke of cheap tobacco, the sound of noisy male talk, the thumping of knee-boots. Yes, things do get gay then: stoves are stoked up in the morning, columns of smoke from the ovens rise into the pale sky above the frozen grey roofs, and in the air drifts the unmistakable fragrance of baking rye loaves. The nights are gripped by frost now, and the sea begins to freeze at the shoreline and the newly-formed ice to crack noisily, while increasingly from inland a goodly odour of warm manure draws from the barns and pens where the livestock shelter. Now the club shows films almost nightly, the diesel generator at the back of the village mutters into the late hours, the council is in permanent session, and all the conversation is of fish, the Plan, the weather, earnings and day-units—enough talk to fill the time almost to February, when the village will empty once again: some to go out on the icebreaker to trap seals, others to begin winter-fishing for navaga in the bay of Archangel where the Dvina comes into the sea.

2

Such a sense of cyclic vacancy as I have described, exists now in the izba where I presently live: an extensive building, tall and constructed in two divisions, the whole comprising many rooms and storage areas. The izba was built for a large family, probably sometime in the 19th century. It is a quiet and echoing place, at night the walls creak softly.

Seen in the daytime, its tidiness takes one aback. The windows are sparkling clean, and stretched along each sill is a little fence of flowering plants—whose glossy leaves have been given a wipe-over as well! The scrubbed floors are white and smell of soap and of the birch besom used to sweep them. At the entrances, to serve as doormats, are remnants of old fishing nets, and their faint tang of the sea and of seaweed is always present inside the building. Curtains of well-blued embroidered towelling flank the diplomas, the photographs and wall-mirrors; the open-work cloths which cover the tables and chests are starched severely, to the point of crackling.

And in that silence lives and on that bygone order attends just one person: ninety-years-old Marfa.

How ancient she is! At times I look at her with a feeling of awe and alarm: her face is so worn and dark, her eyes so lustreless, colourless. How still she sits in those infrequent moments when she pauses to rest! She will never now straighten that bent body of hers, that round, humped spine; those swollen legs will never regain their previous slimness, nor her cold hands become warm again.

Is it possible that she knew passion once, that there was a time when she was pretty? Could a different heart really have beaten in that frame? No, it seems impossible, impossible to believe such things, to imagine her otherwise than she is now.

And yet, she certainly was once young; indeed, according to the old men who remember her long ago, what a village beauty had blossomed there, how unconstrained was her dancing on feast days, how her cheeks had flamed, how firm, slender and strong was that body!

How she had loved her dear Vanya: a thickset young man with a muscular chest, small, white teeth, a bristly, black moustache and an equally jet-black, unruly forelock. How she had grown faint and glowed and trembled when she saw him coming down the road in his rosy shirt and odorous thigh-boots, with what joyful fear had she fled to the back of the house at the sight of him turning into her parents' yard!

Ah, how lovely she had been in those long-ago days, and how she had liked singing, what delightful old songs she knew then, what a ringing yet melting voice was hers, and with what skill, enthusiasm and tireless energy she applied herself to the heaviest and most unpleasant work!

Well, then, what had shrivelled her and aged her, what had chilled her hands, stilled her heart? Surely not those white, spectral, spellbinding nights? Had that awesome night-sun seared her blood? Or perhaps, on the contrary, was it the wearying weight of long winter evenings, passed at the spinning wheel under the crimson glow of a smoky torch?

What did she think, what did she dream about, in those dark hours when the wind whistled and droned, drove hard the brittle dry snowflakes, sharp as burrs; when it rattled windows and coiled perturbingly inside the flue of the baking oven; and when the ice on the shore was breaking with terrible hollow reverberations, and it was a fearful thing to go out into the blackness of a polar night?

And how she had wailed and thrown herself to the ground and keened, later, when in ritual accoutrements she had followed on the path to their graves, first her father and mother, then her brothers and sisters, and finally her husband and children—had looked for the last time down at each of them, powerless to tear herself away! How she had run to the sea then, had thrown herself headlong into the waves, had wanted in those terrible moments to have gone too, gone forever to that sandy graveyard among the sparse and stunted pines!

As things have turned out, I shall be staying here for only a short time, I will be leaving soon and quite likely will never see this shore again, nor these tall cabins which stand so dark in the autumn light, nor this ancient woman of the White Sea coast. Then why should her life so strangely touch me and seem important to me? Why do I observe her so persistently, think about her, question her? When, mind you, she does not like to talk, always answers shortly and in a general way:

'How did I get on in those days? Oh, I just lived.'

'Yes, but how?'

'Well, it's as I say, I lived, pretty well anyhow.'

She is abstracted, not much interested in seizing on a point and discussing it. She looks around absently or thinks about something of her own, something far away and unknown to me.

But then, suddenly, her sailor-grandsons come to her mind, and she becomes more lively and brings out postcards, cards that have taken months to reach this village so far off the beaten track, and which out here in this corner of the North seem in their rare quaintness almost artefacts from a fairy-tale world. She empties a clean kerchief and they scatter on the table. They are glossy and delicately coloured, postmarked Bombay, Rangoon, San Francisco, Colombo...

I read their messages aloud while Marfa listens, her dark face lowered. She smiles vaguely, barely perceptibly. Then she takes some time sorting them, touching the smooth cardboard with her crooked fingers, examining the illustrations. Finally, she folds the kerchief about them and takes them back to their sanctuary in a trunk; and then she returns to her housekeeping in the izba, forever doing something.

She gets up before daylight, and while still bareheaded says her prayers quickly. So soon after sleep her movements are difficult and awkward as she bends to the dark corner where a black Old Believer icon in a dull silver frame hangs between diplomas. Then she ties on her headscarf and goes to the porch, returns to move about the izba's rooms, box-rooms and closets, pokes into the garret, the lean-to shed, goes out to the kitchen garden...

What does she not do in the course of the day! She milks the cow and then drives it along the path out to pasture; she rattles the butter-churn; she feeds the hens and gropes in the henhouse for their eggs; she takes up a rusty chopper and scythes grass and potato-tops and dices them in the porch to feed the young pig; she digs up the potatoes and dries them when there is any sun, then stores them in the cellar; she gets a fire going in the stove and cooks dinner and boils the samovar; she goes to the sea-shore with a basket to gather lilac-coloured bunches of seaweed which the agar refinery buys from her; when there is a delivery of hay she strains herself to the limit to heave it up through the shoot into the hayloft! Comes Saturday, she fires up the bathhouse-copper, drags some twenty buckets of water up to it, does her laundry, darns and irons, then she sweeps and washes the floors of the house and that of the porch and even the wooden footpath outside. Almost every day she will go to help out in the calf-shed up at the yards, thereby earning a few day-units. Her remaining, youngest son, a gloomy widower, himself now grey and often ailing, is staying at the nearest fishing-ground some ten kilometres from the village, and Marfa, once she has rushed through her daily chores on that particular morning, goes to him, on foot, carrying cigarettes, butter, bread and sugar. She gets there in three hours, and without a moment's rest begins to scrub and wash and darn. She even repairs the torn nets. There are only men on those grounds, and Marfa cannot, as she puts it, see all this old-wives' work left undone.

3

Lately she has begun to sleep badly. Some sombre alteration is taking place deep in her being, which she accepts as an omen signifying her approaching death. Her husband, her father and mother, her dead children, appear now more and more often in her dreams. I have seen her rummaging in a trunk, looking over her burial garments: a clean blouse that has gone yellow and become permeated with the wood-odour of the trunk, a spacious white shroud, a gown, an embroidered coverlet, ribbons, linen, black stockings, slippers. She examines them, puts them back, sets them in order—how strange and frightening it is to see it!—with the same attentiveness and concern for the best effect which she gives to any other domestic activity.

'Lack's too late when they're nailing the crate,' she recites with self-satisfaction. She is not frightened of death. She is unshakeably convinced that life is as it should be and she believes in the appropriateness and necessity of death.

'That wee grave's been waiting a good while now,' she says in a gentle tone, as if speaking of something perfectly congenial, and while doing so looking at some point above me with her dim eyes. 'The old ones are there, all rolled into their holes. And my sons. They're all there, waiting for me. They miss me. And I, bless the heavenly Mother, have lived.'

At night when a storm breaks out—and down below us, frightfully close it seems to me, the surf is high and its roaring resounds throughout the whole izba so that the ceiling and walls tremble—Marfa prays on her knees in the icon-corner. Her prayers are not for herself, they are for those out in the Barents Sea, fishing.

'Shelter them, O Lord!' she whispers, and bends till her forehead taps the floor, 'Let them not perish, Lord! Safeguard them, good Saint Nicholas!'

It feels strange, listening to her: as if it was my grandmother praying, or my mother whom I hear in a dream, or my progenitors, peasants all, tillers of the soil, their existence from childhood to death one of ploughing and reaping, who lie forgotten in country graveyards, having brought to life bread and then other lives. It is as if they are praying now not for themselves but for the whole world, the world known to them, for Russia: praying to some heaven-knows how distant from our times Saint Nicholas the Intercessor.

'Send them good weather, send them clear skies and calm waters...' rustles on in the dim room the ninety-year-old voice. Then she goes to her bed and lies there without moving, looking into the darkness. She feels unwell, oppressed by something. Her years are pressing down on her, the years of her childhood and youth, so far away, indistinct now and yet a matter for wonder, like the white nights. And the years of her old age, like a darkening autumn evening.

Marfa lies there thinking of her life. As it returns to her, she seems a young girl again, singing a song. She listens to it as if standing beside herself, listens to the clear, sad voice:

'Ah, mother, weep:
Across the deep
Thy luckless son's away...'

But those tender and melancholy thoughts soon pass, giving place to other, habitual, considerations and cares. She now wonders how she might live to Michaelmas, when all the family will begin to gather at the house. She knows that the cow is old and milks badly and little, so she must remember to tell them to buy a new one; tell them also that the ewes must be driven to the other side of the sandbank where the sea-cabbage has been piling up. And to mow the barley in the kitchen-garden and hang the stooks to dry.

She takes a long time to fall asleep, her body starting occasionally. As she sleeps, her breathing is uneven and shallow; she wakes, changes the position of her numb hands and then again sleeps and does not sleep, hears and understands the night-noises around her, and yet dreams also: returns to dim and long-familiar dreams.

The sea rages more frequently and Marfa goes to the shore often now and stands immobile by the leaning posts of the wickerwork sea-fence, her form starkly black against the pale yellow of the sunset. She looks at the murky, agitated sea, at the never-ending run and roar of the waves across the sandbar, at their ranks after white-maned ranks. Yes, a familiar scene.

Sharp and bitter is the smell of cold, diced potato-tops, the smell of seaweed; clear despite the clamour of the sea are women's voices, the sound of footsteps on the boardwalk paths, the bleat of goats—which in this village is in a peculiarly bass register and abrupt.

Along the road a fisherman-neighbour is coming, his boots loud on the wooden walkway. He has muscular shoulders, is strong, rejoices in his strength. He greets people loudly as he passes, urges them to come to the film being shown that night, puffs cigarette smoke, breaks into a spasm of coughing while his face suffuses with blood. Then, noticing Marfa, he takes on a serious expression and mutters to himself in rough wonder: 'Well! She's out again... waiting for her dead ones, surely. Saintly biddy. And a true Shore-woman, a *Pomorka*... worth lifting a glass to, any day!'

He inhales deeply, squinting with his right eye, singeing his lips, then he drops the cigarette-end, treads it into the sand, spits copiously after it, and goes along the shore towards the point where the fish are being unloaded, rubbing his red neck and scraping the turned-over tops of his high boots against each other. Passing Marfa he bares his head and bends deferentially to her.

The wind turns colder, the sky darkens, the sunset is now wine-coloured, the air limpid. The ruddiness of the higher izbas dims, to the east a few stars begin to appear. It will soon be completely dark, but Marfa will go on standing, her old, blue-grey hands on the fence, and she will look at the sea until the last dim glow of the sunset dies.

13. MANKA

Dedicated to K. G. Paustovsky

1

From Vasintsy to Zolotitsa is thirty versts and there is no road between them, only a lonely trail overgrown with moss and grass and sometimes even mushrooms. More than once the thought has come to Manka that had she not carried the mail over it every day, the trail would have disappeared long ago. Then just let folk try to find their way through the forest!

Manka is an orphan. 'Papa drowned in a storm,' she tells, lowering her eyes and flicking a pointed tongue around her lips. 'And the year after that, Mama raised hands against herself. She was awfully sad. Once she went out of the izba at dusk and ran across the ice and got to a gap, took off her clothes and made a bundle and put it on the edge and fell in…' Blushing, she will add almost inaudibly: 'Mama was a bit wild…'

There is a certain wildness and strangeness about Manka herself, a dreamy otherworldliness; something inhabits her silences and is suppressed in her vague smile, her lowered green eyes. When they were burying her mother four years ago, Manka stood there looking bored and indifferent, keeping her gaze fixed on a spot on the ground between her feet. Then suddenly she was seen to look up and consider the mourners with such an outlandish, wide-eyed frankness, so casual and insolent, that the other villagers felt an intense unease, the men taking refuge in throat-clearing, while the women ceased keening and paled.

It has been two years since Manka took on the work of delivering the mail. By the time she reached her present age of seventeen she had probably tramped in versts the distance to Vladivostok. But she likes the work: her home is a mess, empty and dull, there are no animals to tend, the sky is visible through the long-unrepaired roof of the lean-to, and the stove has not had a fire in it for six months.

She walks easily and confidently, hardly ever tiring: a tall, slim and leggy figure. By the end of summer her hair is bleached, her arms and legs have reddened and then turned brown, her face has grown thinner and her eyes are even more green and arresting.

The sea-breeze here blows evenly in that warm season, bringing to the nostrils an astonishingly strong tang of seaweed, an odour that can carry your heart away. In August there are lanes of brilliant flowers along the banks of shaded little streams that foam yellow and murmur their way

169

through the windfalls. Then, Manka plucks up the flowers by the armful and binds them into dense posies, or resting in the shadow of grey pines twisted by the North's winter storms she decorates herself with daisies and dark-blue juniper berries and imagines herself a bride.

When there is little mail the walking is easy, a pleasant and dilatory routine; but sometimes there arrives a quantity of parcels, rolled-up newspapers and magazines, and then they strap a large basketwork frame on her back, packed tightly and heavy.

'Well lass, what's it feel like?' the postmaster shouts in his high-pitched voice. 'Will you get it there? Should we send for the horse?'

'No, it's nothing...' Manka's answer will be barely audible, while her face flushes and she shrugs her shoulders to settle the frame more comfortably.

By the end of the first verst her back aches and her feet have begun to drag. But how much happiness there will be on such days for the men out on the fishing grounds! How lively they always become, what gaiety erupts, and how laboured and careful and accompanied by what banter is their signing of the receipts! Yes, the fishermen love her on those days.

'Come on girl!...' they shout to her, 'Drop that stuff—there's plenty of time! Sit down and have a bowl of fish-soup with us. Hey, Mitka—get her a spoon!' And some towheaded Mitka will dive into his stowage for a spoon, rub it vigorously with the end of a towel and extend it to her with a regal bow. 'More salmon! Give her more salmon!' they shout—and pink with embarrassment, her eyes lowered, Manka sits and eats, trying not to gulp, moved and grateful for the men's concern and affection.

But the best thing is to walk with just letters and papers, when there is no heavy basket with its straps that cut into her shoulders. Then, on such easy days, what a feast for the eyes spreads before her, what curious thoughts came to her mind along the way! There are three fishing camps that she must call at as she marches towards Zolotitsa. At each place they wait for her with impatience, and despite her wool-gathering she has never failed them, has always arrived on time with their mail. Sometimes they give her tea and cranberry jam while they prise from her scraps of the neighbourhood news. When at last she arrives at Zolotitsa, she spends the night there, and next morning she picks up the outgoing mail on the way home to Vasintsy.

2

The closest fishing camp to Vasintsy is called Voronya. There used to be a quartet of fishermen and a cook there, but with the coming of summer and the nights beginning to grow golden a fifth fisherman arrived.

He was called Perfily Volokitin. He had a lean, firm-featured face and black hair, close-cropped when he first joined the camp. After being de-mobilised in the spring, he had lived at home for a couple of months, thinking eventually to move to town. But suddenly he began going out with Lenka, the prettiest and pertest girl in the village, over whom there had been fights at the club among the boys. He decided to stay and asked for a fishing job at Voronya.

He brought his accordion to the camp and played it frequently, gazing out to sea with a faraway expression. He was invariably cheerful and took to the heaviest work in a way that was keen, prompt and, for the benefit of the stay-at-homes, soldierly. When evening came, he shaved, sewed himself a new neckband, to peep dazzlingly above the collar of his army tunic, polished his boots, angled his forage cap on his head and went to the club in the village. He was always back by first light.

In addition to his other qualities, he was strong and boisterous, a deft and untiring dancer, quick-witted and ironical; and one day when Manka approached him at the club to give him his letters and papers she suddenly blushed and lowered her eyes. After that, both at home and in Zolotitsa she began having trouble sleeping at night, took to thinking long thoughts about Perfily, going over his face and voice, what he said and how he laughed. She imagined—and her cheeks burned bright-red then—that she was living with him in a tall new izba with windows which looked out on the sea, a home that had everything. Finally, having fallen asleep at last, she still muttered and tossed, so that her knees tapped against the wall by her bunk.

She was sleeping in Zolotitsa, in a stuffy, overheated izba shared with a work-brigade of eight carpenters, when just before light she suddenly dreamt about Perfily. Stark, strange, and troubling was that predawn dream, and Manka awoke from it abruptly, her green eyes opened wide and she jerked up into a sitting position, in that first moment of waking aware of nothing but the pounding of her heart.

The carpenter-sleepers snored on the floor and on benches around her, while on the other side of the condensation-beaded windowpanes the white night glowed brilliantly. Manka, unheard by anyone, choked back her sobs and tried to control her tears, for she had come at last to realise that she loved Perfily. She sat rocking in grief, racked with pity for herself and her thin, still-childish body, detesting pretty Lenka, knowing herself a destroyed creature, that her whole life was ruined; and it was only after dawn had come that she fell asleep again, exhausted by her sorrow and with her face still streaked with tears.

After that morning she was frightened to go to Perfily's camp, frightened of giving herself away and provoking the raillery of the fishermen, and she trembled and paled whenever she caught sight of Perfily or heard his voice. On those occasions, her heart faltered, her lips grew dry and there was a soft ache in her breast.

Each time she left Voronya now—half alive, in a state of somnolence, heeding nothing around her—she gradually increased her pace until she was almost running; then on entering into the cover of the forest she fell face down on the dry white moss and sobbed a long time in sweet abandon, weeping from joy and love and loneliness and incomprehension.

Sometimes she pressed through the forest in whatever direction she happened to face, smiling and talking to herself; at other times she emerged on the seashore and sat on a stone ledge, hugging her legs; and as she warmed herself in the sun and looked at the seagulls and at the blue-green placid sea she rocked and chanted in a murmur: 'Seagulls, oh seagulls, take to him my love!...'

And then the memory of her grandmother came back to her, as in a dream, she who had been long dead and departed from this world, came with the recollection of her tales and forlorn crooning. Unbidden words then rose to Manka's mind, words that she articulated with strength, distinctly, wild and oracular words:

'I will go forth—
I, Manka, servant of the Lord!
Revering Thee
And crossing me,
I will pass through doorways
And through portals,
Seeking to enter
Thy fair fields...

'He shall groan!
Love-stricken, moan!
Burn his blood,
Burn flesh and bone!
May his drink draw dry!
May his food not satisfy!
May he die and not die!'

She was possessed by a sensation of dread, her heart beat like a drum, her palms grew damp, and at that moment she desired Perfily even more, saw him as even more unapproachably beautiful.

The sea was motionless and like silk, rising and falling almost imperceptibly, as if breathing. Hazy luminescent clouds drew across the sky, the hidden sun shaping a dully-glowing orb through them; while out in the distance, over the pale blue hump of a cape, columns of blue-white light thrust down like spread fingers, and where they met the sea the water shone unbearably, swelled and seemed to smoke. It was a wonderful, joyous and extraordinarily balmy summer.

3

Then one day, now already in September, Manka, grown even more untamed in the course of the season, approached Perfily's fishing camp and guardedly stopped. The weather since morning had been unsettled, with strong gusts and a sea that was restless and choppy. There had been a short, heavy shower at dawn, and immediately the wet wood of the hut had darkened and taken on an autumnal look, while the windows reflected the weak light with a niggardly dullness. There was an unusual quantity of seaweed on the shore, and the sand was scattered with humid vermilion jellyfish and small yellow-brown starfish.

On the previous day there had been a good batch of salmon in the trap, and today was the festival of the patron saint of Vasintsy, so the fishermen feeling they were due for a holiday had loaded the catch in a karbas and all of them gone to deliver it to the fisheries collection-point. It was an opportunity to steam themselves in the bath-huts and spend a night at home enjoying the celebrations.

Perfily had left with the rest and gone that evening to the club, where he had listened to the accordion being played, had himself given a short and not very interested performance, and then stood about, cracking sunflower seeds and making loud witticisms for the benefit of the hall. After a while he went outside to drink with some of the village lads, as a consequence of which his dark, attractive eyes had gone slightly out of focus and his voice become a touch hoarse. Aroused, he swayed extravagantly on the dance floor, bumped into people, his lean, neat-featured face thrown back in the prisyadka squats, eyelids half-closed, his box-calf boots thumping and squeaking. Then, perfectly pan-faced, he sang bawdy ditties of increasing suggestiveness, to the delighted guffawing of the other young men and the ritual disapproval of the girls.

And all that evening he watched Lenka, watched her with a hunter's eye and with trepidation, and all that he did was done for her. At last, when everyone was being moved out of the hall so that the benches could be set up and the tickets sold for the film, he found her among the crowd, gripped her by the arm and pulled her out to the porch. There, where sunflower husks crunched underfoot and the air carried the odour of the latrine, he pinned her to a wall and, his face pallid with anxiety and desire and his eyes narrowed, he hissed: 'Come on, let's go to your place! Don't you see what you're doing to me?... Come on, we'll go and sit at your place, hey? Just for a while!...'

'My place?—I can sit there any time I want.' Lenka replied promptly and evenly, looking back through the door and trying to hear what was happening in the hall.

'Ah. So you don't want to?...' said Perfily, his tone a mixture of menace and helpless begging, while he smelt Lenka's powder and her hair, 'Found yourself somebody, hey? Some little sailorman, I'll bet. Look out you'll not be sorry, that you won't be rubbing tears away with those little fists!'

'Let go!' Lenka exclaimed, freeing herself with a muscular wrench. Without a glance at him she went back into the club, banging the door behind her; and Perfily had only time to notice how disconcertingly high were her breasts, how firm and apt for embracing were her arms, what a cruel-fine face she had, and how insolently and enticingly her hips moved as she sauntered away.

He went outside into the dimly lighted street, and the night-cold was sobering, but he still tore off a button in his sudden need to throw open his tunic. He wrenched off his cap, and holding it gripped in his hand began walking homeward, trembling with fury and shame, his boots thudding on the boardwalk. At home, not listening to his mother's appeals, he snatched up a bottle of vodka and some bread and lard and went down to the shore, got into a karbas, and two hours later was back at Voronya.

He went into the hut, his body hot from the furious rowing, lit the lamp, and without sitting down at the table poured a glass of vodka and drank it. He gritted his teeth and blinked and ran his fingers absently through his summer-growth of hair. Then he went outside and sat on a log and smoked, looking for a long time and without expression into the darkness. He looked out over the cold sea, where in summer at night the huge dull-crimson disk of the sun rolled along the horizon and where now, more and more frequently, the blue striations of the northern lights trembled, glowed fitfully and then wearily dimmed.

And so, when next morning Manka entered the hut, alerted by the unusual quiet, she found Perfily asleep in his corner-bunk, legs sprawled wide, his muscular belly bare, and his head muffled in a quilted jacket. When he heard the door creaking open he woke, looked dumbly at Manka and rubbed his face.

'Oh, it's you...' he muttered sullenly. He got up and came over to sit at the table, holding his head in his hands. 'Got any letters?'

'No,' said Manka, and she lowered herself down on a bench by a wall and drew her knees bashfully together. She sighed.

'No? What've you got then?'

'Papers,' Manka said. She cleared her throat nervously and flicked her tongue over her lips.

'Oh. Papers.' Perfily looked gloomily through the window. 'There'll be a storm. If it tears up the traps... What's going on over at the village? They've all gone there, every son of a bitch! Having fun!'

He rose with an effort and went to the bucket to get a drink, glancing on the way at the seated Manka.

'How come today you're sort of...' he began dully, and tilting his head back he drank, his throat working.

'Me? What?' Manka's voice was a whisper. Her face turned crimson almost to swarthiness as she looked down and smoothed a patch of skirt on her knees.

'Still living alone?'

'Yes.'

'Lonely, that,' said Perfily without any great feeling, and he continued to look out of the window.

'It's a life,' said Manka with a weak gesture of her hand. Clearing her throat again, she rose and went to the bucket and drank too, happy in the thought that she was drinking from the same mug he had just used.

'I should be going,' she said, some difficulty in her throat making her voice hoarse. She sat down again and lifted a pair of frightened eyes to Perfily. But he was paying her no attention: he was looking out through the window and not speaking.

'Storm's coming,' he repeated at last flatly. 'Those idiots at the met! They said on the radio it was going to be three on the scale, and no wind to speak of!'

Manka looked out too. The sea had darkened and was attacking the shore, and the wind could be heard whistling noisily through the drying-racks. The waves ran quickly now, foaming and overrunning each other, and on the horizon a growing band dark purple in colour was heading to-wards the two watchers.

'Here it comes. And they're away on a spree!' Perfily said bluntly, re-membering Lenka with bitterness, and he went behind a curtain and be-gan pulling on his canvas jacket and trousers.

'Where are you going?' Manka asked, shocked. 'Where are you off to? Do you want to get drowned?'

'Where! Where do you think? The traps are out there! Got to bring the nets in!' he said morosely and went out.

Manka was left alone, her lips parted, listening to the wind and looking through the window at the dark band which had broadened considerably just in those few moments.

Suddenly she got up and hurried out after him. Outside, she felt the wind as a tight pressure on her face; she saw Perfily busy with the karbas and ran over to him.

'Well?' he shot the word at her with irritation, and without waiting for a response he turned his back and began pushing the karbas over the roll-ers into the water.

'I'm coming!' said Manka and put her own shoulder to the boat.

'What?... D'you think it's a kindergarten here?...' Perfily's shouted words were indistinct, and as the karbas started to leap in the water and thud against the sand he shouted to her again: 'Go back to the hut!'

'I won't!' Manka shouted back, her white fingers clutching the side of the boat, 'D'you think I've never seen the sea?'

'Well... then jump in!' shouted Perfily, baring his teeth in sudden gaiety and desperation, 'Get in!'

Manka boarded the karbas easily and then staggered from side to side until she reached the stern. Perfily, flushed, bending forward and strain-ing, up to the waist in water, pushed the karbas off and then pulled him-self up, his stomach over the freeboard, and fell in. He took the oars im-mediately, turned the boat into the waves, and in a moment they were making way, lifting and crashing down, in the direction of the dark stakes marking the position of the traps, some two hundred metres from the shore. Manka plied the stern oar strongly, licking the salt spray from her lips, the wind blowing her hair in every direction. All kinds of thoughts ran through her mind: 'I didn't bring my shawl!' and 'Oy, we'll drown, we'll drown' and 'O what a terrible wind!' and she looked with love at Perfily, his face flushed with exertion, turning every few moments to peer over his shoulders to windward, a figure full of intense purpose.

They reached the first trap, and while still coasting—and without daring to look towards the approaching blackening band—they began at once to pull up the stakes and with them the net, piling everything in a tangle into the boat. Manka pulled at the net and bailed by turns. All her limbs were already aching, her dress was soaked and rucked high up her strong, thin legs, showing her bare thighs blotched with cold up to the edge of her pink drawers. She was embarrassed, but there was no time to adjust her clothing, and anyway Perfily was not looking. The stakes were set deeply into the bottom and he was levering them from side to side, while the karbas tossed and the waves rose higher and higher.

In about fifteen minutes the trap had been taken out and they made for the shore. They were low in the water and Perfily rowed grimly, staring at something that was approaching from the sea. Manka sat facing the shore, steering or baling and afraid to look back.

'Stop there!' Perfily bellowed, 'We'll never make it to the shore—throw everything out! It won't drift back from here!'

They threw the trap gear overboard, and immediately the thundering waves began to take everything towards the shore. They turned the boat back, and now Manka sat facing seaward again, half dead with fright at the scene. A short distance offshore there was no sky, there were no clouds, what filled the space between the upper air and the water was a dark, nebulous movement, a force so frightful that it could not but seem alive—pitiless, arrogant in its imperious advance, wanton—and in that darkness only the crests of the waves showed briefly: cold and tusked white.

The wind this time barely allowed the karbas to reach the second trap. Perfily arched his whole body with each stroke and flung himself forward for the next one, while Manka's arms felt ready to part at the joints from her efforts to steer.

And once again Perfily was gripping the stakes and rocking them backwards and forwards; the boat pitched and rolled, and with each lift of the bow or of the side that he was working from, his upper torso disappeared, and Manka, round-eyed with horror, then saw only his straining buttocks, his legs and his glistening wet boots braced wide in the well of the boat. Each time a stake came away it arrowed out of the water and Perfily fell back, taking with him an armful of netting into the boat. In this trap, a number of salmons were darting about, together with some long gang-fish, but no heed could be given them.

Now the real storm arrived. As it struck, the waves were instantly blanketed with foam, and a spindrift, fine as dust, whipped up around the karbas. From the shore rose a continuous roar where an enormous surge was reaching up the sand almost to the hut, and the water for some distance out to sea was turning a chocolate colour. The second trap had almost all been brought in, there only remained a section of the right wall— when suddenly the karbas poised almost vertically up a wave, tipped sideways, and turned over. Manka, stunned and choking, found herself under it.

She could make out nothing in the darkness, she wanted light and air, wanted to see Perfily; but in her violent floundering she only struck her head against the thwarts, while the sinking net tangled her feet and pulled at her. 'Oh, heavens!...' a voice gurgled in her head, 'Oy, mama dear, I'm gone, it's the end!...'

Something brushed her leg and she kicked out, clutched at a thwart, turned her face up close to the bottom of the boat where there was still a little fish-smelling air, and howled with terror. And then once again a rough, impatient arm slid up her legs, surrounded her hips and dress and yanked her abruptly down. Manka swallowed water, choked and fought in animal panic, writhing and bending backwards; until the same arm as painfully and roughly dragged her up to the surface and pinned her to the side of the boat's ribbed belly. Perfily spat sea-water and pulled Manka and himself up to a handhold on the keel, the clothing on his back blowing over his head, each vertebra of his tense spine standing out with the effort.

'What... were you playing at... you idiot... under the boat?' he shouted happily into her ear. He held her tightly with one arm and the slippery keel with the other. 'Hold on!... It's taking us to shore. We'll get there yet!...' Manka, shaking, coughing, blinded by tears, gasping from the force of salt wind and driven spray, clutched the keel with one hand and held the other around Perfily's neck. She was shocked into silence and numb with cold.

'... mere nothing!' Perfily was shouting happily with all his lungs, and he rattled his boots impatiently against the hull. 'We're still alive! Don't sing o' grief to me, until you've seen the sea!...'

And the sea howled: it was like a huge, ungovernable beast, lifting and lowering on its back the overturned karbas and bringing it always nearer to the land. In half an hour the boat's round sides were flashing in the turbulence of thunderous breakers. A wave would pull it towards the shore, break, and the karbas, surrounded by hissing foam, at first slowly and then more quickly, drifted back out again, to be then lifted by a new wave and thrown shoreward, closer still.

Suddenly there was a moment of silence in which could be heard the hiss of water now retreating along sand, and then a rumbling that grew behind them like the approach of a train. Perfily looked quickly in that direction and almost let go the keel: an angry curve of water, its crest collapsing into minor waves, was bearing down on them. It burst on the karbas, and with insufficient buoyancy to float up the side of the comber the boat went rolling towards the shore, and there it was dumped with a long crunch upon the sand. The last Manka remembered was being spun over and over along the sand, on her face, her back, her elbows, feeling her arms and legs being wrenched and battered.

When she opened her eyes she was lying on the beach, and Perfily on his knees was lifting her head. Embarrassed, she pushed him away, sat up and brought her dress into some sort of order, covering her legs. She felt sick, her head spun, and there were spots before her eyes.

'Alive then, are we?' Perfily said with relief; and then: 'Just wait here a minute...'

He ran heavily across the sand to where the karbas, now upright again, heaved and gleamed in the foam like something alive. Wading in water to his waist he caught the bow and pulled the boat up on the beach. Then he went back into the dirty-white, hissing backwash to catch the netting, and that he dragged up as well by a corner draped over his shoulder, with an effort that had him staggering forward almost level with the sand. He returned to Manka, out of breath, the high tops of his boots flapping and the skirt of his coat streaming. She had remained there all this time without the strength to stand up.

'Now then, what's all this?' he said cheerily. Then with greater care: 'Right, put your arm around my neck—I'll carry you!' and he bent and peered at her anxiously.

But she looked away and forced herself to rise, unaided and rocking like a drunk, a weak apologetic smile on her pale face. They set off side by side, Perfily supporting her tentatively with his hand across one of her meagre shoulders. His boots squelched and he seemed to grow more carefree with each step: he looked back towards the sea and talked animatedly, laughing at himself, at Manka, at the storm—as if it was someone else who minutes earlier had been gripping the keel of an upturned boat, shouting hoarsely, someone else who had strained with all his body's strength and stared with horror at the waves.

4

Perfily lit the stove, pulled off his wet garments in the porch and changed. He brought out for Manka a pair of trousers, a sweater and a coat, and then returned to the porch. He sat there smoking with rapid, avid draws and examined the scratches on his trembling hands. After a minute he called back into the hut: 'Going to be much longer?'

'Wait, I've nearly finished!' Manka answered in panic. She was making what haste she could, pulling off her clinging blouse and skirt and donning the unfamiliar clothing. And as she bent to deal with the long trousers, she happened to brush her arm across her still immature breasts and sighed.

'Well?' Perfily called again from the porch.

'All right. Come in,' Manka told him, embarrassed in her man's clothing. With downcast eyes, she hurriedly carried her wet things outside to wring out and hang up to dry. The wind was abating at last.

'And now...' Perfily greeted her when she returned, 'bring yourself over here. I'm going to doctor us with the latest thing in medical science.' He made her sit on a bench at the table, pulled out from under his bunk the bottle of vodka he had started on yesterday, and filled two glasses.

'Bottoms up!' he said fervently, then paused to look into her face. 'C'mon, drink up! Up with that glass and down we go together. It's against colds, you know. Happy landings everybody!' He emptied his own glass, stood for a moment catching his breath through his open mouth, and then filled a mug with cold tea. Manka drank. She choked and shook her head.

The vodka had an instantaneous effect on her. She flushed and her green eyes grew bright. And then fear and horror crept over her as she became more and more intensely aware of a pressing and acute desire: that Perfily should take her in his arms and kiss her!

And he, glancing at her, suddenly fell silent, and his high spirits faded to be replaced in his expression by something else. He pushed his mug of tea away and stood up. He walked to the door of the hut, and his step suddenly become as light and feline as that of a stalking hunter. Outside, he looked quickly up and down the shore and found it empty. He returned, and there was a tenseness now in his manner as he sat down. He gazed directly and keenly into Manka's face, looked at her flushed cheeks, her soft hair, curling and still not dry, at her golden, lowered eyelashes: and he began to understand the cause of her silences, her strangeness, her downcast eyes and husky voice. The sea thundered and echoed beyond the walls of the hut; here it was warm and dry, the stove crackled and there was a smell of fish.

'Say now, just how old are you? Mm?' he asked in a voice she had not heard before.

'I'd better go...' Manka said weakly, getting up; and then she sat down again.

'So how old are you then?' Perfily asked again, trying to look into her downturned eyes.

'Nineteen...' she whispered the lie. She turned her face away, feeling her hands grow cold and her head spinning. And she remembered then, all at once and as with the sensation of a sudden chill, her summer's grief, her tears, and all the mortifications of first, secret love; remembered her despair in those delusional white nights; and a confused sweet fearfulness gripped her—there sat Perfily, near her, looking at her with terrible eyes: her dreams were being realised! 'What's happening?...' passed through her mind, 'Oh God, he's going to throw himself at me!... Mama, what is this?' And she looked wild-eyed into Perfily's face.

Perfily grunted. Restraining himself long enough to put on a grimace of lovelorn despair, counterpart to Manka's confusion, he slid along the bench towards her. He bent back her face and with his eyes narrowed to slits he hungrily kissed her while his free hand fumbled her thin body.

Manka froze. Then she tore herself out of her numbness. 'What are you doing, damn you! What do you think you're doing?' she cried out.

'I'm lost to girls like you...' muttered Perfily with some unease in his voice, lifting himself to a better position over her.

'You dope!' Manka's cry was hoarse now, and she was almost in tears. 'Go kiss your floozies and keep your hands off me! I'm... I'm not just your anybody!'

'Manka dear, Manya...' Perfily, now baffled, begged penitently, 'wait a bit... I just wanted to be nice to you...'

'I'm not just some girl! Go and kiss your Lenka. Go on, be off to her!' And then: 'I'm... I'm still... I've never been kissed before!' she brought out with an effort, trembling. And turning suddenly and breathing heavily she tore off the coat she was wearing and threw it on the floor. 'Go outside, damn you!' she said in a low voice. 'The mail... I've got to take the mail...'

She changed her clothes, no longer concerned that Perfily would come in from the porch. She was shaking with anger, and by the time she was ready to take up the mailbag a sweet feeling of vindictiveness had grown to suffuse her. Head lowered and ignoring Perfily she left him standing and smoking unhappily in the outer doorway.

She had gone a little distance, when he caught up with her. He was bareheaded and wore a pair of shabby house-shoes on his feet. 'I had these...' he mumbled and thrust some chocolate sweets into her bag. 'For the road... Don't be sore Manya... You'll forgive me, won't you? It's all over with Lenka...' he said desperately and sadly, 'she's a proper bitch, plays around...'

'Go away!' said Manka, not looking at him, 'Leave me alone!'

'Will you come to the club on Saturday?' Perfily asked, walking quickly by her side.

'I've got to do the mail,' said Manka, still looking away.

'Well then, Sunday?' Perfily persisted, 'I've got to tell you something. You'll come, hey, Manya?'

'I don't know,' she replied barely distinctly after a moment's silence, and she quickened her pace. Perfily dropped back and was left behind.

'Yes, likely!' Manka whispered to herself as she hurried, 'What? He thinks I'll just trot over there? Just like that? Ha! You go and wait at your club if you want!' And as she pressed on, head lowered, she heard the sound of the sea, moderating now and softened by distance. 'Thinks he's found himself some dope... What would I go for? Bought by a bag of lollies! He'll be licking his chops back there right now!' She felt among the mail for the sweets and found them, but for some reason did not fling them away as she had intended. And she walked on like that, holding the sweets in her hand.

At a bend in the trail she halted as suddenly as if someone had tapped her on the shoulder. She turned and saw Perfily standing where he had stopped, still looking in her direction. Seeing that Manka had turned, he lifted up his arm, and she immediately hurried on again, barely keeping her pace below a run. Half a verst further along the trail, she stopped again, stooped a little and looked back cautiously, then she turned into a thicket of gold-yellow birches. She lay down on the moss, her face on the mailbag. 'What a mess it's turned into... How am I ever going to take him his mail now?' she thought.

Her face burned and her head spun from the fresh, clean, fisherman-smell of Perfily. She saw close to her once more his dark, excited eyes, distorted by their nearness to hers, and she grew still and suffered over again all the fright, all the happiness, all the shame she had felt that day. And now she heard in her mind—but gaily, vengefully and with informed conviction—that same feral incantation:

'He shall groan!
Love-stricken moan!
Burn his blood,
Burn flesh and bone!
May his drink draw dry!
May his food not satisfy!
May he die and not die!'

14. TWO OLD MEN

1

The watchman's hut stands near the warehouse, an extensive stone structure set on the highest summit above the town. The low, broad squatness of the warehouse gives it an appearance of having sunk weightily into its site over the many years it has stood there, indomitably horizontal to the falling slope beneath it, the side of a humped feature overgrown seasonally with short, dusty grass and said to be the remnant of a rampart that surrounded the town in far-distant times. A little way below that slope the ground declines less steeply towards the river and is a patchwork of old gardens divided by gullies and crooked lanes. The town viewed from the top of the feature is a scene of church-belfries and the roofs of old mansions: the many-balconied homes with sculptured facades, with entresols and mezzanines, that once belonged to the town's merchants. A market-square and its rows of stalls is also visible, there is the green expanse of a stadium, and two small white factories are first revealed by their stacks. Along the edge of the river are boat-repair yards, wharves, and a backwater that lodges abandoned craft and others in various stages of repair. Then there is the river itself, and across and beyond it and disappearing into the tremulous distance lie fields over which winds play all summer and perturbingly-dark cloud shadows roam.

In summer a white veil of dust raised by the traffic on the highway hangs over the town, the heat is unmoving or only varied by parching dry winds, the river gleams blindingly, and in the evenings endless copper sunsets flare through a sultry haze lying suspended over the western steppe. In that season, trucks rising to the warehouse arrive with heated motors and tyres, and the building exhales its particular summer-odours of soap, pine boards, bast matting, petrol, and hot dust.

Comes winter, and snow covers everything. At night, drifts pile high on the streets, and in the morning the horses need to clamber over them until eventually they level them down again. The town becomes cosier then, cleaner, more cheerful; sledges squeak and rasp over the frozen snow, chains jingle on vehicle wheels, and the Sunday market is yellow with horse dung, black with sheepskin coats, and red with new-slaughtered carcasses. The warehouse at that time seems hunkered lower and unwelcoming, its smells deaden in the cold, the snow heaps up along the walls almost to the decorative stonework of the little latticed windows, and only the entryway leading to the double doors, which are low and wide and embossed with metal reinforcements, is always clear and kept packed down by the tyres of vehicles.

The town is ancient and out of the way. Long ago, Raskolniki and sectarians of all kinds, priestless schismatics, Old Believers and such, built in the then surrounding forests their small, secluded monasteries, each more grimly austere and secretive than the next, and lived in them lives of world-renouncement. In the town they sealed themselves inside shuttered houses, held conventicles behind locked doors, and were renowned for the massive forged-iron padlocks they hung on their wells. For years the merchants who travelled from here to Moscow and St Petersburg and lived domiciled in those capitals were a byword for narrowness and uncouthness. But however much they trafficked, did their deals, went on sprees, nevertheless each had his home and his soul in this town and each came back to die in his own nest. Church-building was the major local activity in those times; hardly anything was produced here beyond cast-iron kettles, spoons, and birch-bark baskets. There was a feeling of Asiatic backwardness and enervation: it was a dull, dusty, forgotten place.

Even now, night watchmen do their circuits with a wooden clapper, the old are buried according to ancient rituals, and anomalous great wheels poised above bottomless wells, dug perhaps back in the time of Yuri Long-arm, startle and puzzle the visitor. To this day, women doing their marketing will come flocking to listen open-mouthed to the prophecies of some Colin Holy-fool: one or another dirty, sun-blackened imbecile, dribbling, guffawing and keening by turns.

But last year, twenty versts downriver, began the construction of a great weir, and now tip-trucks carry quarry-fill there around the clock. And also, just within the last ten years, a gigantic kolkhoz has sprung up some distance above the town, and all sorts of foreigners are taken there by ZIM saloon to look at it. In the course of things, such passing visitors stop in the town to stretch their legs: folk in modish tight pants, excessive galoshes, unfamiliar three-quarter-length overcoats, and brimmed hats. They poke around, a little perplexed, click their cameras, duck into a church to peer about for a moment. No one in the town stares at them any longer now; people have got used to the sight of them.

2

During the day in winter the storeman on duty at the warehouse sits in the watchman's hut doing his rosters and inventories at the table, wearing a padded jacket and fingerless gloves; and usually there are also lorry drivers from around the region, smoking and keeping warm. The walls behind the benches, and the benches themselves where the drivers sit, are smudged with auto grease and rubbed to a glossy shine by the sitters' backs and bottoms. In a corner, a pile of damp aspen logs emits a bitter tang into the air. The logs are brought into the hut by Tikhon's day-relief, Fyodor, who has a withered arm and lives in one of the rural hamlets on the outskirts of the town. Above the table a shelf has been nailed to the wall, and on it are scattered oily black machine-nuts, the brass weights of the warehouse scales, old food-cans containing salt and tea, and the odd half-empty packet of shag tobacco or loose cigarettes left behind by drivers.

The ceiling of the hut is black with soot, the floor is dirty and littered with woodchips, for neither of the two watchmen is greatly concerned with housekeeping. A small stove, its adobe surrounds rendered with grey-brown un-whitewashed clay, hums away, the cast-iron plates heated to a raspberry flush, while above the ash-pan an ardent golden light emanates from the narrow aperture that regulates the draught. In times of really hard frost, the gaps between the hut's door and doorframe sprout a curly rime, and ice grows to a depth of two fingers over the glass of the windows. When the thaw arrives, moisture seeps in from beneath the windowsills and there is a general smell of mould, mingled with the fug that always hangs about buildings unlived-in domestically. The door then swells so much that visitors need to shoulder into it with all their weight to enter the hut. In a corner next to the door hangs an old Berdan rifle re-barrelled as a shotgun. Its stock shows the prints of grubby hands, the blueing of the metal has long worn off, and a rag is stuffed into the muzzle as defence against damp. Sometimes out of boredom Tikhon cleans the gun and takes the shells out of the magazine. The cases are metal, greasy-yellow, and held in the palm have a substantial weight and pleasant coolness; they are loaded with buckshot.

Tikhon likes to sit on a block of wood beside the stove, thinking his thoughts and gazing into the open fire-box, and at such times his broad face grows still, the pupils of his eyes contract and his expression softens. His thoughts are heavy, they are old men's thoughts. Unaware of it in those moments, he begins to draw more deeply and often on his cigarette, smokes until his heart beats harder, and he spits frequently into the hissing and sparking coals.

In his youth, Tikhon was known for his amazing, his almost bizarre strength. He worked as a wharf labourer, carrying ten-*pood* bales on his back, with long, effortless strides of his massive legs. He was extraordinary in his wild, indeed elemental, behaviour as well. For example, just like the squat, flat-faced, and scantly-whiskered Tatar workers, he commonly ate raw meat. He would buy a couple of pounds of beef at the abattoir, sprinkle it with salt, and tear at it with his clean, white teeth, narrowing his eyes and crunching through the gristle, while a rosy stream of saliva coursed down his bearded chin. It was a horrible sight.

He lived alone throughout his younger years, was closed-in and friendless, revealing his thoughts to no one, invariably short in his speech. One day his morose figure disappeared from the town and was seen no more for some two years. He returned tanned almost black, his head shaved to the skin, his beard a bleached, gingery tangle, wearing a silk shirt of Oriental cut and on his feet battered dyed-leather kidskin boots. How he had spent those two years he told no one beyond saying that it had been in Persia. For a long time after his return he was apt to insert strange guttural utterances into his speech and he looked on everything even more sullenly and inscrutably than before.

Our people love the unusual, they love strength, power—Tikhon they did not love, they feared him and were awed by him. His fame proclaimed the physically remarkable in him, but also something deep and feral. When he was sober he did not arouse any terror, nor was he in fact particularly interesting, but once drunk he became frightening, a creature capable of all kinds of mad, ungovernable acts.

He seldom drank, but he drank deeply when he did, becoming not so much intoxicated as tranced: his brows then worked, he become ponderous and dull, his gaze grew glassy, crazed. He would intone quavering unheard-of melodic strains, emitting sounds that seemed to lack any words or metre, singing with his head thrown back, his thick lashes half closed over bloodshot eyes, his hairy Adam's apple trembling. Or it should be said more precisely he not so much sang as ululated in a falsetto register—to uncanny effect, since his voice was normally deep and resonant.

On those occasions, he would emerge at midday from a grogshop, having been drinking there since morning. Shoulders hunched, eyes glowering under lowered brows, hands thrust into the pockets of his trousers—a dirty garment, drooping at the backside—he would lurch his way towards the market, examining from head to foot anyone he passed, while a gaggle of loafers and beggars trailed him from a distance, hooting and laughing nervously. Arrived and without uttering a word, his face flushed almost to a violet tinge, Tikhon would begin to methodically tear the tethering-posts out of the ground, terrifying the snorting horses. Next, sweating, dull-eyed and bovine, with an ominous, crazed smile on his face, he would go up to some cart that might be parked there waiting for a load. 'Now, now… What's this? What's this?…' the driver sitting on the cart would mutter down at him, paling. 'Listen! Brothers! Christians! Look here… What… What's this?…' Tikhon would bend, take a grip on a wheel, tense his massive spine, curved from years of lumping sacks and bales, and, straightening, would tip the cart over on its side, horse and all. Panting, he would wipe his tarry hands on the back of his trousers, cast a dangerous look in the direction of the fleeing muzhiks, and then return to the grogshop. Imprecations of: 'Half-wit! Crazy devil!' would follow him, but not too loudly. No one dared to shout them at his face.

Tikhon had been drinking the day he got married. Perspiring and gathering himself, he took a long time to finally kiss the bride, while the guests provoked him with a clamour of 'Bitter! It's bitter!' and watched him tensely to see what he would do. He kissed her, uttered a leonine growl, heaved over the wedding-table—and the drunken company made for the door! They poured from the house in panic, treading on each other in an uncoordinated column, all intent on getting through the porch and out into the street. And that night, trampling with their boots on the garden-beds, they sneaked back, with a fence-picket broke a pane in the window of the connubial bedroom, whistled into the hole, and fled, flattening the wicker fence and scattering in every direction. And for the rest of that night, roaring Tikhon was in pursuit of someone or other throughout the outlying streets of the town.

Subsequently, he had two children, but they both died: one, a boy, of the cholera; the other, who had grown into a young man by then, was drowned under a barge.

Tikhon's aging was again not like the typical process: it did not occur all at once nor gradually but in spells. In a matter of six months he would age five years, deep wrinkles would appear, his legs would become venously knotted and more bowed, his beard increasingly flecked with grey. Then he would go around like that for ten years. When the next phase came, his beard suddenly showed more grey, his hair grew greasy and sparser; and so on.

On rare occasions he would remember Persia, and then he closed his eyes and things would come back to him: the white sun baking down, hot beyond bearing, the noise of the bazaar-streets, the smell of the heated dust and ordure in the narrow, dark laneways. He remembered the way drops of goat-fat dripped on the red coals, and the smoke that then rose in curls of blue; how the men sat in the coffee shops on threadbare carpets, chewing rubbery little pancakes, drinking coffee, bitter green tea, smoking their hookahs with narrowed eyes, then emerging with the whites grown sallow and their swarthy faces glinting with sweat; and how at night the old, worn pavement stones breathed back the heat of the day. And he recalled again the short, un-Russian dusks shading so soon into darkness, the minarets rosy-reddening against the violet heavens, while the mullahs whined their sad, dorsal cries and the true believers fell and fell, pressing their faces to the dusty stones. And then, recalling also the dark, oily water of the bay, the smell of cinnamon and rusty iron, the impenetrable darkness of cargo holds, the emerald-blue expanse of the Caspian Sea, the sharp animal-smell of the milling navvies—Persians, Greeks, Armenians, Azerbaijanis, Russians—Tikhon would close his teeth tightly, put his hand over his heart, and think with helpless melancholy: 'Akh, to go away!...'

But there were in Tikhon's life oddly gentle and elevating moments as well. Each year in July, some two weeks before Peter-Paul Day, he would take out his scythes from where he stored them, ready whetted and wrapped in sacking. He would put on bast sandals, tough as fired clay, would pack a bundle with bread, and he would go off to day-labour in the seasonal haymaking.

He would go a long way, to totally remote places, black-soil flood-flats settled centuries before by cultists and nonconformists. And no sooner had he found himself a place on the riverboat's lower deck, on the humming metal floor, next to a pile of bunker-wood smelling of forests, of ravines and mushrooms, next to the evenly exhaling engine and its yellow-greased, thrusting steel pistons, no sooner did he feel the rapid mutter of the vanes and hear the noise of their turn and splash outside the hull, feel the tremor of speed, of purposeful haste, than his old life left him. For a short time he forgot it, and painfully and sweetly beckoned, called to him again, the endless, dusty roads, the river reaches, the somnolent, sultry and odorous forest margins, all those things long familiar and native and evocative of earliest boyhood.

And then Tikhon started to grow more talkative and tolerant towards others, and he did not touch a drop during all the period of haymaking. He got up before daybreak and began mowing while there was still dew about, in the morning chill, swinging his scythe over a generous arc, never tiring, flushing at most, breathing deeply of the languorous, fresh hay-odour, the clover's honey, and the spicy, heavy dampness of meadow earth.

He relished the free expanses, relished hearing the solo trill of a sky-lark up in the morning's rose-green sky, a shiver would go through him at the sight of a colt drumming by, its pasterns dew-wet and its short tail puffed out and flying. He loved the country children with their sun-bleached hair, shoeless, silently watching and timid to the point of imminent flight, or trotting to the fields carrying afternoon titbits for the workers. He rejoiced in the long summer twilight, the humid grass that cut crisply and sagged over with each even sweep of his scythe, found pleasure in trailing some passing thought that seemed wonderful but what it ever led to he could never quite make out, pleasure in listening to the doleful, lingering, distant sound of bells, the neighing of mares, the thin voices of women singing in a village. And he loved to sleep the short sleep of summer nights, on day-warmed, aromatic threshing floors, seeing in some state between sleeping and waking the myriad lights of the stars, and in the darkness under their radiance the dimly-glowing ripening rye.

But the haymaking would end, Tikhon travelled back to the dust and oppressive heat of the town, to the smells and dirt of its fringe hamlets; and once again he strode over sagging gangplanks with vertebrae-crushing loads on his back, heard the shouts of overseers, smelled the pitch and the bast sacking of the barges, the oozy swill at the river's edge, the dung and urine coming down from the market above and from the grogshops and the tea houses. And again Tikhon began drinking, did stupid things, fought and roared, again everyone called him crazy, and the memory of Persia returned.

Well, Tikhon has been a widower a long time now, he lives alone, has quietened down, become kinder, more normal, more open. He has sprouted a yellowish-white, almost apostolic beard; but as before he is still powerful, has lost neither that terrible strength nor his iron constitution. And, as before, wherever he goes he is accompanied by his renown as a fabulous Hercules.

He has become one of the sights of the district, well-liked now and a source of pride; people tell anecdotes about him to visitors, they have discovered in him both intelligence and Russian shrewdness, and for the last twenty years without fail have elected him to the town soviet. Spotting Tikhon's huge figure, the secretary of the regional committee will brake his car, jump out to greet him and enquire about his health, launch into complaints about the drudgery of committee work, the nonsense and disorder one meets everywhere, will embark on a critique of the Plan, managing in the course of his analysis to mention in passing one or two little achievements of his own; and Tikhon has grown to like this interest in him, the deference now paid him, and he assumes a frown, blinks away the rheumy tears of age, passes his great, discoloured hand over his beard, breathes deeply, evenly, and looks contentedly around, at the streets, the passers-by, the sky and the river below. And the secretary, having extracted the sincerest enjoyment from this encounter and the exchange of insider-talk with Tikhon, feeling gayer and even physically enlivened, gets back into his all-terrain GAZ, while Tikhon walks on, his sheepskin open across his chest in defiance of the cold, his eyes looking mildly and directly into people's faces.

Others greet him, talk with him, stop to invite him to a tea-room, and he willingly responds to everyone with a firm and resonant voice. But he will only go to a tea-room with old friends. There, he takes off his hat, opens his coat even wider, sets his great, felt-booted feet under the table and orders a 'quarter to two' to make himself a 'wee punch'. While he mixes the first of the two glasses from the quarter-litre bottle of vodka and the pot of tea and then drinks it, some young riggers or scaffolders from the wharves come over and ask if they might join his table. They treat him, and he accepts their vodka graciously, downs it without a morsel of food, showing off a little his strength and hardiness, just to please his audience.

Another thing that Tikhon likes is voting. Before elections, he goes almost daily to the campaign centre, reads the magazines and the newspapers, listens attentively to all the speeches, his best ear turned slightly forward. He is always the first to vote, and if he works on the day of an election, then they bring the ballot box to him. He sets his spectacles on his nose and slowly reads and considers the information arriving with the ballot, asks question all over again about the candidate—qualities, place of birth, parentage—then he tells the officials: 'Leave me!' and having marked the leaflet, he carefully folds it with his thick fingers and slips it into the box.

3

Winter days are always so brief: the dull sunset fades quickly, the rosy tinge on the snow disappears, windows deliver a final golden flash, roofs and bell-towers smoulder red... and then come the shadows, crawling across the town and over the river.

Tikhon arrives for his shift towards nine o'clock. He goes around the warehouse with the day-storeman, checking the locks and the door-seals; then, alone, he yawns and makes his preparations for the long night. Having got a good fire going in the hut, he takes the gun and goes out to look over the surroundings, doing what he has done on countless nights before. The sky is black and clean, dotted sparsely with the green blink of tiny stars; the snow glints, thrusts needles of light at the eyeballs, crunches and creaks underfoot. He pads across to the outer edge of the area of snow illuminated by the security lights, peers down at the wide, dark river below. The odour of ice comes to him from there, and as he inhales it he snuffs in as well the smell of the cold gun-metal and of his old sheepskin coat. Each time he passes under one of the perimeter lampposts his shadow shortens and compacts, then with each subsequent step it lengthens, grows wider, huge and quaking, losing itself at last among the house-roofs beneath the rise.

Everything is in the grip of the cold, is petrified and lifeless, save for the translucent column of smoke ascending from the hut's flue straight up into the black sky and casting a faintly trembling shadow on the snow-covered roof of the warehouse. A long way below, street lights burn along the quay where the cargo landings and the debarkation jetties are, but the lamps and lampposts there are indistinct: all that can be made out from the warehouse are the widely-spaced round puffs of light on the snow. An occasional last MAZ truck drives past on the highway, and then the transparent shafts of its headlights slide over the roofs and the streets, tremble a long way out on the river, and the distinctive high tone of the truck's motor is easy to recognise in the distance.

The town sleeps, covered in snow, and even in the darkness everything is vaguely, metallically aglow—streets, gullies, yards, barns, gardens—only the low, recessed portal of the warehouse and the window-squares of neighbouring buildings remain pitch-black.

Then from the direction of a pine-grove behind where Tikhon is standing, a small horse-drawn sleigh comes suddenly into view, seems to fly whistling towards him, bursts into the lighted area and sideslips to a stop next to one of the lampposts. Tikhon walks over to see who the arrival is, and he recognises sitting on the sleigh a young militiaman from the local station. The sleigh-horse is a small, strong beast with curly grey flanks; having stopped, it instantly drops its head and lapses into reverie.

The militiaman makes an effort to rise from the sleigh, even stretches one felt-booted leg over the side, and then for some reason reconsiders, drops the reins, pulls off a mitten and leans over on that side to fish for his cigarettes.

'And a very good evening to you, Tikhon Yegorich!' he calls to the old man. His voice is cheerful and loud and characterised by a dialect which stresses the 'ch' of the other's name. 'Been anything happening here?'

'Up here? When's anything ever happened here?' Tikhon answers with a tired chuckle.

'Is that so? Well then, there you go. We, now, get it by the bucketful,' says the militiaman happily and with a nod of significance. 'I could tell you...' He breaks off and sits smoking, a cloud of blended smoke and breath-vapour rising from him. Then he spits expertly and confides: 'I've just come from a job right now, in fact.'

'Oh? Where?'

'Out Bondaryovo way. Feller cut up another feller, a mechanic... Stuck him nine times with a pocket-knife, the bastard!'

'Killed him?' Tikhon's face takes on a pained look.

'Nah, still alive, for now. He's in a coma. It's a laugh listening to him raving on.'

'And the other one, did they catch him?' Tikhon asks, growing slowly livelier with each question.

'They got him. He's sitting tight in the local soviet over there. They'll send a vehicle to pick him up in the morning.'

'Well then, that's that then.' After a pause Tikhon asks: 'So how did it start?'

'Pah, over a girl!' The militiaman makes a face and puts his mitten back on. 'There's some girl over there. A looker, they say. Anyhow, it was over her.'

'So, what's going to happen to him?'

'Well, we're not letting that one pass, I can tell you. If the other one lives, this lad'll get ten years. If he dies—off to the wall. That's the law.'

'H'm, yes...' Tikhon shifts his weight from one foot to the other, eases the sling of his gun on his shoulder, the snow squeaks under him. 'And all for some woman. What a heap of people get written off that way. It's baffling how often it happens.'

'Why, man, what's baffling about it?' the militiaman returns cheerily, sitting himself more comfortably in the sleigh, 'There's nothing baffling. They're stupid. It's just loose living, that's all. And as for women, where would you be without 'em in life? Take me now; just got married...'

'You don't say,' Tikhon breaks in, interested. 'I heard something. Got married, mm? When was it?'

'Two weeks ago, going on three.'

'Good dowry?'

'Nah, what dowry—she's an orphan! Just you wait a bit, I'll get a bonus for that other case—you remember?—and we'll put on a proper wedding, not just this registry stuff. And, you know, Tikhon Yegorich, I've been meaning to ask you for a while now—made a detour tonight to see you—would you take on giving the bride away and all that?'

'She'll be nice-looking, your girl, I'll bet?' says Tikhon in reply, beaming; and he reaches for one of his own cigarettes and comes nearer to light it from the other's glowing tip.

'You'd reckon!' the militiaman says with ardour, looking down at Tikhon's broad face bent over the two cigarettes. He undoes the hooks on his greatcoat with his free hand and feels in a side pocket. 'Dammit, I left it at home, her photo. I wanted to show you. Man, you should've seen the way I lived before on my own. Now when I get back home and I'm all done in after a shift there's a fire going, hot soup on the stove, and—you know what?—she's got lace curtains hung in the window! I come home, stiff with cold, my nostrils full of ice. Well! She helps me off with the coat, see? Helps-me-off!...'

His voice resonates joyfully, he stretches the sounds of words, repeats himself, all in an effort to spill out this amazing happiness of his which extends so far beyond the mere telling of it. 'Nostrils' he pronounces as 'nose-strils'. 'She hands me the soap, the towel, snuggles up to me, tickles me...'

He laughs and gives up the effort. Tikhon smiles too to himself, a little condescendingly, and rocks; the snow crunches under his boots, he pulls his nose. The sleigh is floored with hay, strands of it hang over the side, and their ends are white-tipped with snow: the smell of summer has arrived in the icy air.

'So that's how we live. And you say—just some woman!' The militiaman's words end huskily, so that he has to clear his throat for a moment while looking at the glow on the horizon from where the dike is going up. 'They're still at it,' he remarks now, in an everyday tone. 'A heap of people've come. It'd be good if they did something like that right here in town.'

'We'd have more thieves.' Tikhon says, smiling.

'Tikhon Yegorich, that's not the point,' says the militiaman, leaning across the front of the sleigh to gather up the reins, 'The thieves we'd lock up, but we'd have a bit more fun around here, that's the thing. I'm off... And about the wedding—we've agreed, right? I'll be relying on you now!'

He adjusts his pistol-holster, blows out one side of his nose, then the other, surprisingly loudly and reedily, and jerks the reins. The frozen and long-unmoving horse, its curly mane frosted white, leaps into joyous action, the runners fire off a glasslike crackle of shots as they detach from the ice grown around them, the sleigh departs with a whistling sound, and then both that and the crisp zhik-zhik-zhik of the horse's hooves dies away. The militiaman has gone, the heel of the foot, which he had provisionally stretched out of the sleigh and never retracted, leaving a slender furrow in the roadside snow.

Tikhon returns to pacing under the lights, thinking about the young wife of the militiaman, smiling and shaking his head. He looks below at the town, stops, listens to something. He is close to freezing. Beating his arms across his body he goes inside the watchman's hut to drink tea.

4

Down in the outskirts of the town, by the river, lives another old man: the former millionaire ship-owner and miller, Kruglov. Summer and winter he goes around in the remnant of a once luxurious knee-length coat of Romanov sheepskin, worn shiny and crackling with age; winter and summer he is seen in the same hat and felt boots, and an old silver-knobbed walking stick never leaves his hand.

Kruglov is a contemporary of Tikhon, and in his youth he too was well-known, indeed known throughout Russia; but his fame was of another kind: he was infamous for his frenetic troikas, his gypsies and his debauches, as wild and inventive as could only spring from the repressions of those ursine backwoods of his time. He—himself gypsy-featured, wiry, with blazing black eyes and darkly hirsute to an unusual degree—was insatiable in his binges, abominations, and depravities, as he was equally single-minded in his industry after each carouse. He went on orgies to Moscow, to St Petersburg, even as far as Paris, astonishing the civilised French with his outlandish carriages and the huge sums he daily squandered in restaurants and public houses, astounding them over there with his seemingly unrelievable world-weariness, his tears, his dancing, his totally incomprehensible, mad practical jokes.

But, it should be repeated, unexpected as it might be from one addicted to such destructive outbursts, Kruglov was also cruelly intelligent and cold-blooded in his other persona as an entrepreneur and wealthy proprietor. He had almost all of the region in his pocket, living deliberately in this out-of-the-way town where governors, councillors, other merchants, even the gendarmerie, were forced to come to him cap in hand and cursing the Russian roads.

Now when Tikhon married, his wife brought him a modest dowry, and he conceived of buying a flour mill in a village not far out of town. He moved there, got the venture started—and in that same first year Kruglov crushed him, cleaned him out totally, leaving him with not a kopek in his pocket and in fact loaded with debts. Tikhon returned to town an even more ferocious and crazy person than before; and subsequently whenever Kruglov saw him on the wharves the tycoon would doff his tall *kartooz* to him in a sweeping gesture that displayed the hat's white silk lining, and, while the overseers guffawed, would bow low to Tikhon and enquire: 'And how is your worthiness today? In good health I hope?...' Tikhon would bare his teeth in reply.

The revolution came for Kruglov like a thunderclap out of the bluest of skies. He was about forty then, a bit quieter by that time, but even harder, more pitiless, more implacably efficient, and his wealth was said to be uncountable. Instantly, with a kind of muzhik intuition, he sensed that the old ways were done for, all this that was happening was too wide and too deep: he understood that he had to clear out, make a run for it. And he almost made it. He had obtained the right passports—English ones—had filled a trunk with fine Vologda inlay-work, all gold and diamonds; but his wife blabbed. She was a simple woman, not too bright, not at all his mettle. The Red Guardsmen came, they confiscated the gold, threw the family out of their house and locked up Kruglov himself in a prison for three months. He came out a different man: thinner, ashen, silent, unremarkable now in appearance; but his soul was more vicious and astringent than ever. And to the day of his death he never forgave his wife his calamity; for fifteen years he never spoke a word to her on any matter of least significance, and when she died he made his ceremonial leave-taking in the church, ritually kissing the iconographic ribbon on her forehead, but he would not accompany her coffin to the cemetery. When he visited the graves of his parents on the yearly Saturday of the Dead, not once did he come near her grave, and in fact he did not even know where it lay.

In his old age Kruglov turned Evangelical, and now he drags out an isolated, unsociable existence, forgotten by everyone and apart from everyone. On Saturdays he goes to the prayer-house, and he devours the Bible, delighted and excited at finding in it an increasing number of portents boding the nearing end of the world. As he did from the very first, he nurses a ferocious hatred for Soviet rule, and from the regime's inception has refused to take part in voting at any of its elections. 'Governors stood before me. Yes, at attention! And get this into your heads—I am an England citizen!' he taunts thus with irony and pride the agitprop officials who come to exhort him. And if they continue their efforts, his contempt for them quickly explodes, he turns pale with fury and stamps his walking-stick on the ground!

Palsy has shattered him now, his eyelids quiver unevenly: first, the left one flickers repeatedly, like the batting of a bird's wing, then the right will lift and fall slowly. His beard is of a dirty tinge and trembles constantly, his bony, bald head is shiny and yellow, sunken at the temples, intimating the skull of a corpse. He is repugnant with the slovenliness and grime of age, and smells unpleasantly even on a frosty day. Still, to this day, he has not lost his hardness. Even now, humiliated, in a continual state of anxiety and uncertainty, decrepit as he is, he will open wide his turbid, sclerotic eyes, swivel his head around while his feeble body is shaken by some momentary subterranean rage, and then it is hard to sustain his stare.

The stubborn constancy of some human passions can hardly be credited at times. In the town lives an individual whom Kruglov has hated for decades, whose name he cannot hear without being afflicted by a fit of quaking, helpless anger. What Kruglov would not give or do to find this enemy brought low, to see him crushed, and to savour the sweet knowledge of his, Kruglov's, precedence and supremacy over this other! How often in his sleepless nights has Kruglov trampled on him, tormented him with fatal mutilations, burned him alive! And this adversary is—none other than Tikhon.

So long and so intensely has Kruglov loathed Tikhon, that the feeling has become a sort of infatuation, a bizarre addiction. Not to approach and speak to Tikhon, not to taunt him, are beyond Kruglov's powers now; and so, in winter, when Tikhon's nights are especially long and dismal, the watchman hears, perhaps three times in a month, the rap of Kruglov's stick, and a short time later sees his familiar and likewise detested figure drawing near. Kruglov grows visible, arrives and comes to a stop under one of the lights.

'Well?' Tikhon says sullenly.

'I've been... I've been at my grandson's,' Kruglov pants, feeling the front of his sheepskin with a trembling hand, 'I was going home and I had this sudden cramp in my chest... Thought I was going to die... Something sweet came into my mouth...'

Tikhon says nothing, he scowls and only looks sideways at Kruglov; he does not like sick people anyway, and never ill himself he would rather avoid feeling a perplexed pity for them.

'My legs shook,' Kruglov continues, having somewhat caught his breath, 'My legs, oh dear, these poor old legs... It's the second time. It can't be long now. I'll die... Who should I say hello to on your behalf; mm, Tikhon?...'

'What do you want here? It's a closed area!' Tikhon cuts him short.

'Oh, nothing. I'd just like to stay around for a moment. To give my property a look-over, for old time's sake. I built all this, you see...' Kruglov's speech is measured, polite, unpretentious. 'It's my old corn chandlery.'

'Yours?...' says Tikhon, dragging the word out in a rising tone of mock sympathy, shakes his head and makes smacking sounds with his lips. 'Well now, will you look at the great man, the big shot!'

'Shut your mouth, fool!' hisses Kruglov and furiously thrusts his stick into the snow.

And Tikhon becomes silent again.

'Not thinking of dying yet?' Kruglov asks, grown calmer; and he gives the massive figure of the other an appraising look. 'H'm, yes. There's still another twenty years in you. Well I'll tell you something, confidentially: me, I'm frightened,' and he winks. 'That old death, you see: I'm frightened... But, anyway, here we stand for the time being, the two of us, side by side. Yes, despite the fact that you're a bum and all the land of Russ once knew me. And here we stand evenly, one with the other. Now explain it to me—why's that?'

'All the land of Russ knew you and forgot you. That's probably why,'

Tikhon says dryly.

'Fool, you're lying!' Kruglov erupts once more; then he collects himself and begins on another tack: 'I never like going home. I get there, I lie down, everything in my head is dreary and sad. There's a pressure on my chest, like earth being heaped on it. It's death, I suppose, letting me know. That's when I really believe in God. I light the lamp, "Lord!..." I say to my-self... In the daytime, now, well, I get by, it's all right. But then comes the night. I lie there, listen, a clock strikes somewhere, once, twice. The birds shuffle a bit in their cage. I've got finches, you know. Nothing else.'

'So then, you can actually love living creatures?'

'Yes, yes, you hit it! I've got to have some living thing by me. When the old woman was alive, at least I had her snores. But now I'm alone, not so much as the breath of a single soul to make a sound near me, only my own heart beating. Beats, wheezes. It's borne a lot, this old heart of mine, borne-a-lot. I don't like listening to it... I thought, one time—what should I do, keep a cat maybe?... But no, I don't like cats, I've got no admiration for cats, there's a feral darkness in them, the hell with them! But I did have a bitch now, Damka. She wandered over, lost devil of a thing. A sizable dog, wasn't anything she couldn't eat. She ate and ate; a barge-full wouldn't have satisfied her. So I killed her.'

'You killed her?'

'Strangled her!' says Kruglov, sensing accurately the controlled antipa-thy in the other's reaction. He smiles and—'There it is, the show's start-ing!'—he thinks to himself, and continues: 'I tried to drive her away, she wouldn't go, got used to me somehow. How am I to feed her? Under this system of yours you can't get enough for yourself—no way I could keep a dog like that fed! I called her out to the shed. "Damka," I said, "Here, Damka." So we went out, I got some rope, put a noose around her neck, she looked up at me, understood what it was all about probably, gave me a whimper, and then I...'

'You mean you had no pity on her? Is that what you mean?' Tikhon rumbles, glowering into the face of the unnaturally cheerful Kruglov.

'Idiot!' Kruglov replies happily. 'Just try to think for a change! What would have been her fate? You know there's never been a dog that died of old age. Something's always taking them off. They get run over or drowned or they go mad; or if it's not that, then they'll shove them into a sputnik and fire them off. It's what God's decreed for 'em.'

'You are nothing but filth!' Tikhon says levelly. 'You're a cockroach and that's just your looks! And as for the evil in you... To do that to a harmless, trusting brute! Your soul is rotten!'

'Gotcha!' Kruglov exults silently. He has attained his objective, the mo-tive for the climb up to the warehouse. But then on an instant he himself starts to shake: overwhelmed by his own ungovernable hatred, his self-possession snaps. 'So! Now you've started to remember the soul! And when you tore the clothes off my back, left me barefoot, did you give any thought then to my soul? Did you? Pull your faces, you bastard, you ba-boon-faced bum! Kruglov lived and let others live! How many of you bloodsuckers battened off me? That building you put your tech school in—that was a poorhouse I paid for in those days. You remember? The church you pulled down—who built that? Hey? And the times you got work lumping cargo—whose was it? And the women I had—oh God, the memory of that—local popsies, one and all! You think they didn't walk off with everything they could lift? I passed on from one to another, passed on, yes, but never abandoned! I built them houses. We lived in those days, lived, I tell you! How can anyone compare this black time of yours—you antichrists, vagabonds, sons of bitches—with those days! I'd be working, sweating seven lathers, spots before my eyes...'

'From all your drinking, you had spots before your eyes,' Tikhon is grimly happy to interrupt.

'Drinking? You know when an idiot's wisest? When he keeps his mouth shut! From drinking? Sure I drank, and the whole town grew rich by it too! Thousands I threw around then, thousands. God, where did they go? I lie sleepless at night, thinking: Why did they ruin us like this? Was life in the past, I think to myself, really worse than now? Memories come back to me, and I itch all over; the old days pass before me and I feel like crying...'

'You think...' Tikhon jeers, smiling vindictively while he swings his arms across the front of his sheepskin and claps his sides, 'You think, and then, my! you break out into tears. The poor cat crying over the mouse. And do you ever think of anything else?'

'I think of something else,' Kruglov says, lifting a trembling arm. 'The end of your lot is nigh; not distant, no! You haven't got much time left to sup on blood. The Bible will fulfil its prophecies—it will! How you will all burn then, how bitter it will be for your kind!... You think the atom is just that? Just anything, you think? No! It is written: And brother will rise up against brother, and the father against the son, and sorrows will multiply, and the heavens will gape, and earth and sky will burn... Aha! You'll be devouring one another then, like the jackals of Araby! Retribution for your ways will fall upon your heads and you will burn, damned ones! You'll re-member Kruglov then! Remember, Judas, who fed you and who it was you flung to the stinking dogs! They robbed Kruglov? So be it. A place has been prepared for me...'

'In hell it's been prepared!' Tikhon snarls back. Kruglov's invective have made him restless, have affected and roused him at last. 'Sad for the loss of your money, are you? Just how did you come by it? Well? Who was it who fed arsenic to your dear old papa? And who drowned that nephew of yours—hey? You don't say anything to that now, do you?—you treacherous snake! How many souls went tramping homeless around the world, how many orphans' tears were poured out because of you! Whose fault was it I drank, carried on like a crazy idiot? "We lived," you say. "Lived." Ha! Would that you went to hell and lived there the way we did! All you can remember is Paris. Hunger and cholera you don't remember—it wasn't your children they were burying! You think I strained my back in your sight, panted till I was hoarse, grew boils all over my hide out of sweet enjoyment? Who wrecked my life, my youth? Wasn't it the likes of you? Murderers all, your mothers be damned! I, I don't remember anything, the whole of my life is like a day. You know why? You lie whining in your bed, broken-hearted over your past, while I sit in that shed there, night after night. I too think, and I can't remember anything, because there's nothing to remember. They didn't shoot enough of you! You should have been tortured for everything, for all those that went hungry, for all of us! We should have buried you where the tree roots would keep you down! You... you drivelling devil... You... I'll kill you! Don't come here, I'll kill you, you'll drive me to it! You know me, you remember me—don't poke at me, don't needle me! I regret it as it is, I chew my elbow that I didn't get to you, didn't liquidate you in '17! Do you hear me, merchant? Here, look, as I sign me now by the holy cross, I'll kill you!'

Tikhon's face has a terrible expression, he grabs Kruglov's coat collar, drags him away from the lights, the collar tears, Kruglov is limp, his heels, almost off the ground, paw the snow, his beard trembles. 'You wait,' Tikhon pants, his breath is rasping, his words a croak, 'When spring comes... the weir'll be finished... It'll flood you out, you stinking animal!...' He gives Kruglov a mighty shove that sends him flying forward and down into the snow.

Kruglov gets up with difficulty and turns to face Tikhon; bubbling and whistling sounds come from his throat, he stutters in his rage, drools, chokes on sobs, 'It *won't* f-flood me!' he shrieks.

'It *will* flood you!' Tikhon repeats cheerfully, his voice returning to its normal resonance, 'Your days are over, you'll croak soon, merchant—your worthiness... And how is your worthiness today, mm?' he suddenly remembers. 'Mm?... Oh-ho-ho!'

'It *won't* flood me!' Kruglov weeps back, 'I'll outlive you! My blood doesn't die!'

Tikhon laughs particularly gaily and vengefully, while Kruglov lifts his beard, tilts his face shiny with tears up to the dark sky and implores with desperation: 'Lord!...' And the rest of his appeal follows as a muttered prayer under his breath, a series of murmurs retreating into the darkness.

He passes from sight, a pathetic figure, tearing at himself, wild with despair, remembering, re-imagining his past powers, sway, pride and vigour, seeing nothing before him for tears. He goes away to pray more, to convince himself once again of the imminent end of everything, to immerse himself in depths of hate for whatever is new, unfamiliar, unintelligible to him, to again tremble and choke when he sights somewhere the huge form of Tikhon. He leaves, to return in a fortnight perhaps, back like an alcoholic, like one obsessed, back to his corn chandlery; and having swayed his way up to it and weakly hunched himself for some moments against a lamppost, he will begin again to torture himself, curse and threaten with terrible vengeance Tikhon and all Tikhon's like, who are creating this incomprehensible new world. Then he will recall with sorrow, with ineffable pain, his old life, his successful ventures, his wealth, even his past failures; and all that he had gone through will unfailingly seem to him now sweet and splendid and real, while what has replaced it is foreign, inimical, unfathomable, and unjust. And again Tikhon will be driven into frenzy, driven to at last roar at him, laugh cruelly at him, lay hands on him.

People are certain—those who know of this incredible and invariable occurrence, this feud which has become one of the town myths, those people who remember Tikhon when he was young, who remember his wildness, his mad acts are convinced—that the end of this thing is inevitable: one day Tikhon will kill Kruglov. And in that conviction they have already justified such a finale. Kruglov wanted it so.

15. THE CHIME OF THE BRÉGUET

It would be a while yet until the sun rose: the nocturnal carts and drays still creaked and squealed in the darkness, a few shops had begun rattling open their shutters, but the great windows of the palaces and mansions remained coldly lifeless.

Dim as the streets were, however, the city's clerks and lower official-dom were already hastening to their offices, pressing forward over the widely spaced stains cast on the ground by fading streetlamps; in the basements and garrets of poorer, decaying buildings lights glowed palely, yellowing the frost-powdered glass of windows and extending misty bands across the pavement snow; up in the lilac sky the first jackdaws were flying noiselessly all in the same direction; and like a swinging pendulum of sound—coming and going over the city, to and fro, from far away and then nearer, sometimes distinct and then merging densely into chords—oscillated a continuous and rhythmic hum of bells: the bells of matins.

It was almost ten o'clock by the time the sun finally appeared, rising slowly, inimically cold and smoky; and it was only then that the rose-and-silver cupola and the columns of St Isaac's began to emerge, the needle of the Peter-Paul fortress to glint dully, the Bronze Horseman to rise eerily through the haze, the outlines of the Winter Palace to grow defined, and the sextet of horses on the archway between the Main Staff blocks to throw its shadows over Palace Square.

The sun seemed to have materialised momentarily merely to cast down a single glance at the splendid metropolis below, as if to ascertain that the memorials and eminences had not vanished or crumbled into dust overnight, and having found them still present it immediately withdrew once more behind a curtain of grey clouds. It was thus that for Lermontov began that St Petersburg day, in a winter-morning's instant of blinding light and almost simultaneous commencement of the day's fading.

He had that morning decided to go to Pushkin.

For long now, Lermontov had suffered from a mortal affliction: a sense of life's pointlessness. What was there in the world around him to value? The military parades and troopings of the guard? The balls and coming-out receptions at court?—events of such peculiar moment for the gallants and ladies of the city—conferrals and ceremonials on His Majesty's name-day or on New Year's Day or at Easter? Promotions into guards' regiments, the dubbing of young women as Maids of Honour and young men as Gentlemen of the Bedchamber? All of it seemed for a long time now wretched and pitiable to him. The mechanical measures of foot-drill, the empty screech of flutes and the pounding of drums, the invariant shouted commands, the put-on grimness of the generals, the manoeuvres and stink of horse sweat in riding-school arenas, the officers' bachelor parties: all these were one wearying side of life. Another side was that of young and not-so-young women with bare, powdered shoulders, ladies of the court and salon, odorous of ointments, of perfume and of the scented sweat-pads secreted in their armpits, a side of card games, of frenzied balls, of the insolent familiarity and tiresomeness of bought love, of the endless round of shallow social occasions, including ones where grief was feigned for those who had departed it all.

One thing Lermontov did love, however—agonisingly and passionately—poetry. And in that kingdom Pushkin ruled. Not the short, restless and frivolous, already balding Pushkin, who might be seen at receptions and about whose wife recent distasteful talk had been circulating, but another Pushkin, someone it was impossible to think of without tears welling up in one's eyes.

Lermontov envied to the point of pain everyone who was familiar with Pushkin and he blushed at the very sound of Pushkin's name. He could have met him—yes, long ago—but he did not want an acquaintanceship of just another man-about-town with him, he wanted to go to him as a poet himself; and he could not do that yet, he did not dare, he had not been ready.

Until today. At last, an oracular voice spoke to him: 'Go!' and he was overwhelmed by a feeling of lightness and of panic. There was something oddly elemental in his decision, as if a coiled steel spring had been suddenly freed and with the imperative twang of a tuning fork had attained its natural shape. 'Yes, it's time!' he said to himself, and he felt a hot, stabbing jolt.

He rose, although he felt ill, ordered his horse saddled, hurried out into the snow and the cold, mounted and galloped off, launching himself on whatever course fate had willed for him.

The meeting seemed now inevitable and nothing could prevent it—but it would not occur immediately, not quite yet; it had to be at an appropriate moment. It would happen, he decided, a little later, towards evening.

And now, an hour after midday, his face drawn from the tension of his determination and flushed with secret feverishness, Lermontov was entering Dumas on the corner of Gorokhovaya and Greater Morskaya

Streets.

2

He arrived at the restaurant at one, fresh snow adhering to his clothes and red-cheeked from the biting chill of his passage. The moment he entered, and while still in the foyer being relieved of his accoutrements, he was surrounded by the warm odours of sauces, roast meat, wine and the heavy fragrance of tobacco. Through the glass doors he made out a sumptuous dining room with low, oval windows, starched tablecloths, overawing flunkeys, and sparkling silver: an ambient, as he entered it, of blue smoke and humming talk.

'If you please, this way, your honour! Such a long time we have not seen you! Your friends are here in a private room,' informed the Frenchified maître d'hôtel while with a fatherly air he preceded Lermontov.

Following him, Lermontov wiped a hand in turn over his damp eyebrows, lashes and moustache, set aright his hussar's pelisse, and as he strode past tables, his spurs jingling, his legs in their blue breeches still unsteady from the ride, he nodded and smiled momentarily in response to engaging shouts from various diners. The maître opened a door, drew back a velvet curtain, bent in a deep bow, and Lermontov entered.

'Ha! Michael lad! Is that you at last?' chorused instantly in a good-humoured discord the three or four hussars who were seated inside, among them 'le beau Mongo' of St Petersburg, Aleksey Stolypin. The room was filled with a tobacco haze pierced by the unsteady glow of candles. All those there sat with unloosened collars, smoking pipes, their flushed faces and shining eyes evidencing a carouse in its opening stages.

The moment he saw Lermontov Mongo leapt up to embrace him and kiss his chilled face. 'So, you've come out into the world at last!' he cried happily. 'Gentlemen, gentlemen, make room there! What will you drink?'

There was a shifting of places, ordering of champagne, more candles, a pipe. One of the hussars, a short blond youth with blue, very slanted eyes, shouted: 'Michael, we're planning to visit the gypsies tonight; Stesha will be singing! What a wonder she is...' and he contorted his face into an expression of rapture. 'I could die listening to her. Will you come with us, Michael?'

'There and to the gates of hell.' Lermontov replied mechanically while accepting a glass of Lafitte. 'That's if this fever of mine doesn't lay me out by tonight.'

'A bagatelle!' broke in a second hussar, one with a dark complexion and dismal expression. He launched a plume of smoke into the air and uttered in a rasping voice: 'I get those fevers too. Mine bed me down with gypsy girls all the time—ha!'

As if some solemn pledge had been uttered, all raised glasses and gulped down half the contents. Eyes glistened yet more brightly, smoke rose, and the talk continued on the subject of women, as it inevitably will when young men meet over a glass of wine.

And Lermontov after the first onrush of high spirits suddenly felt an inexplicable discomfort, grew melancholy and distant.

'Hey laddie, what's the matter?' asked Mongo quietly, looking at Lermontov with a half-serious expression while keeping an ear turned to the conversation of the other hussars. 'So you really are still ill?'

'No, it's just that I've had a lot on my mind recently,' Lermontov replied in the same confiding tone.

'Aha!' said the swarthy hussar of the cheerless face, catching Lermontov's words. 'A hussar should have nothing on his mind; a hussar shouldn't think. Everything's a matter of chance, so what's the point of worrying. If you're lucky, why, you'll break the bank in a jiffy, that's all it comes to. And as for love...' he said, now addressing the room, 'More luck! So, here's a toast to the lady—to luck!'

'Luck?' repeated Lermontov, his glance encompassing them all, 'And who's to say that when your moment does arrive you'll still have the strength and will to...'

'Oh God, more philosophising,' the hussar with the slanted eyes interrupted dolefully. 'You're becoming unbearable, Michael. And I suppose you'll have started to hate women, next?'

Everybody laughed and Lermontov laughed as well, his moustache lifting and revealing his white teeth. 'No, it's impossible to have a moment's serious conversation with any of you,' he said in a lighter tone. 'Give me a pipe, I haven't smoked in a long while. And some champagne. Dear old Mongo...' he turned again in a lowered voice to Stolypin, 'you don't know how glad I am to see you. I had a dream about you last night. I'll tell you later. It's been a queer time for me lately, in general, and I don't know myself what I shall be doing next; whether I'll be on some highroad to vice or to stupidity; not that but both lead to the same end in these times. So, gentlemen—we'll be off to the gypsies then? It's decided?'

He talked and laughed, turning his wan face this way and that, loosened his collar, drank steadily, blew smoke-rings. The candles flickered, heat radiated from the room's small fireplace, its logs spat sparks, and Lermontov sat feeling a limp contentment in that warmth and light. Within a very short time all the regimental gossip was known to him, what the Grand Duke had said the day before yesterday, what the last opera had been and the next would be, and he quickly entered into the disconnected talk around him, contributing to it his own habitual witticisms, cruel jokes, in his turn laughing unpleasantly with his head thrown back.

And then suddenly he remembered about Pushkin and stopped himself halfway through some word. He looked hurriedly towards a window, took his Bréguet out from its fob pocket and depressed the catch. The watch sounded two. Lermontov stood up.

'What's this? What's this? Where's he off to?' shouted the hussars.

'Can't stay, gentlemen, I've an appointment.'

'The devil!' Mongo exclaimed with put-on envy. 'He's got a new affair. When did you manage it?'

'On the contrary, an old one!' said Lermontov. 'So then—until this evening!'

He walked quickly through the dining room without looking at anybody, got into his street things, adjusting the angle of his sabre, and went out to take a sleigh. Finding one waiting, he got in and sat down, quickly bending and lifting his body forward and giving a sharp tug to the skirts of his greatcoat to wrap them more tightly about his legs. He saw the cotton-padded spine of the driver tautening and rounding, heard the whistle of the runners, the muffled thudding noises from the horse in front, and St Petersburg flew to meet him.

Shako tilted over his forehead, his face sunk into the depths of his collar, Lermontov breathed in with a wince the icy air of the sleigh's passage and he thought of Pushkin.

He saw in his memory the figure of the poet as he had observed it from a distance once. It was an evening when Lermontov's unit was rostered for guard duty at the palace. Windows blazed with light, streetlamps glowed around Alexander's Column and on both flanks of the entrance, there were constant arrivals of coaches and carriages over the snow. Tautly squeaking, they ascended the wood-cobbled pavement to the palace doors: new vehicles with springs and shining with lacquer, old ones that were mounted lower, unpretentious and comfortable, and each stopped in front of the portals for just a moment or two. The entryways to a series of connected halls stood wide open, and into the brilliant warm depths and heights within passed generals with plumed headwear, envoys, ancient dames from the time of Catherine II, senators.

And then another carriage drew up, with Gentleman of the Bedchamber Pushkin on board, in a fur coat and a tall, glossy top hat with brim down-tilted front and back, stepping out to give his hand to a descending vision enveloped in furs, his wife. At such evening functions Natalya Pushkina was especially sparkling, young and astonishingly beautiful; but Lermontov hardly saw her, his eyes following the little man beside her, active and quick in his movements and with a somewhat jaundiced pallor and grey lips.

He remembered such things clearly now, in daylight and with the noise of the metropolis around him, the soft jolts of the horse, the shouts of the driver, and he sat on with a feeling of dread.

In the sky above him a struggle of wrestlers was taking place: grey, murky clouds converged and briefly separated again, by turns filling the city beneath them with a shadowy, fantastic light and returning it an instant later to its workaday winter pallor.

At half past two Lermontov drew up at the Rostopchin home. Why was he calling on the countess? He himself could not say. Probably out of habit, just in case—who knew who might be there at one of her salons!

Rostopchina was alone, a young woman with a good, slender figure, bare-shouldered and with large, grey eyes that dominated whomever they happened to turn upon; yet they were eyes that expressed universally nothing, whether considering the frozen Neva through a window or resting on some person, be it the butler or her mother or aunts or the countless aged dependants in her establishment.

It was only when she gazed at Lermontov that those eyes seemed to darken, to waver a little, and to acquire an inner glow. And Lermontov presented at this moment an especially swarthy, unattractive, short, stooped and large-headed aspect, as if he had decided intentionally to display at one instant all his deficiencies. He was particularly nervy and inattentive now in her drawing room, restlessly rising from his seat, pacing the floor, suddenly halting at a window to look out at the river, then resuming his pacing again, bowlegged in his riding breeches, limping, jingling his spurs.

'You haven't recovered from your illness yet, and that is why you are angry,' Rostopchina said at last and sighed. 'Have you some new poems? I would be pleased to hear you read them.'

Lermontov came to a window again and stood looking at the Neva. He folded his arms over his chest and she saw his shoulders lift with the movement.

'You like to interpret dreams, Countess...' he began.

'Stop that!' Rostopchina broke in, 'What are those poems, Michel? You've just come, it seems, expressly to upset me!'

'Explain this dream to me,' persisted Lermontov. 'I open a door and enter a large room; but beyond it is another room, then a third. I walk through room after room, expecting any moment to see something that will astonish me, frightened to see that thing, and yet, it would seem, impatient to see it. Finally, I come to a room that contains a coffin. I see my grandmother. She is lying in that coffin looking up at me. I come close and speak to her—I don't remember now about what—and she sits up and we embrace. She looks at me raptly, and I kiss her cold hands. Then she begins kissing my hands. I feel her trying to bite me through the skin—here!... Countess, you seem to have grown pale,' Lermontov remarked calmly. And then he asked: 'My grandmother—a vampire? Does the dream foretell some evil?'

'No, I'm convinced that troubling dreams always lead to something good. But promise to never again tell such a terrible and uninteresting dream! But I forgive you for one reason.'

'What reason?'

'I know that you are intent on meeting that poor Pushkin.'

'How did you know that?'

'I suppose it must be to do with women being clairvoyant when... they are loved,' she said smiling.

'You are right, Countess. Let the world roast in its own hell, but as for me, I've never been happier than I am today!' And Lermontov gave the floor an emphatic thump with his foot. 'Happier than a drunk singing in a gutter!'

And he almost ran to the porter's lodge, in his spasm of elation carrying outside from that modest chamber an acute impression of its odours of coffee and furs.

Through the turns and rolls of his resumed journey it seemed to him that the sleigh could not go quickly enough, was dawdling despite the snorting of the horse, its flickering legs, despite the passing houses on each side, the glinting windows, the pediments with their columns and lions, the gratings, crowds, other sleighs and sledges, the signboards, despite his driver's feral, grown sensually excited anarchic cries, high-pitched and then falling, irresistible: the medieval exaction of precedence from the pedestrian rout by those mounted, '*Padi-padi-i-i!...*'—Down on your faces! Way! Way!

'Stop there!' Lermontov shouted to the driver after the third or fourth call on other acquaintances, and he took out the Bréguet. 'Turn towards the Moyka and head for Choir Bridge! Go!'

And at five o'clock he arrived at the building by the Moyka River belonging to Princess Volkonskaya, in which Pushkin had his apartment.

3

At five he halted by the Moyka. At five, hotly flushed like a boy, catching a spur in the sleigh-robe, he leapt out at the Volkonsky entrance.

'He is not at home!' they told him. And to his question: 'Will he be back soon?' the answer was brief—'Soon!'

He went out into the frosty cold, wiping his face with his handkerchief and actually feeling a degree of relief that the meeting would not take place quite yet. He got back into the sleigh and continued slowly along the road, considering whom else he might drop in on.

But having gone back over Choir Bridge and taken a right turn, intending to do a circuit via Million Street, Lermontov on an instant told the driver to stop by the Winter Canal and wait for him. Leaving the sleigh, he paced slowly along the short canal, returning more than once to the Moyka.

What was passing through his mind? The elements of some poem perhaps? Or was he thinking that later in the evening he would be on the way to Pavlovsk aboard a rushing troika on an empty road, and then in the redly-ardent light of candles and oil-lamps would listen to the songs of the gypsies?

Dusk began to fall, the street surroundings to fade, grow inert and mat; dispersed downy snow drifted slowly through the air. Lermontov never did turn finally into Million Street but continued instead pacing towards the Neva and back. Beyond the straight, sky-reflecting and vaguely blue band of snow-dusted ice which was the Winter Canal on its way to the river, rose the walls of the Hermitage. Behind that darkening bulk the west was coloured by the last of the sunset, a dimming stratum interrupted twice again: at the Neva embankment by the black hump of the canal bridge, and back towards the Moyka by the arced overpass to the Hermitage.

Lamplighters were beginning to light the streets, windows to glow, and their yellow radiance reached out warmly and benignly into the cold blue-greyness of the departing day.

Then the wind which earlier had gusted lightly completely stilled, and the snow now fell sheer and was so dry and feathery that it did not adhere to Lermontov's shako or greatcoat but drifted away at his slightest movement.

From every direction came the swish and crunch of traffic moving on snow, the snorting of horses, shouts of drivers from smart cabs, voices of passengers, women's laughter. Twice he heard a hail addressed to him, but he made no acknowledgement and did not turn his head.

He came back to the Moyka once more and peered towards the Volkonsky mansion. The lights in Pushkin's apartment were also being lit. The golden stain of a single flame floated from room to room, from window to window, and those glowed increasingly brightly with each added touch delivered to the candelabras inside. But then curtains were suddenly wrenched across each square, and all were extinguished and replaced by intervals of weak, coldly blue luminosity.

For the last time Lermontov took out the Bréguet and with a frozen hand pressed it open. The watch chimed six o'clock. And at that moment he saw a black carriage approaching and crossing Choir Bridge from the direction of Palace Square. He started and shuddered. It was the carriage of Baron Heeckeren: he recognised it immediately and caught his breath. At once, all the talk in recent days of an imminent duel between Pushkin and the Baron's favourite, d'Anthès, flooded back to him.

The carriage approached like a catafalque. He began walking towards the bridge, first uncertainly, then more and more quickly, stumbling as his feet caught in the long skirts of his greatcoat.

He was almost running by the time he crossed, and even so he was too late. The doors of the mansion's entryway were open, people carried something through, something heavy, awkward; he could hear their laboured breathing, heard a faint, breaking voice, lights flickered within; and then in a space between people's backs he saw for one brief moment a drooping, trembling head in the act of painfully lifting. Pushkin's head.

As if moving in a dream, he went to one of the group, a man in a military uniform doing something with rapid actions near the carriage. 'What is it?' he asked him. 'Dead? Tell me, for God's sake!'

Konstantin Danzas, Pushkin's second, did not reply.

'Ah!' Lermontov exclaimed in a choked voice, and gripping Danzas by the lapels of his greatcoat he shook him so that the other's hat rocked. 'He's killed!...'

And then he saw Danzas more clearly: he was crying, all of his large frame was shaking, his cheeks jerked with such disfiguring pain that his face had almost lost its human cast.

Lermontov staggered away. Just short of the bridge he stopped and put his hands on the rails that enclosed the Moyka and stood looking down at the iced-over river. 'So that's how it goes...' something said inside him, 'How it goes...'

He went on, over the bridge and towards the sleigh, slipping and somehow recovering on strengthless legs, his eyes fixed ahead. He fell once on the frozen ground and it took a moment of graceless effort to return to his feet. He ran his tongue over his moustache and felt the cold and salty taste of it. The recumbent driver, his bulk enlarged by a layer of snow, gave Lermontov's face one glance—and he hurriedly descended to help him into the sleigh, with frightened concern to tuck the heavy sleigh-robe about him.

'Home!' said Lermontov in a weak, hoarse voice, throwing himself back and furiously kicking aside the heavy cold scabbard of his sabre, and the sleigh jolted forward. He had never been conveyed at such a rate before, and yet it did not seem to him rapid enough: the Neva's reflection blinded him and he shut his eyes, while through clenched teeth angrily and wretchedly he kept demanding: 'Faster! Faster!'

And when he arrived and had bounded from the sleigh without a backward glance at the overheated horse, its body steaming with vaporising snow, Lermontov, his steps lumbering, faltering, burst into his room, and not pausing to do more than tear off his pelisse and tug free his collar he collapsed on a divan.

Eyes tightly shut, his body lying for a long time in a distorted pose, unaware of his discomfort, he hardly breathed, while all the day's events and scenes forced their return through his mind: the restaurant Dumas, the visited houses, the halls and stairways and talk and laughter, the streets; and amidst it himself, the pained relentless witness of it all.

And then he remembered again that night at the Winter Palace, the distant piping and whistling of a mazurka repeating with unreal gaiety the same, monotonous motif, while a murmuring crowd moved onwards together, all in the same direction, quietly and in deferential progress, with only a rustle of clothing and hushed comments. And among it, in concord with the couples before and behind him, just as they did, one was there who offered a hand to something bright, pale and glittering, superbly dressed in stuffs light-coloured and brilliant: his wife. And he, that figure, paced on, like those in front and those behind, into the depths of the palace, into halls that opened on each other endlessly, one and then another and another: paced onward, the gentleman of the monarch's bedchamber, with the tired face and ashy, African lips.

Lermontov wrote his inflammatory poem on the death of Pushkin that night.

Six weeks later—after a period of imprisonment in the *ordonnanzhaus*, interrogations by a military tribunal, ordered to the Caucasus and newly accoutred in the uniform and shaggy sheepskin cap of the dragoons—he was travelling on a post-chaise to his new billet.

The little bells on the harness-bow above the shaft-horse tinkled musically, villages of wooden houses, blackening and greying in the beginning thaw, passed now on one side now on the other, bare withes curving up from the receding snow waved in the wind. The dark road was already visible beneath the cambered, granulating snow, and Lermontov's hooded carriage settled often and moved heavily and slowly.

St Petersburg was distant behind him; it had become finally completely empty without Pushkin.

Lermontov's thoughts were dim and troubled. He was going a long way away, going—by a similar literary presaging as had told Pushkin's fate—to fight in five years' time the duel in which he himself would be killed by a pistol-shot to the heart.

16. ANTLER COTTAGE

1

She has been convalescing at the seaside rest home for some days now. She arrived here after a long illness and at first would not venture out but just sat inside the echoing, cold veranda, dispiritedly watching the squirrels jumping in the pines outside.

On the fourth day she wakes early while the morning beyond her window is still in the half-darkness of a long spring-dawning. She dresses and goes out though the porch door and stands on the steps until her face is turned rosy by the chill air, by the smell of March snow and the sight of the pine-covered hills, by the morning's clarity and silence. Her first steps are careful as she goes down the path, thawed yesterday and frozen again overnight, and she holds her arms slightly out from her sides, ready to balance herself. Where there had been shallow puddles, the ice breaks crisply under her soles, and the clean sound, sharp and loud in the calm morning, stirs at the edge of her memory a response from something heart-achingly sweet and secret, distant now and concealed even to herself. She moves further away from the house, not looking back, walks up the rise of a hillock and finds below her the iced-over sea with a black line of free water near the horizon, sees her surroundings grow lighter and the sun at last rising, still lustreless and weak.

She returns a little later, smelling of the frost, and passing through the dining-room acknowledges with a shy murmur the greetings of other residents, her face lowered, hiding her smile, her still-dazzled eyes.

Like all who are emerging from an illness, she has inexplicable radiant moments, and her happiness is particularly fresh and keenly felt because she is sixteen, has enigmatic dark, limpid eyes, because she is alone and free to do what she wants, because her imagination is naive and fanciful. Awesome and quaint and fairyland-like is how she perceives everything around her.

Each morning she trembles with happiness when she hears the deep, kindly voice of the announcer on the house-radio: 'Runā Rigā! Pareizs laiks...' Each morning, with a crunch of one heel and then the other, she places her feet exactly into the prints she made yesterday, and swaying thus from one to the next returns to the hillocks, where among the pussy-willows she stretches her body forward, her thin face turned upwards, and breaks off withes loaded with catkins that she takes back to put into a vase. And each day she goes further, all alone in the pine woods, comes out on the seashore and walks on the ice, fearfully, out, out, and then stops, hardly breathing, terrified to move, while she feels the ice swaying and shifting beneath her like a sentient thing in discomfort.

On her way back, she stops to examine with pensive and wistful curiosity the boarded-up holiday cottages that have been standing empty throughout the winter. Her growing interest in them elicits for some reason a thrill, gay and intrepid, such as one might feel while secretly and pleasurably leafing through a book of fairy tales past the age for such things.

She makes no friends at the home, speaks fleetingly and politely in a little voice, almost bobbing a curtsy as if she were still at school, reddening, fumbling, afraid to look at others. She likes her solitude, her freedom and her outings, likes them increasingly and dismisses from her mind the thought that she will eventually have to leave this place. But the more reclusive she is, the graver and more adult she tries to seem, the more clearly her girlhood shows.

One day a young man passes her on skis. He wears a knitted pullover and his legs are thin, appearing in their tights almost fleshless. He slows his career, stops and stands looking back at her. But she hurries on, fixing her eyes on her feet and pretending indifference, not noticing how panicked her movements have become. After that, he appears often in the area, skiing up the rises, halting and looking about; but he does not pass near her again.

The cottages in the forest are a pretty sight, one nicer than the next. The sun is shining, blue-green shadows lie at the base of fences and at the foot of trees, squirrels jump from one pine to the next, dense moss grows yellow and green on concrete fence-posts; and at night the clock on the steeple of the kirk tolls slowly, and from a distance sometimes comes the two-tone call of an *elektrichka*. The rest home is old and fires off explosive little creaks, ice rustles down the drainpipes, and there is a constant far hum from the sea; a keen, astringent odour of dry granulated snow, of pine bark and pungent, sappy pine nodules is always present. With every passing day, the sunset tarries longer, is visible through ever more transparent air, the sky above the flush deepens and seems colder, while in the east the points that are stars grow more acute and azure. And when the sunset passes, its glow departing behind a thin yellow curtain that turns green and then lilac, the trees then and the cottages with their see-through verandas, the kirk and the cross above its steeple, stand starkly black against that waning background.

At night the girl flies over the hills, hearing quiet music and feeling her heart beat from fright and rapture. When she wakes, giddy and still insubstantial to herself, she decides with adolescent earnestness that she must really take herself in hand, consider what this thing is that is happening to her. And what is happening is something out of the ordinary, totally mystifying to her. She has almost stopped replying to letters, she is in love with the stretches of silent forest, with the music she hears in her dreams, with being alone. She loves everything which seems abandoned and speechless, loves the quiet, sunny clearings with their scattered overgrowths of purple-willow shoots and copses of silvery-grey balsam firs, loves the rocky grottos in the cliffs beside the sea.

In the evenings a fire burns in the fireplace of the home's parlour, a room scattered with old-fashioned furniture. Birch logs set upright in the hearth crackle and spark, crimson-purple shadows dance on the walls, there is a pleasant smell of smoke, and the big windows at the western end glow coldly with light. And that is the occasion she waits for: she tiptoes down there, curls up in a lounge chair and looks with wide, shining eyes into the fire. Sometimes, after glancing at the windows, then assuring herself from the sound of talking in the distant dining hall that no one is approaching, she goes to the old walnut upright and lifts the lid of the keyboard. The ivory keys are yellowed, stiff and cold. She presses a pedal and strikes one of the keys and hears a tired, fading hum. She would like to recall the music she heard when she was sleeping. She stretches her fingers over a chord, then another, her fingers grow cold, she shivers; it seems to her that she almost had it and will remember it in another moment... But no, it's not like that, not like that at all... And so she carefully closes the lid again, her breath leaving a trace of mist on the piano's varnish, and she returns to her chair to curl up again and go on looking with an absent smile into the fire, to listen to it crackling and smell the strangely sad yet satisfying and inexplicably domestic odour of birch smoke. 'What's the matter with me?' she thinks in wonder. 'Why do I feel this ache in my heart? And why should that pain seem so dear to me?'

For some time now, one in particular of the empty cottages has caught her attention. It stands a distance back in spacious grounds under trees and is barely visible at first behind its fence until one approaches nearer. The doors are clearly fastened tightly, the windows are covered by jalousie shutters, it has a high and sharply-peaked roof of dark tiles, and the snow is banked up almost to the top step of its porch. Nailed to the front wall, a little under the attic window, is a set of deer antlers, brown and shining as if lacquered, and that window unlike the others is for some reason not shuttered, and its glass, as also all the glass of the veranda on that side, gleams palely with the tones of the sunset. The snow around the house is clean and undisturbed by humans: perhaps the reason why the surrounds of the cottage seem unusually extensive and secluded. The fence is also uncommonly high and solid, with the exception that in one place a couple of broken palings have allowed dogs to wriggle through, and their prints have left a deep, clear trail to a large pine. From that pine, lighter lines of prints fan out for reasons unknown into the depths of the property.

'Antler Cottage,' is the name the girl has given the little building and the enclosed land about it. And now she hardly goes anywhere else but walks there daily, noting with glee and satisfaction as she draws nearer that only her own recent footprints are to be seen and none other. She takes a seat on a convenient stump on a little rise, tucks the skirts of her overcoat tightly against the back of her knees, and sits there a long time, very quietly.

She passes the time thinking about the sealed-up house. She imagines its empty, dark rooms vibrating with silence, the stillness within at night, the needle-thin rays of moonlight penetrating through fissures in the shutters.

But the glade about her is full of glittering motes, full of light, and the sun is so warm that the resin on the sunlit side of the pine trunks softens and runs, the stems of pussy-willows poke up out of thawed snow-funnels, perspiring, and their pliant, mist-grey offshoots are already downy and swelling with sap.

2

It all happens on a day when the spring air is especially warm and spicy, a day when one's head might spin and mind be bemused, when the heart pines with indeterminate longing, pines mutely and dwindles within itself. The girl gasps quietly and claps both her hands to her mouth as she looks wide-eyed at the cottage—there, up in the attic, the window has opened and someone, a little man, looks out!

He clambers over the sill, backside first, feels with his feet for an antler and stands on it. At that moment a ladder, long and narrow, is thrust out of the window. The little man lodges the bottom of it on the ground and steps down the rungs, arriving on the snow outside the porch. A moment later down the ladder comes another diminutive man. 'Goodness—trolls! It must be trolls!' the girl concludes. 'The gnomes of legends—and they live in that enchanted house!' And she jumps up from the stump, stands, and follows open-mouthed the actions of the pair.

They are dressed in a style long unseen: breeches that descend to stockings, low-hemmed lilac sleeveless jackets, night-caps with tassels; both are bearded and have an air of self-conscious dignity, both smoke ancient meerschaum pipes. Having sat themselves down side by side on the warm top-step of the entry, they remain there, feet dangling, their faces lifted to the sun, resting motionless. An occasional cloudlet of smoke comes first from one, then the other, escaping lips that in both individuals are surrounded by whiskers of a greenish hue.

The smoke drifts sideways towards the peering, unseen girl: and all the strange aromas of southern lands, wisps of equatorial fragrance, waft to her nostrils, and she inhales repeatedly, deeply, while the day's light airs tremble and unravel themselves into tempered streams, and on all sides there is a rustling of snow dropping, constantly detaching and dropping from the firs and the pines. The trolls stand suddenly, and with a busy attitude walk one behind the other across the sky-reflecting azure snow. At a thicket of pussy-willows they seem to take a long time sniffing for something, unearthing rootlets, examining them, holding them close to their eyes. That done, they wipe their hands and begin to play, showering the downy, round willow-catkins on each other, running unhurriedly about the yard, and all the while preserving that mien of studied self-importance, their pipes never leaving their mouths. Their sober frolic ended, they stroll to the porch, climb back into the garret, pull the ladder up and in, the window slams—and once again the cottage appears uninhabited.

Hardly breathing and intoxicated by the sunlight and the trolls' smoke, quietly and carefully controlled, the girl returns to the rest home, in trepidation that her face will reveal to others there this thing that has happened to her, that she might be asked questions, that suspecting people might begin to elicit from her what occurred.

And all that day she is not herself, she looks at her surroundings with the eyes of a wild creature, tormented by doubt, unable now to believe what she had seen; and in a turmoil of impatience for the arrival of night, she lies down on her bed fully clothed and thinks of the trolls. Sleep is impossible, her face is hot, her lips have dried and cracked. The clock in the kirk's steeple beats the hours, the home is silent; but it seems to her that someone is walking from room to room, pausing occasionally to look out of a window, touching the keys of the piano in the parlour.

Fainting with anxiety and dread, feverish, ecstatic, she rises and stands for a moment, listening, watchful and rigid. She goes outside, and on the steps again is startled almost to pain by the silence, the sharply-brilliant blue stars, and the odour of snow.

Too frightened to look about her she hurries breathlessly through the park-grounds of the home and out into the lane, past sleeping houses, shuttered shops, under streetlights, her heels tapping over the ribbed paving of a footpath; and finally she turns towards the sea, the woods and Antler Cottage.

The streetlights have been left behind, and in their absence surrounding vague objects suddenly abate and acquire a bluish hue, while the darker pine trees and firs seem to advance upon the path. Between their trunks the moonlight shines bright and revealing; the fence now appears, standing on the edge of its own sharply-bordered and profound shadow; elsewhere the snow glints and seems to smoke.

Approaching the cottage, she stops and rises on tiptoe, looks towards it through the thinning trees and—glimpses light! Yes, escaping from a jalousie! As in a dream, she arrives at the fence and follows it to the broken palings, crouches low and crawls through the hole. The line of frozen pawprints stretches before her and she follows them; her paces are long and she pauses repeatedly on the indented little trail to consider each move.

At the tree she turns sharply; the level snow to the cottage is firm, its surface granular, and each step produces a sound like a knife cutting a watermelon.

She stops before the porch. A fire is burning in the cottage, for a thin column of smoke rises from the chimney and casts weak, wavering shadows on the snow. Music is audible, a flute and some unidentifiable string instruments: the hollow piping void of resonance but sweet, the muted strings strummed in measured chords, give voice and cadence to some graceful, slow-lingering old melody. Why, the very one she had heard in her dreams!... And at that moment they come back to her, those light, spectral-shadowy, frightening and wonderful dreams, and she recognises everything: the way she had nightly flown here, gliding from hill to hill, launching herself to swim in air, between spaced pines, drifting down long rays of moonlight. And sounded, sounded then that inhumanly beautiful music!

She nears a window, looks upwards between the louvered slats of a shutter: a flickering saffron light is playing on the ceiling inside, alternating with monstrous moving shadows. Clutching her hands tightly to her breast she peers through the gap between two shutters.

Waves of ruby luminosity issue from an open fireplace, and in that light she makes out a rough-hewn log table standing in the middle of the room, surrounded by a number of like crude chairs with tall backs. On the table is a small wine-cask, beside it are pewter mugs and a round cheese. Trolls are sitting at the table. They are many. All are bearded, comically serious-important, drinking, eating, playing cards and smoking meerschaums. With the same solemn expressions, other trolls sit on tree-rounds by the hearth, and the most ancient of them, his cap pushed partly over his eyes, his hands raised acutely-curved by the side of his head, is the flautist, playing, while the rest of the group near the fire gravely and tristfully pluck the strings of lute-like instruments, and only the faces of yet others, dancing to the music, reveal an exceptional modicum of liveliness. Their dance is archaic, its movement flowing and circular, of a pattern regularly disparted by elegant deferential bows. And all the room is filled with a haze of pipe-smoke intermittently haloed by glimmering rings of light emanating from rosy, thin candles set in bronze holders.

'What does it all mean?' marvels the girl to herself. 'What a wonderful place! And—what if I should go in to them?...'

She leaves the shutter, mounts the top step of the porch and tries the door. To her surprise, it opens—the music immediately grows louder and more distinct: the cottage resounds with it, seems itself to play it, the old beams to sing and the furniture, forsaken by the owners, to sway to it.

The girl crosses the veranda—a porch enclosed with varicoloured glass—feels her way down the corridor, timidly pushes the door to the room where she had seen the trolls at their entertainment... and instantly the flames on the hearth blow out, the music breaks off, the startled dancers halt!... The trolls glare with wild looks at her. She wants to say something kind to them, speak a friendly word... but she cannot, she is unable to utter a sound. And yet her eyes glisten and her face is flushed with confusion, with eagerness to understand, with delight, all her being is reaching out to the trolls... and they grow calmer.

But their secret is destroyed. They all stand, clear away the meal-things from the table, gather the cards, collect at a trapdoor in the floor and lift it open. The coals in the fireplace, then the candles, save a last, are extinguished, and one by one the trolls descend: gravely, slowly, each bowing to the uninvited guest before disappearing beneath the boards.

One troll remains, the oldest, the one with the most important bearing and the ugliest: the flautist. And the girl looks questioningly, appealingly at him, waits for him to say something. But he does not speak and goes to the trapdoor. Holding that last candle in his hand, and about to follow the others, he pauses, turns and fixes his eyes on her. An inkling of hidden good-will is in that look, an intimation of something wonderful, astonishing awaiting her. His eyes pass some message to her, his thousand-year-old face, with its prophetic knowledge of the sorrows and joys of life, is conveying something... but she is unable to understand, and her wanting to is like an ache in her. He raises a finger to his lips and nods to her significantly, and then, descending, he blows out the candle and closes the trapdoor over his head.

She feels her way, now with some difficulty, out of the dark building and sits down on the top step. Her cheeks are burning and her heart is beating hard. 'Why would he not speak to me?' she thinks painfully. 'But— of course—they can't, not with us. Yet, he did want to say something, I saw that. How very interesting!'

Suddenly she feels a presence behind her and, turning, sees the old troll again. He is considering her, but as before there is kindness in his look, and his face in the moonlight is even more evocative of mysterious capabilities, of knowledge and fateful insights. But he is so small and delicately frail that she would like to reach her hand out and stroke his beard, touch his little cap. Silently he nods to her, leaves the porch and skips down from the top step, gesturing to her over his shoulder. She rises obediently to follow him, and he leads her to the shuttered window through whose slats she had peeped at the festive trolls, and points to the same gap between the two shutters. Cold apprehension steals over her, but she puts her eye to it. And a quiet little scream escapes her.

Instead of the room, she sees a day brilliant with sunshine, hills striated with pine trees—and there the familiar skier is rising and sinking noiselessly over the undulations: she can make out his sunburnt face with its concentrated look, his strong, thin figure, can see the manner in which he throws wide his skis and how vigorously he thrusts down with the poles.

She watches and watches, then turns to the troll; but he has gone. Silence is all around, the moon is bright, the emerald stars have opened wide their radiant lashes; and fall, constantly fall the snow-caps, down from the pines and the fir trees, leaving with every descent the lightest trail of powder suspended for a moment in the moonlight.

3

Next day she wakes late, when rays of smoking sunlight have penetrated her transom window and lie in straw-coloured ruled squares on the floor. And once again she senses the new day with an expanding rush of amazement and unspeakable happiness. She rises to the voice of the announcer—'Runā Rigā!'—to the fresh frosty air coming through the window-vent, to the smell of coffee and the warmth of the home. All morning, out of sight of everyone, she sings, she dances in imitation of the trolls, falls at times face-down on her pillow in paroxysms of reasonless hilarity.

In the afternoon she can bear it no longer and she sets out for the cottage. But when she arrives she is afraid to look at it or so much as turn her head towards it. It seems to her that the trolls will be angry if they see her there again. But she can do nothing else, she cannot stop herself. Distracted, she brushes away with a red-mittened hand the morning's soft snow from her usual stump and sits down. Then she takes some deep, open-mouthed, vaporous breaths, and, finally resolved, lifts her eyes to the cottage.

It is again uninhabited. Its jalousies are tightly shut, the antlers glow wanly on the front wall, and the window above them is closed. There are no trolls. She looks for her prints of the previous night, but sees none, and feels a jolt in her heart and bitter disappointment. So, she had not been here at all, then!

She slides off the stump, walks with determination to the fence and without any attempt at concealing her actions wriggles through the hole. Within, she bends to peer at the blinding smooth snow, even feels here and there below its powdered surface with her fingers. No, she finds nothing, just the frozen-hard trail of dog-prints leading to the pine. She goes to the cottage and walks around it, touches the door—locked and immobile—recognises the window the troll had pointed to, seeks out the gap. But the shutters too are tightly sealed. No, there are no signs anywhere; and there were no trolls, there had been no music, candles, fire on the hearth. And her pain at last becomes unbearable: desolate and alone she bursts into tears, blubbers, rubs her wet cheeks with her mittened fists.

Between the pines comes the skier, swooping down a slope, lifting glittering snow-dust, rising up another slope and then accelerating down again towards a third hillock, up and down along the seashore, diminishing, obscured by his self-created mist.

She recognises him instantly and, tearful and snuffling, from a corner of the cottage she follows his course. She can believe nothing now, and when he drops momentarily out of sight she wipes away her last tears and goes to see whether he really had left some trace.

Her boots fill with soft snow as she clambers and pants up a rise—and from the top she does see a deep woolly line with round little pits on each side and the drag marks between them of the skier's poles! She looks about in renewed excitement, recognising everything that she had been shown by the troll: a bright March day, blue fir trees, deep-green pines, an extent of sea free of ice!... Hope and happiness overwhelm her. She may once again believe in, know the reality of, magical things, of dreams and fables! She smiles joyfully, lifts her face, grown pink, grown pretty, extends her neck, and lifting a hand to shade her still-damp eyelashes she calls—'He-e-y-y!...'—and listens with delight to the clear and ringing echo.

And caught by that jubilant, exultant cry, the distant skier digs his poles forward and halts. He turns his face, flushed by the speed of his run, stands waiting; and hearing nothing more he throws his skis about and comes back on his tracks towards her.

And she stands hidden behind a pine tree, her heart beating, listening, wondering if there will be a responding call. She is so happy, standing there with her coat fallen open, with her little red cap—a cap almost like those the trolls wear—with her thin, bared neck, her wide dark eyes in a countenance so happily flushed...

What response is she seeking from the trees and the sea and the spring? What is that music she hears, where does she fly in her dreams? Why was it so important to her to know what the troll might have said? What brings that expectant smile, that look of certainty and rapture to her face as she meets each new day and waits... for what?

Who will unravel her or construe her visions; who will tell us what the poor girl is waiting for?

17. IN THE MIST

From some distance through the mist came the distinct high ring of metal striking on metal, the sound coming unhurriedly and in measured intervals: ting!... ting!... ting!...

'Hear that?' asked Kudryavtsev.

'Yep!' the agronomist replied. 'Looks like we were heading the right way all along. Let's have a smoke.' Not waiting for a response and blowing a gusty sigh he sank down to the ground, laid his shotgun beside him and rolled on his flank to reach in a back pocket for his cigarettes.

Kudryavtsev, one of the kolkhoz mechanics, had gone hunting with the district agronomist; but the afternoon had come to nothing, nothing had been bagged. They had waited a long time at a spot where the ducks usually passed on their evening flight, had peered towards the west till their eyes ached; dusk came, and it was then that this thick mist had caught them, down there on the river flats. They struggled back through damp thickets, floundered in a boot-sucking swamp, rustled their way through sedge, and had finally become totally disoriented.

And now, from not too far away, came that chiming sound, and they both knew instantly that it was from the workshop at the edge of the kolkhoz, and so they relaxed and stopped for a smoke.

'See any stars?' asked Kudryavtsev after a while: he was short-sighted.

The agronomist raised his head and looked up. 'Nope,' he said at last, yawned, and lay back. 'It's one hell of a fog all right; and they said it was going to be clear tonight.' The cartridge-belt around his big belly was taut and he wheezed when breathing. He pulled at his cigarette infrequently but deeply.

Kudryavtsev had lain down too; but he suddenly sat up and slapped his thigh and with quickened breathing drew several loud inhalations through his nose.

'What's up?' asked the agronomist.

'Oh, I don't know; I guess I just felt suddenly happy for some reason,' said Kudryavtsev, laughing, and then asked: 'Are we having a drink tonight?'

'Pal, need you ask?' said the agronomist, and he also grew livelier. 'I keep thinking about that duck: I'm damned sure I picked it off. Pity we couldn't find it. But you saw me drop it, didn't you?'

'Me? No. When I turned to look, you were tearing into the reeds.

Raising spray higher than your head, you were,' laughed Kudryavtsev happily.

'Nah, you never see anything! There were three, flying along the bank, above the trees. They would have been a hundred paces when I banged off at them. Two turned away but the last one came down. Couldn't have come down straighter—right into the reeds. Ekh, if only we'd brought a dog!'

And there in the mist was that metallic ringing, softened by distance, repeated over and over; and Kudryavtsev said nothing, overwhelmed by this unexpected and inexplicable sense of happiness that had suddenly come over him just a moment ago. Is it the mist?—the thought passed through his mind. Or the hunting? Or that hammering: reassuring, telling of the presence of people nearby, people not yet gone to bed, still at their employment?

He remembered his wife, with whom he had recently had, as he thought, a final quarrel. He had exploded, and after that had ceased paying her any further attention, for whole days staying silent in her presence, going out at night to drink with the agronomist or some of the tractor drivers. He had only to see her resigned face to be seized with fury, and then he said abusive things to her, and it pained him as well when he said them.

And—there you are. All that had passed, had been, as it were, sucked out of him, and now all he wanted was to be good and that everybody around him should be happy and kind to one another.

'Let's get going!' said the agronomist and struggled up. 'Back empty-handed, dammit. A bit of duck would've gone well with the drinks.'

'Well, you know something, I'm happy just the same,' said Kudryavtsev, walking behind the agronomist and looking at his ample back.

They went on, calmly now, talking loudly about the recent summer, how hot it had been; and they talked about the harvest at the other collective farms. And then suddenly they came out onto a road, glistening like a ribbon of oil after the previous day's rain, the first rain for a long time.

All that summer the heat had been immovable: the wheat, flax, clover, beans, all were parched. There was that certain feeling of lassitude in everything, which is always present in such endless, exhausting droughts, and the dust on the roads was two or three fingers deep. But at last the end of August had come and the sun was losing its strength, and now what one sensed was more like an impression of heat; and something feverish seemed present in nature, something bitter and hidden and urgent, as is often the feeling during an Indian summer, early as it was for that. The nights were already beginning to grow misty and cold and left heavy dews behind, and the moon passing close above the forest shone red through the mist.

Yes, the summer had gone on and on, baking everything and turning the soil into dust; right up to yesterday, when at last there had fallen an abundance of rain and some hail as well. With that, it was suddenly the beginning of autumn and the first yellow leaves appeared and the red-brown plantains kindled into notice along the less-used cart tracks.

Kudryavtsev had gone past on this road three days earlier and seen the flax burnt to a ginger colour shot through with a chocolate tinge, the leaves moving with a dry rustle in any breath of air. And now the crop had been pulled up, and as the two passed through a grove of birch and aspen the odour from the fields was one of baths and permanganate, while nearer the road, where the flax had been dampened by the rain, it was more like that of bleached wet laundry.

'Listen,' said Kudryavtsev to the agronomist's back, 'I feel like a kid, I just want to jump and skip! You know, I heard that hammering, there's this mist all around, I saw you sitting there smoking, and it just came over me...'

'Oh, what did?' said the agronomist, and he stopped to let the other come up beside him.

'I don't know. Happiness, I guess,' said Kudryavtsev in an uncertain tone, and he gave a short, embarrassed laugh, 'That's how it gets you sometimes, in autumn. There's all that miserable weather, and then suddenly a blue window opens up there in the clouds, and you look at that blue, and in front of you the puddles on the road get brighter, and you remember all your past springtimes and how happy you were.'

'H'm, yes...' said the agronomist, and mused for a moment. 'That's life all right—remembering. I should have looked a bit longer...'

'What... what did you say?' asked Kudryavtsev, returning from his thoughts.

'I'm saying that I should have looked for that duck.'

The hunters were nearing a ruddy glow flickering through the mist and soon made it out to be a fire burning in the open outside the workshop. A number of tractor drivers, identified by their oily overalls, sat around the burning logs, their figures casting long shadows outwards in every direction. Approaching, the two also saw a caterpillar tractor with a broken track, its drive-wheels glinting with a velvet gloss from recent work over miry ground, the links shining in the firelight. Three men were busy around the machine: one was underneath it on his back, only his feet showing, the other two were working in their own shadows, trying to re-join the track by blows of a hammer, but the links kept parting.

'A good evening to all, lads. Do you need a hand there?' asked Kudryavtsev loudly, feeling his heart going out towards these people who were still at work so late.

'Hallo. And who might that be?' the one under the tractor asked, and he peered out for a moment. 'Oh, hallo. No, there's only half an hour left in it. They'll all be away shortly,' the last words come out muffled, as he returned under the machine.

'Have you pulled up the Haritonovsky section yet?' asked the agronomist, bringing an ember from the fire up to his cigarette.

'Well, not exactly...' someone answered after a moment's silence. 'We did start on time.'

'Better watch out...' the agronomist warned, 'The rep from the regional committee will be here tomorrow night.'

The two stood around a little longer, poking at the fire and enjoying the smell of grease and metal; and then they went on, and as they went past the first houses of the village they re-slung their guns barrel-down and quickened their steps.

The inexplicable feeling of happiness and contentment was still with Kudryavtsev. His tiredness left him and he kept thinking with increasing tenderness about his wife. He would make up with her the moment he got home.

'You know what?' he said to the agronomist, 'I think I'll stay home tonight, I don't really feel like drinking.'

'Oh?... All right. You do as you like,' the agronomist said, surprised.

The club was near now and they could hear the scratchy sound of a record on the radio-gramophone and see the glow of the large lamp at the club's door.

'Should we cross to the other side?' Kudryavtsev offered.

'Nah, there's just as much light over there,' the agronomist said sullenly. 'They'll see us anyway.' But he pulled the peak of his old forage cap lower over his eyes and at the next step stumbled, accentuating his lumbering gait. There were couples sitting on benches and standing by the club's fence and for some reason no one was talking, perhaps they were all listening to the music. They turned their eyes now towards the approaching pair.

'Shoot up much today, comrade agronomist?' a raspy voice called out.

'Yeah, his foot!' said another voice, and there was laughter.

'You can talk,' the agronomist sent back after a moment: annoyance affected his breathing. 'Wouldn't have popped a sparrow in your time.'

The two friends parted outside Kudryavtsev's house.

'Sure you won't come?' the agronomist asked, half turned to go.

'No,' said Kudryavtsev, 'I'll stay home.'

'Well... see you then.'

Kudryavtsev stood for a moment outside his porch, smoking and scraping his boots mechanically on the step. The gun weighed on his shoulder but his body felt light. Happiness, he thought—where does it suddenly come from when you feel it like this? If it was love, now, well, then of course that's understandable; or some particular bit of luck happening to you; or success, when your work and everything is going well and in full swing... yes, then it's all clear and there's no need to ferret into the thing. But to come to you like this, for no reason, in some dark and miserable moment... All at once something brilliant flashes inside you, your heart beats faster, and you know that you'll remember this day for a long, long time... And what a fine night this is—actually, what a wonderful thing it is to be alive!

'Zoya!' he called to his wife. 'Come out for a moment!'

And while she was looking for something in the house and her shoes pattered softly about on the floor and she opened the door into the porch to come outside to him, he drew deep breaths and coughed and inhaled into his lungs more of the cold mist, heavy with sharp odours from the kitchen garden, heard now from a distance the club's music, thought of the tractor drivers standing illuminated by the red flare of the fire.

'Will you just look at this mist, dear!' he said to his wife, and he put his hand on her warm shoulder. 'Can you see any stars up there?'

He wanted to see the stars, for some reason.

18. FLIMFLAM

1

Fuddled by the day's heat and a heavy meal of underdone, undersalted fried fish, Yegor the buoy-keeper lies sleeping in his hut.

Yegor's hut is new, unfinished and bare: it does not even have a stove and only half the floorboards have arrived from the mill. A pile of bricks and damp clay lie heaped in the entry-porch, loose oakum hangs from gaps in the log walls, and the glass in the new window-frames is still un-puttied and buzzes softly in harmony with the calls from passing steamers. Ants trail along the sills.

When Yegor wakes, the sun is setting and its radiance suffuses the faint mist rising over the fields; the river has acquired a golden stillness.

He yawns, yawns again, extending the sweet pangs of his awakening; then, after a motionless moment, he twists and stretches convulsively. Eyes still somnolent, he begins to roll a cigarette with quick, limp fingers and soon is avidly smoking, inhaling deeply while moist sucking noises escape his lips. He clears the sleep-fug from his throat by great, pleasurable coughs, tears with horny nails under his shirt at his chest and sides, his eyes grow limpid, take on a vacant look, and his whole body fills with a lush and gentle lassitude.

His smoking done, he goes into the porch and gulps with relish some water from the bucket kept there: cold river-water, odorous of leaves and roots, that gives to the mouth a pleasantly acrid taste. Then he takes the oars and the kerosene lamps and goes down to his dinghy.

There is a matting of trampled sedge in the dinghy's bottom and a quantity of water has collected in the stern, making the hull float lower at that end. The thought passes through Yegor's mind that he should bale it out, but he cannot be bothered. He sighs, looks at the sunset, then up-stream, then downstream; at last, bow-legged and straining from the added weight in the bilge, he pushes the dinghy fully out till it floats beside the bank.

The stretch of river which Yegor serves is not of any great extent: he lights the lamps on four buoys, two above and two below the hut. Each evening he ponders over the easiest way to do that, whether to row up-stream first or downstream; and now he stands for a moment considering that question. Finally settled in the dinghy, he rattles the oars into place and with his feet tamps the sedge down and pushes the lamps further along the bilge. And he begins to row: up, against the current. It's all flim-flam anyway, all meaningless, he thinks, as he loosens up and warms up with jerky strokes of the oars, snapping quickly forward after each stroke and then straightening again, looking sideways as he goes at the bank's reflection on the calm water, darkening on one side, flushing rosy on the other. The dinghy leaves behind a dark trail on the golden river, and pre-cisely-spaced rings of curling water on each side of that trail.

The air is cooling, swallows crisscross just above the water uttering high-pitched chirps, fish splash near the banks. At every splash Yegor nods in satisfaction as if each fish is known to him by name. The smell of wild strawberries, of hay and dewy shrubbery drifts to him from both shores, the dinghy itself carries the smells of fish and kerosene and sedge, and from the water rises a barely visible haze tanged with the odour of the river depths and the mysteries thereof.

Yegor lights the red and the white lamps in turn and sets them on their respective buoys; then, lazily, the oars almost motionless, he drifts like a figure in a painting down to the downstream buoys and sets on those their lighted lamps. The glow from each buoy is bright and visible at a distance in the deepening twilight. Now he rows with more effort back to the bank below the hut. He leaves the dinghy, goes up and has a wash and looks for a moment at his face in the mirror. He draws on a pair of jackboots and dons a fresh shirt, sets his old navy cap firmly on his head at a jaunty angle, returns to the river, crosses to the other side and fastens the dinghy to the bushes. A moment later he has risen to the river flats and he stands there gazing over them towards the last of the sunset.

The flats are quite covered in mist now and redolent of their own hu-midity. The mist is so dense and milky that from a distance the expanse before Yegor appears as if in flood, and as he passes through that white-ness he seems to float almost submerged in it and dreamlike, everything below the level of his shoulders invisible. As he walks he notes ahead of him the protruding tips of hayricks, and a long way beyond them the black line of the forest under a still and now fading sky.

He rises on tiptoe and cranes his neck. After a moment he detects a distant pink headscarf above the mist.

'E-ye-ee!...' he calls in a carrying tenor.

A faint 'A-a-a...' comes back to him.

He increases his pace along the path through the flats, then ducks his head below the mist and darts forward like a quail. He veers aside and drops down prone, greening his knees and elbows on the grass, his heart beating as he peers in the direction where he had seen the pink head-scarf... A minute passes, then another, and no one appears; there is no sound of footsteps, and Yegor can contain himself no longer. He rises and looks up over the breadth of mist. As before, he sees only the sunset, the forest line, the dark tips of the hayricks, and about him the vague, dove-grey surrounding dimness. She's gone to ground! Joyously and impatiently he dives again into the mist, again waits in ambush. He gathers a great breath until his face reddens with blood and the rim of his cap cuts into his forehead. Suddenly, with a start of surprise, he sees quite close her shrinking, hesitating figure.

'Stop!' he roars like a madman, 'Halt or I'll shoot!'

And with a thudding of boots he is after her, and she, squealing and laughing, runs, drops something from her purse, he overtakes her, they roll together on some soft, mushroomy, fresh-smelling patch of mole-diggings, and they hug each other tightly and happily in the mist. Then they get up and go back to find what she had dropped, and afterwards they slowly wander back across the flats to the dinghy.

2

Yegor is quite young but a drunkard already, and his wife had been one as well: a tattered and wasted little bird of a woman, considerably older than he was when they married. One autumn the ice had broken under her and she had drowned. She had been at the village, three kilometres across the river, getting vodka, and drinking and singing on the way back had arrived at the bank opposite the buoy-keeper's hut and shouted:

'Yegor, you beggar, bane o' my life, come out and look at me!'

He had emerged from the hut in a merry mood, his sheepskin coat thrown over his shoulders and a foot-rag trailing from one of his bare feet; he had watched her coming over, twirling her purse over her head, watched her stop in the middle to do a little dance, wanted to shout to her to cross over more quickly. But before he could open his mouth the ice broke, and in an instant, before his eyes, his wife had disappeared under the water. He had dropped his coat, had run in his shirt sleeves, the foot-rag unwinding further, had run barefoot over the ice, and as he ran the ice everywhere crackled and swayed and sagged gently under him. He fell down on his stomach and crawled to the edge of the hole, and all he saw was the black, vaporous water. He had howled like a dog, his face contorted, and then crawled back. Three days later he had boarded up the hut for winter and gone to his parent's home in the village.

The next spring, during the thaw, he happened to be ferrying young Alenka who lived in Trubetskoe, and when she started to fetch out her money Yegor suddenly rattled off: 'Nah, don't worry, don't worry... it's all flimflam. Drop in sometime, I'm on my own and it's dull here. And there's a few things to wash too. You get lousy without a woman. And I'll give you fish...'

And when one evening some two weeks later Alenka was returning from somewhere and dropped in on the way back to her village, Yegor's heart beat so hard that it frightened him. For the first time in his life he got dithery with a girl, running outside to make a twig fire between bricks to boil the sooty teapot, asking Alenka about her life. Halfway through something that he was telling her, he fell silent for such a long pause that it alarmed her to the point of tears, and he was just as much flustered himself. Then he had gone away to the porch, had washed himself and put on a clean shirt and taken her across the river, and because it had already become late he had walked with her a long way across the flats.

Now Alenka comes often to him in the hut and stays with him for three days at a time, and when she is with him Yegor is carefree and humorous, and when she is away he is lonely, cannot think what to do with himself, nothing seems to go right and he sleeps long and has bad and troubled dreams.

Yegor is strongly built, has a prominent Adam's apple, tends to listlessness, and walks somewhat pigeon-toed. His face is broad and rather flaccid, with a hooked nose and an immobile, dreamy expression. In summer the sun and the wind tan him almost to blackness, and then as a consequence his grey eyes appear blue. 'Look at you: a misfit; unfinished...' he jeers at himself in the mirror, especially after a few drinks. 'The devil fathered you off a drunken she-goat...'

This spring he suddenly decided to stay in the hut on May Day. Why he did not to go to the village as he had earlier intended, he himself does not know. He lies restless on his ratty, unmade bed, whistling gloomily. At mid-day his little sister runs over from the village and her thin wail comes to him from the other bank: 'Ye-go-o-or!...'

Sullen, Yegor comes down to the water.

'Ye-gor-ka-a...' she draws out the diminutive, 'They say you've got to co-ome!...'

'Who-oo says?' Yegor shouts back after a pause.

'Uncle... a-sya and Uncle... e-dya.' she shouts, the 'V' and 'F' lost in the distance.

'Why didn't they come themse-elves?'

'They can't co-ome, they're both dru-unk...'

Yegor's face is a mask of boredom. 'I've got work—tell 'em I've got work to do-oo!...' he howls back, although of course he has absolutely none; and he thinks bitterly to himself: 'Ekh, how they'll be kicking their hooves up now, over there!' imagining his drunken relatives, his mother, the tables with snacks and pasties, the incessant music, the yeasty taste of the home-brewed beer, the village girls in their holiday best, flags hanging from the izbas, films in the club. He spits gloomily into the water and trudges up the steep slope to the hut.

'... go-or, co-ome...' chimes and beckons to him the voice from the other side; but Yegor pays no attention.

His attitude to everything is one of indifference and mockery, and he is uncommonly lazy. He has plenty of money and it comes easily to him, for there are no bridges on the river near here and he takes everyone across, charging a rouble per trip, or two if he is in a bad mood. The job of a buoy-keeper is light, only work fit for a pensioner, really, and it has de-bauched him, spoiled him utterly.

Yet, sometimes a vague uneasiness seizes him, most often in the eve-nings. Lying beside the sleeping Alenka, Yegor remembers the days of his service in the Northern Fleet. He remembers shipmates with whom he lost contact long ago, remembers vaguely and idly their voices, faces, even snatches of their conversation. He remembers a low, hazy shoreline, the northern sea, the awesome polar winter-lights, the small, stunted, blue-grey firs, the moss, the sand. He remembers a lighthouse, its blinding, smoky light creeping by night over a dead forest. But all those things come to him devoid of excitement and from a distance.

At times a strange disturbance agitates him, confused and alarming thoughts pass through his mind: that the coast is still as it was and the slate-roofed barrack buildings still stand on the shore even now, the light-house flashes at night, in the barracks there are sailors, double-tiered bunks, the crackle of the radio-loudspeaker, conversations, letter writing, tobacco smoke—everything, everything is still there, but he is not there, as if he had died, as if he had never lived there, had not served, as if it had all been an illusion, a dream.

Then he gets up and goes to the edge of the river and sits or lies down under a bush, wrapped in his sheepskin coat, and he listens keenly and looks through the darkness at the lapping reflection of the stars on the water, looks at the bright, far-off glows of the buoy-lamps. There is no one at those moments towards whom he need adopt the usual poses of daily life, his face becomes melancholy and thoughtful, he feels a torment in his heart, wants something, wants to go somewhere, wants to live a different life.

From up the Trubetskoe reach a dense, velvety, three-toned hoot grows slowly to the ear and as slowly fades again. In a little while a steamer appears, all bright with lights, hissing with vapour, its side vanes thrashing the water rapidly; and now it releases another hoot, and that hollow sound, and the sounds of its engine, and of the splashing water return trembling to it from the riverside forest. Yegor looks at the ship and his yearning grows.

He imagines the passage ahead, imagines scented young ladies asleep in bunks, travelling to unknowable destinations, imagines the soft-sweet smell of steam vapour, and the polished brass in the en-gine-room, the ventral warmth of the machinery. The deck and rails are dew-wet, the watch up on the bridge is yawning, Yegor sees in his mind the helmsman making his adjustments with the wheel; and on the upper deck there will be solitary passengers sitting wrapped in overcoats, looking out at the darkness, at the tiny lights on buoys, the occasional red bonfire of fishermen, at an illuminated factory or power station: and it will all seem delightful and wonderful, those small landings will beckon, inviting you to descend and remain there in that cold and dewy stillness. And there will always be somebody lying asleep on a deck-bench, with his jacket pulled over his head, legs curled up, to be wakened for an instant by the sound of the hooter or the clean freshness of the air or the touch of the boat drifting to rest against a landing.

Life is passing him by! What is this vibration overspreading his heart and reaching beyond him, trembling towards all things around him, what is that ringing? What calls to him and disturbs him so during the dark hours in the dead of night? Why should he feel such a longing: to the extent that these pleasant, misty fields and the peaceful forest and his easy, free and infrequent work all suddenly weary him? Why, how splendid after all is his native countryside, with its dusty roads, tramped-over countless times since he was a boy, its villages with individual ways and sayings, its girls with changing natures in each one, villages he had gone to so often at dusk for kisses in the rye-fields, where he had fought frenzied, bloody fights! How joyous it is to see the blue-grey smoke of a campfire drifting over the river, and the lights of the buoys, and the lilac-coloured spring snow on the fields, and the boundless, turbid following floods, and the cold sunsets spread over half the sky, and the heaped-up leaves from last year rustling in the gullies! And a wonder is the autumn, yes, even with its melancholy; a joy, with its fine little rains and the matchless cosiness of the buoy-keeper's hut in that season!

So why does he wake, who calls to him at night in the tenor of a stellar cry reverberating thinly, tensely, across the river? Ye-go-or!... And he feels restless and feverish, far things draw him—towns, noise, lights—and a longing grows to find work somewhere, to engage in genuine work, its honesty avouched by bodily exhaustion and contentment.

And trailing his sheepskin coat he goes into the hut, lies down beside Alenka, wakes her and wretchedly and hungrily presses close to her, is aware only of her, like a child, is ready to cry. Eyes closed tightly, he nuzzles his face against her shoulder, kisses her neck, is melting with happiness, with warm love and kindness towards her; and he feels on his face her responsive, quick and tender kisses, and he no longer thinks of anything else, wanting nothing else than that this, at least, should go on forever.

Then they whisper to each other, although they could just as easily speak aloud, and Alenka, as always, tries to persuade him to settle down, to give up drinking, marry, go somewhere and get a job that would have people respect him, have them write in the papers about that unique talent of his.

And after half an hour, become calm and languid and mocking once more, Yegor mutters his favourite, 'Ekh, it's all flimflam!...' but the remark comes out in an absent and inoffensive manner, he content in his heart to let her go on endlessly whispering, endlessly urging him to begin a new life worthy of him.

3

It often happens that people passing up or down the river in motorboats, and sometimes also in kayaks or even on rafts, stop to spend the night at Yegor's hut. On each occasion the progress of events is much the same.

The travellers kill their motor and one of them scrambles up the bank. 'Hallo there, landlord!' he shouts to Yegor with confident heartiness.

Yegor does not respond. He snuffles and goes on fiddling with his new fish trap.

'A good day to you, sir,' the traveller begins again in a somewhat more careful tone, 'Would it be possible to stay the night here?'

And again the only response is silence. Yegor even holds his breath, so intent is he on his fish trap.

'How many of you are there?' he asks at last.

'Just the three… But we'll… you know…' The other's approach is by now one of no more than timid hope, 'We'll pay of course: don't imagine…'

Without interest Yegor begins an interrogation that extracts who the people are, where they are going, where they have come from: all slowly and with long pauses. When there is nothing left to inquire about, he gives them reluctant permission: 'Oh well… I suppose you'd better stay.'

The others get out of the boat as well, and the visitors set about unloading it, dragging it up on the bank and turning it over; then their rucksacks, canisters and kettles and the motor are all brought into the hut; a smell of petrol begins to circulate inside it, and the odours of travel, of boots; space is at a premium. And now Yegor becomes livelier and begins to lend a hand, feeling a flow of gaiety buoying him at the imminence of drinking. He bustles about and talks incessantly, chiefly about the weather; he shouts orders at Alenka, starts up a generous crackling fire outside the hut…

And when the time comes to pour the vodka, Yegor's eyelids droop and his eyes glint through the gaps, he hardly draws breath in his silent agony and fear that he will be passed over. He reaches out a powerful, horny-nailed dark hand to the proffered glass and utters the toast in a firm, companionable tone: 'To new mates!' and he swallows, and his expression hardens momentarily.

His descent into drunkenness is quick, happy and easy. As he becomes drunk he begins to lie—fluently, persuasively and with great enjoyment. Mostly he lies about fish, for some reason being convinced that people passing through here are interested in little else.

'Around these parts, the fish…' he begins carefully, as if restraining himself on the subject, 'are of many kinds… True, there aren't as many now as there used to be, but… I say but…' he hawks, pauses and lowers his voice, 'those who know how… Why, just yesterday, for example, I caught a pike. Not a big one, I must say; wouldn't have come to more than twenty-five kilograms... I was going out to the buoys in the morning and heard it splash. I cast right away. While I was seeing to the buoy she took the hook—yep, down to the gut!'

'A pike—twenty-five kilograms? Where is it?' they ask him.

'Oh, I took it to the workers' compound and sold it,' he says without batting an eyelid, and then he goes on to describe the fish in detail.

And if anyone gets suspicious—and there is always someone, and Yegor waits impatiently to hear the doubt raised—why, he flares up, takes hold of the bottle as if it was his, pours himself exactly a hundred and fifty grams, knocks it back, and then lifts his intoxicated, dumb-reckless eyes to the doubter and says: 'Why then, you want to come out tomorrow? What're we wasting our breath for? What motor's that you got?'

'An LM-1,' they tell him.

Yegor turns and looks at it for a moment where it leans in a corner.

'That? Flimflam! Slavka's got a Bolinder I gave him, that I brought home from when I was with the Fleet. Put it together myself: an animal of a motor—twenty kilometres an hour! Against the current, I'm saying. Well? Want to bet on them? I put up my Bolinder against that flimflam thing! Well? There's been one who took me on—lost his shotgun on it. Mm, what? You say you want to see the shotgun? A handmade little job, a Tula. Animal of a gun! Last winter I got...' he thinks for a moment, his eyes gone glassy, 'three hundred and fifty hares with it! Well?'

And the visitors, irritated and at a loss as to how to pin him down, move the subject to something else, the stove: 'Friend, how do you get on here without a stove?'

'A stove?' Yegor's voice by now has grown to a shout, 'Who's going to put it together? Do you know how? Do it! The clay's there, the bricks—all the stuff's there, in fact. Put it together and I'll give you a hundred and fifty for it. On the nail! Well? Do it!' he persists stubbornly, knowing quite well that what he is asking is impracticable and that therefore the victory will be his again, 'Well then?'

And at that moment he notes that there is still some vodka and that the guests are scoffing and laughing to each other, and he goes out into the porch and puts on his service cap with the 'crab' insignia, opens the collar of his shirt to show his old striped service-vest, and returns.

'With permission...' he announces with a drunk's exaggerated politeness, 'Boatswain's mate of the Northern Fleet reporting! Request leave to congratulate the ratings' mess on the anniversary of the Communist and Socialist Revolution! All the forces of peace—to the attack! And the devil's dam drag down the enemy by the leg! Bottoms up!'

They refill his glass. Alenka, in an agony of embarrassment, prepares the beds for the visitors, feels the hot tears ready to overflow her eyes, and with an almost distracted impatience waits for Yegor to begin the act that will astonish these people.

And Yegor begins.

Eyes dazed, he suddenly sits down on a bench, leans back heavily, positions his shoulder blades against the wall behind him and shuffles his feet to get comfortable. Then he raises his head and begins to sing.

And with the first sound of that voice, the conversation of the others instantly ceases—they look at Yegor with incomprehension, with alarm.

He does not sing the usual ribaldries of the countryside or the latest popular songs, although he knows them all and is constantly humming them; no, he sings in the old, old Russian manner, drawn out as if releasing the notes unwillingly, a touch huskily, as if the sound was rendered thus by that long egress. He sings as he heard in his childhood the old people sing. He sings now one of those ancient long lays whose interminable o-o-o's and a-a-a's enter into the very soul of the listener. He does not sing loudly, in fact his execution is rather playful and trifling; yet there is so much power and penetration in that quiet voice, so much of the genuine Russia, the land of the old *bylina* epics, that in a moment everything else is forgotten, his coarseness and silliness, his drunkenness and noisy bragging, forgotten is the road, forgotten tiredness—it is as if the past and the future have met and nothing remains but this moment in which that extraordinary voice rings and winds through the brain, clouds the mind, and one just wants to go on listening, head propped on a hand, body bent forward, eyes closed, scarcely breathing, just holding back the tears...

'The Bolshoi for you! The Bolshoi!' they all cry together, the instant Yegor finishes; and they all, excited and moved and with a shine in their eyes, try to press their help on him, they all want to write to some radio station or newspaper, to telephone someone. There is a joyfulness, a festive jubilation in everyone; while Yegor, content with the praise, a little tired now, a little deflated, returns to indifference and dismissiveness and his broad face has once again grown vacant.

His image of Moscow's Bolshoi Theatre is imprecise: the flying horses above the facade, the divisions of light between the portico columns, the glittering hall and the sounds of the orchestra are to him only what he remembers from some newsreel. He stretches lazily and mutters: 'Oh, all that's flimflam...' and then inconsequently: 'Ah, well, you know, they've got all sorts of theatres over there...'

And no one grows angry with him, so glorious his standing is now with the others, so heroic and incomprehensible he seems to them.

But this is not all the measure of his greatness.

4

No, it is not yet the whole measure of his greatness, is perhaps only a quarter of it. Its perfection appears when, as he himself puts it, 'there's something tugging' at him, a condition which occurs once or twice in a month, when he feels particularly dejected and out of sorts.

At those times, from the moment of rising he mopes and he drinks. True, he drinks sparingly, from time to time making some listless remark to Alenka, like: 'Oh, hell… What about it? What d'you think… mm?'

'About what?' Alenka feigns incomprehension.

'Oh, I don't know. Let's have a song… or something. A duet, eh?' he asks dully, and sighs.

Alenka smiles rather haughtily and says nothing, knowing that the time is not yet ripe, that Yegor's peculiar mood has still not quite irreversibly suffused him. And so she goes back and forth about the buoy-keeper's hut, busy with cleaning something, with washing, she goes to the river to rinse laundry, returns…

Then the moment comes, and it comes usually in the evening, and Yegor is no longer considering any 'duet' now. He gets up, his hair rumpled, face morose, looks out of one window then another, goes outside for a drink of water. Then he returns and thrusts a bottle of vodka into his pocket and picks up his sheepskin coat.

'Going far?' Alenka asks innocently, inwardly all atremble.

'Let's go!' says Yegor roughly, and he passes over the sill with his pigeon-toed gait. His face is white, his nostrils are distended, and the veins stand out on his temples. Alenka walks beside him, coughing and clearing her throat, knotting a woollen scarf around her neck. She knows that he will first mount a steep part of the bank, will look up and down the river, thinking for some moments as if he were pondering what best might suit things; she knows that he will then go to his favourite place, a derelict, flat-bottomed barge upside down at the water's edge among birch saplings, and that this is where he will sing with her. But it will be nothing like the singing that the travellers hear. In their presence he sings, as noted, somewhat negligently, to some extent as an act of self-indulgence, and certainly not in full voice, no!

And so Yegor in fact does stop at the water's edge, does think for a minute and then goes silently to the old barge. There, he spreads his coat out on the ground and sits on it with his back against the hull and first extends and then crosses his legs until they satisfactorily prop the bottle that he has set between them.

The sunset is in full flush, the mist has flooded the fields up to the dark tips of the hayricks, the forest on the horizon is a black line. The birch foliage above him is motionless, the grass fresh, the air warm and calm; but Alenka starts to shiver and she presses against Yegor. He extends a trembling hand to the bottle and takes a mouthful, shudders and coughs and feels his mouth filled with sweet saliva.

'Now…' he says, and he turns his head away for a moment to clear his throat, then readies her in a whisper: 'Just the second part, mind. Watch me!'

He draws in a lungful of air, tenses himself and begins in a mournful and trembling high, clear tenor:

> 'On the mirror of the ocean, O!
> On the slumbering blue water
> Of a far sea, O!...'

Alenka, frowning and in a torment of expectation, waiting for her cue among those endlessly drawn-out vowels, comes in now, low, ringing and with perfect timing:

> 'Drift a fair fowl and her youngling,
> Swan and cygnet, dam and daughter,
> Light as floating snow...'

But she does not listen to her own singing, to her own low and wan, fervent voice—how can she! She only feels Yegor's gentle hand gratefully pressing her shoulder, hears only his voice.

O what sweetness is in this song, what torment! And Yegor, now limpid now tense, one moment reduced to huskiness, the next ringing with the timbre of metal, dwells upon those ancient words, so unlike our times, so folk-simple, sung for centuries:

> 'Gold the sand that lies below them, O!
> Ne'er a yellow grain is stirred
> In that bright sea, O!
> Meek that passing, never marring
> Aught beneath braw bird and bird
> Nor the still sea's glow...'

What is this strangeness?—and yet how painfully familiar, as if Alenka had lived long, long ago and was returning now from that far time when she had sung like this and listened to the voice of Yegor weaving its enchantment:

> 'Whence that baleful eagle-shadow, O!
> Like a cloud that goes
> O'er the wide sea, O!
> Blue-grey eagle coming, coming:
> Sad fore-ken in bosom grows
> Of the coming woe...'

Yegor's voice is a moan, a weeping. With deep anguish he gives himself up to the song, rests his ear on his palm, head turned away from Alenka, and his Adam's apple trembles and his doleful lips tremble:

'See the growing of the billows, O!
Claws of water landward score,
See the roiled sea, O!
Empty now and breast-down bearing
White and foam-soft to the shore
On the storm-tide's flow...'

Oh, that dove-grey eagle! Why does he need to plunge upon the white swan, why did the grass droop, why the sudden darkness and the stars falling? O that these tears might end soon, that this voice, this song might cease!... And they sing, feeling only that their hearts will break and that at any moment they will fall on the grass dead, beyond the powers of any mystic waters to resuscitate, beyond resurrection, after such happiness and such anguish.

And when they finish, worn out, empty and happy, when Yegor silently lays his head down on Alenka's knees and sighs deeply, then it is that she kisses his pale face and whispers, choking on the words: 'Yegorka, dearest... I love you, my wonder, my golden one...'

'Flimflam!...' he wants to say, but he says nothing. His mouth has dried, and a sweet taste is left in it.

19. ON THE ROAD

1

The winter passed mildly, much as usual, the snow going quickly and leaving the ground smoking with vapour wherever it lay under the full radiance of the sun. Now colts kicked at the sides of their stalls and nibbled at the stablemen's hands, and the farm-bulls grew restless, snorted hoarsely, vented breathless, choking bellows and jerked at the oaken posts they were chained to. At the forest edges thrushes performed their aerobatics, in the twilight starlings, black and glistening like nuggets of coal, whistled, and the scent of bird-cherry blossoms rose with stupefying intensity from the ravines. Stripped to a shameful nakedness by the winter, the countryside began to clothe itself anew with the budding growths of rowans and birches and fence-arcing lilac withes.

Before long the green of the fields could be discerned through a light layer of heat-haze, and the roads grew dusty with the early prospect of a dry summer. It was then that Ilya Snegirev began preparing to go to Siberia again.

He had decided to return quite some time back, in February in fact. It was during a night when Ilya, worn out by the day's driving, had come out of the office-cabin of a state forestry camp, had stepped into a clearing strewn with the detritus of logging and walked to his truck. The vehicle stank of petrol, as did his padded jacket and trousers, his hands and his cap. His sense of smell now was such that he only recognised the odour of dust in summer and frost in winter.

But on that February night the thaw had started and the sky glowing in the distance was tinged green just above the dense blackness of the trees. The arriving spring was so tangible that Ilya could almost feel it as a presence all around him. He drew in a deep lungful of the night air, blew his nose through his fingers, and as he climbed into the chilled cab he determined there and then that he would go.

This was not the first spring that had drawn him away from familiar surroundings: he had been to other oblasts, and had actually gone to Siberia itself once, spending a miserable summer there the previous year and returning in autumn in a state of seething disgust. He had not liked living in the workers' barracks, and as for the region itself, he was sure that he had developed a loathing for it: from its bloodsucking taiga-insects to the tense, thin whine of the MAZ trucks they employed on the roads over there.

When Ilya had returned from Siberia that time, the ground at home was banded black and white where ridges of early snow lay across the bare earth, the woods were naked and dead, the grass was brittle and trembled in the wind, and at night cold gales swept over the fields and sheeted them over with temporary sleet. The winter snows came, the ground freezing and thawing by turns, and Ilya settled happily back into his previous life.

He drove day and night: to the station, to the forests, and even to the neighbouring districts, sleeping wherever he found himself at the time, his only concern being to warm up some water before daylight, fill the radiator and get the truck started; that done, he would drink a quick mug of tea with whoever had put him up, while chatting about some matter with him and listening with approval to the motor turning over outside.

He liked to travel at night along deserted roads, when he was often taken by the feeling that he was the only one awake in the whole world, sitting in a vehicle that swayed and pitched and flung its dazzling oblong of light ahead, up and down, now just in front of the wheels, next extending almost to the very horizon. At night, on those lonely stages, it came naturally to think about the past, to forget his resentment towards Siberia, and for unpleasant things about that region to fade and vanish, leaving in the memory only the beauty and grandeur of its mountain ranges, its furious, un-Russian rivers, and the awesome concrete curves of the dams.

And so, having decided on that February night to go back there, Ilya drew his final pay a week before his departure in May.

2

Now each morning he wakes up in a holiday mood, and in the evening, wearing his best clothes, he goes around among the neighbours to say good-bye: a handsome young man, quiet but cheerful, with the air of someone who is conscious of being unexpectedly free amongst those who must still labour—'looking like his name-day's arrived', as the country expression goes. After a while he loosens up and begins talking about Siberia. He talks long and interestingly, and the faces of his friends grow gloomy: they too would like to go there.

He returns home late and takes his boots off inside the porch, stepping quietly into the izba in his socks, knowing that his mother will be sleeping. After having spent most of the last week at farewell parties, he stays home that last night, preparing for the road; and for the first time he sees the loving, sad expression on his mother's face, notices that her eyes are red and swollen. He goes to bed thinking of Siberia, then of his mother who will be left alone, and he swings between excitement and sadness. He cautiously lights a cigarette and finds it difficult to get to sleep.

Next morning, and imprudently late, he starts out from home. He will have no one see him off except his mother, because he dislikes good-byes. His mother has been crying all morning; now as she walks quickly through the village beside him she is breathing hard, but she keeps talking, telling him about all sorts of unimportant things.

The road leaves the village and takes a sharp turn to the right, and at the point where it emerges from copses and begins to follow the fields a truck loaded with bricks approaches them, coming from the direction of the station. The vehicle is the one that Ilya drove, and Mishka Firsov, Ilya's neighbour and friend, is at the wheel now.

The two Snegirevs move off the road as a light mist of spring-dust raised by the truck settles about them. Mishka shouts something at them in passing, then brakes, jumps out of the cab and comes back towards them.

'So, then—you're really off? Still can't believe it,' he says to Ilya, and holds out his hand to him. He, now, smells of petrol.

'Yep,' says Ilya.

'Sure you'll like it this time?'

'Don't worry, I'll like it all right,' Ilya mutters, and he looks steadily out across the fields; he can hear next to him how his mother is breathing unevenly in her effort not to cry.

'Ekh, too bad. Looks like we've had our last fling then, us two,' says Mishka, and he looks back towards where the truck stands shuddering, its motor running. 'Well then, take care... Here, have a cigarette, for the road.'

They smoke for a while and no one speaks.

'And how is it with little Tamara?' Mishka suddenly remembers, 'That been all sorted out?'

'Little Tamara?' Ilya's tone is even, 'What about little Tamara? She can come over if she wants.'

'Oh sure, I see... Well, shake!...'

'Right,' says Ilya.

They would have embraced, but there is a sense of awkwardness and they just grip each other's hands.

'Going to get the train now?' Mishka asks.

'We left late,' says Ilya shuffling his feet.

'I was going to say—I'll be coming past in about an hour and a half and could've given you a lift... But, anyway—bon v'yage...'

Mishka runs back to the truck, and Ilya and his mother continue along the road. In a moment they hear behind them the truck being revved and the sound of it departing, labouring through its gears.

The mother walks silently now, she has tugged forward the top of her head-scarf to shade her face from the sun. Then she says distractedly: 'I tell you, Tamara's a paragon compared to your other girls.' She pronounces the word 'paragon' with care and seems for a moment to regain her spirits at her success. 'And she really does care, you know. Not like those other silly ones...'

Ilya remains silent. But his mother is seized now by the need to talk: and she talks about Tamara, talks to him about the new roof that the house will have this summer, of her hope of getting a good horse when the time comes to plough their plot of kitchen garden, returns to Tamara... Ilya looks at his watch and moves on more quickly. His mother hurries, her steps are awkward and now her thoughts are becoming confused.

'Oh dear...' she says. She has suddenly stopped.

Ilya stops too. He catches her eyes turned up to him, a faded, short-sighted, tender look, and he rubs the bridge of his nose. His mouth is a wry line and he feels numb, but he thrusts out his chin and cocks his brows to take on a cast of impassive interest in something across the fields.

'Just let me give you... to you...' his mother says, and she makes a quick sign of the cross over him. 'Go on, go on. You'll want to go more quickly, and I'm taking... I'll come too... more slowly...'

'I'll write to you, Mama!' says Ilya, his voice coming out high-pitched. He kisses her clumsily, 'Don't you go getting ill now!'

'Keep out of fights... You'll dress warm, won't you? Maybe it's still cold there, in that Siberia,' she says, trying not to cry.

'Now, now, Mama, stop that!' reassures Ilya, too firmly, 'It's not the first time I'll be going there, is it? Look after yourself and write to me about what goes on. And I'll send you money from the first pay!'

He hugs her again and then turns and goes quickly up the road. His breathing through his nose is laboured, as though he had been running, his eyes sting and there is a tormenting tickle in his throat that is difficult to clear.

Some two hundred paces onwards he starts to feel better, he breathes more evenly, and he has stopped rubbing the bridge of his nose. His face adopts that expression of busy abstraction it had worn all during the previous week.

He looks up at the lacy stratus clouds, flexes his cheek muscles, swallows; and suddenly, unbidden, he sees the northern Yenisei flowing between huge cliffs, sees the hills, the taiga, the dimly lamplit workers' camps caught in the glow of a polar night...

After another two hundred paces he turns. His mother is slowly following after him, shielding her eyes with her hand. Ilya stops, takes out his handkerchief and waves it, but she does not respond.

'She doesn't see!' he thinks sadly, and he sighs and walks on.

Just as he begins to walk away from her—ever more quickly, ever further from her, more decisively—his mother stops; radiantly smiling, she waves to him with her hand. It seems to her now that her son has turned and is looking at her. She can even make out his face, and it is a surprise to her that she can see it so clearly through her tears.

A long way away, to the side, over the fields, Ilya catches sight of a dot bouncing along a boundary path: it is a girl running towards the trees. 'My mother ran like that once,' he thinks to himself with tenderness, dejectedly, and he looks back. His mother is so far behind now that it is impossible to tell whether she has stopped or is still progressing along the road, plodding after him.

But she is still following, she cannot bring herself to stop and turn back, the tears run down her face and she wipes them with a corner of her scarf. She does not need to hold them in now, she is alone among the fields now. 'Lord...' she thinks, 'They've no need of their homes... where they were born. They go, they go... The whole world is moving; oh, Mother of God, what a time has come on us! He used to run in his little shirt... barefoot... a fair little thing. And then, all at once—flown away!...'

She halts, sobs, and gazing under her palm looks into the distance. Ilya has long gone now, dissolved into the blue haze of the horizon, but the mother thinks she can still see him: he has turned and is waving to her, waving good-bye.

She takes deep breaths, pauses often, feebly waves back...

20. TO TOWN

1

It was early morning and Vassily Kamanin was walking on the road to Ozerishche. His boots were covered in mud, his swarthy neck was long-unwashed, the whites of his lacklustre eyes were yellow, and the grey stubble on his face grew practically to his lower lids. He pressed on with an uneven gait, as if his legs were badly hinged to the rest of his forward-straining body, his progress not much assisted by a chill wind nipping at his back. Dirt-spattered late sorrel growing by the roadside swayed in the wind, fields recently scarred by the autumn ploughing stretched unendingly on both sides, looking like furrowed mine-waste cratered by pools of water glinting with a leaden pallor. It had rained all the previous week.

The night before, Vassily had drunk heavily at his in-laws, parents of the boy one of his daughters had married sometime previously, and now his head ached and his whole body ached as well, as it always did anyway in bad weather. There was a foul taste in his mouth and he spat often, each time raising his head with an effort to peer glumly into the distance before him; but all he kept seeing were the muddy, ravaged road, dreary rain-darkened hayricks and a low, grey sky which across its whole dull extent right to the horizon showed no hint of any sunlight filtering through it nor any promise of change. He noted mechanically the drier parts of the road, but his attention strayed at moments when his thoughts especially preoccupied him, and then he slithered and stumbled heavily, even as his thin body lurched ever forward.

Vassily lived in Mokhovatka, in a spacious old izba that stood somewhat apart from other households. Mokhovatka before the war had been a large village, and the Kamanin place then was one in a row of other such comfortable structures. When the Germans retreated they burned the village to the ground, but that one house was miraculously spared. After the war Mokhovatka was rebuilt in a new location a little distance away, and the Kamanin family found themselves now on the outskirts, on the road that led away from the village. Vassily had been offered help to move the house, and had indeed from time to time given the possibility some thought, but it never came to anything, and so they remained where they were.

His three daughters married in rapid succession, all going away to live in town, and the izba came to feel very empty. He took increasingly to working on private jobs, for he was a good carpenter and made money by it, but as the years passed he soured, drank a lot, and when drunk grew sullen and beat his wife. His wife's name was Akulina, and he had not liked her for a long time now.

Before the war, he had been recruited to work on a big project in a city, spending a whole summer employed on it, and from that time the thought of going to live in town had never left him.

Every autumn, when work slackened off, he was suddenly overtaken by a deep longing, and then he became indifferent to everything, lying for hours out in the yard with his eyes closed and thinking of life in town. Actually, he could not stand city people, abusing them as parasites, but his mind was on the amenities of city life, the parks, restaurants, picture-theatres, stadiums: with those he was positively enamoured, to the extent that he hardly dreamt of anything else.

He came close to leaving a number of times, even arranging to sell the cow, but Akulina whispered to him at night, urging him to think of the land, of the home and surroundings that had given them birth and a live-lihood; she told him that she would pine and die in town. Anyway, for whatever reason, he hesitated and year after year stayed on.

In the kolkhoz everyone knew of his passion and they tormented him about it. 'Still here?' they laughed. 'So, what happened this time?'

'Just you wait. The night-cuckoo outsings the day one...' he would reply enigmatically with a humourless smile, while inside him anger at his wife simmered.

In spring Akulina fell ill. At first it was thought she would get over it, then she began going to the clinic. She took the powders and mixtures prescribed for her, downed the bitterest medicines in the sure, unques-tioning belief that they would cure her; but she did not get better, on the contrary her health kept deteriorating. Rather more recondite methods were tried then: ancient crones took to visiting the Kamanin house with bladders of holy water and root infusions. Those did not help either: Akul-ina's eyes grew sunken, her temples hollow, and she began to lose her hair. She grew thinner so quickly that she seemed to melt before people's eyes, and those who had seen her in good health not long before, now on passing her would stop to stare after her. It became frightening to lie be-side her, so bony had she become and so dreadfully did she moan in her sleep; and so Vasily started sleeping on some fresh hay in the yard.

At this time he worked all day in the fields at the haymaking, arguing often with the brigade leader; but his mind was elsewhere: his dark, bushy brows knitted, he thought constantly of his wife and was more and more firmly convinced that she would soon die. He returned one evening with a load of hay and bags of grain: the advance on his next season's units of work. Tired, his face darkened by the sun, he sat down on a bench and leant forward with his chapped hands on his knees and looked glumly at

Akulina.

Frightfully wasted, with dark, dry eyes frantically mobile, and yet still bearing remnant features of the handsome woman she had once been, Akulina was setting the table for him. When she had finished she remained standing, her back against a wall, breathing with difficulty, her mouth open like a dark hole and her face covered in perspiration.

'Vassya!' she pleaded, 'In the name of Christ, take me to town! Get me there! I'll be dead soon for sure... I can't stand it any longer. I'm sick all over, Vassya!'

Vassily went on noisily spooning soup into his mouth, unwilling to let her see his thoughts by looking up at her.

'Take me to town, Vassya!' she said very quietly, and she slid down and sat on the floor, still backed against the wall. 'I can't eat anything, I just bring it up. I can't even keep milk down now... We've got the animals, Vassya. They've got to be looked after, and it's hard for me. I'm on my hands and knees. I creep along, it's easier like that. And inside me, it just burns, it burns! Take me to town, let those professors look at me. I don't believe in anyone here anymore. And I feel so bad. Oy, so bad.'

And so, Vassily was going now to Ozerishche to see the chairman of the collective farm, to ask for a horse for his wife, and at the same time to make the case that he should be released from the farm.

He was in a bad mood, his temples throbbed and he was furious with everyone: his wife, the brigade leader, the neighbours. Cursing, he tried to gather his thoughts and plan the best way of asking the chairman to release him so that he might go and live in town.

2

He arrived at Ozerishche an hour later and was so worn out by then that his legs were buckling under him.

The chairman's house stood out from the others by its size, it had a covered porch supported on posts, an iron roof, and its yard was spread not with the usual straw but with woodchips. The grounds were enclosed by a high fence, and as Vassily entered them a glimpse into the kitchen-garden in the rear revealed to him the dark cubes of beehives under apple trees. While he carefully scraped his soles on the boot-grate he thought to himself for the umpteenth time: 'Should get some bees: there's value in 'em...' then, remembering what he had come for, he grunted, and with an uncharacteristic feeling of nervousness opened the door into the dark, cluttered entryway.

The house was untidy, grimy and smelled of baked milk and sour cabbage. A sewing machine was on the kitchen table and cuttings of cloth were strewn on the floor under it; a row of socks hung from an electric cord linking the light-globe to the radio. The man of the house was evidently away, and Marya his wife, a solid, swarthy peasant woman, was bending with legs apart at the stove, her skirt stretched tightly across her buttocks, her face hotly lit by the radiance from the open fire-door: she was working a pair of tongs with vigour.

'Hullo,' Vassily said in a surly tone, and took off his cap. 'Where's Danilich?'

'What do you want him for?' asked Marya in a like tone, not turning to him.

'Something I got to see him about.'

'He's gone to the fields, went on light.'

'Is he coming back soon?'

'He said for breakfast; or lunch; can't tell.'

'I'll wait,' said Vassily and sat down heavily on a bench, facing the stove. He took out a pouch of shag, then remembering that Marya did not like people smoking in her house he put it away again. He did not really want to smoke anyway; he felt a nauseous weakness throughout his whole body and there was a buzzing in his ears.

His head drooped and he fell into thought. He thought that his wife would die soon, that he would need to make a coffin for her, and he had better get hold of some good boards smartly. Then he thought he would have to kill the ram, or maybe even a second one might be needed for after the funeral. All the relatives would be coming out of the woodwork, would want to stuff themselves, you bet... He started to think next about selling the house and the stock, who might want to buy what and for how much, and then about where he would move to after that. Smolensk might be a good place to start with: he would go to his oldest daughter there, then see; there would be money enough, Lord be praised... Yes, he would look at getting a little place in town.

He turned then to his arguments, going over them again, arranging them. The chairman could not possibly object. In fact in his mind the thing was settled already: the chairman could do nothing, he would have to give way.

'So what brings you to these parts?' the woman asked again. She put the tongs in a corner and went to sit at the table.

Vassily had been so involved in his ponderings that he did not catch immediately what she had asked; he started as if jolted from sleep and looked at Marya's ruddy face, her full lips and blue, slightly protuberant, amused and unfriendly eyes.

'It's my wife: she's sick,' he said at last, 'I've come for a horse to take her to town. And then... some other matters of my own.'

'Oh. How old's Akulina?' she asked without interest.

'How old?' Vassily thought for a moment, 'Let's see. I'm fifty-five. Now, she's two years younger...'

'I see,' said Marya.

She remained silent for a moment, in some thought of her own, then she bent over the sewing machine, bit through a thread, smoothed out a piece of material, and the izba was filled with an even, measured whirring.

Vassily's eyes closed again; he wanted to stretch himself out on the bench, cover his face, think of nothing, and just go to sleep. The thought that he must wait for the chairman to come so that he would argue and demonstrate to him that he, Vassily, could no longer live at the kolkhoz, and after his talk that he would need to trudge on that muddy road all the way back to Mokhovatka, chilled him and filled him with distaste. Sharp pains between the shoulder blades nagged at him and the skin on his chest and arms felt as if there was something crawling over it.

Soon the hum of the machine stupefied him, and he did indeed cease thinking of anything, so that he started again when heavy footsteps sounded outside in the porch and the chairman came in.

He was a thickset man with a small, pale face irregularly grown with tufts of whitish hair that gave him the look of one of those pictures of old Skoptsy sectarians, the ones who practiced self-castration. He had arrived on horseback and was frowning and rubbing the back of his thighs as he entered the izba. He bent at a window, looking at something outside, and Vassily turned to look too: a boy was leading a tall, bony stallion away, following the line of the fence; the horse had a clipped tail and was throwing its head up and side-stepping.

'How did it go?' Marya called out to her husband as she moved back to the hearth and picked up the tongs again.

The chairman, still in a semi-crouch, turned to reply to her, but seeing Vassily he checked himself, straightened up and extended a cold, humid hand to him. He crossed the room and heaving the sigh of a deeply tired man sat down on a bench with his back to the other window. He hauled off his jackboots and continued sitting bare-footed, wriggling his naked toes. His eyes rested for a moment on his wife's back, and the expression in them became somnolent and remote. Vassily too turned to look at Marya as she strained to move the cast-iron pots about on the stove, he looked at her strong back and suddenly thought to himself: 'Devil take her, but she's a choice one!'

'Well, how are things your way?' the chairman asked Vassily. 'Getting that hay in?'

'We are!' said Vassily, shifting his glance hastily away from Marya; then he added: 'We're getting it in, but I don't know how soon we'll finish. It's this early rain: everything's wet. And we're shorthanded: people are staying inside.'

'What the hell's that brigade man of yours doing?' said the chairman, frowning. 'How many times do we have to say things here? Get the hay in! Don't wait till the rain comes! He'll get a flea in the ear when I come over!'

Vassily shifted restlessly on his bench, while the chairman sighed again and looked around towards his wife: 'Is that going to be much longer?'

'In a moment,' she muttered back.

Vassily was at a loss. The chairman had not asked him why he had come, and it did not seem right to begin on his own to set out the arguments of his request. Suddenly, every sentence he had prepared as he had sat waiting flew out of his head and he felt utterly ill again and the thing he most desired at this moment was to take a stiff shot of something and go to bed.

'We've been looking at the fields out Bukatinsky side,' said the chairman, brightening up, 'With a correspondent from the regional paper. The flax looks like it might come to something. He said he's going to do a piece on our farm girls.'

Without turning, he felt behind him for a newspaper that rested folded on the windowsill, brought it around and tore off a small square. He stretched out his right leg and pulled a shag-pouch out of the pocket on that side, rolled a cigarette and lit up.

'Well now, you don't say...' said Vassily with exaggerated surprise, and he hurriedly joined the chairman in rolling and puffing on his own cigarette, 'So, they'll write-up something. That's what they do—write-up things...'

'God, look at 'em filling the place with smoke!' said Marya angrily, and she stamped out, banging the door behind her.

'What was it you wanted to see me about?' the chairman asked, grinning at Vassily and throwing a wink in the direction of the departed woman.

Vassily shifted his feet, settled himself lower on the bench and looked down.

'My wife's very sick,' he began. 'I want to take her to town. The road's just a mess, the trucks can't go on it. A horse, Danilich...'

'A horse?' the chairman groaned, and he scratched his head. 'But didn't she go to the clinic here?'

'She did, but I think she needs an operation.'

'Oh well... all right, I guess. I can't do anything today, though. But I'll tell them to give you one tomorrow. You can be away tomorrow morning.'

Vassily began again with a gloomy face: 'And another thing is, my health's started to go bad too, I don't know why...' Then he interrupted his own train of argument; remembering that such things are not done dry he suddenly urged: 'Look Danilich, why don't you drop in at my place sometime, ha? I've got some home-brew: my daughter's sent me the sugar from town. We could have a drink. It's not a bad brew, the wife made it the other day, not bad at all. There's a bit of lard as well: that pig came to not much short of three hundred pounds. You should call in.'

The chairman smiled: 'I could make it over one day, I suppose.'

'And as for me, Danilich...' Vassily went on happily, riding on the moment of good humour, 'I've made up my mind to... you know... say good-bye to the kolkhoz.'

'What—what's that? Good-bye?' The chairman stopped smiling, 'How do you mean?'

'Well, it's like this...' said Vassily gathering himself, his eyes shifting in every direction, 'It's like this: I've not got any more desire to work here. The wife's ill, I've got daughters writing to me, calling me over... And, actually, what's there for me here? And what's more, I've been thinking of doing it for a long time. The old chairman was for letting me go, ask anyone! Let the others do the work, I've had enough. I can always find some carpentry to do in town. What work have I got here?...'

'What have you got?' the chairman stared at Vassily as if he was seeing him for the first time, 'Are you mad? Or have you forgotten what we were talking about at the last meeting?'

'Hell, the meeting, the meeting...'

'Just a minute—I'll give you the meeting! No work? This autumn we're doing a new shed for the calves—what's that, do you think, nothing? Then, the club's being rebuilt—that's not work? And the frames for the forcing beds—not work?'

'Yes, that's so; but let the others do it. And don't you try keeping me here, either. I'll go anyway. I still know what my rights are, well enough!'

'You know, do you? And d'you know that the kolkhoz is short of people?'

'That's got nothing to do with me. That's your lot's affair, keeping people so they don't want to run off. From a good place, they wouldn't want to! And as for me, I want to live a little. I'm not some old relic, you know, who's got nothing going for him but to sit by the stove all day. And what's the kolkhoz got me? Where's the culture? There's nowhere even to go for a drink.'

'So, you've had a poor, hard life here, ha?...' the chairman bent forward, his yellowing face looming down at Vassily as on a prey, 'All that work you've done for the kolkhoz's been killing you, ha-a?'

'Don't go making your noises at me! You'll choke yourself! And don't go getting on any high horse either!' Vassily snapped back, his eyebrows rising, 'Whatever I've got I carried home on my bloody own bent back! You people who run a kolkhoz wouldn't give away snow in winter!'

'Right! Let the others work, let them struggle! And you—you're off to town?'

'I've got a wife that's dying...' Vassily felt his head buzzing and his breath coming to him unevenly, 'She's got to get to town. Now how about that?'

The chairman stood up. 'The kolkhoz will see that you get a horse.'

'So, you won't let me go!' Vassily said, also rising.

'The man wants to go. Seems he's made his pile. Wants to cut.'

'Yeah, yeah, my pile! So big the devil couldn't shovel it into the stove in a day!' Vassily sneered.

'That's about the size of it!' the chairman hissed, 'You're so dab at working on the side—well, you'll build us the calf-shed, and the club, and you'll get the frames in! And after that, we'll see!'

'The calf-shed? Here!—that's for your calf-shed!' Vassily made a crude gesture.

The chairman turned his back and went to the window. 'That's it, we've talked, now make tracks! You know what the Party's position is, I suppose you can read? Then that's the end of it! We'll call you when we have the next meeting, and then we'll talk again!'

'Fine!' Vassily flung on his cap, 'Fine, and greetings to your mother!... We'll see, ha? We'll see if we can find a bit of rope for that neck of yours too!'

Banging the door behind him Vassily staggered through the porch and went heavy-footed down the steps, sniffing and snorting with chagrin, grinding his tobacco-stained teeth; he walked rapidly down the road, pan-icking a brood of hens that had been roosting on a wattle-fence.

'A fine talk, that! You really had that one thought out! The son of a bitch!...' he muttered to himself, wiping his perspiring face, 'I should have known—talking gets you nowhere without a half-litre to start it off!'

And all the way back he cursed himself for not having had the sense to bring a half-litre.

3

Next morning Vassily drank some beer and went to the horse-yards, com-ing back half an hour later riding a horse. Having tethered it to the porch he returned with some hay and heaped it in the cart and tamped it down. After a moment's hesitation he gave a little of the hay to the horse and then went inside. He had decided the previous evening to kill the ram: it was market-day in town and the ram had been coughing with the croup for the past two weeks.

He told Akulina to get ready and then he picked up a long, narrow Ger-man bayonet and went outside. The ram, black with a white patch on its neck, big-boned and old, put up a struggle to remain in the pen, baulking and trembling.

'Smelled something's coming, hey?' Vassily muttered, and a malicious smile grew on his face. He rested a moment after his first attempt and then grabbed one of the animal's warm, twisted horns. The ram kept its limpid eyes turned on the open door of the pen.

'Well—say your prayers!' said Vassily, and he threw the beast to the ground, pressed his knee down on its soft flank and forced back its muzzle with his palm. The ram kicked free from under Vassily's knee, but with his breath wheezing now he pinned it down again and bent its head back, stretching its throat. He clenched his teeth, took aim at the patch of white hair, and with a vicious thrust cut through the neck there.

The ram shuddered and went limp under Vassily's knee, and a gush of blood that was almost black in colour poured from the gaping wound onto the straw and dung scattered on the ground, some of the blood staining Vassily's hands. A faint trembling passed through the ram's body, its eyelids flickered, and then the eyes, which had up to then been turned towards the light, grew dull. The calf, sniffing curiously from its corner of the pen, suddenly snorted and plunged several times against a side wall.

Vassily stood up and dropped the bayonet. He carefully extracted his pouch of shag and with bloody fingers began rolling a cigarette, wetting the paper liberally with saliva, not taking his eyes from the ram. Now it twitched and stretched, the eyelids closed completely; then the back legs kicked out strongly, and the next moment the whole recumbent body, still on its side, was in rapid and measured motion, the legs developing a gay little trot that scattered hay and droppings about the pen.

After the ram had grown still, Vassily hung it on a rack and quickly and deftly skinned it, separating the inner blue-grey tissue of the skin from the carcass and cutting through the leg-tendons. Opening the steaming stomach, he took out the warm liver and cut off a piece and chewed it, crunching it with his teeth and staining his lips and chin with blood.

Akulina came out of the porch, neatly dressed and with a bundle in her hand. It held a change of underwear in case she was to stay in hospital. She got into the back of the cart with some difficulty, drew a raincoat over her knees and sat there waiting for Vassily. She looked with sadness and tenderness at the dark fields, at the stream below them, sat eyeing her surroundings as if seeing them for the last time and saying good-bye for ever to them, to her home and her village.

Soon Vassily came out of the house, holding in his hands something bundled like a swaddled child. It was the carcass of the ram, now cut up into sections and wrapped in a sack. He put it in the front of the cart and walked away to give the animals their feed and to lock the house. Akulina suddenly became aware of the sweetish smell of the newly slaughtered meat. She had liked the smell in the past, that being always a sign of the arrival of a festival in the neighbourhood, but now it made her feel ill, and she covered her mouth and nose with the end of her scarf.

Vassily washed his mouth out with some more beer, then having locked up he stood on the sill, tucking his shirt in under his belt. He had washed and shaved that morning and had donned a clean shirt and now appeared younger and in a happy mood.

'Vassya!' Akulina said to him, 'Look at all this—isn't it pretty? I bet I'll die in town. It's so sad to leave it all. You know, my heart is just breaking.'

Vassily glanced round at the fields with their dark hayricks and the black ploughed furrows, at the stream, at the roofs of the village, darkened by the recent rains; he spat and said nothing. Then he untied the horse and harnessed it to the cart, jerking savagely at the horse's mouth as he inserted the bit, making its lips bleed. He checked the hay in the back of the cart, boarded, and flicked the reins. The frightened horse set off at a rapid pace, and the cart was soon swaying in and out of the wide ruts.

Akulina sat in the back with her shoulders hunched and her hands pressed to her breast, looking forlornly at the izbas passing on both sides. She looked at the rowan trees, filling now with saffron-red clusters of berries, and at the birches, and scenes of her life in the kolkhoz kept coming back to her, memories of her youth and marriage, her children. And her love for what she saw grew and pained her, realising with each moment that she would perhaps never return to this place she had been born in, perhaps would nevermore see those who were dear to her, and the tears rolled down her sunken cheeks. She just wanted one thing: to die in her own home and be buried in the cemetery of her native village.

Women who happened to be outside, stopped what they were doing, looked at her silently and bowed their heads to her. And Akulina responded to them through her tears with a stiff, embarrassed smile and bowed gratefully back each time, her forehead almost touching the sides of the cart.

Vassily kept urging the horse on. His flushed face had a tense look of happy expectation. He was thinking that he would deliver his wife to the hospital, carry on to the market, sell the meat, then he would drop in on his relations, and afterwards go to the restaurant at the station. He would sit there and drink light wine and look out at the passing trains. Waitresses in little white aprons and with caps fastened by hairpins would serve him, a band would play, and the air would be full of the odour of good food and tobacco.

And at a convenient time, after discussing it with his people, he would decide what to do next, what would be the smoothest way to get out of the kolkhoz and move to town, how he would go about selling the house and the stock and so on.

21. THE KABIASY

Zhukov, the director of the club at Dubki, had been delayed during a visit to a neighbouring village. The problem lay in the fact that it was August, and although he had arrived in good time to deal with his affairs, had gone wherever he needed to go, talked to the people he had come to meet, still the day had turned out to be long and moreover rather pointless; everyone seemed busy and in a hurry: it just happened to be one of those hectic times in the season.

He was a young chap, somewhat green, had been working at the Dubki club for less than a year and was therefore still active and full of enthusiasm. He himself was a native of Zubatovo, a large settlement, but he had been transferred and was now established in a tiny room attached to the club.

He should simply have gone back to Dubki when he heard there was a vehicle going there on which he could have had a lift, but on the spur of the moment he reconsidered and decided to call on an old teacher of his, to have a good talk with him about cultural matters. As it turned out, the teacher had gone hunting, and although expected back at any moment his absence dragged on. Zhukov sat waiting at the man's home, irritated by his own nonsensical decision and aware that he should have started back for his kolkhoz long ago. He sat there to no purpose for two hours, smoking and keeping an eye on the window and maintaining a dreary conversation with the housekeeper, even dropping off into a momentary doze, to start awake again when some cattle came past outside, driven on by the shrill cries of peasant women.

Finally, when further waiting was clearly hopeless, and cross at the whole turn of affairs, Zhukov drank a glass of sour kvass, which had the instant effect of setting his teeth on edge, and then left to walk back. The distance to Dubki was twelve kilometres.

As he was going over the bridge on the road out, he caught up with Matvey. The old man had stopped to run his tongue along the edge of a freshly-rolled cigarette. He was wearing a frayed padded coat and some ragged item of winter headgear and he held a shotgun clamped under one arm. He watched the approaching Zhukov without much sign of friendliness.

'So, Matvey!' Zhukov recognised the other man straight away, although he had only seen him in passing a couple of times before, 'What—

are you off hunting too?'

Matvey resumed walking slowly up the road, considering his new cig-arette while he felt under his coat for matches. He lit up, inhaled a couple of times, giving effect to a long bout of phlegmy coughing, then with a scrape of rough nails on the material of his coat he returned the matches to the recess they had been fished out of. Only then did he reply:

'Hunting? Who's hunting? I guard the orchard, nights. Got a bush lean-to thing over there.'

Zhukov still had a disagreeable taste in his mouth from the kvass and he spat before lighting a cigarette himself. 'I see,' he said, 'Not that you'd lose much sleep doing that, mm?' He spoke absently, still cursing himself for leaving so late—with a truck to take him there, for goodness' sakes! And now he had to walk.

'Sleep? If only t'were like you say!' Matvey paused, then added curi-ously: 'I'd sleep, all right, if they'd but let me...'

'Who, robbers?' asked Zhukov, interested enough to be ironic.

'Robbers? Ha!' Matvey dismissed the notion scornfully. His ancient form seemed momentarily to move more freely and erectly, he appeared almost to swagger in some private knowledge. He paid little heed to his young companion but walked on, looking to each side at the rapidly dim-ming evening fields, and what he said next may not have been meant to be heard: 'Robbers? There's more round here, nights, than them that comes to rob, brother!'

'Well, who then? Young ladies?' laughed Zhukov, and at that moment he remembered Lyubka, whom he meant to visit later that night.

'It's them... you know...' Matvey muttered.

'Come on, out with it man, don't pull the elastic forever, let's hear about it,' said Zhukov and spat again. 'So who the hell are they?'

'The Kabiasy, that's who!' said Matvey in an odd tone, and he looked sideways briefly at the other.

'Aha, at last—the answer to the mystery!' laughed Zhukov, 'You best go tell that stuff to your old lady, Matvey! And, by the way, who or what precisely are Kabiasy anyway?'

'They're—just that,' Matvey said sullenly. 'You ever fall in with 'em one day, you won't have to ask!'

'Devils, eh?... Or what?' said Zhukov, a little wary now of provoking the old man.

Matvey squinted across at him with a measuring look and then growled back reluctantly and barely distinctly: 'Sort of. They're black. Some with a bit of green...' Then he stopped and took out of his pocket two brass cartridges, blew away some strands of shag tobacco clinging to them and said: 'Look at that!' showing him the ends of the cartridges where cardboard wads tamped the shot.

Zhukov peered down and saw that a cross had been scribbled in ink on each wad.

'And they've had the right words said over 'em too!' announced Matvey with a nod of satisfaction, as he put the cartridges back in his pocket. 'I can deal with those fellers all right!'

'But what do they do? Do they come around bothering you?' asked Zhukov, taking care not to smile.

'Not so much as they'd like,' replied Matvey weightily. 'They don't come right up to the lean-to. They just... They come out of the dark, one and then another. They sort of get into a crew under the apple trees, rustle about, break twigs. Tiny wee things: they stand this high, all in a row...' Matvey moved his palm side to side vaguely above the road. 'Sometimes they sing songs.'

'Songs now?' Zhukov could not help it: he burst out laughing. 'Sounds like you've got the very best on offer at our own club—why man, musical nights even! So what sort of songs are they?'

'Oh, different ones. Sometimes they're very sad. And then another thing—they call out to you: "Matvey! Hey, Matvey! Come you here, come you here!"'

'And you?...'

Matvey laughed good-naturedly: 'I tell 'em what I think of 'em. Them and their dam too. "Shoo!" I say, "Get ye gone," I tell 'em. But then they start to muster together and to creep up to the lean-to, and then I loads my magic cartridges, and ke-rack!—let them have it!'

'Get any?'

'How? You can't get 'em!' Matvey pronounced disdainfully. 'D'you think you can kill them things that dwell in the dark world? I just flush them away a bit, until dawn comes, till the first rooster calls.'

'Yes...' Zhukov sighed after a moment of silence, 'Bad, very bad...'

'Eh? Who, what?' asked Matvey.

'No, it's this program of mine that's no good. I'm responsible for educating you lot, leading you away from this sort of thing,' said Zhukov, frowning: he had just a moment ago remembered one of his many duties as club director. 'They've got me employed on promoting atheism, and now I hear this; that's what's bad. And of course you've been spreading that rot all over the village, I suppose? Frightening the girls?' He looked sternly at Matvey, 'Kabiasy indeed! Why, you old... you're no more than one of them yourself!'

'What—who is?' asked Matvey, and his face turned suddenly incensed as he understood what the young man had said. When he spoke again, a moment later, his voice had taken on a peculiar intonation: 'You'll be going through the forest shortly, I'll warrant?'

'Well, what about it?'

'Look out then, when you get there... look out you don't make it home... that they don't take you off with 'em!' And he turned sharply away without another word, without a good-bye, and headed rapidly across a field towards the darkening line of the orchard, his resentment clear in the set of his diminishing figure.

Alone on the road, Zhukov smoked and looked around. Darkness was approaching and the sunset in the western sky was beginning to fade. He could hardly make out the kolkhoz he had left behind, just the odd dark roof still visible between poplars. Some distance to his left the birch forest mentioned by Matvey stretched in stepped layers to the bounds of the horizon, the view suggesting someone having made innumerable vertical strokes with a white pencil on a dark background: where the pale trunks of the birches were closest to the viewer, the strokes were wide apart, then they converged in the middle distance, and finally the white melded into a continuous band at the furthest twilit limits of the trees.

Also on the left, he saw a lake, in its stillness seeming soldered there, the surface of the water even with the flat ground around it. It was the one bright thing in the growing gloom on that side. A fire had been lit by the lake's edge and the smoke drifting from it across the road carried a whiff of dampness from the descending evening dew.

To the right of the road, a series of sparred towers marched across the dimming meadows and through clearings that stretched between fingers of the same birch forest on that side, the van of the procession disappearing over distant hills. The towers looked like great, silent creatures from another world, left behind on this planet, creatures that now wordlessly and with uplifted arms trekked westward towards a gradually brightening greenish star, their home.

Zhukov looked back again, still hopeful that some vehicle might overtake him and give him a lift; but there were none and he walked on. As he did so he kept studying the fire by the lake, and he became aware that there was no one near it, nor was there anyone on the lake; and that solitary fire, lit by unknown folk for an unexplained purpose, made a strange impression on him.

He had started walking with a not very determined pace at first, smoking and looking around, expecting to see if not a vehicle then perhaps someone else going his way, but the road was empty in front and behind: his surroundings, as far as humans went, were deserted to the very horizon. He suddenly began striding forward with a serious swing.

He had covered some four kilometres by the time night fell. Soon, the road alone remained visible in the dark, and it too disappeared occasionally where bands of mist drifted across it, for it was a moonless night. Each time he entered one of those bands he sensed a chill creeping about him, and he was glad for the renewed warmth when emerging on the other side.

'What a lot of backward citizens we still have after all this time!...' he mused as he walked onwards with his hands thrust into his pockets, still thinking of Matvey, so amazed by his recent impression of the old man that even his eyebrows worked in the intensity of his communion with himself concerning him. How suddenly he had altered, become irate, even somewhat haughty towards him when he had laughed at that nonsense. 'Yes…' Zhukov thought, 'definitely more work's needed on the campaign. More work. Atheism's got to be drummed into their heads, these superstitions rooted out!' And as he walked onward, those reflections so excited him that he would dearly have loved to have had someone there with whom to converse about culture and other matters intellectual.

Then he turned to thinking that it was time he should move to town, to enter an institute and further his education. And, as he often did, he began imagining himself directing a choir. Not like the one in the club at the kolkhoz—the stage there did not even have a back or wings, and the kids smoked in the hall and never remained serious for a moment—but a hundred-member establishment, in Moscow perhaps, a real cappella choir! As always with such dreaming, he felt a joyous quickening and in a few moments grew lost to things around him. He paid no attention either to the stars or to the road in front of him, walking as his feet led him, clenching and unclenching his fists and knitting his brows in accordance with his thoughts, singing snatches of songs, laughing at his efforts, all unconcerned that someone might hear, and even feeling happy that he was alone, unencumbered by any other presence. And in that mood he arrived at an old farmyard close to the road, and there he sat down on a piece of timber to have a rest and smoke a cigarette.

There had been a privately-owned farmstead at that place once, but after the collectivisation it had been demolished, and all that remained now was an old barn, open and empty. The barn appeared to have no door, it was a derelict building, dark and leaning to one side, and the blackness of the hole that was its entry gave the impression of being particularly intense.

Zhukov sat with his elbows propped on his upthrust knees, facing the road and with his back to the barn. As he smoked, his body gradually cooled. He had stopped thinking about the conservatorium, and now his mind had turned to Lyubka and the possibility that he might finally get to kiss her.

Then he felt that someone was standing behind him, looking down at him.

He tensed. Suddenly he realised that he was sitting in darkness, alone in the midst of empty fields, and around him were black, strangely-shaped forms that might be bushes, or might—not be! He recalled Matvey again, and his last-uttered angry warning, and then his mind returned to the unpeopled, silent lake and the fire burning beside it… with what object?

Slowly he turned, not breathing. He looked into the entry of the barn— the barn roof floated in mid-air! Stars glinted where the sky had poured through gaps in it, and now those luminous spills uncannily buoyed that dark oblong!… But as he blinked, the roof and the wall-frames joined together once more. Then, beyond the barn, something pattered away towards the fields, uttering a series of anguished exclamations: 'Oh-oh-oh-

oh!...' repeatedly until they faded in the distance. Zhukov's nape-hairs stood on end—he leapt to his feet and was on the road in a single movement!

'That's it!...' he whispered to himself, 'I'm done for!' and he took to his heels. The wind whistled in his ears with the speed of his flight, on each side of the road things crackled, made snuffling noises in the bushes, a cold wind pursued him, its breath chilling his back. 'Cross yourself, quick!' he thought, as he felt icy fingers clutching at him from behind, 'Lord, into Thy hands...' he began—and having crossed himself he stopped both recitation and running. Out of breath, he turned around.

But there was no one there and nothing else on the road or in the fields, and as for the barn, that was now out of sight. He wiped his face on his sleeve. The road lay before him, solid to his feet, and without taking his eyes off it he shouted a hoarse and disgusted 'Ha!' which startled him again. Then he cleared his throat, listened all around, and while trying this time to keep his voice steady uttered a loud and challenging 'Ho! Ho! Hey!...'

Having got his breath back, he made off again at a rapid pace, unsettled and aware with flushed unease of the considerable distance he still had to cover, aware of the night in a way he had not been until then, and of the darkness around him, and that Matvey's forest was ahead of him and quite close.

The road descended to a stream. As in a dream, a pair of giant leaps took Zhukov across the bridge, over the dark and willow-congested water and to the other side, uncertain as he left the timbers whether the hollow booming beneath his feet had been real sounds or reverberated only in his imagination. 'You wait, you old fake, I'll get to you, you wait!...' he addressed Matvey in his mind; but it was an anxious speech, formed, he was conscious, while ascending the slope where the forest began.

His arrival at the first birches declared itself by an instant sensation of dew and dampness. Something vaporous seemed to exhale out of vegetative depths: rotting things, mushrooms, still water, pine needles, breathed odours that drifted into the warmer surrounding field-air. On the right of the road, the darkness under the trees was dense, concentrated; on the left, the fields were slightly more visible if still not precisely defined; above, the stars were increasing in abundance as the night advanced, and on their faint background of smoky luminescence the tops of trees stood out as distinct silhouettes.

An owl broke out of the forest darkness, left its roost with a slight rustle, flew over Zhukov and settled on a tree a little ahead of him. He recognised the flight but try as he might could not locate the bird, he only saw how behind him the dead branch on which it had been perching continued scribing up and down as if with a pointing finger a small arc across the stars.

He went on and disturbed the owl again, and it began to fly around him, circling over the fields on the left and disappearing into the darkness on the right. The horizon beyond the fields still held colourless traces of the departed sunset, or else perhaps the air in the sky there had been burnt clean and more ethereal by it, and Zhukov could see the owl passing like an inaudible black stain across that slight pallor.

In his preoccupation with the owl, Zhukov stumbled over a root and cursed the bird. He found himself unable to look—dared not so much as glance—sideways at the forest or back behind him whence he had come; and when he did lift his eyes from the road to the way ahead—an icy chill scoured the whole length of his spine! A little in front of him, on the left of the road, three figures had crossed over from the forest. Three Kabiasy stood waiting for him!

They were small, as Matvey had described them. One croaked a giggle at him: 'Hee-hee-hee-ee...'; the second uttered that mournful 'Oh-oh-oh-oh!' wail Zhukov had heard a little while ago at the barn; the third called out imperatively in the tones of a quail: 'Come you nigh! Come you nigh!'

Zhukov's teeth thudded together. He froze. He could not even cross himself this time: his hand hung limply at his side, devoid of strength.

'A-a-a-a!...' he bellowed, so that the forest rang—and a moment later he realised that what he had seen were three small fir trees. Trembling like a setter approaching its quarry, he took one step towards them, then another... behind the saplings something rustled and took flight with a nerve-rending shriek, heading out towards the fields... 'A bird!' Zhukov whispered in near-panic to himself.

He made an effort to calm down, took a deep breath and straightened his shoulders under his sweat-dampened shirt. Once he had passed the saplings his spirits improved a little and he took out his cigarettes and felt for matches. The instant he found the box it struck him that if he lit a match he would become visible to the whole forest. Whom he would be seen by, he did not know and was afraid to consider, but he knew that he would be seen.

He squatted on his heels, and peering round from that position he pulled his jacket over his head and struck the light under it. 'I'll go by the fields!' he decided: he had had enough. The road was now entering a salient of the forest where both sides would soon be dense with trees, and if the fields were frightening, that seemed more bearable than going this way further into that defile!

Forcing his way through the hazelnuts that bordered the road here, he broke out into the open and began making his way forward through the fields on a curve which followed the edge of the forest. He gave a wide berth to anything particularly dark that he met on the way, yet managed to make progress, keeping his eyes attentively on the right. The owl still flew above, all around him things soughed or squealed, and from time to time there came suddenly to his hearing, from the very depths of the forest, out of some ravine perhaps, a sound which was half-scream and half-moan: an ejaculation that hung quivering in the air, rolling its echoes along the treed edge.

By the time the birches ended, and the ribbon of dusty road could in the starlight be detected ahead of him, winding unthreatened by shadows again, Zhukov's breath was whistling from his efforts and apprehension. He stepped back on the road and without lifting his eyes broke into a jog-trot, his elbows pumping close to his sides like an athlete. He went on and on like that, while the wind flowed past his ears with a bass hum and the tree line fell further and further behind, until had he looked it would have shown as a barely distinguishable black streak. But he kept his eyes fixed on the road, determined to look at nothing else; and his spirits grew lighter, he gradually fell into the rhythm of his running, at last even break-ing into a monotonous and artificially gay little song: 'Ti-ta-ta, ti-ta-ta...' Until—again!—he checked himself as if he had hit a wall—and he stood staring, round-eyed, transfixed!

What he saw was no tree, nor was it a bird: those were now known to him. This new thing which riveted him to the ground this time was alive in some inexplicable and terrible way, and it was moving along one of the field-paths towards the stretch of road where he stood! There was noth-ing human about it nor was it a cow or a horse: it had a monstrous shape! Zhukov began to distinguish noises made by it as it loomed closer: a crack-ling of dry steppe-weed being crushed by the thing's passage on the path, a soft bouncing sound, a repeated clicking...

'Who's that!' a voice shouted to him.

Zhukov said nothing.

'Hey, do I know you?... You there!' sounded the voice again, nervously, from the edge of the road now.

Zhukov understood at last that he was being addressed, that some per-son was coming towards him, and that person was wheeling a bicycle. Still he could not reply. He continued standing there, panting.

'That you, Zhukov?' the other asked uncertainly, as he came close and finally peered into the face of the silent figure, 'Hello there! Why didn't you say something when I called? I was thinking—who could that be? Got any matches? Let's have a smoke, what?...'

Zhukov recognised Popov from the district Komsomol, one of the com-mittee members. His hands were shaking so much that the matches rat-tled when he passed them to Popov.

'Where've you come from?' Popov asked after lighting his cigarette, 'You know what? I got lost. I was coming to see you lot and went right past the turn. Deep in thought, you bet...' he giggled, 'Rode on till I hit the Gorki road, and from there came this way by the boundary-path... I say, is some-thing the matter?'

'Wait...' Zhukov said hoarsely. He felt weak all over and his head was spinning, 'Wait...' He stood there in the darkness, an embarrassed smile on his face, unable to control the lassitude that he felt now, trying to brace up, breathing in with short gasps. Inhaling like that, he recognised the scent of the roadside weeds: they were dusty plantains and their scent and the odour of dust seemed to permeate the night.

'Are you ill or something?' Popov asked with the beginnings of concern.

Zhukov nodded.

'Right, get on!' Popov said authoritatively, and he turned his bicycle. 'Hold on to the handlebars! That way!' By unsteady punts with one leg he got up some speed and as the bike wobbled forward himself attained the saddle. Blowing the hair from his eyes he began pedalling hard for Dubki.

Zhukov sat on the frame, uncomfortable and ashamed. He could feel with what difficulty the bicycle moved through the thick road-dust, while Popov's hot breath gusted down his neck and Popov's pumping knees kept nudging into him. They said nothing until the lights of the kolkhoz appeared ahead, and at that point Zhukov at last made up his mind to act: 'Stop here, just here, here will do!' he blurted out.

'Keep still, keep still!...' Popov panted, 'The clinic's not far...'

'No, no, stop now!' Zhukov said grimacing, and he dragged one foot on the ground.

Popov braked, expelling a breath of relief. They extricated themselves from the bicycle and stood for a moment without speaking, not knowing what to say. They had stopped next to the horse-stables, and the horses within, hearing voices, moved restlessly in their stalls and their hooves thudded on the wooden decking. A strong and rather pleasant odour of horse dung and tar came from the building.

'Here, let me have a match again, will you?' Popov asked. He lit a cigarette and wiped the perspiration from his face and neck, unbuttoning the collar of his shirt.

'How do you feel now, better?' he asked hopefully.

'Yes, I'm over it now,' Zhukov reassured him quickly. 'I had some kvass. That's what it must have been.'

They went slowly down the road, hearing the abating sounds of a large settlement preparing for rest and sleep.

'How are things going at the club?' asked Popov.

'Oh, all right. You know how it is...' Zhukov replied absently, 'we ought to have a clean-up but everyone's busy. August of course.' And then, as if he had just remembered something, he turned to Popov and asked: 'Say, have you ever heard the word "Kabiasy" before?'

'Mm? What? "Kabiasy"?' Popov thought for a moment. 'No, never. What's it about? Something in one of your musical pieces?'

'Oh, no, it just came to mind,' said Zhukov.

They arrived at the club and shook hands. 'Take the matches, I've got more at home,' Zhukov said.

'Right!' said Popov, taking them, 'And you go and drink some milk. That's always good for an upset stomach.' He mounted his bicycle and rode off to call on the chairman of the collective.

Zhukov passed through the dark entry of the club and unlocked his room. He drank some cold tea and had a cigarette. He sat in the dark listening to the radio for some time, then he opened the window and lay down on the bed.

He was almost asleep when suddenly everything in him seemed to revolve and he saw from a height, from a high hill as it were, the dim fields, the deserted lake, the dark rows of towers with their upraised arms, the fire by the lake... and he felt the vitality, the life which filled such things and filled all the huge expanses that radiated from them in all directions throughout the darkness of this very night-hour. As he lay there, he experienced again all the incidents of his journey, all its traumas up to his arrival here, but now happily and with a joyous affection towards the night, the stars, the smells, the rustles, the cries of living things...

He wanted now once again, as he had wanted before, to talk with someone about culture, about high things—eternal things, for instance. He thought of Lyubka. He sprang up from his bunk, shuffled barefoot for a moment while finding his things, got dressed, and went out.

22. QUIET AS A MOUSE

1

The old muzhik who owned the barn which was to be their quarters came out to them that first afternoon: he was barefoot, his face was puffy from the stupor of an after-dinner drowse, and while holding up his sagging trousers with one hand he addressed them in a nearly impenetrable mumble:

'Now that—and I did agree... It's just that it's summer now, that's what I mean... It ain't nothing—have a good time, God be with you! But now that everything's dry... So if you ain't minding, what I mean is—smoking in that hay! If it should, and God help us it should...'

And a minute later he was sitting in the doorway with them, himself puffing on his own drooping cigarette, breathing noisily, blowing his nostrils with his thumb, telling them that the shepherds hereabouts saw wolves every day, that the heath-cocks in the forest-reserve just came at you in swarms, and out in the fields behind every hayrick it was a frightful thing to behold the number of quail.

They were two young men come to hunt. The clearly junior was Sasha Starobelsky, a student, still almost a boy, thin and self-conscious and apt to perceive all the novelty of that first evening as a confused and happy buzz.

Only yesterday, leaving Moscow on the way to rendezvous with a friend, he could hardly tear himself from the window of the train as it passed through the Smolensk countryside. He noted with wide-eyed interest the passengers getting on and off at each station, was both tense and ingenuous towards those sitting beside him, and in general showed all the anxieties of his first independence and the excitement of the coming hunt and prospect of staying in a village.

But at Vyazma, into the carriage came Serge Varaksin from Myatlevo way. He tossed up on the baggage rack a bundle of strongly and evilly odorous empty sacks, propped a watermelon on the seat beside him, cut it open with a crunching rip of his knife and commenced sucking and chewing wedges of it while making an unreserved examination of the other passengers.

He was thick-lipped, had bloodshot eyes and pinkish, pudgy hands, and he had been drinking and was in a gay mood, for at Vyazma he had done well in the sale of a quantity of pork. He began addressing Sasha as 'Student' almost as soon as he laid eyes on him; and, discovering that the boy was on the way to do some hunting, he began describing with passion the infinities of wildlife around Myatlevo.

'You listen to me, Student!' he said to Sasha. 'What I'm telling you is solid. I'm an electrician. I get called out from our sovkhoz to go all over the oblast, and—where did you say you were going?'

'To the Vazuza reservoir,' Sasha happily revealed.

'Ha! I've been there. I've been everywhere, know the whole oblast up and down. Just ask me anything about hunting! Your Vazuza's not worth a cracker! You wanna hunt? Go my way to Myatlevo. I've got a pal in a village. We've got everything there. There's quail, the lakes are black with ducks, there's geese. I'm telling you facts!'

And the harangue went on and bewildered poor, credulous Sasha to the point of powerlessness, until he was almost dizzy with inconceivable happiness and the feeling of how marvellous it was to be alive.

The thing progressed as if with a will of its own. They got out at Myatlevo in the dark and without further ado began walking along a road through fields. And at that point, even before the train had left, Sasha felt that he was taking a step out of his previous life and into something abruptly unlike anything he had known before, into some indistinct and mysterious new stage.

On the horizon flashes of summer lightning blinked and blinked, as if the faraway forests and meadows were emanating electricity; the night was moonless, but the stars were so bright and abundant that they illuminated everything, everything glowed: from the long filmy clouds to the shrubs and the fields, the infrequent, narrow boundary-paths, the hayricks and the little copses of fir beside the road. Along the road there was a smell of earth and dry plantains, on each side things made crisp munching noises, chirked and squeaked; black telephone poles appeared and were passed, and each time in the vicinity of the poles a weak but distinct choir of sound grew audible: a puzzling hum, since there was no wind to cause it.

They walked over timber bridges, rickety and splintered by the passage of caterpillar tractors, the bridges spanning old anti-tank ditches, long since become scrub- and reed-choked canals, in which black, oily glints of water occasionally showed through the vegetation.

In the train, Serge had said that it was fifteen kilometres from the station to his own village, and at the time Sasha thought the distance a trifle; but now they seemed to walk and walk, passing fields on both sides and copses and grey obelisks marking the wartime mass graves, yet the road just kept stretching on and disappearing into the darkness ahead. Sasha grew tired; he was sure that they must have gone fifteen kilometres, maybe twice that, and he was beginning to feel that there would be no end to the road, no end to the night and its secret noises.

And then, just as a faint current of anxiety was starting to tingle inside him, his companion suddenly hissed: 'Sh! Stop there!' Serge had halted and was listening for something, holding his breath. 'Student, get your gun out!'

'W-what for?...' Sasha asked. But he took his shotgun out of its sheath.

Serge made no reply. Sasha hurriedly opened his rucksack and felt about for the waxed-cardboard box of cartridges, those admirable small cylinders with shiny brass bases that he had packed away at home.

'We could be done in—that's why!' Serge replied finally. 'I'm carrying money, five hundred roubles—now d'you understand?' He spoke coarsely, with satisfaction in frightening Sasha, while he himself suddenly tensed as what he had just said sank in. 'C'mon let's move on!'

Now, looking from side to side more often, they almost trotted on-wards, at times taking quicker ways over trails that cut across bends in the road. Sasha panted under the weight of his heavy rucksack and gun, while Serge pressed on ahead, the soles of his boots clattering noisily on each return to the compacted road surface.

They came at last to where there were hayricks and where a combine had left a swathe of shining hay on the road, they tramped over the hay, and it was springy and crackled lightly underfoot. A river appeared, and in the distance beyond it were the pale shapes of buildings. They crossed the water by leaping between reed-grown sandbanks, and so finally arrived at Varaksin's sovkhoz and his house. By then there could be no thought of eating: they went to bed and straight to sleep. And next day, in the sharp cold of earliest morning, they hitched a ride to their goal, the village of Kunino.

2

Having settled into the old peasant's barn, the following day at dawn Sasha had been the first to wake and emerge from under his sheepskin coat. He had shaken Serge, and now, with the sun slowly rising in a bright but still colourless and chilly morning, the two were walking one behind the other through a water meadow, leaving behind them their damp, green boot-prints. The nearer they approached the reserve, the more ea-gerly Sasha thrust forward, despite the increasing denseness of the mar-ginal shrubs and saplings. His face was drawn with concentration, he walked in a part crouch and had unshouldered his gun and cocked it well before the beginning of the thickets.

Serge, on the other hand, sauntered behind indifferently, yawning at almost every step such prodigious open-mouthed yawns that his heavy cheeks trembled and his eyes narrowed to slits. He cast vague glances up at the clean, turquoise-blue sky, and then each time he did so he stumbled over some hummock.

'Hey, Student!' he called at last to Sasha, and his voice was a smoker's early-morning rasp. 'You know what? We're a pair of dopey Papuans!'

'Why?' Sasha asked after a moment, not looking back.

'Look, mate...' Serge caught up with Sasha and grew livelier, 'we're wearing out our boots here and there's no point to it. We ought to be looking out for a bit of skirt. That would make sense. Some fat-faced village tart, hey? You hear me, Student?'

'Oh Serge, stop that,' said Sasha, blushing, and he increased his pace.

'Some of these gals around here...' Serge began again and cleared his throat—in trying to keep up with Sasha he had begun to wheeze and his nostrils flared—'You get a-hold of a handful of their...'

'Serge, please, don't make so much noise,' Sasha pleaded over his shoulder.

And just as he was bending forward to resume walking—and as always happens when one is unprepared—a heath-cock burst into sight, seemingly out of nowhere, and with a crazy gabble zigzagged up and away through the birch trees! Sasha was left flat-footed, shocked and goose-pimply all over. An instant later he let off a shot after the bird, but of course it was too late.

While he extracted the empty case he turned a pained look on Serge, who on his part contorted his face and eyebrows into an expression of apology and sorrow. The two went on, more quietly now, alert and taking care with their movements.

By midday the sun had grown hot and Serge would go no further: he sat sprawled in the shadow of a bush. He had gone through Sasha's rucksack and was wolfing into boiled eggs, bread and cold greasy lamb, washing the food down with a bottle of well-shaken milk he had also found in there.

Sasha had made a circuit through the forest and returned. He too was overcome by the heat, and now he lay on the ground and for some time had been looking up at the sky until the expanse of it made him dizzy. He had something to eat but ate without interest; nor did he listen to Serge with any great pleasure: who, sated and lying with his belt loosened, had returned to his previous subject. With eyes sleepily fixed on something in the distance he lectured Sasha, while yawning, belching, and poking in his teeth with a matchstick:

'Now you take the young ones—they're not the real goods, keep away from them. Movies, the club, dancing... They expect all that stuff from you and then they want ideas too. And then come the tears, the blaming—it wears you out. I've been frazzled before by girls. Nope, get yourself a real woman...' he hawked and spat thoughtfully. 'A woo-oo-man!'

'O come on, Serge,' Sasha pleaded in a pained voice. 'Haven't you got any shame?'

'Listen, you infant, I'm giving you some education,' Serge laughed, growing animated, fidgeting happily and throwing one leg over the other. 'And forget your usual heifer, too—you get yourself a widow; and not a young one either but, say, about thirty-five—it's about there that you get the choice stuff. Find a widow—or a divorced one. Looks a bit of a dog, not too nice now—she's not going to waste her time with palaver about marriage and stuff. She'll give you her heart and soul, though. And how!... Oh, so tenderly she kissed me, a-a-all thro-o-ugh the night!' he shouted the line, and laughed and slapped his thigh. 'Student!' he began again, fixing his bloodshot eyes on Sasha. 'We're a pair of dopes, daft Papuans, eh? When the villages here are loaded with 'em! Come on, let's get out of here!'

'Oh, go to blazes!' Sasha said. He picked up his shotgun and went back into the forest. Serge thought for a moment, then he got up and followed him.

3

But on the evening of the fifth day Serge did not go hunting. He dusted his boots, threw his jacket over his shoulders and went to the club.

Sasha set off alone, rambling among the hay-stubble as it grew golden and then rosy under a descending, dimming sun. He started a quail, fired well and ran quickly to pick it up, and the bird was firm and warm in his hand. He put it into his bag and smiled tiredly and wiped the sweat from his brow.

It got dark quickly, and with that the day grew cooler at last. Coming to the river, Sasha undressed behind some bushes and then his unmuscular, thin body flashed whitely for a moment as he ran and threw himself with a squeal into the water. He swam for some time, undulating the water that had been still and black beneath the riverbank.

Refreshed and feeling light of step and spirit, he returned to the village and gave his bird to the old woman. He did not want dinner and only drank some milk still warm from the cow; then he went up into the loft, let his last thoughts lull him in their usual way and soon fell asleep.

Serge came back late that night. He clambered panting up to the hayloft, took off his boots and clothes, stretched, yawned, and got under his sheepskin next to Sasha. But his preparations were evidently incomplete: he kneaded his pillow, turned this way and that to make himself comfortable and warm, then he nudged Sasha.

'Well, what happened? Bag anything?' he asked, lively and obviously in a good mood.

'A quail,' Sasha murmured sleepily.

'That so? Well brother, I've been courting quail myself tonight. Big time,' said Serge, and he lowered his voice for greater effect: 'Did I cut me out one hell of a bint! Lives in that third house from the edge, you know the one? Nineteen years old, the bitch. Finished tenth grade.'

Sasha was annoyed but could not help remarking: 'You said you didn't like the young ones.' The effort at sarcasm brought him to total wakefulness, and in the darkness the smell of his pillow and of the hay rose pleasantly to his nostrils.

'That depends on who and what, my friend,' Serge replied without a moment's hesitation.

'How on earth did you meet her?' asked Sasha after a pause.

'Nothing to it, I can find skirt anywhere! You wanna know how to play them a line, how to write letters for instance, just ask me.' He sat up, felt for his trousers, found and lit a cigarette and lay back in the straw. He continued: 'Say now you're writing to some girl, some Lyuba, say, from one of these boondocks. You lay it on with things like: "Warmest greetings to you, Lyuba, from one as yet unknown to you: front-line electrician Sergei Varaksin. Concerned as we are with maintaining a heroic vigilance over the wellbeing of the Soviet people, I would be interested to know how you get on in your daily life and studies..."' Serge shouted with laughter at that point and then went quickly on: 'Or something like this: "You, dear Lyuba, wrote in your letter that you believe in platonic love. Although you don't yet know me well, I'm sure we could remedy that lack if you would allow me to write and to meet you. Then you would see that as to your question about modern friendship I am in total and unreserved agreement with you and offer you my own, Lyuba. Do write to me what your thoughts are in that connection. And meanwhile, dear Lyuba, I send you my photo and hope in return to receive one from you." And on the back of your photo,' he guffawed, 'you write "Love me as I do thee, and we'll be friends for eternity" or "May this lifeless image remind you of a living heart."'

'God, you're a rat!' said Sasha, also grinning. 'But what happened tonight?'

'What rat? What rat?' Serge replied excitedly. 'You haven't learnt to blow your nose yet, you haven't a clue! They just lap up that language. You with your philosophy and your poetry will get left for dead, for a lonesome shag on a rock. Boy, you should meet my mates at work, they'd work you over, make something out of you! You're all right to look at, but... Oh well, anyway, tonight I got to the club—and what a dump it is! Where I am we've got a new one, with columns; they spent two years building it. All they've got here is some kind of a big izba with one inside wall and no partitions. So I got there, lit me a fag—I'm just explaining the setup—people arrive, just girls for a start, you couldn't see any males. The feller who plays the squeeze-box comes and makes his noise, and the girls pared off and started to dance. I went over to one and invited her for a shuffle. We go around and I suggest to her, innocent as anything, that we could get better acquainted outside. And what a juicy piece of ham she is! Bursting at the seams, jowls all a-flap: a Japanese god, I think to myself, a tartlet to my very own taste! But no, it turns out she's got me taped, she's biding her time, but it's not for the likes of me. Best I pull my snout out of that bucket, it's empty! So, all right, I step back, all modest-like, and keep my eyes peeled.

'Then I spot one alone. A young 'un, pretty as a peach. She's taking in the scene, and I see she's got nice red lips, a brunette—I've had it up to here with the blond ones! And I notice that she's only dancing with the other girls, giggling and carrying on—when they're not taken up, they always herd together like that.

'I catch her looking at me once, then again; so I go over and get her clear of her buddies; and just then the generator gives a knock and the lights come on and she looks even nicer. They put on the records and we danced a couple of times and I got to ask her about herself. She told me she looks after the calves at the farm. I suggest we go outside for some fresh air, and we go out through the porch, into the yard. Yeah, and all the fellers in the place are collected there—they're all Youth League types round here, know a thing or two, sharp lot of parasites. They're standing there, smoking, and they sing out to her: "Galya! Galya!"—that's her name—and they flash torches at us. So I take her a bit to the side and tell her that I've got something to say to her, and she sort of trembles. They always, these girls, go for that trembling thing. Just take 'em by the arm or put a hand on 'em and they start shuddering something grim.

'So she's trembling and I'm leading her up the road, and I look back—there's no one. And there I sort of move in close on her; but I keep mum, sort of cough and make out that I'm the shy and unsure kind. "Are you cold? Why are you trembling?" I ask her. "I don't know why," she says. Straight off I put my jacket over her shoulders. There, Student, is your first lesson—give her your jacket! The moment I had it on her, she went quiet as a mouse.

'I went with her like that up to her place, and I tell you that the best thing I found out was that it was on the way to here. If she'd been an outsider, from Gorki down the road, say, you'd be mad to have anything to do with her. As it turned out, we're neighbours. We went through her yard and out the back and I found a bit of a log to squat on. And I talked on about life, let it pour out, made intellectual noises, the stuff you see in the papers—they love that ideas-talk. And then I'm all over her. She pranced away a bit at first, but then got used to it, sort of went weak, started breathing, the bitch, jerking about. Give me a week—a week's what this agrarian campaign needs, no more. I've sorted her out already!'

'You're a louse!' said Sasha.

'Wanna make a bet on how long? Well?' offered Serge cheerfully, and not waiting for a reply, still grinning, he turned away, settled himself comfortably, and in a few moments was asleep, his palms together under his nose. Sasha remained awake for some time longer and saw Serge's body twitching once or twice as he slept.

4

It rained on and off for some days, and with that change signs of the coming autumn suddenly appeared. The roads dampened, roofs and walls grew darker, slow clouds rolled down from the north. It became cold and the hay in the barn where the two slept felt humid now, and in the morning getting up from under their sheepskins was harder.

But then the rains stopped, and everything glowed once again with the radiance of a late summer: spiderwebs in the fields and in the bushes shone golden, sunsets long bled and turned yellow then greenish just above the skyline. Dew fell again in the morning, the air was keen, and more and more often roofs and the grass were sprinkled with a crisp hoar-frost; starlings flew in clouds over the village gardens and the fields and the copses of mountain ash. Winnowing was taking place in numberless threshing sheds, and the air was full of the distant knock-knocking of working motors; trucks rolled continually in the direction of the cities with loads of grain, and a light dust hung like dry mist above the roads.

Serge disappeared on his amorous expeditions. He had completely given up hunting, and so Sasha went on his own, went stubbornly, morning and evening, although he too now was impatient to go to the club. He had no one now to exchange a word with and he grew moody, seemed to lose weight, the features of his face and his cheekbones in particular to become more distinct and his eyes transparent and larger. He looked with more attention at any girl he happened to pass.

Serge came back late each night, rustled the hay, lay down wheezing and restless, smelling of perfume and powder. If Sasha was asleep Serge woke him to update him on the latest happening with Galya.

And then one night Serge returned just before dawn and without un-dressing, only dropping his boots, he remained sitting on the edge of the loft, dangling his legs and smoking. He called to Sasha: 'Hey! Student! You asleep?'

'Yes. What is it?' Sasha answered ill-humouredly.

Serge paused, flicked away his cigarette, then cleared his throat, spat, and said: 'You owe me half a litre, Student. You lost!'

'You're lying!' said Sasha, sitting up.

'Why should I be lying? The militia ain't grilling me,' Serge said evenly; and from the touch of listlessness in his voice Sasha knew that he was not lying.

And Sasha without understanding what he was doing began putting on his boots; all he was aware of was that there was an ache in his heart and misery and self-pity and he felt as if something distasteful, something shameful had happened to him. Serge, meanwhile, slumped back on the hay, folded his hands under his head, stretched, chuckled and began talking:

'I spotted three days ago that she sleeps on her own, up in their hay-loft. I didn't let on, I was still trying to sweet-talk her then. But I wasn't getting anywhere, no way... Hey, where're you going?'

'Nowhere,' Sasha said, sinking back, and he began aimlessly ruffling the hay with one hand.

'Oh, I thought... We said good-night tonight as usual, she went in and I stayed outside the gate...' He suddenly laughed. 'Their neighbour's a mad old coot, always worrying that his garden's been broken into. He's out all hours in his sheepskin, patrolling the place with a shotgun. Everything around was quiet, the village had shut down, so I thought to myself—now, an apple would be nice! While I was trying to hop over the wicker fence I got my leg caught, and granddad came out—"Who's there, I'll shoot!" he calls out. I heard him cock his gun—click! I dropped flat on my face and just lay there, nose in the dirt. All my back sort of froze. Hell, I thought, you're in trouble: a load of shot in the backside and it's the end of your romancing. But nothing happened, he went off after a while. I pulled down about five apples and—back across I went. I was going to bring you a couple but it sort of slipped my mind. Must have ate the lot; sorry.

'So I'm sitting on a log eating apples and thinking the situation over. It's getting so cold my arms and legs have gone stiff, and all round it's pitch black. I finish the apples, take off my boots, and I'm on my way into the barn! I'm tiptoeing, ghosting—I was a bit nervy I can tell you, trying not to breathe while I went up the ladder! Quiet as a mouse. I stick my head up above the floor of the loft—where is she? Then I spot her lying just under the eaves. I worm along the floor towards her... Say, where're you off to?'

'Go to hell!' Sasha shouted shrilly, groping violently with one foot for the cross-beam. 'Animal! Idiot!' He could say no more: he was choking.

Dressed in his underwear and boots, he flung out of the barn and onto the lane outside, and near a bridge over a little stream that flowed under the lane he found a log and sat down on it, hunched over, trembling with the night's chill and his own feverishness, his unhappiness and disgust.

About five minutes later Serge came out. He was dressed and had put his boots back on. He looked around, and finding where Sasha was he went over to him and sat down on the other end of the log.

'What's the matter, Student?' he asked with a chuckle. 'Feeling a bit sour are we, a bit green-eyed? I told you lots of times to give away that bloody hunting, you dope. Everything's got its own time. D'you want?—I'll introduce you. Galya's got a friend who's on her own, who's looking for someone. She doesn't look as good, but she'd do you. What d'you say?'

Sasha sat turned away and said nothing. He felt bitter and very alone.

From the direction of the village came the sound of voices, and then several dark figures appeared, moving together down the lane, the wavering glow of cigarettes tracing their approach. When they reached the bridge they stopped in silence. They seemed to be looking for something and they turned towards Sasha and Serge.

'Him?' one of them asked uncertainly.

'Dunno, let's see...'

And they veered in the direction of the sitting pair and came nearer. Serge got up. He stood facing the group, legs spread apart, his hands in his pockets. Sasha did not understand what was happening, but a feeling of dread suddenly came over him and he stood up as well.

'Got a smoke?' someone in the group asked Serge.

'In the barn...' said Serge, and his voice sounded odd.

'Hang on a minute!' said a short, stocky young man with an army cap, and separating from the group he caught Serge by the sleeve as he began moving away. 'You know Galya?'

'Hey now, let go!...' Serge said weakly.

'You remember what you got told at the club, you bastard, don't you?'

'Oh, come on fellas...' Serge mumbled, beginning to shake. 'I'm just the same as anyone else here, a country bloke. Don't now, don't... I won't have anything more to do with her...'

'You won't have anything more to do with her!' the one who was holding Serge repeated with suppressed fury. 'Oh, I get it!'

'Yeah, yeah, straight! I'll go away tomorrow. Honest!'

'You'll go away! Oh, I get it...' the stocky one repeated senselessly and with the same frightening restraint.

But here a second figure joined in and approached the two with an apologetic cough. This was a tall, supple-looking youth in riding breeches and high boots, who for some reason wore a posy of white flowers in the pocket of his jacket.

'Easy there, Pete-boy...' he said in an unnaturally caressing tone, leading his colleague a step aside. 'I've had a word with him myself. He's one of us country blokes. There's no need to give him a hiding, is there?...'

And he drew down one shoulder and launched such a punch to Serge's chest that his own forced-out gasp audibly accompanied the swing of his arm. Serge fell heavily, then quickly leapt up again, but instantly two more of the group were on him and knocked him off his feet once more.

Sasha wanted to stop them, but a big lad gave him a backhander—not a serious blow, but enough to make his ears ring—then grabbed with one brawny hand the collar of Sasha's undershirt, and while twisting it beneath Sasha's chin murmured to him: 'Best take it easy pal... Don't want bloody teeth now, do we?' and holding Sasha back at arm's length he turned to what was occurring nearby in the darkness.

And there the others, nudging into one another, interfering with one another, were hitting and hitting something on the ground, a thing which emitted cries and grunts with every blow. Most effective was the tall young man with the posy, who, while skipping nimbly into openings for another and yet another clout to Serge's head or stomach, kept up a breathless plea: 'There's no need, fellas... Come on... Quit it... What have I done?...'

Suddenly a woman's shout, high-pitched and full of consternation, shrilled from one of the nearby yards: 'What in heaven's name are you all doing out there?'

The one who had been holding Sasha—his attention on the beating such that he was unaware he was shaking and garrotting his captive—

let go the collar and threw himself towards the others, pulled them apart, and in a moment they had all disappeared across the night-dampened meadow that stretched behind the dark backyards of the nearest houses.

Left alone, Sasha craned forward and froze with horror at the sight of Serge's slumped form near the bridge; and when people ran up and flashed torches and began asking what had happened and why, his teeth chattered and his knees shook and he could make no reply.

They carried Serge into the barn, laid him inside the doorway, aimed lights at him, felt him all over and examined his head and trunk; and Serge kept turning his face to one side and then the other, made snoring noises, spat out blood, and at intervals broke into fits of sobbing.

'Nah, he's all right!' said one of those who had looked Serge all over, and he wiped his hands on some straw. 'He'll have himself a spell in bed out of it, that's all.'

A panting nurse in a white gown arrived from the village infirmary. She swabbed Serge, put tincture on him and bandaged his head. Straw was thrown down from the loft, then a pillow followed, and having made a bed for him and laid him on it everybody dispersed.

All night long, Serge moaned, blew his nose, spat blood and abused Sasha, Moscow, and hunting.

Next morning, Galya came hurrying to the barn—and when Sasha saw her he was astonished at her loveliness and how artlessly frank she was in showing her love for Serge, and yet how timid and how shy she was.

'My God, what did they do to you? What on earth happened?' she whispered breathlessly, looking with horror at Serge's swathed head.

'Yeah, right, right! Just you look!' Serge moaned bitterly, pulling the bandages aside to show her the dark bruises, and he glared with puffed eyes at Galya. 'See it? It's all because of you, you bitch! I'm getting out of here. Today. To hell with the capers they play around here!'

'Sergy dear,' she said sinking down on her knees, 'Don't now, don't talk like that... We'll go to the militia, we'll report them...'

'Go to hell!' said Serge, turning away.

Galya glanced at Sasha. Her face was overspread with a painful blush and there were tears brimming in her eyes. Sasha snatched up his gun, hurried out of the barn, crossed the meadows, and thrust into the forest. He was overcome again, as he had been yesterday, with sorrow and self-pity and envy.

And, as if from spite, it turned out to be a wonderful day, especially calm, especially mild, a day totally of summer and yet with the pale and melancholy light of autumn.

All that day Sasha drove himself, walked and fired, desperately wanting to clear his head, to drive away unhappiness with fatigue. But he could not seem to think about anything other than Galya.

Quite as a mouse! And he thought of the scene in the girl's barn with a bitter smile.

And he stumbled over tussocks again, clambered through ravines, ate raspberries and wild currants, tasting their intoxicating, sultry tang. He fired and walked on and fired, and he heard the echoes ringing and snapping back from the forest and saw the smoke of his shots settle like a veil on the grass.

He returned to the village, pinched and worn out, and when he opened the door of the barn he understood immediately and with contempt that Serge had gone.

'The swine!' he thought, and putting his gun down on the straw he went out to find the old peasant. The man had just got up from sleep and was sitting inside the izba on a bench, his face puffed and vacuous, one dark hand vaguely waving away the flies buzzing above the oilcloth on the table.

'Serge?' he repeated, and thought for a moment. 'Oh, gone,' he said. 'Quit, a while back today. He wasn't too happy. Gave me two roubles,' he added sadly and with a wry smile. 'Two roubles. How about that?... And yourself? Staying on? Up to you, there's plenty of hay in the barn. Who was it that got at him? Not the Levoshkinski boys? I just poked my head out, and there's the militia heading for there. Some job they did on him!'

He tottered to the stove and reached above it for some brownish-green leaves of home-grown tobacco and began shredding them between his palms.

'A bit o' baccy I got growing here...' he muttered, yawning. 'How was it, the hunting, got anything? It's a thing for them that likes it, of course. And did they sort it out, what it was about? You didn't hear? Well, well...'

He rolled a cigarette, lit it and pleasurably released a plume of smoke, after which he was overcome by a spasm of coughing that brought a flush to the very top of his bald head. He screwed up his face and wiped the tears from his eyes with the back of a rough hand.

'Nastya!' he called out in the direction of the porch. 'Pour us some of that brew. A couple of pannikins... No, not from there...' he called again, recognising something in the clatter made by his wife. 'That one, in the bucket!'

And when it had grown quite dark, Sasha returned to the barn, and having pulled himself up into the loft he collapsed on the hay. Dulled by the beer, depressed, he lay there rubbing the feeling back into his face. He suddenly had a melancholy desire to go home. 'The hell with this, I'm going!' he decided. 'I've got my friends in Moscow; girls; I'll go and play football. I'm clearing out of here!'

He called to mind the girls he knew in Moscow, and his face flushed with confused thoughts. And the life which he had been leading for so many days recently—the hunting, the shame on Galya's face (but now also the wantonness which he was beginning to imagine he had seen on it), Serge, the sound of the grain threshers, the night-time beating, the glimpsed beauty of early autumn—all of that at once began to seem dis-tant, to be retreating somewhere; precisely as he had sensed his life at an earlier point falling away behind him when he had late one night got off the train at the Myatlevo station.